# IMPLEMENTING OSI NETWORKS

# WILEY SERIES IN DATA COMMUNICATIONS AND NETWORKING FOR COMPUTER PROGRAMMERS

**SERIES EDITOR:**
**Gerald D. Cole**, Independent Consultant

David Claiborne • Mathematical Preliminaries for Computer Networking
Gerald D. Cole • Computer Networking for Systems Programmers
David Claiborne • Personal Computer Networking
Gerald D. Cole • Implementing OSI Networks

# IMPLEMENTING OSI NETWORKS

**GERALD D. COLE**

John Wiley & Sons, Inc.
NEW YORK / CHICHESTER / BRISBANE / TORONTO / SINGAPORE

***Library of Congress Cataloging in Publication Data:***

Cole, Gerald D.
Implementing OSI networks / Gerald D. Cole.
p. cm.
Includes bibliographical references and index.
ISBN 0-471-51060-2 (paper)
1. Computer networks. 2. Computer network protocols.
3. Computer network architectures. I. Title.
TK5105.5.C578 1991
004.6 — cc20
91-23907

Printed in the United States of America

10 9 8 7 6 5 4 3 2 1

# CONTENTS

# 4

# THE OSI UPPER LAYERS 145



# 5

# BASIC BUILDING BLOCKS AT THE APPLICATION LAYER 181

## 6 APPLICATION PACKAGES 211



## 7 OSI PROFILES: SPECIFICATION, IMPLEMENTATION, AND TESTING 245

# SERIES PREFACE

The Data Communications and Networking for Computer Programmers Series provides the information programmers and software engineers need to effectively deal with new data communications and networking technology. The series focuses on the educational needs of the computer systems analyst, systems programmer, and systems engineer, building on their existing computer knowledge base. The series as a whole provides an integrated view of such real-world topics as analyzing networks, implementing network protocols, developing local area and wide area networks, interconnecting networks, creating multivendor networks, and understanding network standards.

Because the breadth of the data communications field is beyond the scope of a single book, the information is presented in a series of books. Each book deals with a different aspect of the wide range of data communications topics. This division of information allows the different books to build on a level of knowledge defined by the other books in the series. When one book is used by a programmer, the other books in the series provide an established source for additional information. Overlap between the books is limited to essential information.

The authors of the series are working professionals in different networking and data communications areas. Each author writes using his or her experience in solving actual data communications problems in system development. The authors relate the data communications aspects to concepts already understood by experienced programmers, using similarities to extend the programmer's understanding from familiar computer programming concepts to different aspects of data communications networking. In many respects, data communications and networking can be viewed as a specialized form of I/O systems.

The complexity of data communications and networking, however, is not overly simplified. Unique data communications topics such as network error control and recovery, sequence and flow-control management, distributed fault recovery mechanisms, and concurrent operation of atomic actions across the multiple resources of a network, are all addressed in detail. While the books emphasize similarities, aspects that differ are highlighted, still allowing the programmer to maximize the benefits from his or her existing knowledge.

*Gerald D. Cole*
Series editor

# PREFACE

The objective of this book is to explain Open Systems Interconnection (OSI) and computer networking in a way that is useful to implementers of computer systems and applications that run on them. The audience is expected to include computer systems analysts, system programmers, and application programmers.

The intent of the book is to describe OSI in easy-to-read terms, given that the reader has some familiarity with data communications and networking concepts. Every attempt has been made to avoid the seemingly endless stream of verbose OSI terms such as CONNECT DATA OVERFLOW SPDU, (abandon) request primitive, GIVE TOKENS SPDU with token item parameter, and association-responding-reliable-transfer-protocol-machine. The OSI specifications are filled with such nomenclature, and these specifications are a necessary part of implementing OSI systems. However, these specifications are not the proper starting point for learning about OSI.

On the other hand, articles and books on OSI fill several bookshelves. Much of that information fails in the other extreme. Readers are left with too sketchy an understanding of what OSI is really about and what it can (and cannot) do for their systems. This book is targeted toward the center position. It provides the overall perspective of layered architecture with a detailed description of the services and protocols of each layer. It stops short of including all OSI details, but it does give examples so that the reader who needs to consult the detailed specifications will be able to do so.

The book begins with a description of the OSI Reference Model and the general concepts of OSI. It then covers the important issues of naming and addressing, as well as communications services. These topics are pervasive across the layers of protocol. The bottom two layers of OSI are considered point-to-point protocols, including the physical layer, the data link layer, and the overlapping media access control (MAC) sublayer of local area networks.

Current LAN standards are considered in sufficient detail to see their strengths and weaknesses and how they fit into OSI standardization efforts. Next, the network and transport layers are considered end-to-end services. Since these two layers are closely coupled, they are discussed in a single chapter.

The upper three layers provide support to applications. The OSI session layer provides synchronization, dialogue control, and other services that pass through the presentation and application layers. The OSI presentation layer allows applications to negotiate data representations. Associated with the presentation layer is the abstract syntax notation (ASN.1) that provides a notation for the representation of data structures, including application protocol header information.

The application layer service packages provide two forms of support to applications. First is a set of commonly used building blocks, such as the commitment, concurrency, and recovery package for applications that require atomic operations. Then there is a set of application-specific packages for file transfer, remote login, electronic mail, and similar uses. Thus, all three of the upper layers provide services to applications and are of particular concern to system developers.

Since OSI is intended to provide interoperability across multi-vendor computing environments, it is important to be aware of the potential problems influencing interoperability. This is the subject of a chapter covering profiles, conformance testing, and interoperability testing. Profiles define subsets of protocols that are to be implemented, with the idea that interoperability is more likely if only the needed portion of protocols is implemented. Conformance testing is intended to determine if an implementation complies with a test suite. The final *proof of the pudding* is actual interoperability testing with other vendors' equipment.

Network management is considered an OSI application layer function that deals with data about each of the other layers. Network management is the subject of a separate chapter and may be skipped if not of interest to a given reader. However, anyone developing applications that employ networking should have at least some knowledge of network management capabilities. Hopefully, that knowledge will provide insight into potential problems and performance limitations that may affect an application.

The final chapter is a brief look forward to see what is in OSI's future. Expected trends include more distributed applications and transparent forms of networking, greater use of connectionless forms of networking, and attempts at vendor enhancements to OSI implementations. The future also holds better conformance and interoperability tests and improved migration strategies.

In this book the approach is to provide a comprehensive analysis of each protocol, with an emphasis on the services it provides and the way it performs its functions. This approach has been successful in courses taught by the author at several universities including UCLA Extension and the University of Southern California. More recently the author has used this approach in courses offered by Learning Group International.

The author acknowledges the cooperation of Learning Group International during the writing of this volume, and thanks that organization for permission to include in this book figures developed by the author for use in Learning Group's networking courses.

*Gerald D. Cole*

# 1

# INTRODUCTION

Open Systems Interconnection (OSI) promises to end the dependence of computer system users and administrators on a single vendor's networking products. The idea is that IBM, DEC, Unisys, Hewlett-Packard, and other systems will all be able to share access to information and other computer services, without requiring that the user attempt to translate between differing internal representations of data. Don't throw out those terminal emulation boards and software, and don't *trash* the DECnet, IBM System Network Architecture (SNA), or Transmission Control Protocol/Internet Protocol (TCP/IP) networking software right away. Getting OSI in place and fully operational will take time — probably the rest of the decade.

OSI is a large and complicated subject. Unfortunately, people often limit their views of OSI to the OSI Reference Model and the resulting OSI protocols. The basic components of OSI include not only the OSI Reference Model and protocols, but also the OSI profiles, implementation agreements, conformance tests, and interoperability tests discussed in Chapter 7. People also often overlook OSI network management, which is the subject of Chapter 8. However, an understanding of these areas is dependent upon a solid understanding of the OSI protocols, and that is the principal focus of this book.

What are open systems? It is often easier to define a new concept by stating what it is not. The opposite of an open system is a closed, vendor-proprietary system. In this case, the information about the networking approach is vendor-proprietary data. That leaves the possibility of a published, open-literature networking approach that is still owned by a particular vendor. Is that open? And what about public domain networking descriptions such as TCP/IP? Is TCP/IP an open system? One could debate these matters at length, and many people have. For this discussion, the issues are moot. An open system is one in which the protocols follow international standards developed from the OSI Reference Model.

OSI standards come about from the joint efforts of two major international standardization groups. One is the Consultative Committee for International Telephone and Telegraph (CCITT). The other is the International Standards Organization (ISO).

CCITT is an agency within the United Nations, with one voting member per country. This voting member is typically the post, telephone, and telegraph (PTT) from each country. The PTT is the government-directed monopoly that provides the postal system, telephone, and telegraph services. The United States does not have a PTT, so the State Department represents the U.S. in the CCITT. Every fourth year the CCITT issues its standards in the form of recommendations (to distinguish them from regulations). Regulations carry the force of law. Recommendations generally do not, at least not in the U.S., although they do in some European countries.

A full set of CCITT recommendations contains about 20,000 pages, packaged as 60 volumes taking up four linear feet of shelf space. Few people purchase the entire set in any case, because it costs several thousand dollars. The principal recommendations of concern are in three of the approximately two-dozen different series: the V-series on modem-related standards, the X-series on digital networking standards, and the I-series on Integrated Services Digital Network (ISDN) that covers digitized voice and data. The principal concern in this book is the X-series.

The second major international networking standardization organization group is ISO. Unlike CCITT, ISO is a voluntary group, but it too has a member from each country. The U.S. representative to ISO is the American National Standards Institute (ANSI). The ISO charter is much broader than that of CCITT. However, the two organizations have overlapping interests in data communications and networking, as shown in Figure 1-1. The figure shows the broad charter of ISO — everything from screw threads to solar energy, including data communications and networking. The figure also shows CCITT living up to its name, developing standards for telephone, telegraph, networking, and messaging systems. Other organizations actively participating in OSI standards development are the European Computer Manufacturers Association (ECMA) and the Institute of Electrical and Electronics Engineers (IEEE).

Both ISO and CCITT are developing standards for data communications and networking. The idea expressed in the figure is that both CCITT and ISO develop their own versions of standards and then attempt to reconcile their differences through a coordination process to bring them into technical alignment. Both publish their own versions as standards. Both make a good bit of income selling their copyrighted standards; as a result, those standards are not as freely available as comparable documentation such as the TCP/IP standards.

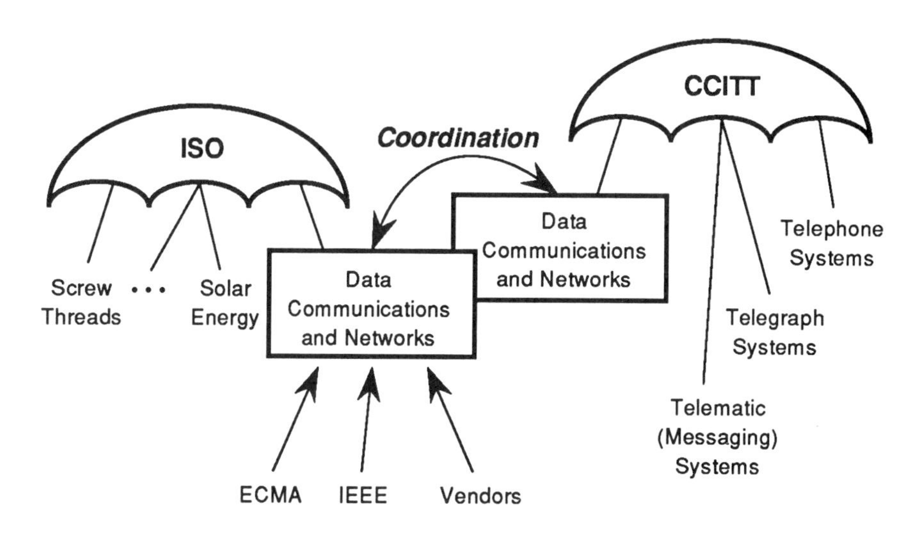


*Illustration courtesy of Learning Group International*

**FIGURE 1-1** ISO and CCITT interests overlap in OSI.

Both CCITT and ISO have published a wide variety of networking standards including the basic document for Open System Interconnection, namely the OSI Reference Model.

# THE OSI REFERENCE MODEL

The OSI Reference Model is relatively brief (approximately 50 pages) and describes how computer networking should be accomplished in terms of seven functional layers. Its primary purpose is to serve as a framework for the development of standards at each layer. In effect, it provides a top-level specification for the services that each layer is to provide and the functions (i.e., mechanisms) to be implemented that will provide these services. For example, a typical service of a layer is to provide error-free delivery. The corresponding function (mechanism) is to provide error detection and recovery. Figure 1-2 summarizes the OSI Reference Model.

The OSI Reference Model was developed during 1977-79 based on existing computer network architectures such as SNA, DECnet, and TCP/IP. That makes it more than a decade old. However, it has become a living set of documents: various addenda include issues such as addressing, network security, and connectionless service, none of which were considered in the original effort. The basic reference model is documented as CCITT X.200 and ISO

- **Definitions of basic terminology**
- **A layered computer network architecture**
- **The definition of services and functions of each layer**
- **A top-level specification for protocols**
- **A framework for the development of standards**

**International Standard**  **7498**

Information processing systems - Open Systems Interconnection - Basic Reference Model

First edition -
1984-10-151984-10-15-

**UDC 881.3.01** **Ref. No. ISO 7498-1984 (E)**

*Illustration courtesy of Learning Group International*

**FIGURE 1-2** The OSI Reference Model.

7498-1. The security architecture is ISO 7498-2; naming (or addressing) is ISO 7498-3; and the management framework is ISO 7498-4. There are also two addenda: ISO 7498-1/Addendum 1 for connectionless data transmission and ISO 7498-1/Addendum 2 for multipeer data transmission. Figure 1-3 shows the extensions.

The OSI Reference Model provides a layered set of network services. In many ways, it is analogous to the layers of an operating system. In both cases, the top layer provides services that are directly of concern to the applications programmer. Similarly, the bottom layers provide detailed control of hardware devices such as disk controllers for the operating system or local area network (LAN) interface boards for the network. In both cases, the intermediate layers provide increasing levels of service, with one layer building on and adding to the services of the layer below it.

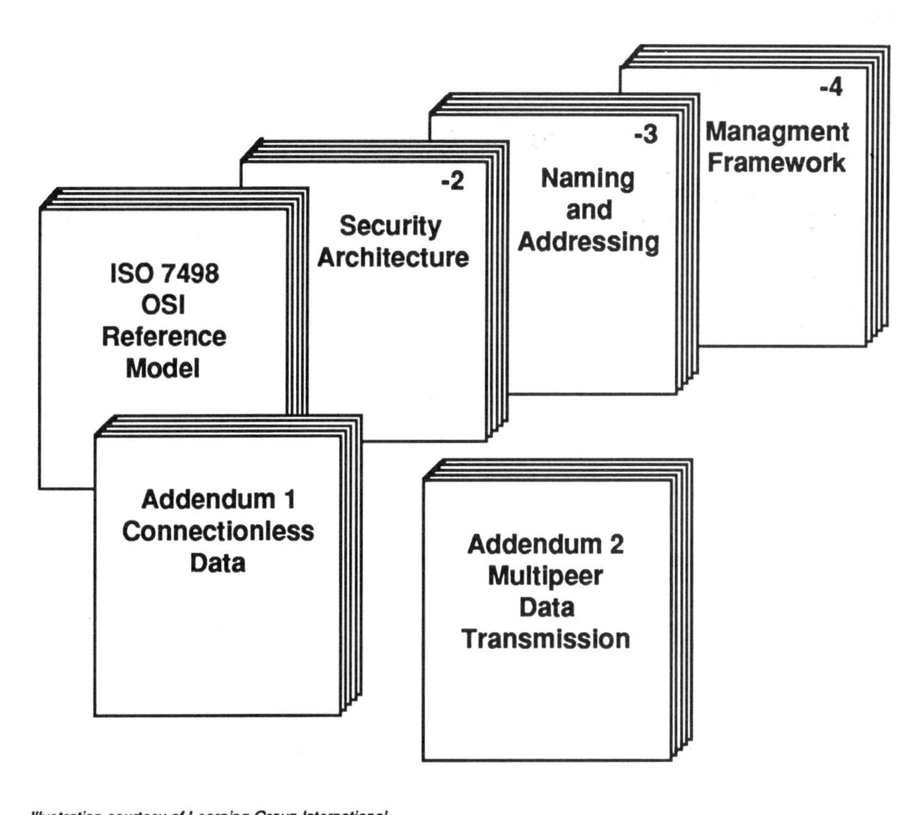


*Illustration courtesy of Learning Group International*

**FIGURE 1-3** Extensions to the OSI Reference Model.

Unlike operating system layering, the OSI Reference Model requires strict adherence to passing through all the layers. Skipping over one or more layers is a violation of OSI layering principles, as is operating an application directly on some lower layer. That does not mean that it has not been done. The first version of the CCITT electronic messaging system, the 1984 X.400 recommendations, bypassed the then fledgling presentation layer and operated directly on the session layer. The Manufacturing Automation Protocol (MAP) group devised a Mini-MAP protocol suite that gutted the middle layers of the OSI protocol suite.

Figure 1-4 shows how a file is to be transferred according to the OSI Reference Model. This example describes the services provided at each layer. The user's application program makes a call on the file transfer protocol at layer 7 (application layer). That layer in turn uses the services of layer 6

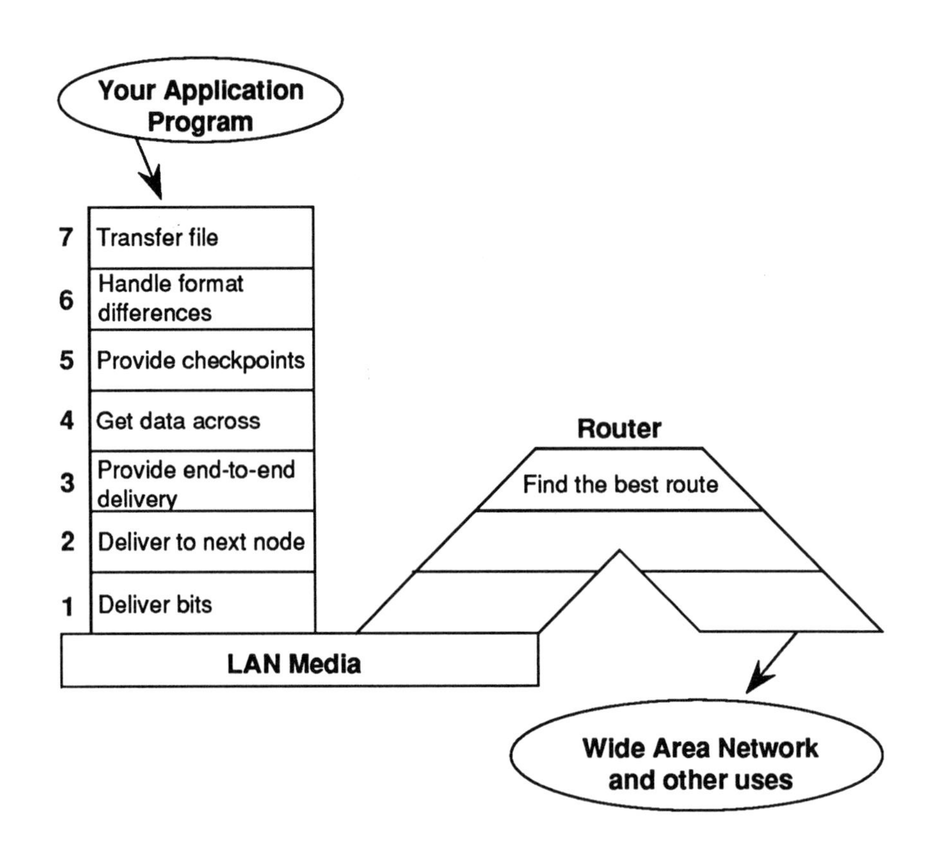


*Illustration courtesy of Learning Group International*

**FIGURE 1-4** An example of OSI layering.

(presentation layer) to handle format differences such as the character set representations of the data. Layer 5 (session layer) provides a checkpoint capability so that recovery can proceed from a checkpoint in case of a computer or communications system failure during the data transfer. Layer 4 (transport layer) is responsible for the end-to-end data integrity; layer 3 (network layer) finds the path from one end system (computer) to the other. Finally, the bottom two layers are responsible for the delivery of data on a point-to-point basis, e.g., between the originating computer and the router.

In a second and somewhat more detailed example, consider an application program that expresses its desire to access an individual record in a remote file.

It makes a service call, which maps the user request into the required commands at the file transfer, access, and management (FTAM) protocol.

FTAM *knows* about operations related to files but not about the specific implementation of files at the other computer. However, the remote FTAM provides the appearance of a virtual file. Like any use of the term *virtual*, this means that the external appearance of the object or effect may differ considerably from the real situation. (Consider, for example, the concept of virtual memory.) This virtual representation of the actual file is the basis for all operations performed. It is the responsibility of FTAM at the host to map the virtual-file-related requests into a form suitable for the file being accessed.

FTAM relies upon the services of the presentation layer to convey the information from one computer to the other in a way that preserves the semantics (meaning) of the information, but maps the syntax (form and format) from one machine environment to another. These required services are negotiated at the time the logical connection between the two end systems is established. (OSI services as originally conceived are the basis for connections that need a connection request or response exchange, during which parameters for the connection can be negotiated.)

The session layer, in turn, ensures that the data are safely stored on disk at the destination end system. To do so, the use of synchronization points, which will confirm that the data units are safely stored, is negotiated. The half-duplex (two-way alternate) operation might also be negotiated. The session layer subsequently enforces the flow by means of a token that only one computer has at any given time.

The session layer builds upon the services of the transport layer, which provides data integrity. The data are transferred in transport layer packets (called protocol data units in OSI). Data integrity means that there are no defective packets, no packets are missing, none are out of order, and none are duplicated. Exactly one correct copy of each packet is delivered in the proper order to the recipient.

The network layer provides a service to the transport layer so that the transport layer does not need to know about the nature and interconnectivity of the network over which the data is transferred. It does not need to know about maximum packet size limitations or how to find a path (route) across the network.

Data link layer protocols provide a data delivery service along several cascaded point-to-point links. These include links within the network and between the host and the network. The delivery service is in terms of blocks of data, i.e., some number of contiguous characters.

The physical layer at the bottom provides a mechanism for delivering bits. Its job is to adapt the bits into a form suitable for transmission over the media (e.g., a telephone circuit, a satellite link, or a LAN).

In this example, each layer built upon the services of the layer just beneath it and in turn propagated the services from lower layers to its own service interface. This is the basic concept of adding value at each layer.

# CONCEPTS AND TERMINOLOGY

The OSI Reference Model not only provides a framework for the definition of computer networking protocols, it also implicitly provides a common set of concepts and terminology. These can be quite useful, since for the first time a universally understood set of concepts, terms, and acronyms exists. In addition to the concepts and terminology from the OSI Reference Model, many other concepts and terms have evolved during subsequent protocol development.

While the OSI Reference Model introduced some new concepts, its principal role in this regard was to codify previous concepts that existed in various forms and under various names. These concepts and others developed during the evolution of OSI protocols are discussed below. These are in six major areas: open systems, layering issues, connection aspects, endpoint names and addresses, data units, and the data flow between systems.

## Open Systems

Open systems are those that can interoperate by using OSI protocols for communications and applications support. A set of terminology exists that applies to the computer systems involved in OSI networking.

1. **Real system** — An autonomous computing environment consisting of one or more computer devices and the associated hardware, software, operators, and networking capabilities. The personal computer, the workstation, the set of workstations and servers, all the way through the mainframe and its existing network constitute a real system.
2. **Open system** — The portion of a real system that supports OSI by implementation of OSI services and protocols. Not every OSI service and protocol must be implemented. This leads to the concept of profiles or selected subsets of OSI that must be implemented.
3. **Real open systems** — A real system (one or more computers) that does indeed implement OSI.

4. **End systems** — OSI communications are established between end systems, which are often called hosts.

Other systems (called intermediate systems) may be invoked between two end systems. They are relay systems since they simply send the protocol data units on towards the destination end system. As indicated in Figure 1-5, these relay systems may be simple repeaters (at the physical layer), bridges between local area networks (at the data link layer), routers (at the network layer) between any kinds of networks, or application layer gateways. Technically, the concepts of end and intermediate systems apply to the role that they play in any given instance, not necessarily the hardware/software configuration. A given system might be an end system in one instance and an intermediate system in another. However, the terms are generally used to refer to specific types of systems as that is the most common situation in practice.

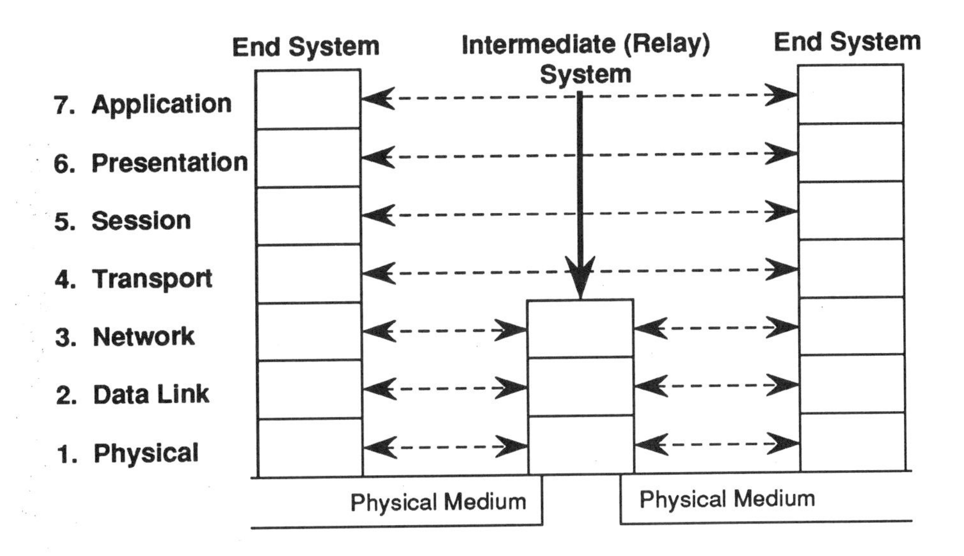


*Illustration courtesy of Learning Group International*

**FIGURE 1-5** Communication involving relay open systems.

## Layering of Protocols

One of the most common principles of networking is layering. A form of modularity, layering goes further to include a hierarchy of the calling sequence of the modules. Several terms and concepts from the OSI Reference Model are indicated below.

1. **Layered protocols** — All networking protocols (at least beyond simple point-to-point protocols) are layered. The basic idea is to take a complex problem such as networking and divide it into a series of smaller problems, a subset of which is assigned to a given layer. Figure 1-5 shows the OSI layers.
2. **The N-layer** — OSI layers have certain general concepts and characteristics. These are typically located at the N-layer. For all but the bottom and top layers, there are N-1 and N+1 layers as well. The N-layer builds upon the N-1 layer and provides enhanced services to the N+1 layer. It is similar to the department manager who builds upon the services provided by lower level branch managers to provide even better services to the upper level division manager. Everyone contributes, and the whole hopefully equals or exceeds the sum of its parts.
3. **The N-entity** — The entity at each layer in the OSI model, typically the implementation of the protocol at that layer. Each protocol layer is a separate implementation and may be assigned to a different programmer. It may be a separate process, depending on the impact on the system.
4. **Peer entity** — Each protocol level entity has a corresponding peer entity at the other end system. The only component of the other end system that the first end system communicates with is the peer entity. Don't even consider saying anything as innocuous as *Have a nice day* to anyone other than the peer!
5. **Peer-to-peer communication** — OSI reinforced the earlier concept of peer-to-peer communication within a given protocol layer. Some earlier protocol implementations were guilty of protocol layer violations in which layer N-1 spoke directly to a remote layer N. A classic example is the original ARPAnet (Advanced Research Projects Agency) *request for next message* sent from the destination packet switch to the sending host. This worked reasonably well within a single network but did not handle the case of internetworking. A more recent example is in LANs in which the receiving hardware sets a flag to indicate if the

packet is addressed to it; this flag is interpreted by the sending host. This works reasonably well in a single LAN, but it introduces ambiguity when a bridge device connects two LANs. OSI considers the specific concerns of peer-to-peer communications, as well as communications between layers.

6. **Strict layering of protocols** — OSI introduced the concept of very strict layering. Every layer should be involved in every application usage of the OSI protocol suite. In previous protocol suites such as TCP/IP, the concern was limited to retaining a hierarchical structure while allowing applications to build upon whatever layer (or subset of layers) were considered appropriate.
7. **Sublayer** — A layer within a layer. For example, the internet protocol is a sublayer within the network layer. Similarly, the logical link control of local area network protocols is a sublayer of the data link layer. Unlike regular layers, sublayers are optional and need not be employed in every protocol suite; as a result, they can be bypassed as appropriate.
8. **Protocol suite** — A particular selection of protocols at each layer. One might consider all possible protocols to be the entire contents of a menu in a restaurant. A meal consists of individual choices at each layer — appetizer, soup, main course, and dessert. An OSI protocol suite is a set of protocols for each of the seven layers chosen from the possible OSI protocols available, as in the following example.

   **Application**: File transfer, electronic mail, and virtual terminal.
   **Presentation**: Basic American Standard Code for Information Interchange (ASCII) and Extended Binary Coded Decimal Interchange Code (EBCDIC) character sets and related representations of data in DEC and IBM host systems.
   **Session**: Two-way alternate flow of data.
   **Transport**: Reliable, sequenced, flow-controlled delivery.
   **Network**: Basic X.25 connection-oriented network service.
   **Data Link**: Point-to-point communications on links and LANs.
   **Physical**: Telephone (modem) and LAN circuits.

   A variety of such protocol suites are possible, and several are discussed in this text. Sometimes called protocol stacks, in the food and menu analogy they relate to a stack of pancakes — one protocol per pancake.
9. **Service definition** and **protocol specification** — Each layer (or sublayer) is described in terms of two documents: a service definition and

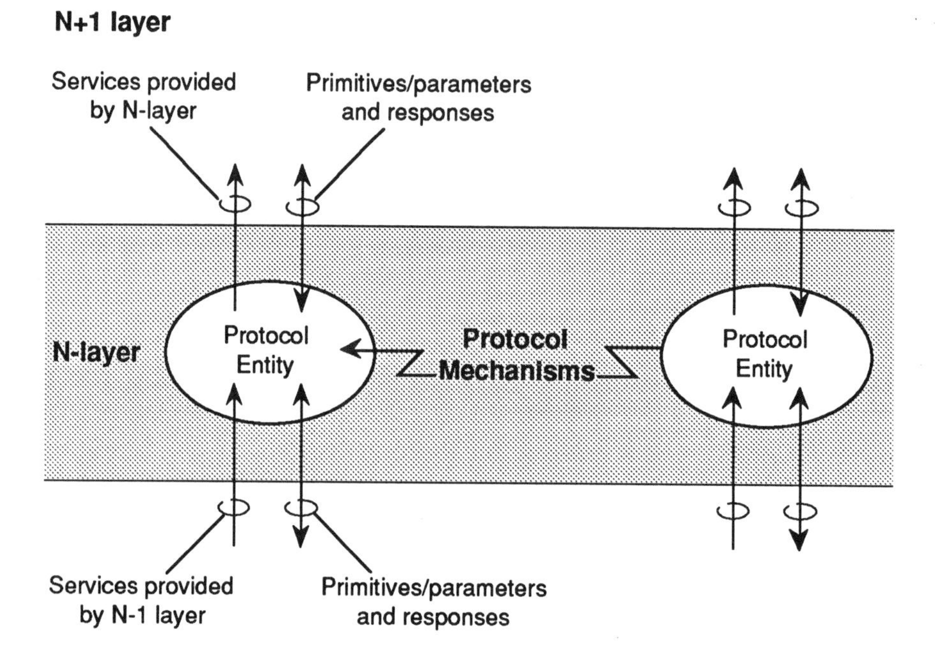


*Illustration courtesy of Learning Group International*

**FIGURE 1-6** Layer model services and protocols.

a protocol specification. The service definition defines the services provided by this layer (or sublayer) to the next higher layer. The protocol specification defines the set of communication conventions that guides the peer-level entities in the two end systems. Entities can be either software implementations or hardware devices. Figure 1-6 shows service and protocol distinctions.

10. **Service user** and **service provider** — Any given layer is the service user of the layer below it and the service provider of the layer above it. Certain functions (e.g., abort of a connection) may be initiated by either the user or provider.
11. **Pass-through services** — Connections at a given protocol layer provide a well-defined service but may not actually generate the service. This is especially true at the network and transport layers (which are

often considered together). If the network layer provides a service, it can be propagated directly upwards as a transport layer service. Reliable and sequenced delivery is an example. If the network layer provides a service, the transport layer can simply pass it along. These are sometimes called pass-through services. Therefore, different classes of transport protocols provide the same service in different mixes of transport versus network-provided services.

## Connections

The OSI Reference Model was connection-oriented from its beginning. Subsequently, an addendum has added consideration of connectionless operation, but the emphasis is still on connections.

1. **Connections and connectionless communication** — The original concept of a connection was a login-to-logout sequence of events. In current OSI work, a connection is a mutually agreed upon form of communications associated with reliable, sequenced, flow-controlled delivery. All three services rely on memory about the past, e.g., what protocol data units have been sent but not acknowledged, what the next sequence number should be, and how much additional data can be sent. This memory is known as state information. In contrast, connectionless communications are more like simple transactions and typically do not have this state information. While connectionless operation may involve some level of error and flow control, the only sequence control involved is duplicate detection. Although connection versus connectionless wars have been fought for some time, many examples of *inter-marriage* exist, and the distinctions are often blurred by current, non-OSI practice.
2. **Connection-oriented services** — OSI services and protocols are primarily connection-oriented and operate on the basis of establishing a connection and negotiating the properties of the connection. Data units are transferred, and eventually the connection is released. The basic requirement of a connection is that data are delivered with error, sequence, and flow control.
3. **Error control** — The ability to detect and correct errors, usually by means of an error-detection code and retransmission based on the expiration of a timeout if no acknowledgment is returned.

4. **Sequence control** — The capability of maintaining the proper order of data units and ensuring that none are missing or duplicated. Sequencing is the second inherent property of a connection.
5. **Flow control** — A mechanism by which a receiver can advise the sender of its ability to accept more data. Flow control is a pervasive capability that must exist between all point-to-point (as well as end-to-end) entities. Flow control is the third inherent property of a connection.
6. **Connection establishment primitives** — Typically the connection establishment is based on a full OSI handshake as shown in Figure 1-7. The handshake consists of an originator request delivered to the other system as an indication. A response completes the handshake; it is delivered across the network and arrives as a confirmation at the originating end system. During this exchange an agreement is negotiated regarding the possibility of connection and its parameters (such as maximum packet size). After establishing a connection, transfers may

- **Some operations have a full handshake.**

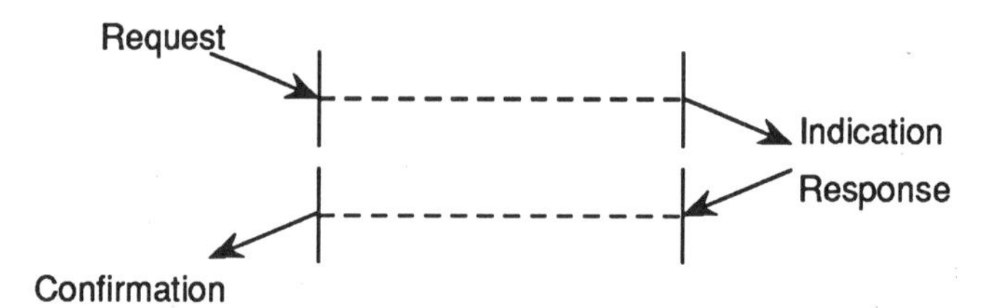


- **Other operations are not confirmed.**

- **Still other operations may be initiated by the service provider.**

*Illustration courtesy of Learning Group International*

**FIGURE 1-7** Handshake: request, indication, response, and confirmation.

be by means of simple request and indication primitives. Indications may also result from service provider operations.

7. **Negotiation** — When a connection is established, various properties of the connection can be mutually agreed upon by the negotiation process. These properties include the maximum protocol data unit size and options such as error checking. If a parameter is not negotiated, it will have a default value. If the originator of the connection requests some non-default value for a parameter, the responding end system can always negotiate the value to be closer to the default value or accept the requested value. The responding end can never negotiate a value further from the default, nor can it introduce new parameters into the negotiation. At the upper layers, services are negotiated in terms of functional units. Negotiation is not found in connectionless protocols.
8. **Functional units** — Unlike the transport and network layers, the higher layers do not provide a common (single) service level. Instead, they provide a variety of functional units that can be negotiated at connection establishment. Each functional unit provides a different service. One functional unit may control the end system that can communicate in a half-duplex manner, while another functional unit may be related to crash recovery in a file transfer. Not all applications need all functional units; therefore, they are negotiable. However, a non-negotiable *kernel* component is required in all implementations.
9. **Normal data** — Once the connection is made, user data can be exchanged. Actually, a limited amount of user data can also be exchanged in the connection establishment and/or connection release protocol data units, but that is a bit like starting a conversation over the telephone before identifying the party at the other end or saying something important immediately before hanging up. Both are possible, but neither is considered acceptable. Normally, one would establish the connection and then send user data.
10. **Expedited data** — Connections may include the capability to send expedited data. Expedited data transfer involves the ability to establish a second data channel over which special urgent data can be sent without being subject to flow control over the principal channel. The idea is to provide a separate, out-of-band control channel.

## Endpoints — Names and Addresses

Both connection and connectionless services require that the applicable endpoints be identified. In the analogous telephone calls and postal messages, one must provide at least a phone number and an address respectively. The party sought typically has both a name and a number. Frequently the name is available but not the number. The network needs the number. Just as people use a directory service (phone book) to find a number, a network employs directory servers.

The official word for name in OSI is title. If people addressed each other as *Mr. President* or *Ms. Programmer*, the word title would be a reasonable synonym for name.

1. **Title** — A permanent identifier (name) associated with an N-layer entity. The most common instance of the use of a title is with an application.
2. **Global title** — Consists of two parts, a title domain name and a local title. A global title is unique within all OSI.
3. **Title domain name** — A globally unique name for a title domain, e.g., an administrative organization responsible for further assignment of names within that domain.
4. **Local title** — An assigned name that is unique only within a title domain.
5. **Directory service** — Provides a mapping of an N-layer title into an N-1 layer address. This mapping is typically from an application title to a presentation layer service access point by an application-layer directory service.
6. **Service access point** (SAP) — An abstraction and generalization of previous *ad hoc* mechanisms that existed in non-OSI protocols to express linkages between the protocol layers. For example, in a typical TCP/IP protocol suite, an application such as file transfer identifies its peer protocol by a TCP port number. The fact that TCP (as opposed to the user datagram transport protocol) is being used is indicated by the next protocol in the IP header. The use of IP (as opposed to DECnet, etc.) is indicated in an Ethernet *type field*. Finally, the particular LAN destination is indicated in an Ethernet destination address field. Each of these fields provides a piece of information required for its delivery, much the same way that each component of a postal delivery address provides information needed during the delivery process. OSI has adopted the SAP for each of these components (except for the network address of the computers themselves). SAPs are the internal software addresses. A SAP is an abstraction, while a SAP address provides a concrete indication of the desired protocol service. By following a

sequence of SAPs, the application data finds its way down through the protocol layers on one end system and back up through the layers of the receiving end system. A given SAP provides a particular service such as secure delivery or high throughput delivery. Several higher-layer protocol entities can use a SAP at any given time. The uniqueness of each entity is maintained by the separate reference point identifiers (sometimes called connection endpoint identifiers), shown as dots inside the SAP ellipse in Figure 1-8.

7. **SAP address** — Concrete representation of a portion of an overall address that specifies a traversal of the OSI protocol suite. The information provided by the sequence of SAP addresses is the same for every installation of a given service. As such, it is provided by a directory service.
8. **Connection endpoint identifier** — An identification number associated with a connection that uses a given SAP. These numbers differ from one installation of a given service to another and are established (and meaningful) only for the duration of a connection.

## Handling Data Units

The data transferred between peer entities and across layer boundaries are grouped into manageable blocks of bytes; in OSI the blocks are called data

- **A service access point (SAP) exists at a layer boundary.**

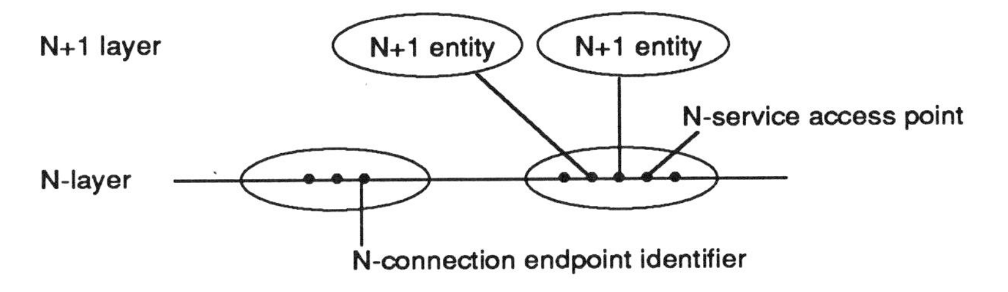


- **A SAP is a number associated with a given service.**

*Illustration courtesy of Learning Group International*

**FIGURE 1-8** Service access points.

units. This section introduces concepts and terminology related to these data units.

1. **Octet** — The OSI term for byte. In the U.S., an eight-bit data unit is a byte; in OSI, it is an octet. Some countries use the term *byte* for six-, seven-, or nine-bit units. An *octet* is always eight bits in length.
2. **Protocol data unit** (PDU) — A protocol data unit is to OSI what the packet was to pre-OSI networking. OSI terminology is often rather verbose. Why say three words when one will do? Just as byte can mean different things in other parts of the world, so can words such as packet, frame, or message. OSI says PDU to be precise. Of course, it may also be that OSI likes dealing with acronyms and does not work well with one-word names.
3. **XPDU** — OSI appends a letter to PDU to relate it to a specific layer. Therefore, TPDU means transport PDU, while NPDU means network PDU. This further specifies the data unit of concern in a given discussion. In general, the XPDU is the unit of information that is passed between peer protocol entities at layer X.
4. **Protocol control information** (PCI) — A PDU consists of two parts. One part is the PCI, which has been called the header in non-OSI protocols. The second part is what the protocol layer considers data. Together they make up what in non-OSI is called a packet. The PCI contains all the information needed by the peer entity to process the PDU. This information may include an error check, a sequence number, an indication about the type of information in the PDU, or an indication if this is the last piece of a multi-part transmission.
5. **Service data unit** (SDU) — The unit of information that passes across a layer boundary and is treated as data. In OSI the data unit that passes from layer N to layer N-1 at the sending end (computer) is the same SDU that passes from layer N-1 to layer N at the receiving end. This allows complete logical units of information to preserve record boundaries. Figure 1-9 shows an SDU at layer N+1 becoming the data portion of a layer NPDU. The remaining portion of the PDU is the PCI.
6. **Interface data unit** — While an SDU is the information transferred across a layer boundary, this does not mean that the entire SDU must come across in one giant block. Interface data units convey all or part of an SDU. Each interface data unit consists of interface control information and optional interface data.
7. **Segmentation** — An SDU becomes the data field in the next lower layer if it fits within the maximum allowed PDU size. There are three

possibilities. It may be too large, too small, or just right (not unlike Goldilocks and the three bears). If it is too large, it is divided into two or more segments, and each segment indicates whether it is (or is not) the last piece. The process of putting the pieces back together is called reassembly. If it is too small, it may be blocked with others as described below. If it is just right, it fits in the PDU by itself. If reassembly is needed, enough control information is required to determine where each piece fits and when all the pieces are present.

8. **Blocking** — Has a different meaning in computer networking than in voice/data communications (in which it means the inability to get a call through the switching devices). In networking, blocking means combining two or more SDUs for transmission. Blocking can occur when the SDUs are so small that it is not efficient to send each as a separate PDU. The SDUs can be blocked into one PDU and deblocked upon reception. The deblocking operation requires that sufficient information be carried along to pull out the separate pieces. This is typically done by conveying a length field with each SDU.
9. **Concatenation** — Similar to blocking but differs in the type of data units involved. Concatenation combines two or more N-layer PDUs

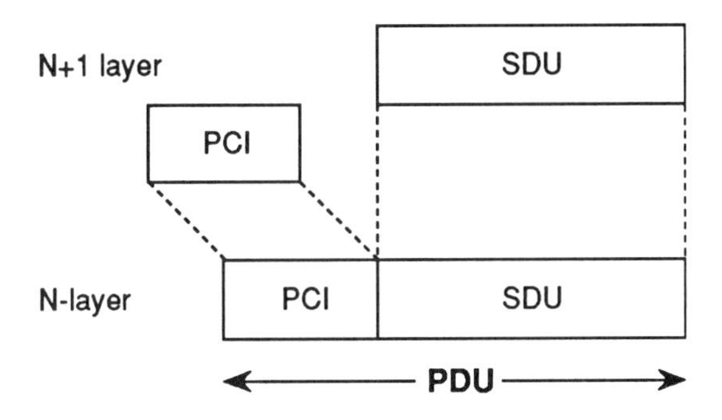


- **PCI — Protocol control information.**
- **PDU — Protocol data unit.**
- **SDU — Service data unit.**

*Illustration courtesy of Learning Group International*

**FIGURE 1-9** OSI data units.

into one N-1 layer SDU. An example of concatenation is to combine an ACK (acknowledgment) PDU with a data PDU in one transmission. The inverse operation in the case of concatenation is separation. Enough control information must be conveyed to allow the individual PDUs to be separated. This is also accomplished by carrying a length field with each PDU.

## Flow of Data

Several aspects about the flow of data need to be considered. These include dialogue control (whose turn is it to talk), path control (where does the data go), and reestablishing the synchronization of flow between systems.

1. **Two-way simultaneous** (TWS) — A form of dialogue control in which there is no control. Either side can send whenever it wants. It is similar in concept to full-duplex data communications (called duplex in some circles).
2. **Two-way alternate** (TWA) — The first thing to remember is that TWA is not an airline, at least not in this context. Instead, TWA means taking turns in a given dialogue. This sounds like the half-duplex operation of the good old days of data communications. In half duplex, the two sides take turns using the entire bandwidth of a telephone channel. TWA is intended for a higher purpose. For simplicity an application may be designed to handle only one transaction at a time. It finishes one before it begins the next. TWA dialogue control ensures that this is the case, since the requester does not get a chance to ask another question until the previous question is answered.
3. **Token** — A control mechanism that allows either end of a connection to perform a predefined operation such as sending a PDU (as in TWA above) or releasing the connection. A token can be requested and later sent by primitives of the protocol. Token ring and token bus LANs provide a limited form of this token control, namely who can transmit next. However, the concept of a token in OSI is much broader than this limited form.
4. **Orderly release** — Both end systems are allowed to complete transmission before releasing (ending) the connection. Connections are comparable to telephone calls. No one hangs up the phone without making sure the other party is also finished.

5. **Abort** — Exactly the opposite of the orderly release. In the telephone analogy, one simply hangs up rather than allowing the used car salesman to finish the pitch. The computer might abort a connection if a non-recoverable exception condition occurs or if a security violation is detected.
6. **Reset** — Used to resynchronize the entities to a known initial state for processing associated with one connection. An example is resetting sequence numbers on data transmissions to the initial value (typically zero). The reset operation may signal the loss or duplication of data, as would be the case if several outstanding (unacknowledged) PDUs were followed by a reset command. The reset may be initiated by either the provider or the user.
7. **Multiplexing** — Another aspect of the flow of data relates to the relationship between these flows at different OSI layers. For example, a communications circuit (real or virtual) at an N-layer may be shared simultaneously by several users at the N+1 layer through multiplexing. Examples include several X.25 virtual circuits sharing the same data link layer connection and multiple transport connections sharing a single X.25 virtual circuit. Multiplexing is almost never performed above the transport layer, although serial (non-simultaneous) reusage of transport and session connections is possible.
8. **Demultiplexing** — The opposite of multiplexing. PDUs that share the N-layer connection must be sorted into the separate N+1 layer connections upon arrival at the destination. A connection identifier must be included in each PDU prior to sending it and can then be used at reception to identify the applicable N+1 layer connection.
9. **Splitting** and **recombining** — A data flow may be split into parallel data streams and later recombined. For example, a host might have multiple data link and physical layer connections to a packet switch and could split traffic so that it could use the higher aggregate data rate of the multiple links.
10. **Routing** — One of the responsibilities assigned to the network layer is to provide a path across the network. Many possible paths exist, whether going through alternate packet switches within a network or through alternate networks in an internet. The routing function provides the best path. In some cases, a static path is established when a connection is made, while in other cases, the path is dynamically adapted based on failures or congestion.

# NAMING AND ADDRESSING

Naming and addressing were not included in the original OSI Reference Model but are the subjects of an addendum. The basic concepts of names and addresses are the same in OSI and earlier protocols. Names are user-convenient text strings that relate one-to-one to network resources. Addresses are binary, hex, or decimal representations of the actual location on the internetwork. Mapping between names (which people like to use) and the numeric values (which the network needs) are typically performed by a directory service. This is analogous to using a telephone directory to map a person's name to the appropriate telephone number.

Almost all name/address systems are hierarchical and can be used to sort out the communications to specific endpoints. This approach applies to the telephone system. It is possible to call another employee simply by dialing four digits. To place a local call outside the organization requires dialing three more digits. To go beyond the telephone area, an additional three digits must be dialed to specify the area code. Finally, adding a few more digits to dial a country code is necessary to make an international call. This demonstrates the hierarchical structure of a telephone numbering system.

The postal delivery system also operates with hierarchical addressing. Consider the address of a postcard mailed from the United Kingdom to the United States, with an address as shown below.

Mr. Sam Smith
Mail Station 123
The XYZ Corporation
1234 Shadygrove Lane
Yourtown, Yourstate 98765
U.S.A.

The first portion of the address to be interpreted is the nation field, which gets it to the continental U.S. There it is sent to ZIP code 98765. If Yourtown is very large, this demultiplexing operation gets the postcard to the proper post office within Yourtown. If Yourtown is very small, the demultiplexing is to a postal unit that knows about Yourtown. In either case, demultiplexing gets the postcard to the proper mail distribution center. From there, the proper carrier for 1234 Shadygrove Lane gets the postcard and delivers it to the XYZ Corporation at 1234 Shadygrove Lane. At this point, the postcard arrives at the proper building. The final demultiplexing identifies the mail station number and the addressee. Each of these fields, from U.S.A. to Mr. Sam Smith, is a component of the address. The portion of the postal address that gets the postcard into the correct building is analogous to the part of the network address that gets the packet to the right physical computer. The remaining portions of the address (the mail station number and the addressee's name) are internal (or logical) rather than physical addresses.

The same structure exists in OSI. One portion of the address gets the packet into the correct computer; the remaining internal addresses specify software components within the computer. In OSI terminology, the internal portions of the address are service access points. The data string consisting of the physical address plus the internal SAPs is the complete address. At any given protocol layer, only one field is of concern, but all are required for ultimate delivery.

In OSI networks, the network SAP (NSAP) plays a major role. It gets the information delivered to the proper network layer delivery point, i.e., to the proper transport entity. The importance of the NSAP is that there are so many alternative components of the address up to that point. Above the transport layer, there is no further multiplexing. The transport SAP (TSAP) connected directly to one session SAP (SSAP), which in turn is directly connected to one presentation SAP (PSAP). In contrast, below the NSAP are various choices on the network layer protocol, the data link layer protocol, the physical address of the computer, the subnetwork number that it resides on, and the organization identifier for the local set of interconnected subnetworks. (See Figure 1-10.) The NSAP concept allows one to sort all this out.

- **ISO 8348 describes a structure for universal addressing.**

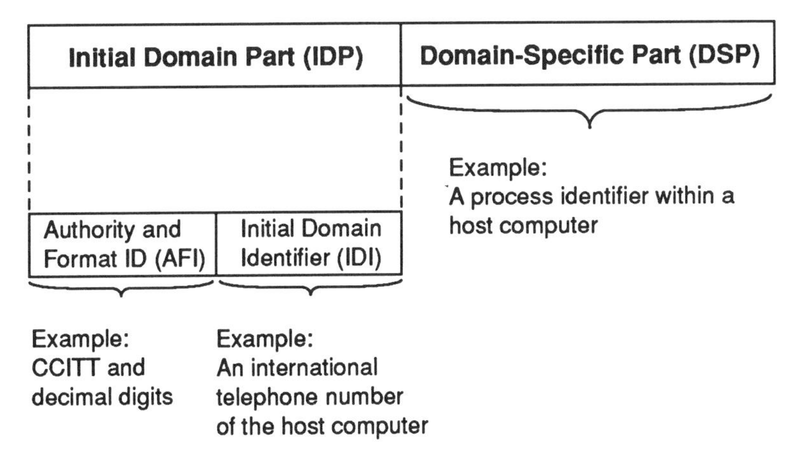


*Illustration courtesy of Learning Group International*

**FIGURE 1-10** Network SAP addressing.

The NSAP consists of three fields: the authority and format identifier (AFI) field, the initial domain identifier (IDI) field, and the domain-specific part (DSP) field. If that is not enough new terminology, the combined AFI and IDI fields are the initial domain part (IDP). The authority and format field identifies the responsible organization (the authority) such as CCITT and the format of the IDI such as decimal digits, packed two per byte. Another example is when the authority is local and the format of the IDI is an octet string. Examples of the defined AFI values and the corresponding authorities, IDI formats, and DSP syntax are demonstrated in the following table.

**TABLE 1-1** Addressing components.

| AFI Value | Authority | IDI Format | DSP Syntax |
|---|---|---|---|
| 36 | CCITT | X.121 decimal digits ≤ 14 digits | Decimal digits |
| 37 | CCITT | X.121 decimal digits ≤ 14 digits | Binary |
| 46 | ISO | ICD, 4 decimal digits | Decimal digits |
| 47 | ISO | ICD, 4 decimal digits | Binary |
| 48 | Local | Local definition | Decimal digits |
| 49 | Local | Local definition | Binary |

Note: ICD = International code designator

The IDI identifies a system or a group of systems under a single administrative domain of control. An example of an IDI is an X.121 international address of a computer in terms of its country code, network number, and computer number. The DSP is then a locally defined format for address information in the domain specified by the IDI value. An example of an NSAP address will help clarify this structuring of address information.

Consider the software and hardware configuration shown in Figure 1-11. The NSAP to be uniquely identified is to specify the user of the network layer service. In this example, that user is the connection-oriented OSI Transport Protocol. The user is distinguished from another user by the NSAP selector. An alternative user of the network service might be the connectionless transport protocol, for example. The network service in this case is the OSI Internet Protocol. That form of network service is selected by the link SAP (LSAP). Both the NSAP selector and the LSAP are internal software addresses of the indicated computer. The next component of the hierarchical address is the physical address of the computer, in this case a six-octet local area network

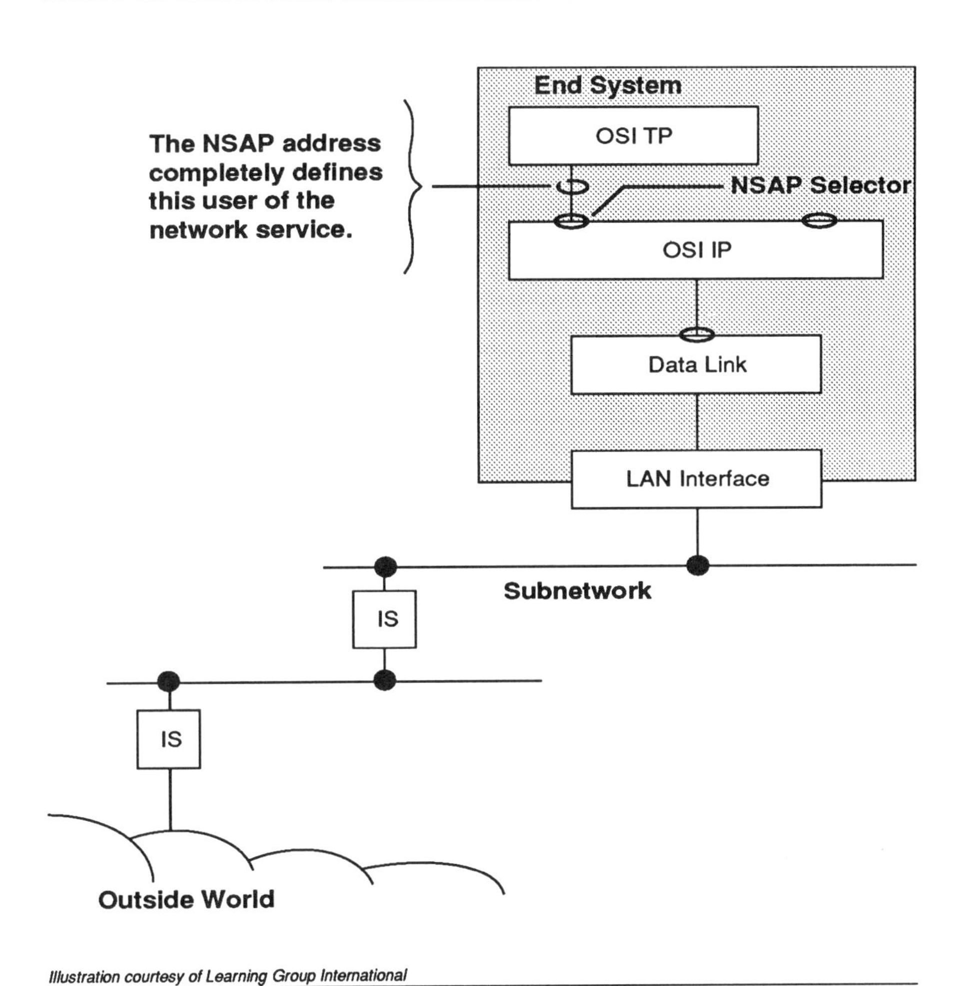


*Illustration courtesy of Learning Group International*

**FIGURE 1-11** The NSAP identifies a specific user of the network service.

address. This computer is on a subnet network that has been assigned a subnet address; the address developed up to this point is shown below.

Address = <subnet address> <LAN address of the computer>
<LSAP> <NSAP selector>

One might inquire where the numbers that fill in these fields come from. Who assigns them? How are the numbers' uniqueness ensured? The internal SAP values are assigned by the standards organizations. The OSI transport protocol will always have the NSAP selector value of one, and the LSAP will always have the value of Hex FE when the OSI Internet Protocol is used. These can (and should) always be the same in all systems. However, the LAN interface address cannot be the same for any two systems on the same network; it must be unique. This is ensured by the method used to assign the address at the time the interface is manufactured. A vendor is assigned a three-octet value by the standards committee, and the vendor assigns the other three octets as a serial number for the interface. That brings us to the subnetwork address. How is it assigned? What makes it unique? To accomplish this goal, yet another field must be added to the growing hierarchical address, namely the organization identifier responsible for the subnetwork.

Address = <organization identifier> <subnet address>
<LAN address of the computer> <LSAP> <NSAP Selector>

The DSP portion of the address is now complete. The addition of the organization identifier solves one problem but creates yet another. Who assigns the organization identifiers? That is easy; just use the next field in the hierarchy, namely the IDI field. Once again, who assigns that? Finally, the point of responsibility is reached. The AFI field is an internationally recognized authority that can determine the syntax and semantics of the IDI field.

Follow this example back down a specific hierarchical structure, namely that used by the federal government in the Government OSI Profile (GOSIP). GOSIP is discussed in detail in Chapter 7, but the concern here is with the NSAP address structure and interpretation as shown in Figure 1-12.

The AFI field is decimal 47, which is assigned to ISO. This AFI value specifies the syntax and semantics of the IDI field. It is a four-decimal international code designator (ICD). The AFI also implicitly defines the syntax of the DSP part of the address. In the case of an AFI value of 47, the syntax is binary.

ISO has assigned the ICD values 0005 and 0006 to the National Institute of Standards and Technology (NIST) in the U.S. for use in GOSIP. NIST is using the ICD value of 0005 for the entire federal government and is the agent responsible for assigning the organizational identifiers associated with that ICD. NIST has delegated similar responsibility for assignment of organizational identifiers for ICD 0006 to the U.S. Department of Defense.

When NIST defines an organizational identifier to a government agency, bureau, or commission, it also delegates responsibility for assignment of the subnetwork identifiers to that entity. Within a subnetwork, it is the subnetwork administrator's responsibility to assign the next level of addressing, the end-system identifier, as appropriate. The end-system identifiers may be either physical addresses (called subnetwork point of attachment addresses) or logical addresses.

The NSAP address is adequate to get a PDU delivered well inside the software of the destination host. At that point, additional SAPs are required for the PDU to work its way up the protocol stack. These additional SAPs (called selectors) are octet strings of predefined lengths — typically two octets each. GOSIP defines a TSAP value of one to represent the OSI session layer protocol and defines an SSAP value of one to represent the presentation layer. The SSAP value of two has been assigned to the 1984 version of X.400 messaging system, which operates directly above the session layer. The PSAP value of one has been assigned to the application layer file transfer, access, and management protocol. Other PSAP values will be assigned as they are integrated into subsequent versions of GOSIP.

The addresses of concern to application entities are the NSAP address and the sequence of transport, session, and presentation selectors. None of these selector fields has global significance, any more than the street address in the analogy had global significance. An address of this form is associated with an application entity within an application process. (An application process name is a title; it typically contains multiple application entities that represent the various service elements needed to perform the desired application function.)

There are two principal addressing concerns, namely the NSAP address and the application entity address (which includes the NSAP address). These two levels within the protocol suite must access directory servers that can map between local (user-friendly) names and the application and network addresses.

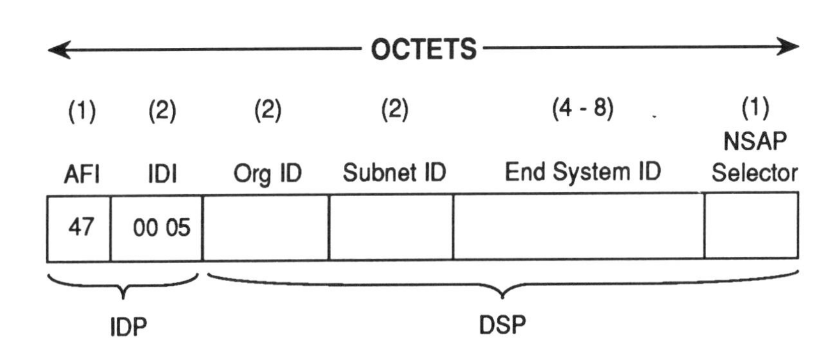


*Illustration courtesy of Learning Group International*

**FIGURE 1-12** U.S. Government NSAP address structure.

# COMMUNICATION SERVICES

The intercommunication of data between OSI end systems is performed at the lower four layers of the OSI Reference Model. The physical layer adapts bits for delivery across various media. The next three layers all provide the same kind of service, namely reliable, sequenced, flow-controlled delivery of data packets. The data link layer does this on a point-to-point basis, the network layer does it across individual networks, and the transport layer does it on an end-to-end basis. But why should they all provide the same service? All three layers are capable of providing this service, but not all do so in a given protocol suite. By the time the transport layer is reached, some combination of the data link, network, and transport layer protocols provides this service. That can be done by any number of combinations of providing error, sequence, and flow control at each of these three layers. For example, systems operating over X.25 networks often provide error control at the data link layer and sequence and flow control at all three layers. Other systems operating the TCP/IP protocols provide error, sequence, and flow control at the transport layer.

Services provided by the transport protocol are typically those of reliable, sequenced, flow-controlled delivery, i.e., a connection-oriented protocol. In contrast, the Internet Protocol is typically connectionless, providing best-effort delivery service. The transport layer is always required, but the internet sublayer is optional. (Being optional is a basic characteristic of the sublayer concept.) While both connection and connectionless transport services have been defined for OSI, almost all usage to date has been on the connection-oriented form of service. In the interests of completeness, connectionless OSI transport service and protocol will also be explored.

As indicated, the basic connection-oriented service of the transport layer is reliable, sequenced, flow-controlled delivery of data from the upper protocol layers. A secondary requirement of the connection-oriented service is to provide an out-of-band expedited data channel for limited amounts of special (typically urgent) data. In OSI, only one expedited data PDU can be outstanding at any given time on a connection, and no further normal data PDUs can be sent until the expedited data PDU is delivered and ACKed.

The services of a connection are to provide error-free, sequenced, and flow-controlled delivery of normal and expedited PDUs. Each of these basic services is considered in more detail in the following paragraphs.

1. **Error-free delivery** — Obtained by means of error detection and correction (EDC) mechanisms. The errors themselves may be intro-

duced on the communications links or within the communications processors. The communications links are by far the most common source of errors, especially with analog telephone switching circuits. In some networks, these are the only errors considered, and EDC can be on a link-by-link basis at the data link layer of the OSI Reference Model. Once PDUs have passed through the data link layer, they are in a safe environment, and no further EDC mechanisms are needed.

In some other networks, the links may have error characteristics that are many orders of magnitude better than telephone links, or the switching equipment may be of uncertain quality. The latter is especially the case when the routing of PDUs is automatically determined by the network and end systems have no knowledge of the particular path that PDUs are taking. This means that the switches as well as the links are possible sources of errors. End-to-end EDC are common in these instances.

Other networks may have a combination of link-by-link and end-to-end error detection and recovery. This may seem like a *belt-and-suspender* approach, but it has merit. Errors are detected and corrected as quickly as possible, avoiding the wasted channel capacity involved in delivering damaged PDUs, only to have them discarded at the destination end system. Link-by-link error recovery also provides diagnostic information regarding where the error is being introduced.

2. **Sequenced delivery** — Just as the error-free delivery service could be provided by either link-by-link or end-to-end mechanisms, sequence controls can also be provided by either of these two approaches. If every link along the path ensures that PDUs are kept in proper sequence and that none are lost or duplicated, then sequence control can be provided at the data link layer. The service is then propagated up through the network layer with no required value added to the transport layer, which likewise propagates the service to the session layer. However, if there are any connectionless links (such as some LANs that may drop PDUs) or if PDUs may be lost, duplicated, or have the order changed within switches, sequencing controls are required on an end-to-end basis.
3. **Flow-controlled delivery** — One might also attempt to provide flow-control service at the transport layer service interface by cascaded data link protocols, since they also have flow control mechanisms such as *receiver not ready* and *receiver ready*. If a destination or intermediate

node becomes short on buffers, it can issue a *receiver not ready* command. However, this would stop all flow across the link, including many end-to-end transport connections. What worked well for error and sequence control does not work for flow control. Flow control should be at a finer granularity so that individual connections can be independently controlled. Flow control must remain as a transport layer mechanism, even when it is also provided at lower layers.

There are many different ways in which transport layer services may actually be provided, depending on the mixture of transport, network, and data link protocol support. The basic service is the same, regardless of the method used to provide it.

## Summary and Conclusions

The OSI Reference Model establishes a set of well-defined terms and concepts that can be used for precise descriptions of a variety of networking needs. However, the fundamental purpose of the OSI Reference Model is to serve as a framework for the establishment of standards. Looking closely at the OSI protocols at the various layers and sublayers reveals that it is very effective in this regard.

The next two chapters will investigate in detail how the four lower layers combine services to provide the end-to-end delivery mechanisms required by the upper layers. The lower four layers will be examined in a *bottom-up* manner, beginning with the physical and data link layers and their point-to-point services between computers (end systems) and relay devices (intermediate systems). An investigation of the end-to-end services of the network and transport layers will follow. This bottom-up approach is used because the layers add value and understanding as they build upon one another. For example, the concept of a fixed window size is introduced at the data link layer, but at the network layer it becomes a negotiated parameter, and at the transport layer it is continuously variable. The bottom-up approach builds both services and understanding of concepts.

# 2

# POINT-TO-POINT COMMUNICATIONS: THE PHYSICAL AND DATA LINK LAYERS

The bottom two layers of the Open Systems Interconnection (OSI) Reference Model are concerned with the delivery of information (in terms of bits and packets respectively) between two directly connected computing equipments. These computing systems are not necessarily end systems because they include intermediate systems such as routers.

Whether the physical and data link layers interconnect end systems or combinations of end and router systems, the interconnection between these systems is by definition point-to-point because there are no intermediate protocols. This definition assumes that physical layer communications are not based on protocols. The physical and data link layers are closely related and are discussed in this chapter. Similarly, the network and transport protocols are closely related and are discussed in the next chapter.

## THE OSI PHYSICAL LAYER

The physical layer is a rather unique layer within the OSI Reference Model because it deals more with hardware and electrical issues than with software-implemented functionality. The basic purpose of this layer is to deliver bits from one end of a wire to another, where the entities at the ends of the wire may be either end systems or intermediate systems such as packet switches, routers, or bridges. The physical layer is concerned with bit serial transmission, clocking, synchronization, modulation, and multiplexing, among other matters. That discussion begins with a look at what the OSI Reference Model says about the physical layer.

## The Physical Layer in the OSI Reference Model

The OSI Reference Model states that the physical layer includes the mechanical, electrical, functional, and procedural means to activate, maintain, and deactivate physical connections for bit transmission between data link entities. This physical layer communication is across a medium such as cabling, but the media itself is outside the scope of OSI.

The OSI Reference Model indicates that the physical layer is responsible for the mechanical, electrical, functional, and procedural means of communications. The *mechanical* aspects include the connectors and pins that interconnect the various devices. The *electrical* aspects include the signal voltage levels and transitions to represent binary one, zero, and non-data symbols. The *functional* aspects include the commands and responses that make up the vocabulary of the physical layer controls. Sequences of these commands and responses make up the final aspect, namely the *procedural* means of communications.

The OSI Reference Model also states that the physical layer includes the means to activate, maintain, and deactivate physical connections for bit transmission between data link entities. The need to a*ctivate* the physical connection includes the need in some instances to establish the physical layer connections such as direct-dial telephone circuits. In cases such as local area networks (LANs), the physical layer mechanisms are permanently in place. The need to *maintain* the physical connection includes any controls required to ensure that the physical connection is kept operational. Finally, the need to *deactivate* the physical connection involves procedures for disconnecting the physical connection when appropriate, such as a direct-dial telephone call.

The protocol data unit (PDU) and service data unit (SDU) aspects of the physical layer are especially unusual when compared to other layers. There is no PDU in the conventional sense of having protocol control information and user data observable at the layer. The SDU is a bit (or a byte if the transmission can be characterized in eight-bit intervals).

The physical connection endpoints may have addresses or identifiers associated with them. Telephone numbers could play this role in the direct-dial example. For simple point-to-point cabling, there is no equivalent. Similarly, there is typically little or no support for error detection and recovery, sequencing, or flow control. One could envision some form of forward error control being used, but that is normally not the case with physical connections. Sequencing is inherent in that the bits are delivered one after another in the same order that they are sent; there is no way to get out of order. It is possible for a bit to be lost, which is one of the concerns of sequencing. Finally, flow control may be nonexistent or by means of XON/XOFF character transmissions.

## The Basics of Physical Layer Data Communications

Whether the physical layer communication connection needs to be established or not, its basic characteristic is that of a communications channel with a predefined data rate and bandwidth. These two characteristics are closely related in theory and practice. To get high data rates, one needs high bandwidth. As a rule of thumb, one needs about one hertz (cycle per second) of bandwidth to get one bit per second (bps) of data rate. As shown in Figure 2-1, a telephone channel has a bandwidth of about 3,000 hertz, and therefore can communicate at approximately 3,000 bps. Some operate at 1,200 bps and others at 9,600 bps, but all are well within this rule of thumb.

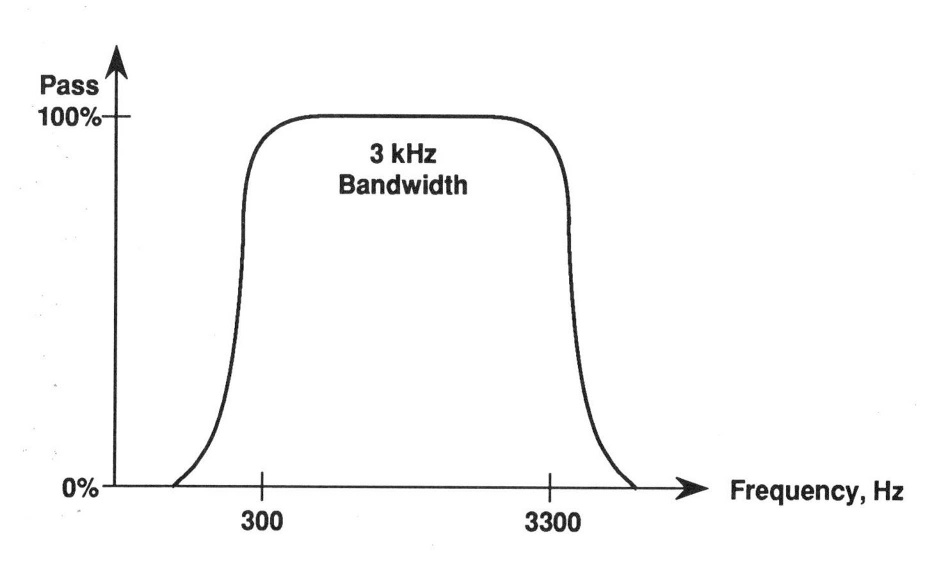


*Illustration courtesy of Learning Group International*

**FIGURE 2-1** A telephone channel has a limited bandwidth.

The theoretical relationship between data rate and bandwidth is stated by a simple but profound result derived by Claude Shannon years ago, namely:

Maximum data rate= bandwidth * log base 2 [1 + S/N]
where S/N = signal-to-noise ratio.

A numerically convenient example is for the signal power to be seven times that of the noise, so that the logarithm value is three (i.e., two to the power of three is [1 + 7] or eight). This says that the maximum bps data rate is three times the bandwidth. The rule of thumb of one bps per hertz is well within this maximum.

Shannon's result theoretically applies to Gaussian (random) noise, but that is not the most common source of noise on terrestrial circuits. Gaussian noise produces random, isolated bit errors, while terrestrial circuits are primarily affected by burst errors, i.e., a cluster of bits, many of which are in error. A burst error comes about by some disturbance that forces all the bits to be either binary one or zero for a period of time. Not all bits of a burst are in error because some bits are intended to be the value that is being forced. The burst length is the bit count from the first bad bit to the last bad bit in the bit cluster.

Even though Shannon's result does not directly apply to burst-error conditions, it does provide a theoretical upper boundary on the achievable data rate over a given bandwidth. It also validates the rule of thumb of approximately one bps per hertz as being based on something more solid than observations of previous implementations.

Data communications are generally by means of bit serial transmission in which addressing and other control information are sent in the same communications bit stream (or band) as the data. This leads to what is called in-band control. An example of in-band control is encountered every time the telephone is dialed. The familiar dual tone frequencies are heard as the keys on the telephone are pressed. The control (dialing) information is sent in the same frequency band as voice conversation. The telephone system operates with a protocol that expects the first several sounds (dual tones and ringing indicators) to be control information, and then the remaining sounds are the user's data such as the voice conversation.

Telephone conversations are normally conducted in a manner so that only one person is speaking at any given time. In data communications terminology, this is called half duplex. Either side can transmit, but only one side at a time. In contrast, data communications may be full duplex, in which both sides can transmit simultaneously. In OSI, this latter capability is called duplex. In higher-layer protocols, these two capabilities are called two-way alternate and two-way simultaneous, respectively.

While data communications are typically bit serial, there may still be both bit and byte distinctions in the data stream. Therefore, an SDU may be either a bit or a byte. When bytes are being recognized, they are often encoded in a character set such as the American Standard Code for Information Interchange. ASCII is the U.S. version of the OSI International Alphabet Five (IA5). Countries measure currency differently and use symbols such as the dollar and pound signs. The familiar # symbol in the U.S. is not so familiar in countries that have a different graphic applied to this IA5 bit pattern.

The ASCII code set (see Figure 2-2) contains many special patterns that are reserved for support of pre-OSI data link protocols, such as data link escape (DLE). This book ignores these character representations because it is about OSI. However, two examples should be discussed to explore how flow

| b7 → | | | | | 0 | 0 | 0 | 0 | 1 | 1 | 1 | 1 |
|---|---|---|---|---|---|---|---|---|---|---|---|---|
| b6 → | | | | | 0 | 0 | 1 | 1 | 0 | 0 | 1 | 1 |
| b5 → | | | | | 0 | 1 | 0 | 1 | 0 | 1 | 0 | 1 |
| Bits | b4 | b3 | b2 | b1 | **0** | **1** | **2** | **3** | **4** | **5** | **6** | **7** |
| | 0 | 0 | 0 | 0 | **0** | NUL | DLE | SP | 0 | @ | P | ` | p |
| | 0 | 0 | 0 | 1 | **1** | SOH | DC1 | ! | 1 | A | Q | a | q |
| | 0 | 0 | 1 | 0 | **2** | STX | DC2 | " | 2 | B | R | b | r |
| | 0 | 0 | 1 | 1 | **3** | ETX | DC3 | # | 3 | C | S | c | s |
| | 0 | 1 | 0 | 0 | **4** | EOT | DC4 | $ | 4 | D | T | d | t |
| | 0 | 1 | 0 | 1 | **5** | ENQ | NAK | % | 5 | E | U | e | u |
| | 0 | 1 | 1 | 0 | **6** | ACK | SYN | & | 6 | F | V | f | v |
| | 0 | 1 | 1 | 1 | **7** | BEL | ETB | ' | 7 | G | W | g | w |
| | 1 | 0 | 0 | 0 | **8** | BS | CAN | ( | 8 | H | X | h | x |
| | 1 | 0 | 0 | 1 | **9** | HT | EM | ) | 9 | I | Y | i | y |
| | 1 | 0 | 1 | 0 | **10** | LF | SUB | * | : | J | Z | j | z |
| | 1 | 0 | 1 | 1 | **11** | VT | ESC | + | ; | K | [ | k | { |
| | 1 | 1 | 0 | 0 | **12** | FF | FS | , | < | L | \ | l | \| |
| | 1 | 1 | 0 | 1 | **13** | CR | GS | - | = | M | ] | m | } |
| | 1 | 1 | 1 | 0 | **14** | SO | RS | . | > | N | ^ | n | ~ |
| | 1 | 1 | 1 | 1 | **15** | SI | US | / | ? | O | — | o | DEL |

*Illustration courtesy of Learning Group International*

**FIGURE 2-2** ASCII code set.

control might be implemented. OSI approaches will build on this simple concept. The device control 1 (DC1) ASCII character is better known as XON, and DC3 is known as XOFF. To stop the flow of data, send an XOFF in the opposite direction. To allow it to flow again, send an XON. These are separate ASCII characters at the physical layer. At the data link layer, their equivalents are separate supervisory control PDUs. The concept is the same.

## Media

While the OSI Reference Model does not include the physical media itself, the media choices are too important to be ignored. The principal cable choices include telephone unshielded twisted-pair, shielded twisted-pair (data-grade), coaxial, and fiber optics.

Telephone unshielded twisted-pair (UTP) cabling is not necessarily what might be expected. Not all telephone wire has adequate twisting to be acceptable for data transmission. The type of UTP that is installed for modern private automatic branch exchange (PABX) usage is needed. There may be insufficient spare wires in UTP cables to use existing wire for data transmission. In addition, it is generally agreed that mixing data and voice pairs in the same cable should be avoided when analog voice signals are being used, since the ringing signal can readily cause crosstalk in the data pairs. The attractive aspect of UTP is not so much that it may already be installed, but rather that people are familiar with how to install it and to manage the cable plant subsequently. UTP is used in a wide variety of networking applications including PABXs, Ethernet, token ring, and many proprietary LANs.

Data-grade twisted pair differs from UTP in two major ways. First, data-grade cabling is shielded with a braid of fine wires or metalized foil (or both). Secondly, data-grade twisted pair has thicker copper wires, providing less resistance. Data-grade twisted pair is used in many IBM token ring LANs.

Coaxial cable has an inner conductor and an outer conductor separated by insulation. As a rule of thumb, the larger the diameter of the coaxial cable, the less signal loss it will introduce. On the other hand, the larger the diameter, the more difficult it is to install, and the more it costs. This is particularly the case for rigid cable that may have a solid aluminum outer conductor. Coaxial cable is used in many Ethernet-style and token-passing bus LANs.

Fiber-optic cable has enjoyed a growing popularity over the past few years. Its usage had been lessened by many of its unusual characteristics. These characteristics include its extremely small diameter, the intricacies of installing connectors and performing splices, and the different kinds of test equipment that are involved. A growing base of personnel now know how to work with fiber, and the costs of the cabling and connectors have decreased considerably.

A wide range of fiber-optic support products such as cables, connectors, and light sources exists, but the most common applications can be characterized by the following choices. Most cable that will be encountered in an OSI application environment is 62.5/125 micron, multi-mode, graded-index fiber. The outer diameter of the glass is the industry standard 125 micron (micrometer) size. The inner core diameter is the AT&T-preferred size of 62.5 microns. This has been adopted widely by others as well. The multi-mode aspect means that the light transmission supports multiple colors of light. (It is really infrared, so the color differences are not really visible.) Different colors travel at slightly different speeds, resulting in the spreading of the pulse width and a reduction of its brightness as the optical signal proceeds down the cable. A partial answer to this problem is to use the graded index in which the color that travels the fastest is given a somewhat longer path to take. The colors get to the end at about the same time. One of the most common types of fiber-optic connectors encountered is the ST (straight tip) connector.

All of the above media have a plastic-like coating. The major concern related to this material is whether it burns and gives off smoke. If it does, it cannot be used under raised computer floors, above false ceilings, or in areas that are part of the air conditioning system. In these areas, much more expensive, plenum-rated cabling must be used.

## Topology

Associated with the media consideration is the issue of topologies. The cabling system may be structured in any of three basic physical layouts or topologies.

The first physical topology is a simple bus that interconnects a number of personal computers, workstations, and larger systems along a single cable. This topology normally uses coaxial cable, attaching each computer by means of a transmitter/receiver (sometimes called a transceiver). The bus structure is conceptually simple but complex to manage and troubleshoot.

A variation of the bus physical topology is a tree in which several bus segments are connected together by relay devices. These devices regenerate the signals and isolate certain cabling and interface problems so that they do not propagate out, affecting the entire tree. Computers can be attached along the cable segments as with the bus.

A tree-like topology may also be developed utilizing hub devices that fan out to attach many computers to the network. Since the physical connections between the hubs and the computers, as well as between the hubs themselves, are point-to-point circuits, they can be of any media choice. Since the computers are attached at the end nodes on cables rather than along the cable segments, this topology is given a different name. It is called a star.

In a star topology, each PC, workstation, or other computer is connected to the network by means of a cable to a hub, and eventually back to a central wire closet. This is the cabling approach of the voice telephone system. The important issues related to the star cabling system are (1) the increased linear footage of cable, (2) the availability of trained labor for installation, and (3) the ease of maintenance of the network in isolating and removing damaged cable segments. Employing one or more central wire closets and unshielded twisted-pair wiring, the star topology has become very popular.

## Clocking and Synchronization

Bit serial data transmissions are sent from one computer to another at a selected data rate such as 1 megabit per second (Mbps). Both the sending and the receiving computers must be initialized to use the same data rate. One approach is using separate and independent clocks at each end to provide the timing. This can be done when the data units are very short (such as individual characters). The clocks of the two ends are synchronized by means of a start indicator (or start bit). The start bit is a binary zero preceding the character.

Between characters, the signal is held at the binary one state, so the start bit can signal the beginning of a new character. The time between characters is unknown, so this approach is called asynchronous. The word synchronous means that one knows something about the timing of the next event, in this case the next character arrival. The letter a in front of the word synchronous means that this is not the case.

Once a character transmission starts, the bits follow in the predetermined timing sequence. The send and receive clocks are sufficiently accurate to convey the eight bits of a byte without excessive accumulation of drift and resulting bit errors. Suppose that the receive clock interval is 1.01 times that of the sender, a 1% error. The arrival of the eighth bit will be off by 0.08, which will still allow the receiver to sample its zero/one value reasonably close to the center of the bit time. However, if the attempt were made to send a 100-bit data unit, this accumulated error would be off by one full bit time, resulting in an error. The asynchronous approach only works for short data units such as individual characters.

For long transmissions, the need is for more accurate clocking, i.e., for a closer match between the clock rate of the sender and the receiver. Instead of requiring extremely precise clocks, which would be very expensive, an approach is used by which the receiving station can recover the clock signal of the transmitter from the incoming signal. This is called synchronous transmission (see Figure 2-3). Synchronization, including clock recovery, is typically by means of a phase locked loop. It can detect when transitions actually occur in the received signal versus when its clock predicts that they may occur. The resultant difference or error signal is used by the closed loop

---

- **In synchronous clocking schemes, timing is recovered at the receiver by the transitions in the data.**

Example: Received data

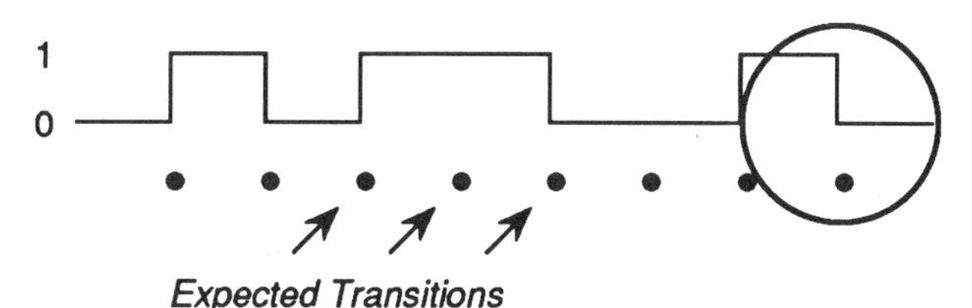


- **Receiver clocking errors can be corrected by noting the difference between expected and actual timing of signal transitions.**

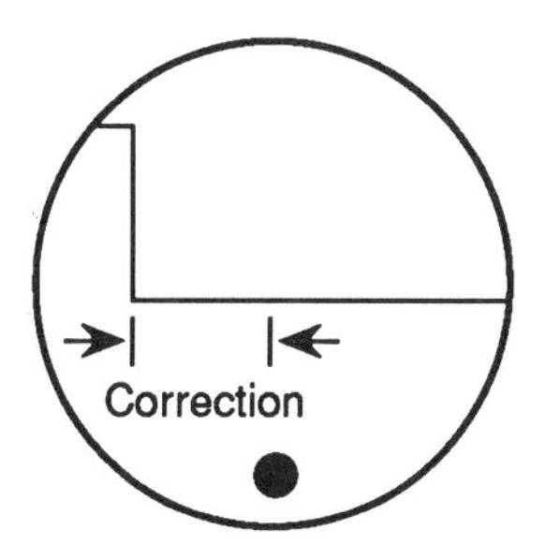


*Illustration courtesy of Learning Group International*

**FIGURE 2-3** Clock recovery in synchronous transmission.

system to make a correction in the receive clock. If the transitions occur frequently, the receive clock will be kept synchronized. However, if a large number of bits go by without any transitions, the clock synchronization may slip sync, and either gain or lose a bit, thus introducing an error.

The key to accurate clock recovery is in the encoding scheme. It is necessary to ensure that there are an adequate number of transitions in the binary representation of the signal. Suppose that the encoding approach is that of RS-232, in which a binary one is represented by a negative voltage and a binary zero is a positive voltage. As long as a reasonable mix of ones and zeros exists, there will be transitions, and clock synchronization will be maintained. However, there is no assurance that a long string of ones or zeros will not be transmitted, either of which will eventually result in a loss of synchronization.

An ideal scheme would seem to be one in which every bit has a clock transition. Suppose that a binary one is represented by a positive transition, i.e., from a negative voltage to a positive voltage, and a binary zero is represented by a negative signal transition. A long string of ones or zeros would not affect the synchronization in either case. This encoding approach is given the name Manchester encoding. It is used in some LANs including Ethernet and is shown in Figure 2-4, along with another encoding form called

---

- **Some encoding schemes have more transitions than others, and therefore better opportunities for clock recovery.**

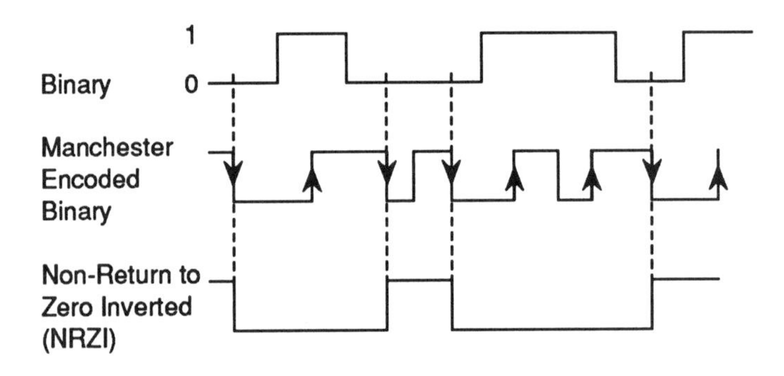


*Illustration courtesy of Learning Group International*

**FIGURE 2-4** Manchester and NRZI encoding examples.

Non-Return to Zero Inverted (NRZI), which does not have nearly as many transitions.

The token ring LAN uses a somewhat different approach in which there is still a transition for every bit, but that uses a different way of representing zeros and ones. In differential Manchester, a binary zero is represented by a transition at the time boundary between bits, while a binary one does not have a transition. An example of differential Manchester is shown in Figure 2-5. The difference between Manchester and differential Manchester is primarily in the polarity aspects of the signal. Differential Manchester does not depend on the polarity of signal changes, while conventional Manchester does. Therefore, twisted-pair wiring, which is the most common token ring media, can have its connections inverted and still operate properly. It is much less likely that the center conductor of an Ethernet LAN coaxial cable segment will be connected to the shield of another coaxial cable segment.

Both Manchester and differential Manchester have excellent clock synchronization properties, but both require more bandwidth than would be

---

- **With differential Manchester encoding, transitions always occur at the center of each bit (except for intentional encode violations).**

- **Ones and zeros are represented by**
  No transition at a bit boundary if a one.
  A transition at a bit boundary if a zero.

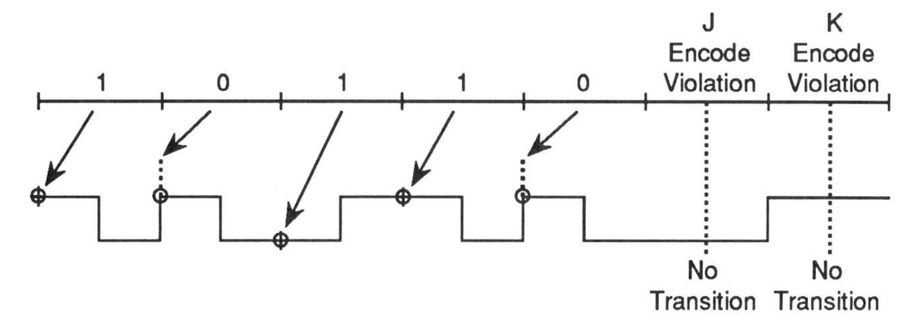


- **These encode violations are called J and K.**
  They are utilized as a pair.

*Illustration courtesy of Learning Group International*

**FIGURE 2-5** Differential Manchester encoding.

required by alternative approaches such as Non Return to Zero Inverted. The excessive utilization of bandwidth is usually not a problem; the coaxial cable or twisted-pair cable has plenty of bandwidth. Only the lower portion of its bandwidth is needed to transmit the digital signal. As a rule of thumb, one hertz of bandwidth is needed for each bit per second of data transmission; the cable has several hundred megahertz of bandwidth — more than enough for 10 Mbps of data transmission. However, to conserve bandwidth (as in broadband LANs) or to reduce the required switching rate (as in Fiber Distributed Data Interface (FDDI) LANs), NRZI encoding is used.

The tradeoff between the ease of synchronization and the conservation of transmission bandwidth is typical of alternatives faced in the design of a network. The optimal solution is dependent upon the particular circumstance.

## Baseband Transmission

When digital data are applied directly to a transmission medium such as a cable, the result is baseband transmission. The medium (or carrier in this case) must be capable of handling digital signals. For example, baseband data cannot be transmitted over a telephone channel because it does not pass frequencies below 300 hertz or above 3,300 hertz. A typical baseband signal representation has frequency components both above and below the telephone channel range. The frequencies below 300 hertz may be due to a direct current (DC) component caused by long strings of ones and/or zeros. The frequency components above 3,300 hertz are due to the rapid rise and fall times of digital signals.

Baseband transmission is performed over a pair of electrical conductors, either in the form of twisted-pair cable or by means of the inner and outer conductors of a coaxial cable. Electrical transmission on cables always involves a pair of wires, just as a pair of wires are required for 110-volt appliance power cables. Fiber-optic transmission typically has two fiber strands as well, but for a completely different reason. One fiber is used for transmission, and the other is for reception.

In any baseband system, there is always a distance versus data rate tradeoff. The third element in this tradeoff is cost. Both distance and data rate can be simultaneously increased by purchasing better (more expensive) cable. Otherwise, the product of distance and data rate remains approximately constant in the tradeoff. The better quality data cable has three metrics of concern: its electrical resistance per foot of length, its electrical capacitance per foot, and its shield of fine braided wire and/or metalized foil. Both the

- **EIA RS-422 balanced electrical drivers and receivers.**

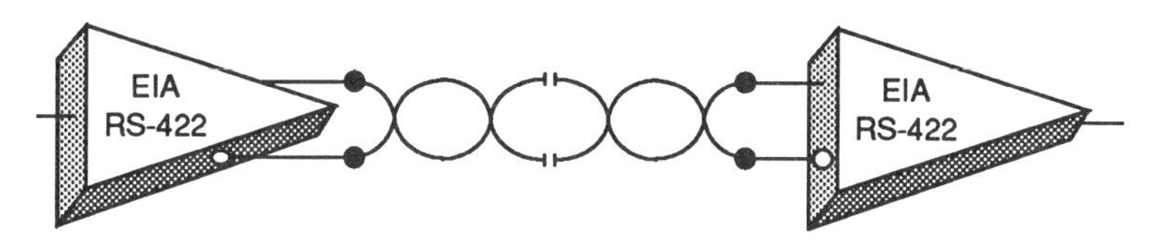


*Illustration courtesy of Learning Group International*

**FIGURE 2-6** Balanced twisted-pair wiring.

resistance and capacitance should be as low as possible. The resistance is a function of the wire diameter, as indicated by its wire gauge number. The larger the diameter, the smaller the gauge number. Typical telephone twisted-pair wiring is American Wire Gauge (AWG) 24, while data-grade cable is AWG 22. Capacitance varies based on many cable factors, including its cross-section geometry and its insulation materials.

Any twisted-pair cabling used for data transmission should live up to its name and be twisted. At least one twist per foot is needed, and considerably tighter twisting is often required. The point of having the two wires twisted together is to reduce electrical interference. The twisted cable itself produces less interference because the signals from the two wires tend to cancel each other. It is less susceptible to outside interference for the same reason. When used with balanced drivers and receivers as shown in Figure 2-6, electrical interference is minimized. The receiver is sensitive to the difference between the two input lines, while noise causes both to change by the same (common mode) amount. The driver and receiver shown in the figure are EIA-422 devices, which correspond to the CCITT V.11 recommendation. There are also unbalanced drivers and receivers (EIA-423 and CCITT V.10), but they do not have the electrical interference rejection capabilities.

## Modulation-Related Issues

In many instances, a digital signal must be converted to analog form, as when the need arises to transmit across telephone or television analog channels. In these cases, modems are required. They modulate digital signals into an analog representation for transmission and demodulate the analog representation back into the digital signal upon reception. The word modem is a contraction of these two functions: *mo*dulation and *dem*odulation. When modems are used, bandwidth is a concern. As in the discussion of NRZI, the encoding schemes used for baseband are not appropriate for modulated approaches.

A modem is an example of what Consultative Committee for International Telephone and Telegraph (CCITT) calls data circuit-termination equipment (DCE). The modems at each end of the telephone link terminate the phone company portion of the inter-computer communications. That is at least the case when modems must be purchased from the post, telephone, and telegraph monopoly, as is true in many countries. In the U.S. modems are available from many sources.

The interface between the computer, called data terminal equipment (DTE) by CCITT, and the DCE is the RS-232 interface. In CCITT, this interface is specified by two recommendations, V.24 and V.28. In both cases, the interface includes separate data lines for transmit and receive and a set of out-of-band control lines, as shown in Figure 2-7. These out-of-band control lines are discussed in detail later.

The principal purpose of the modem is to adapt the digital signal into an analog form by modulation and to recover by the opposite transformation at the receiving end. This modulation may be by any of several means. In this

- **Data terminal equipment (DTE).**
- **Data circuit-termination equipment (DCE).**

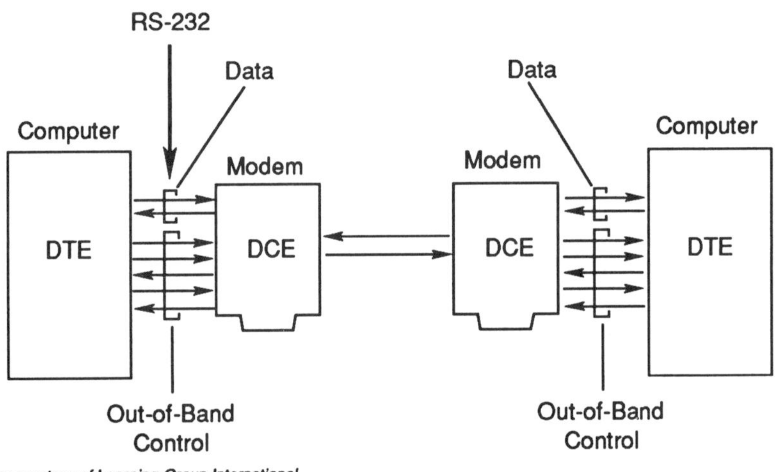


*Illustration courtesy of Learning Group International*

**FIGURE 2-7** DTE, DCE, and modems.

context, modulation refers to the changes that one can make to a sine wave carrier signal. The sine wave goes upward in voltage, peaks, drops to a negative maximum value, and proceeds to repeat the cycle over and over again. One of the simplest forms of change to the sine wave (or modulation) is frequency shift keying (FSK). In FSK, binary ones are represented by a specified frequency or tone, and binary zeros are represented by a different frequency or tone. The frequency shifts between these two values are shown in Figure 2-8. When performed at low data rates over a telephone channel, one can literally hear the bits being transmitted. FSK is most commonly used when the modem cost is to be minimized at the expense of bandwidth utilization.

Since bandwidth is often limited, alternative approaches that provide more bps per hertz of bandwidth must be considered. A common alternative is the use of phase shift keying (PSK). Instead of modulating the frequency or tone of the analog signal, its phase is changed to reflect the pattern of ones and zeros that is to be sent. Phase is not nearly as simple a concept as frequency or tone. The ear can hear tones but is not sensitive to phase.

Phase modulation changes the relative time at which the sine wave makes its zero crossings in its endless cycle of positive and negative swings. Two sine waves can vary in phase anywhere from zero to 360 degrees, a full circle of variations. If a digital signal is modulated to be represented by either of two phases, a direct analogy with FSK is apparent. Phase is being modulated

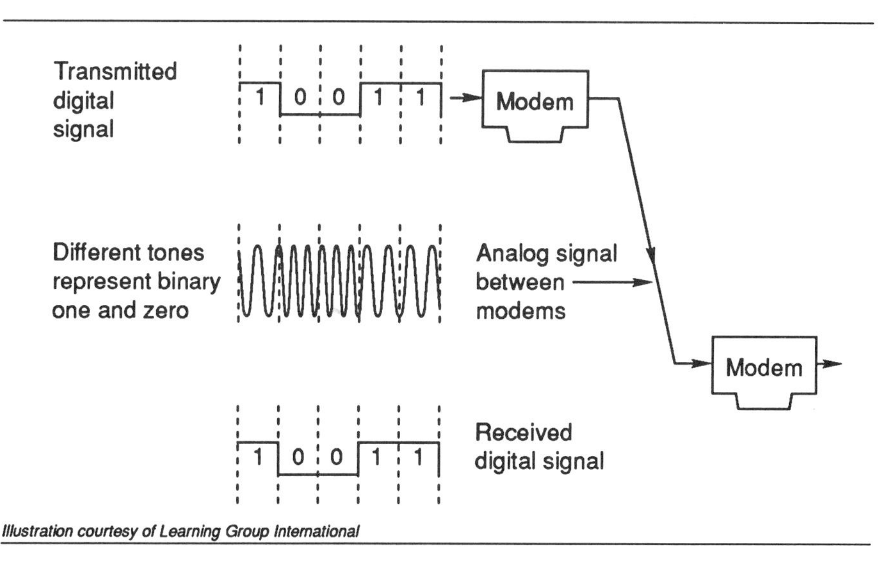


**FIGURE 2-8** Modems modulate the digital signal.

instead of frequency. However, phase is typically divided into a number of finer grain units such as 0, 90, 180, and 270 degrees. That would provide four possibilities or two bits' worth of information instead of one bit in the FSK example. Why not go for 0, 45, 90, 135, etc. phases and get three bits of information? Maybe dividing the phase into even smaller units would yield four or more bits per signal.

The problem with attempting to divide phase into increasingly smaller units is that any noise-induced signal variation is likely to cause a misinterpretation of the received signal and introduce errors in the recovered digital signal. A better approach is to add yet another form of modulation. Suppose that in addition to eight possible phases, there are also two possible amplitudes of the signal for each phase. That would make 16 possible receiver states, each of which would represent four bits.

The rate at which the phase and amplitude of the sine wave are changed is called the baud rate. For most modern modems, this baud rate is 2,400 changes per second. If only one bit per signal interval is conveyed, a data rate of 2,400 bps is achieved. However, two bits per baud may be conveyed to get 4,800 bps, or three bits per baud to get 7,200 bps. The same applies to four bits per baud to get 9,600 bps, all the way up to eight bits per baud to get 19.2 kilobits per second (Kbps). At that point, the data-carrying capacity of a voice-grade telephone circuit is pretty well exhausted and data compression or other means must be employed to get higher data rates. These other means include using digital telephone channels such as T1 (1.544 Mbps) or fractional T1 (56 Kbps and up). T1 channels use pulse code modulation (PCM) that varies the pulse representation rather than varying a sine wave. In T1, the pulse representation is its digital encoded form.

RS-232 modems operate up to 19.2 Kbps and provide a standard interface to the computers. A closer look at the RS-232 interface (see Figures 2-9a and 2-9b) reveals it has two grounds: a safety (protective) ground and a signal ground. The protective ground serves the same function as the third prong in a 110-volt outlet. The signal ground provides a return path for the data and control signals. The data lines are for transmit (pin 2) and receive (pin 3). Two separate and independent lines provide full-duplex capability.

The next group of control lines is the most important set for many applications. Request to send (RTS) goes from the computer to the modem when it wants to send a character (when operating in local echo mode). The response to RTS is clear to send (CTS), which allows the character to be sent. In remote echo operation, the RTS and CTS handshake is performed once at the beginning of operation. Data set ready and data terminal ready are signals that the modem and computer respectively are ready for operation. Ring indicator indicates an incoming call.

The remaining signals are of considerably less importance and use. The next four signals provide a variety of controls, followed by the clocking signals, which are for synchronous operation. There are two forms of transmit clocking, depending on whether it is to be provided by the computer or the

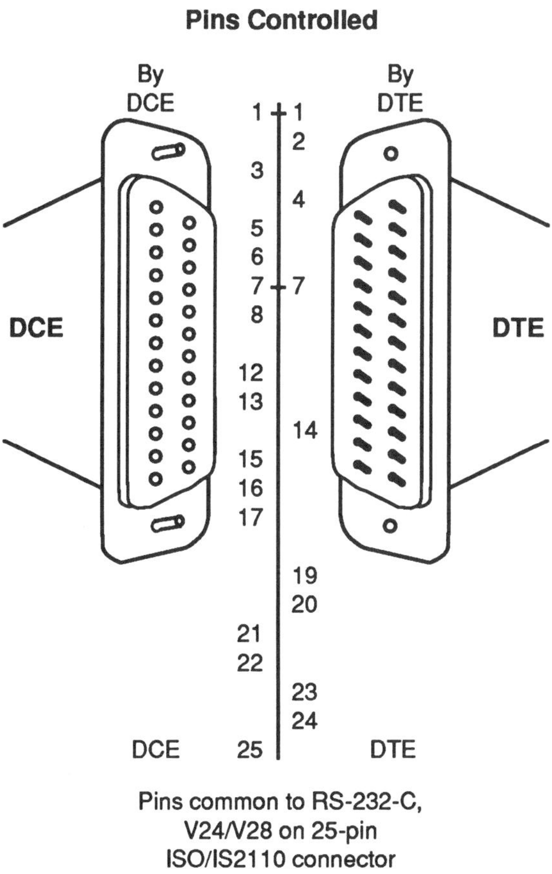

*Illustration courtesy of Learning Group International*

**FIGURE 2-9a** The RS-232-C interface.

| RS-232-C Interface | | | Signal Type and Direction | | | | | | |
|---|---|---|---|---|---|---|---|---|---|
| | | | GND | Data | | Control | | Timing | |
| 25 Pin | EIA RS-232-C Circuit | RS-232 Description | | From DCE | To DCE | From DCE | To DCE | From DCE | To DCE |
| 1 | AA | Protective Ground | X | | | | | | |
| 7 | AB | Signal Ground/Common Return | X | | | | | | |
| 2 | BA | Transmitted Data | | | X | | | | |
| 3 | BB | Received Data | | X | | | | | |
| 4 | CA | Request to Send | | | | | X | | |
| 5 | CB | Clear to Send | | | | X | | | |
| 6 | CC | Data Set Ready | | | | X | | | |
| 20 | CD | Data Terminal Ready | | | | | X | | |
| 22 | CE | Ring Indicator | | | | X | | | |
| 8 | CF | Received Line Signal Detector | | | | X | | | |
| 21 | CG | Signal Quality Detector | | | | X | | | |
| 23 | CH | Data Signal Rate Selector (DTE) | | | | | X | | |
| 23 | CI | Data Signal Rate Selector (DCE) | | | | X | | | |
| 24 | DA | Transmitter Signal Element Timing (DTE) | | | | | | | X |
| 15 | DB | Transmitter Signal Element Timing (DCE) | | | | | | X | |
| 17 | DD | Receiver Signal Element Timing (DCE) | | | | | | X | |
| 14 | SBA | Secondary Transmitted Data | | | X | | | | |
| 16 | SBB | Secondary Received Data | | X | | | | | |
| 19 | SCA | Secondary Request to Send | | | | | X | | |
| 13 | SCB | Secondary Clear to Send | | | | X | | | |
| 12 | SCF | Secondary Received Line Signal Detector | | | | X | | | |

*Illustration courtesy of Learning Group International*

**FIGURE 2-9b** The RS-232-C interface (continued).

modem. There is no corresponding choice at the receive side as the clock is always provided by the modem.

The remaining signals pertain to secondary channels, one in each direction. The secondary channels are low data rate (e.g., 75 to 150 bps) paths that are used for control purposes. They can be used in half-duplex operations to turn the direction of traffic around and for modem management systems.

Three signals that do not appear in RS-232-C but are included in RS-232-D (now often called EIA-232-D) relate to loopback testing. These signals allow the computer to loopback either the local or the remote modem. The third signal is a test mode indicator that shows the current loopback state.

It is often necessary to interconnect two computers that are physically close together and as a result do not require modems. Interconnecting the respective RS-232 signals on a pin-for-pin basis is inappropriate because transmitted data must be connected to the other's receive data pin, not its transmit pin. Similarly, RTS should be sent back to one's own CTS input. Data terminal ready is usually connected to the other side's data set ready so that each knows the operational status of the other. Other signals may also need to be asserted, but these vary by vendor.

## The X.21 Direct Digital Service

CCITT has recommendation X.21 that provides a direct-dial, synchronous, digital service. It avoids the need for modems and provides potentially higher data rate and lower error rate data circuits. X.21 provides the same form of operation as other direct dial systems, with on/off hook controls, the equivalent of dial tone, dialing (sending an ASCII character sequence), receiving the indication of ringing at the other end, and responding to an incoming call. These are all call progress indications.

The development of the X.21 interface took a quite different approach than that of RS-232 with its multitude of out-of-band control lines. X.21 uses its transmit and receive lines, along with in and out control lines to convey control information by the states of these lines, plus coded patterns that are sent and received. This should simplify processor-based implementations because the number of input/output (I/O) lines is minimized.

A variation of X.21 that was developed by CCITT is called $X.21_{bis}$. It is based on RS-232 and provides most, but not all, X.21 functionality. Some call progress signals are not implemented, and data rates are limited to those of RS-232. The principal use of $X.21_{bis}$ is with X.25.

## Multiplexing

Regardless of whether a communications channel is an X.21 digital circuit or an analog modem channel, it may have more bps than a single user needs. The way to share this bps/bandwidth resource is to multiplex two or more users on

- **Several forms of multiplexing are available.**
  Frequency Division Multiplexing (FDM)
  Time Division Multiplexing (TDM)
  Statistical Time Division Multiplexing (STDM)

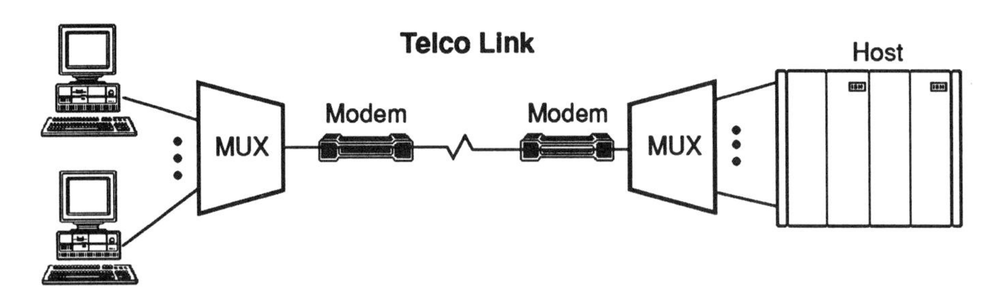


*Illustration courtesy of Learning Group International*

**FIGURE 2-10** Multiplexing allows a communication link to be shared.

one channel as shown in Figure 2-10. Multiplexing means sharing. This multiplexing may be by means of either time division multiplexing (TDM) or frequency division multiplexing (FDM). In TDM, several users share the total bandwidth of a channel on a time basis. In Figure 2-11 first one user has the entire bandwidth and data capacity, and then another in a round-robin

- **Each user gets the channel's full capacity for a period of time.**
- **Each user gets a time slot in each frame.**

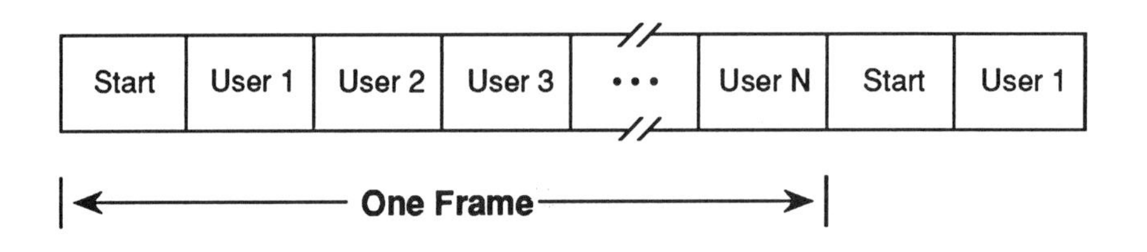


*Illustration courtesy of Learning Group International*

**FIGURE 2-11** Time division multiplexing.

fashion. The problem with this form of multiplexing is that each slot in the TDM frame is dedicated to a particular user and therefore is wasted if that user has nothing to communicate.

A more effective way to perform TDM in bursty communications is to use statistical TDM or stat mux techniques. An example of statistical multiplexing is shown in Figure 2-12 in which a five-bit user_ID tag is appended to each character for transmission. This allows up to 2**5 or 32 users to share a communications channel on an as-needed basis. Even with the additional overhead of the tag bits, stat mux techniques typically support three to four times more users than a fixed allocation form of TDM. Making the stat mux operation more general, carrying more than one character and more control information than just the user_ID, would result in packet switching. Packet switching is simply statistical multiplexing as applied to blocks of characters over more complex topologies than point-to-point circuits.

A different form of multiplexing is FDM that shares the resources in a different way. In FDM, a fraction of the channel bandwidth is given to each user on a continual basis. This is an alternative way to divide the bandwidth/

---

- **Few users fill every slot assigned to them, causing wasted slots.**
- **A better approach is statistical TDM:**
  A user character is "tagged" with the user ID.

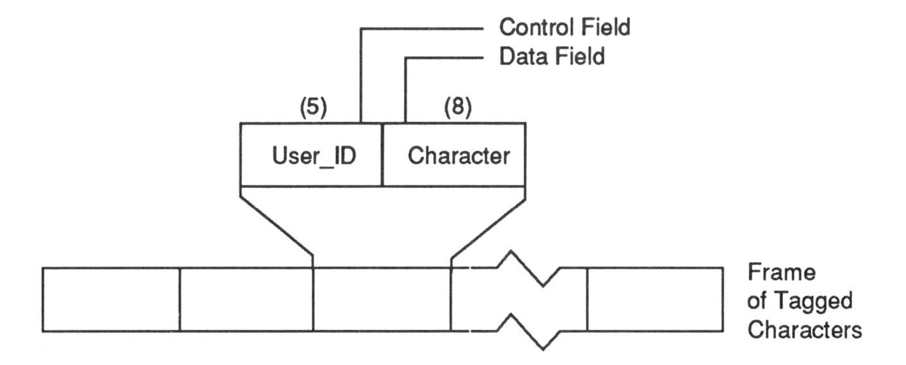


*Illustration courtesy of Learning Group International*

**FIGURE 2-12** Statistical time division multiplexing.

time resource across a set of users as shown in Figure 2-13. FDM is typically used when a wide bandwidth channel such as a broadband LAN or a satellite channel is to be shared by a number of users.

While TDM and FDM are the primary ways of sharing a communications channel, other approaches do exist and are beginning to be exploited. One of the most promising is code division multiplexing that is sometimes called spread spectrum. It shares a single bandwidth on a continual access basis by spreading the signals across a larger bandwidth. It recovers the transmitted signal by correlation techniques and a known sender/receiver pseudo-random bit sequence that codes the transmission, allowing its recovery from other signals in the same bandwidth.

## Decibels

The physical properties of communication channels include signal loss (attenuation) and gain (amplification). These effects are often stated in terms of decibels. Negative decibel values relate to loss, while positive values relate to gain. Decibels (dB) are logarithmic ratios. For example, if an amplifier has a power gain of 100X, its dB gain is

dB gain = 10 * log base 10 (100) = 20 dB.

- **Two channels**
  Used in modems.
  One channel for each direction.

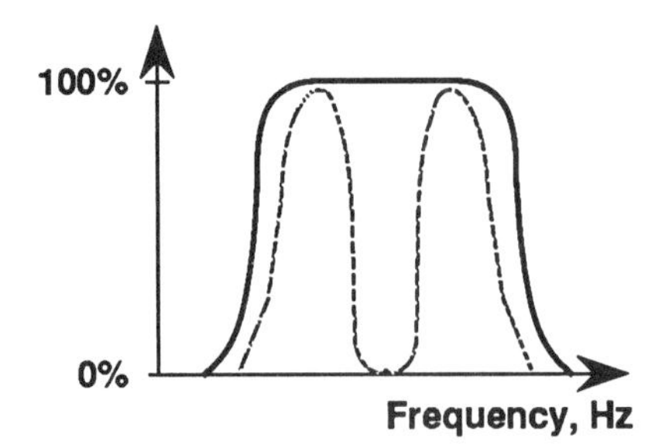


- **Multiple channels**
  Send separate data on each.
  Use with broadband LANs.

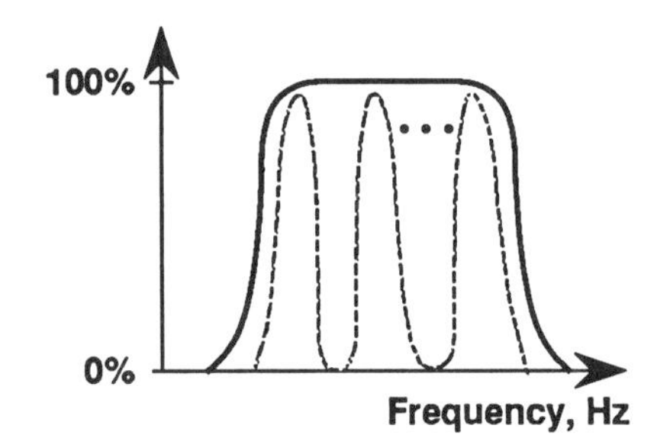


*Illustration courtesy of Learning Group International*

**FIGURE 2-13** Frequency division multiplexing.

A gain of 10X is 10 dB, while a gain of 1,000X is 30 dB. Thus, decibels are like the scale used to measure earthquakes: a small increase in the numeric scale may indicate a large increase in the effect.

The attenuation of a cable (e.g., a fiber-optic cable) may be 3 dB per kilometer. Since this is attenuation, consider this to be –3 dB. To put an amplifier in before the signal power dropped to one tenth (-10 dB) of its original power would require doing so about every 3 kilometers. An amplifier that boosted the signal by +10 dB would restore the signal level to its original value.

These examples are expressed in terms of signal power. However, it is often necessary to work with voltage rather than power. Power goes up as the square of the voltage. If one doubles the voltage applied to the toaster from 110 volts to 220 volts, the power goes up by a factor of four, not a factor of two, and the toaster goes up in smoke. When dealing with logarithms, squaring means multiplying logarithms by two, so the dB relation becomes

dB gain = 20 * log base 10 (voltage gain).

An amplifier that has a voltage gain of 10 has a 20 dB gain. One that has a voltage gain of 100 has a dB gain of 40 dB, and a voltage gain of 1,000 is 60 dB. These are twice the corresponding power level dB values.

Decibels are inherently ratios, but it is often necessary to express actual values in the logarithmic decibel form. This leads to a variation of decibels that are tied to a specific voltage value, namely one millivolt, or 1/1,000 volt. That is not nearly enough voltage to get the toaster to do anything at all, but it is fairly typical of many communication signal levels. In this case, 0 dBmV is one millivolt, while +20 dBmV is 10 millivolt and -20 dBmV is 0.1 millivolt. What would +40 dBmV be? That's right — it is 100 millivolts.

## CCITT V-, X-, and I-series Recommendations

Physical data communications standards are typically those of CCITT's V-, X-, and I-series recommendations. The V-series recommendations are for handling data over analog modems, the X-series recommendations are for digital data networks, and the I-series recommendations are for integrated voice and data digital networks. The V-series includes modems and the international equivalent of the familiar RS-232 interface. The X-series includes X.21 synchronous digital-circuit switched networks at the physical layer, and higher-layer protocols such as for X.25 packet-switched networks and many

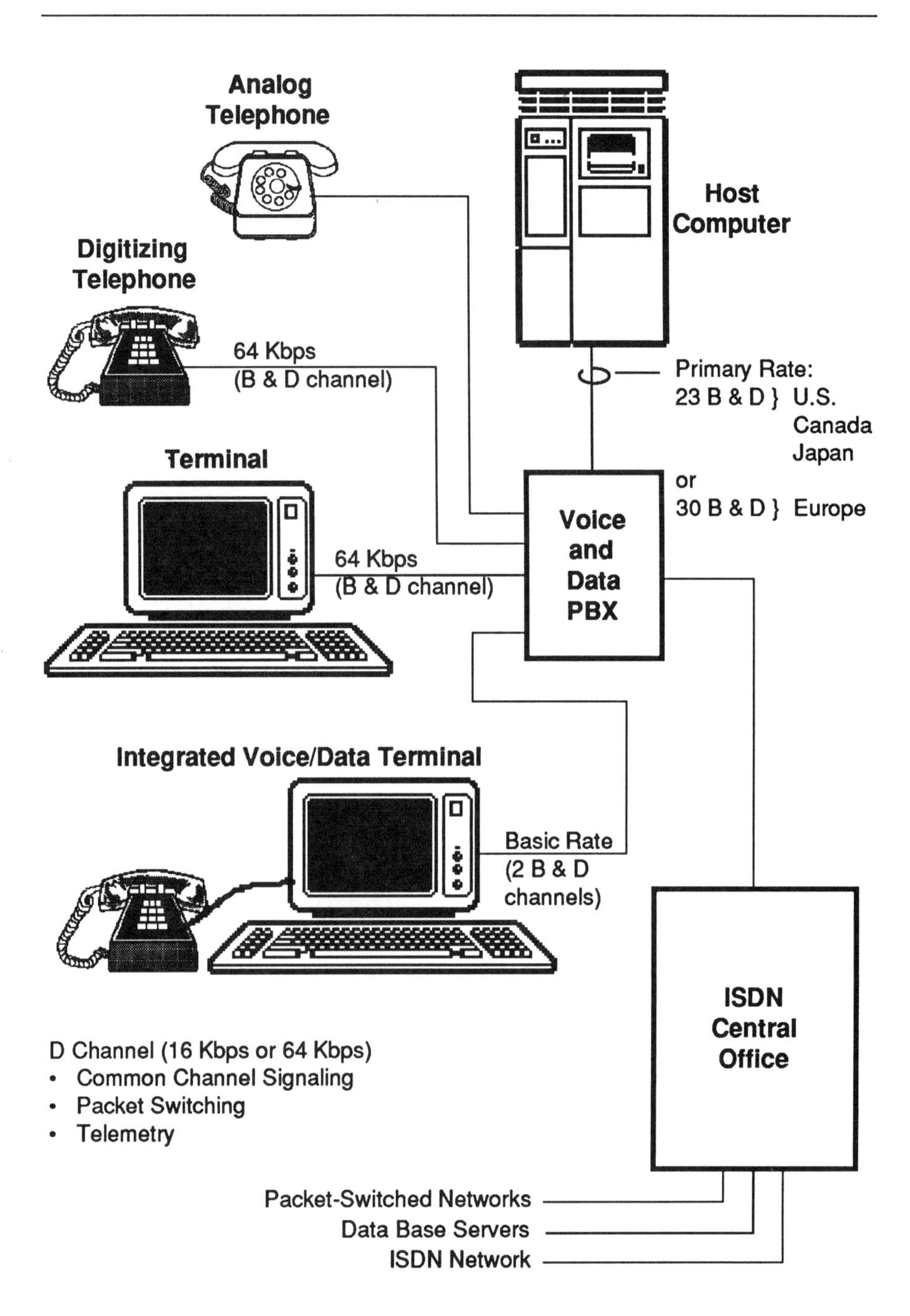


**FIGURE 2-14** A private automatic branch exchange (PABX).

of the OSI higher-layer protocols. The I-series is to specify the Integrated Services Digital Network (ISDN) voice and data network.

Some of the V- and X-series recommendations have already been discussed in this chapter. A summary of ISDN is also appropriate since it is rapidly developing as a major form of data, as well as voice, communications. The combined voice and data communications of an ISDN private automatic branch exchange are shown in Figure 2-14. The B channels are 64 Kbps and can support either digitized speech or data. The D channel can be either 16 Kbps or 64 Kbps and can be used for signaling, packet-switching, and telemetry. When used to support a telephone and/or a single data circuit, the 16 Kbps D channel is used. The 64 Kbps D channel is used when many B channels are to be supported, such as between the PABX and a computer.

The twisted-pair cabling between the telephone/data terminals and the PABX supports two B channels and one D channel. In ISDN terminology, this is 2B & D, or the basic rate. A higher-speed channel can be used between the PABX and a computer. It is known as the 23B & D, or primary rate. In North America and Japan, these circuits are currently called T1 and consist of 24 voice/data slots within a frame at a data rate of 1.544 Mbps. Much higher data rates are being developed for what is often called broadband ISDN.

## Summary and Conclusions

The physical layer protocols are primarily aimed at delivering bits (or bytes) from one point in the network to another. While many of the general concepts of protocols such as handshakes, state machines, and standardized recommendations appear at the physical layer, they typically do not reflect the concerns of protocol data units, recovery mechanisms, and other such mechanisms found at the other layers.

The discussion next proceeds to a special case of the physical layer and an associated media access control (MAC) sublayer for local area networks. The MAC sublayer does not fit well with the OSI Reference Model, although the MAC concepts were developed after OSI became available. The OSI Reference Model was developed with wide area networks (WANs) in mind. WANs do not have concepts such as broadcast addressing, token-passing, and carrier sense. As a consequence, the MAC sublayer is sometimes considered to be part of the physical layer, and other times it is considered to be part of the data link layer. It does not really make much difference which layer it belongs in. It is simply another piece of the layered OSI architecture.

# THE LAN PHYSICAL AND MAC LAYERING

Local area networks are a special form of networking whose popularity has literally exploded. Almost every company that deals with information has at least one LAN. One reason for the growth in popularity has been the development of OSI standard forms of LANs. Yes, that's plural. Like most of the alternative standards, there are many from which to choose. But the situation is not nearly as bad as it was a few years ago when there were literally hundreds of different proprietary LANs from which to choose.

The LAN standards developed as part of OSI come from the Institute of Electrical and Electronics Engineers (IEEE) and the American National Standards Institute (ANSI). The IEEE standards are the 802 series of standards as summarized in Figure 2-15. The ANSI work has produced the FDDI form of LAN that is similar to the IEEE 802 LANs in its protocols and operations.

The IEEE 802 LANs are structured into several layers. The 802.1 considerations, which are shown as the dotted box in the figure, are not actually a layer, but represent general and architectural issues. These include addressing,

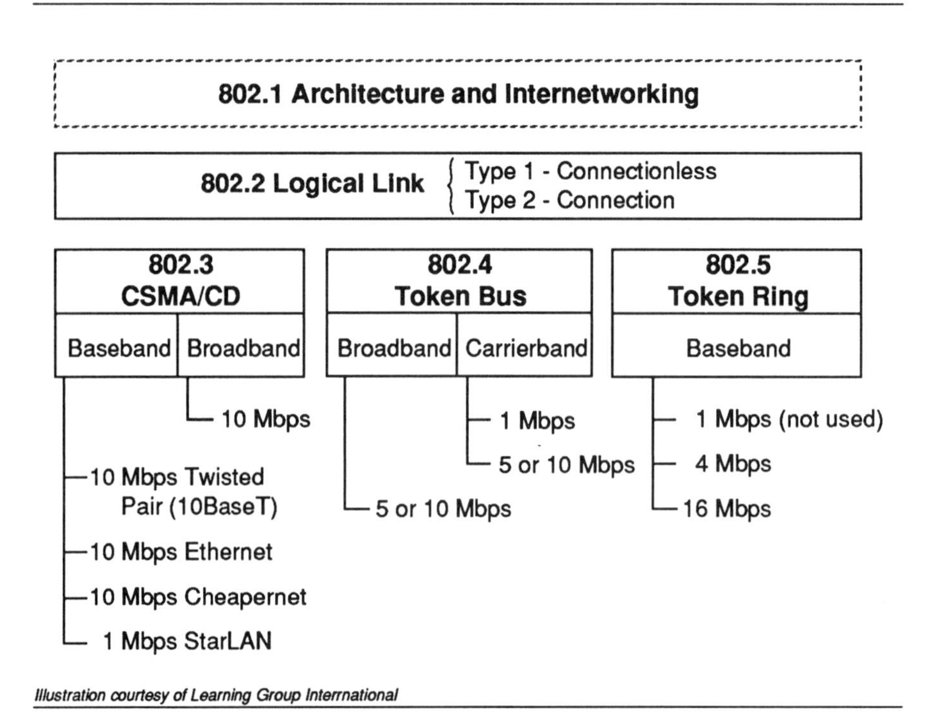


**FIGURE 2-15** IEEE 802 specification variations.

internetworking, and network management. The 802.2 logical link control (LLC) sublayer corresponds to the OSI data link layer and is discussed in the next section. As shown in the figure, there are both connection and connectionless forms of the LLC. The basic LAN standards are as follows:

1. IEEE 802.3, which is based on Ethernet.
2. IEEE 802.4, which is a token-passing bus.
3. IEEE 802.5, which is based on the IBM token ring.

## The IEEE 802.3 CSMA/CD LAN

The IEEE 802.3 standard specifies several forms of Ethernet-like LANs, ranging from one to ten Mbps and including both baseband and broadband implementations. They operate with a carrier sense multiple access (CSMA) contention mechanism, as well as with the collision detection (CD) method of resolving access attempts in which two or more users simultaneously attempt to transmit. The original form of Ethernet in which each device attaches to a thick (0.4-inch diameter) coaxial cable with a transceiver (called a medium attachment unit (MAU) by the IEEE) is shown in Figure 2-16. A variation of

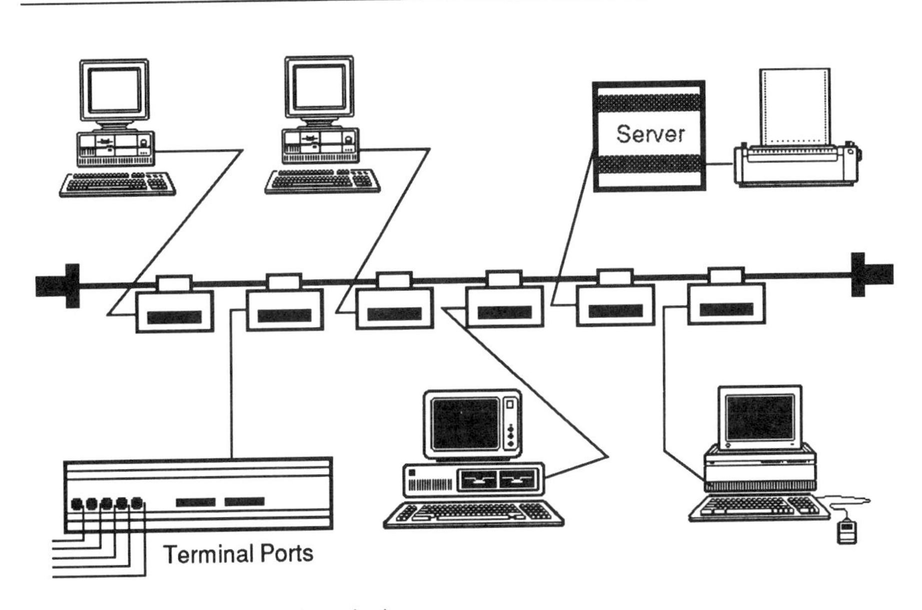


*Illustration courtesy of Learning Group International*

**FIGURE 2-16** A small Ethernet LAN.

this approach is called Cheapernet, ThinNet, ThinWire, or ThinEthernet to reflect its reduced cost (in terms of cabling and transceiver implementations) and its thinner cable (0.2-inch diameter). Two forms of CSMA/CD operation over unshielded twisted-pair (telephone) wiring are shown: the 1 Mbps StarLAN and the 10 Mbps 10BaseT. In addition, a broadband version also operates at 10 Mbps. It is typically used when one already has a broadband network installed and wants to add a few 802.3 nodes.

A large, multisegment 802.3 LAN is shown in Figure 2-17. Repeaters are shown to interconnect the individual cable segments. Repeaters are included in the system to extend the distance beyond that which signal attenuation would have otherwise dictated. The repeaters may be in the form of either a single box placed between two cable segments or two half or remote repeaters that can be up to 1,000 meters apart. There are both distance and repeater

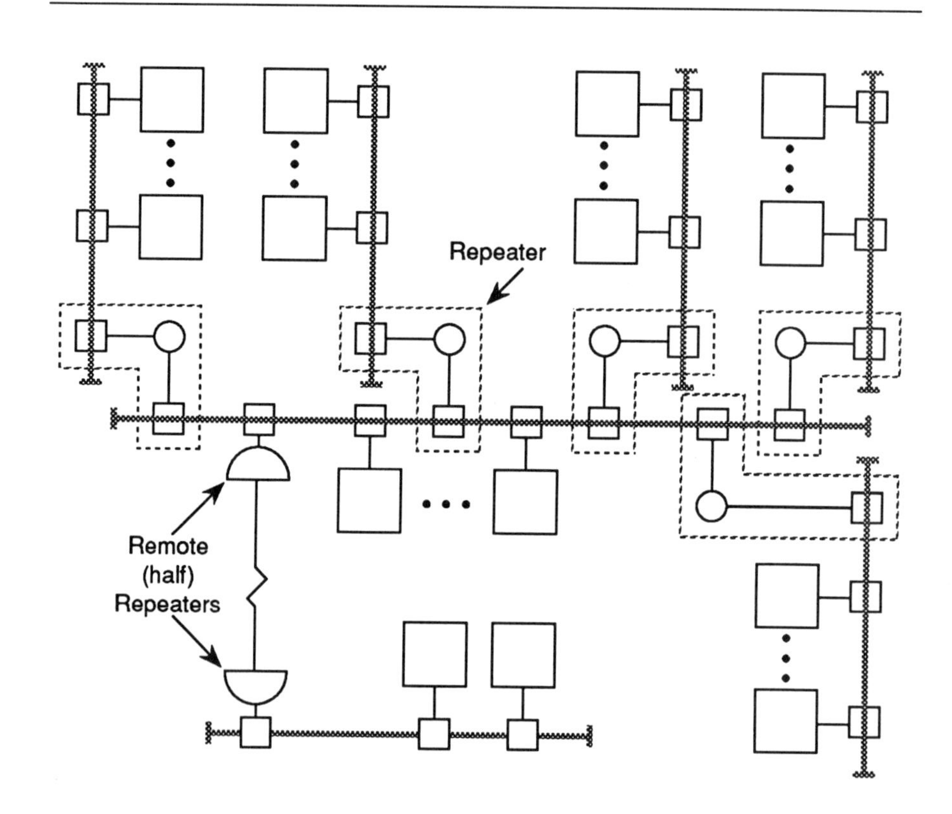


*Illustration courtesy of Learning Group International*

**FIGURE 2-17** A large (multisegment) LAN.

count limitations in an 802.3 LAN; the maximum end-to-end distance is 2,500 meters, and no more than two repeaters may be on any end-to-end path. When half (i.e., remote) repeaters are used, this maximum count is increased to four.

Repeaters operate at the OSI physical layer, forwarding all traffic with only a small delay to regenerate the portion of the preamble that is lost in obtaining synchronization. However small, this delay is the reason for the limitation on the repeater count, since delay reduces the effectiveness of collision detection. (Collision detection does not help unless the transmission can be quickly aborted.)

Collisions and collision detection are a key aspect of IEEE 802.3. It is generally agreed that a CSMA/CD LAN should not be subjected to a traffic load in excess of 40% or collisions will cause a significant increase in access delay and a reduction in effective throughput. Access delay is increased since the CSMA/CD operation doubles the average timeout before retrying for each successive collision. This is called binary exponential backoff because it doubles and redoubles the timer, leading to an exponential growth in the backoff (retry delay). This is generally not a problem, since typical LAN traffic loading is less than 10%, and collisions are infrequent. However, the worst-case situation is that the access delay might grow to 1,000 times its normal value, causing concern in real-time systems applications.

Collisions are a major limiting factor determining the size of an Ethernet or IEEE 802.3 network. These size limitations are both in terms of the geographic size, a maximum end-to-end distance of 2,500 meters, and the maximum number of active users, namely 1,024. But these limits can be easily extended by breaking the network into several subnetworks and interconnecting the subnetworks by means of bridges.

Bridges are devices that contain a processing component and two interface cards — one per subnetwork that it interconnects. One might envision a bridge as a PC with two plug-in cards, although bridges are normally especially designed CPU/memory configurations without the generality of a plug-in backplane. The bridge checks each packet sent on each interface to determine if it should be forwarded (i.e., copied) over to the other side. This filtering operation is based on the MAC destination address. The bridge knows whether each destination address should be forwarded. The bridge *learns* one key piece of information about each node on the LAN. For each node, the bridge learns if it is on the side of interface card #1 or #2 by observing the source addresses on packets as they pass by. Once the bridge has seen node #A as a source address on interface #1, it knows that address #A is on that side of the bridge. Until then, it forwards all packets so none are lost.

The *learning bridge* approach of IEEE 802.3 is called the spanning tree method. The distinguishing topological characteristic of a tree is that there are no closed loops. This means that there are no redundant paths, and the network has a connectivity of one. Any single outage will sever the network into two disjointed pieces. Fortunately, this is not really a problem because the bridge configuration can include one or more bridges in a standby mode. The bridges automatically configure into a tree, sorting out the active/standby configuration by resolving conflicts based on bridge addresses.

The reason a tree configuration is required in the spanning tree approach is the way that broadcast addresses are handled. The issue is whether a bridge should copy a broadcast packet to the other network. If the answer is yes, then each broadcast packet will be forwarded again and again, forming an endless looping of these packets if there is a closed path. The spanning tree approach precludes this problem.

The design challenge in developing a bridge (or the procurement challenge in buying one) is handling the worst-case situation of packet filtering and forwarding rates. The worst case IEEE 802.3 packet rate is approximately 15,000 packets per second on the subnet. This is based on the minimum packet size and the 10 Mbps transmission rate. It is desirable for a bridge to be able to handle this worst-case filtering rate, and many bridge products meet this specification. Many others filter about half this packet rate, but are also about half as expensive (or sometimes even less).

The second parameter of concern for a spanning tree bridge is the copy rate. Some high-end bridges can forward the entire 15,000 packet per second rate, while most others can only forward about half that. Those bridges that filter some lesser rate can typically forward only about half of their filter rate. For example, an inexpensive spanning tree bridge can filter about 8,000 packets per second and can forward about 4,000 packets per second. An important parameter that is not always found on bridge data sheets is whether the bridge can filter and forward several (e.g., a half-dozen) back-to-back packets. This situation involving closely spaced back-to-back packets often occurs in a file server when a request is made for a portion of a file. An actual test of a product under consideration is a good idea in this case, or one might configure the subnets to have a file server and its clients on the same subnet.

The spanning tree bridge makes its decisions about forwarding and develops its *learned* tables on the basis of the destination and source MAC sublayer addresses.

The IEEE 802.3 packet format is shown in Figure 2-18. It has the characteristic structure of an IEEE 802 and FDDI packet, namely a preamble

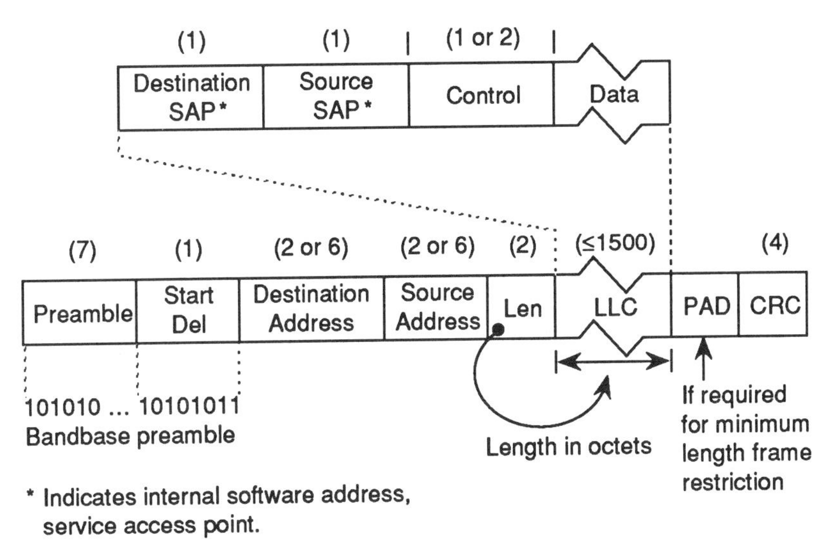


*Illustration courtesy of Learning Group International*

**FIGURE 2-18** An IEEE 802.3 packet.

followed by 48-bit destination and source addresses, and ending with a 32-bit cyclic redundancy check (CRC). The latter is actually called a frame check sequence.

Unlike other LAN formats, the IEEE 802.3 frame does not include an end indication. The Manchester encoding simply stops at the end of the packet. The 802.3 format is also unique in that it has a minimum (as well as a maximum) frame size. The minimum LLC field in the frame is about 48 bytes (called octets in OSI). A minimum frame size allows reliable discrimination between a *runt packet* caused by a collision and a valid short packet. The maximum LLC field in a packet is 1,500 bytes. This allows the length field to convey the Ethernet type field information on Ethernet packets that may coexist with IEEE 802.3 packets on a given LAN.

The IEEE 802.3 standard has been adopted by the International Standards Organization as ISO 8802-3, with amendments to cover medium attachment units (MAUs), repeaters, broadband, StarLAN, fiber-optic usage, management, and operation over unshielded twisted-pair (10BaseT) wiring.

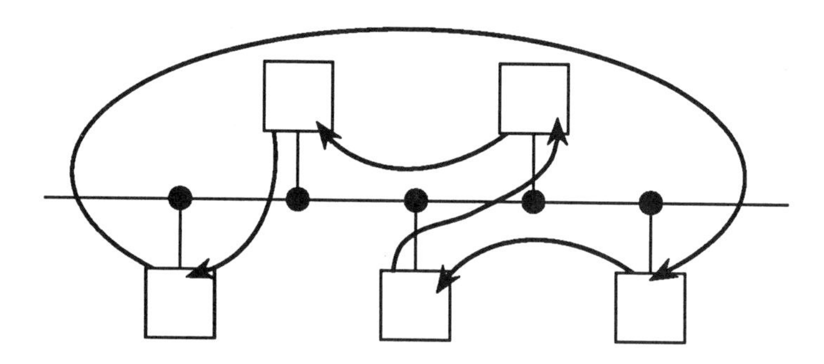


*Illustration courtesy of Learning Group International*

**FIGURE 2-19** The token bus supports an orderly flow of control.

## The IEEE 802.4 Token-Passing Bus LAN

The IEEE 802.4 token-passing bus was included in the OSI standards to support the manufacturing automation protocol applications in factory environments. General Motors was the driving force behind this LAN standard. GM wanted both the multi-channel capability of a broadband LAN and the reasonably deterministic access time of a token-passing access protocol. The basic concept of a token-passing bus is shown in Figure 2-19. Each node on the network receives the token, can hold it for up to a specified time interval, and then must pass it on to the next node based on order of address assignments.

The token is simply a short packet with no data field and with a specially defined pattern in the frame control field. The general format of a packet or token is shown in Figure 2-20. It differs from that of IEEE 802.3 primarily in its frame control field, but the similarity may be misleading. IEEE 802.4 implements not only a different access method, but also provides priority access. A low priority node may access the network only when it is lightly loaded, where the network load is indicated by the token rotation time. In a lightly loaded network, the token comes back around very quickly, while in a heavily loaded network, it takes much longer.

The frame control field provides a variety of special controls for allowing new nodes into the token-passing sequence, for recovering from a lost token

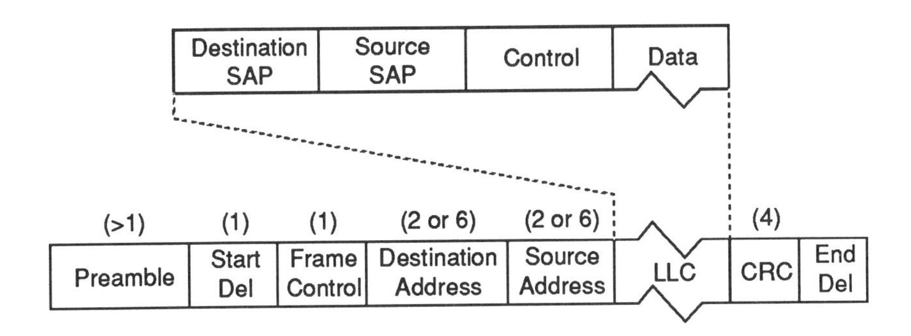


*Illustration courtesy of Learning Group International*

**FIGURE 2-20** Token-passing bus (IEEE 802.4).

or node, and for allowing an orderly removal from the token sequence. This form of control, which is not needed in CSMA/CD (carrier sense, multiple access, collision detection — Ethernet's control strategy) networks, is completely distributed among the nodes of the network.

Token-passing bus networks may operate with broadband (multiple channel) or carrier band (single channel) technology. In either case, modulation techniques are used to reduce the effect of electrical noise in the factory environment. Broadband LANs use cable television (CATV) amplifiers, taps (access points), splitters, and head-end components. In a broadband system, all transmissions are sent from a node to the head-end, and then back out to the receiving nodes. This provides a constant signal level at each receiving node and the head-end, regardless of where the signal originated. In keeping with the CATV tradition, the original transmission from a node to the head-end is called the reverse direction and the regenerated transmission from the head-end to the other nodes is called the forward direction. These terms make a lot of sense in CATV usage in which video programming is placed on the network at the head-end and sent out to all nodes (subscribers). The terms seem almost backwards for broadband LAN applications. Maybe things do not have to be intuitive, as long as they are standardized.

Bridges are used in IEEE 802.4 in essentially the same way as in IEEE 802.3. The spanning tree algorithm provides the same ability to have backup bridges in place but not concurrently operational to share the load. The IEEE

802.4 networks have an inherent tree structure, with the backbone and its bridges being at the top of the tree. The spanning tree algorithm allows this regardless of the specific addresses assigned to the bridges.

The IEEE 802.4 standard has been adopted as ISO 8802-4. There were no amendments at the time this book was written.

## The IEEE 802.5 Token-Passing Ring LAN

Like the token-passing bus, the token-passing ring provides an orderly scheme for allowing access to the shared LAN media. The media alternatives for the token-passing ring are twisted-pair wiring (either shielded or unshielded) and fiber-optic cable. Coaxial cable could be used, but it almost never is, and it certainly is not included in the standard approaches. Broadband is never used, not being appropriate for the token-ring approach.

---

- **The physical topology is usually a star network, connecting each node back to a wire closet.**
- **The topology simplifies maintenance.**

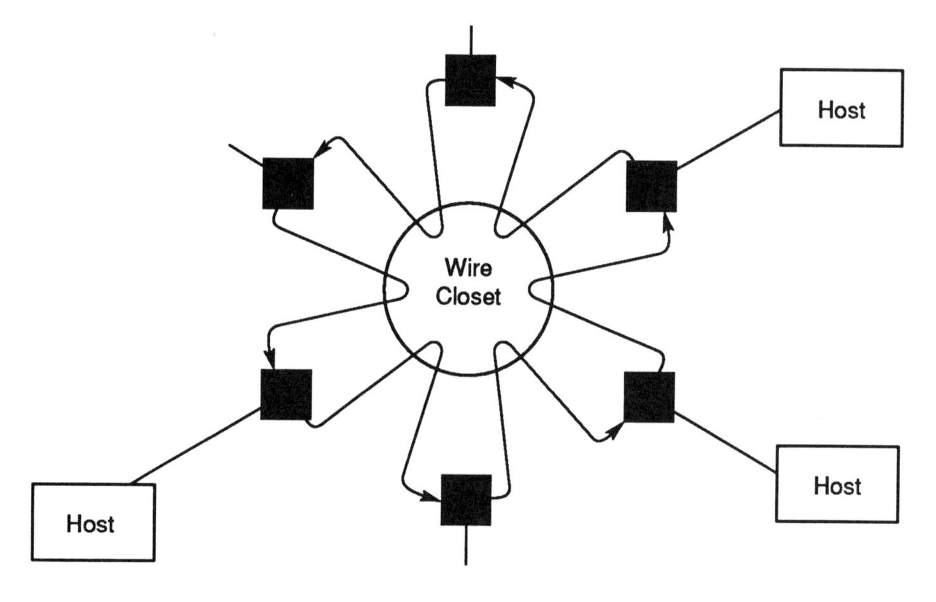


*Illustration courtesy of Learning Group International*

**FIGURE 2-21** The token-passing ring.

In a token-passing ring, a token passes around a logical circle that is almost always physically a star configuration (see Figure 2-21). All lines go to and from the center of the star, which is a wire closet not unlike that used for years in telephone wiring. In fact, a single wire closet may be used for both data (token ring) and voice cabling. Wire closets may also be interconnected, providing one per floor of a building or establishing a hierarchical closet structure.

Each node around the ring serves as a repeater, receiving and regenerating the signals as they pass through. One or more nodes may also be the ultimate destination of the packets being transmitted. The nodes will copy the packets as well as regenerate them (Figure 2-22). As indicated in the figure, each node also delays the signal by one-bit time while it stores each bit in the square box. This is necessary to allow the token to be captured by flipping a bit in the token, making it become the first part of a packet transmission. The figure

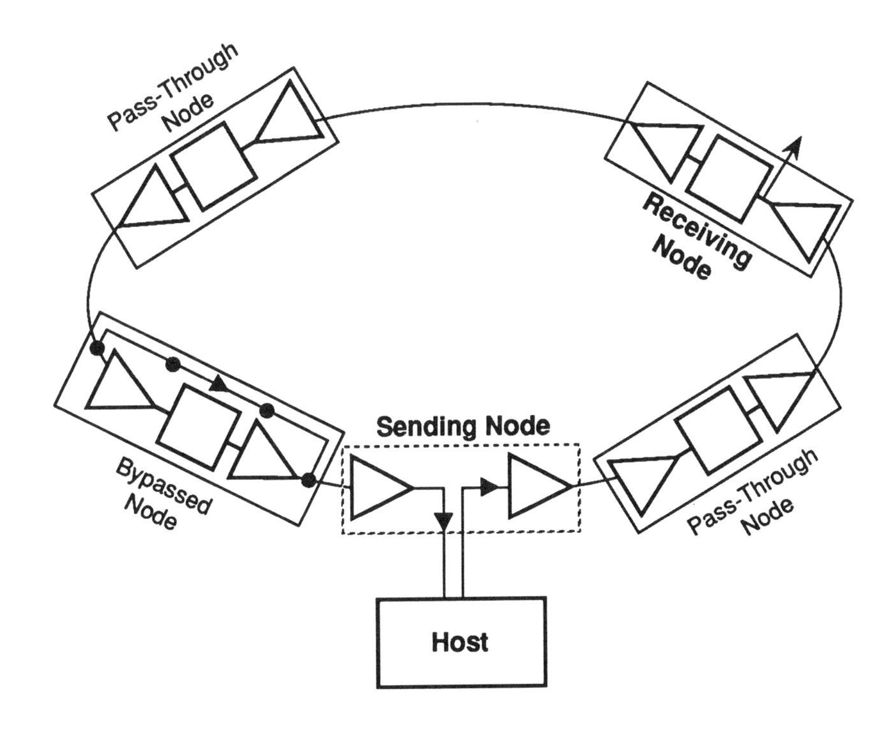


*Illustration courtesy of Learning Group International*

**FIGURE 2-22** Token-passing rings operate in a circular environment.

also shows a bypassed node that passes the signals through a relay when a node is powered down or otherwise unable to function as an active node.

Note that packets are not removed from the LAN by the receiving node, since other nodes may also be intended to copy them. For example, broadcast packets are addressed to all nodes and must go completely around the ring. As a result, it is the responsibility of the transmitting node to remove its packet.

A single token ring can only support a limited number of nodes, just as any other LAN approach has some maximum node count. In IEEE 802.5 token rings, this maximum value is based on clock skew. Each inter-node cable segment and its corresponding clock recovery circuit introduces a small amount of timing jitter or clock skew. As the square pulses that are sent become more rounded, the exact timing of the rise and fall edges becomes obscured. The poorer the quality of the cable, the more signal distortion and skew is caused. As a consequence, token rings over unshielded twisted-pair can support a maximum of 72 nodes, while token rings over shielded twisted pair can support up to 260 nodes.

To exceed these limits, add bridges (as in IEEE 802.3 and 802.4). But it is not quite that simple. IBM, which is the dominant player in IEEE 802.5, prefers a source routing approach to bridging rather than a spanning tree approach. The two approaches are poles apart:

- In source routing, each packet includes a list of bridges along the path. In spanning tree, this is not the case; no list is needed or provided.
- In source routing, the hosts or end systems learn the routes in terms of the sequences of bridges to pass through. In spanning tree routing, the bridges *learn* whether they should forward packets.
- In source routing, the hosts or end systems *learn* how large the packets can be and still traverse an end-to-end path across a series of bridges. In spanning tree, this is not an issue if all its LANs support the same maximum packet size.
- In source routing, each bridge need only look to see if its address is in the source address list. In spanning tree, each bridge must search a table of 48-bit destination addresses to see if they are to forward each packet. This affects the implementation strategy. Source routing bridges have an easier job and may be implemented from old personal computers that would otherwise be used for *door stops*. Spanning tree bridges must operate more quickly and are almost always special purpose boxes.

The IEEE 802.5 packet format (Figure 2-23) is similar to those of IEEE 802.3 and 802.4. The main differences are the additional access control and

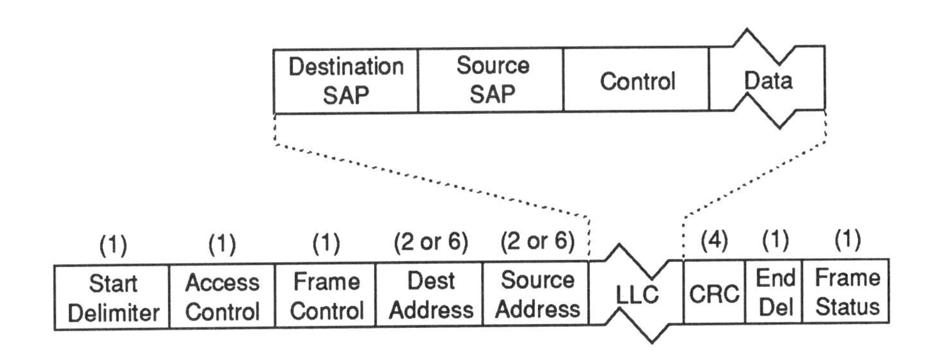


*Illustration courtesy of Learning Group International*

**FIGURE 2-23** Token-passing ring (IEEE 802.5) packet format.

frame status fields. Many interesting features are tucked away inside these fields, particularly the access control byte that is shown along with the rest of the token in Figure 2-24. When a token comes around, the receiving node first sees the start delimiter. The node does not yet know it is a token or the start of a packet. Next, the node sees the priority field. If this is a token, the node can use it only if the node's priority is equal to or greater than that expressed in this three-bit field. Finally, when the token bit is in the node's one-bit delay box, the token is recognized by noting that it is reset to zero. If

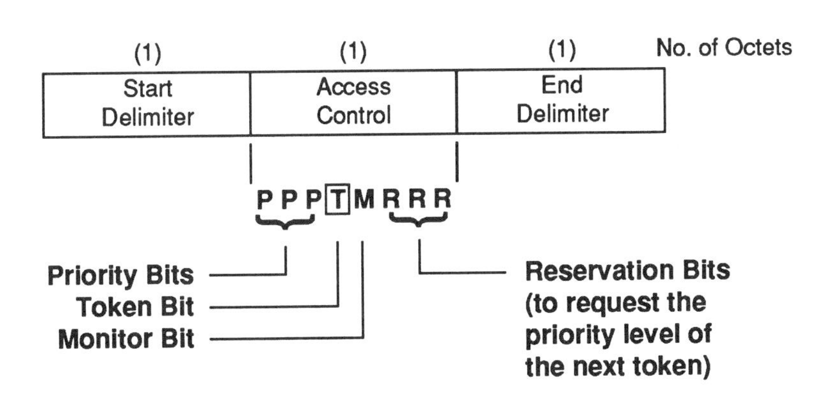


*Illustration courtesy of Learning Group International*

**FIGURE 2-24** The IEEE 802.5 token.

the node's priority allows the token to be used, the node flips this bit and proceeds to send its packet, utilizing the access control field as a part of the packet header.

The access control field also includes a monitor bit, which is used to recover from various token-ring LAN failures. In either a token or a packet, this monitor bit is initially reset to zero. When either the token or the packet passes a node called the active monitor, this bit is set to one. Neither a priority token nor a packet should ever pass by the active monitor again with the monitor bit set because each goes around the ring exactly once. An exception to this rule occurs when a node is unable to reset things back to normal. The active monitor can detect this condition and perform the required resetting.

The active monitor approach seems to introduce a single point of failure in the token ring, but this is not actually the case because a new active monitor can be elected as needed. Periodically the active monitor announces its presence by sending out a special control message. Each node expects to receive these messages periodically, and when a timer is exceeded, one or more of the other nodes begins a recovery process to elect a new active monitor. A special control message is sent, utilizing one of the frame control field values and alerting all other nodes that a new active monitor is being elected. Each node compares the source address of the control message with its own, over-writing its own address into this field if its address is larger than the current value. The net effect is that the highest active address on the LAN becomes the active monitor.

The access control field of the token (or what used to be the token but is now the front end of a packet) contains a set of reservation bits. These bits represent a bid as to what the priority of the next token should be. Any node can raise the bidding, as long as it is authorized to use the higher-priority token. When a packet is being removed from the ring, the node checks the reservation bits to determine what priority the next token should be.

The destination and source addresses of the token ring are identical to those of other IEEE 802 LANs except that a special situation is considered for source addresses. Source addresses can never be group addresses; they must always be individual addresses. Therefore, the leading bit of the source address could never be a binary one based on the defined encoding approach. IEEE 802.5 uses this extra bit as an indicator that a source route list exists in the packet. Within any ring, such a list is not needed. When going outside a ring, the list is necessary.

The source host must know if a transmission must go outside of its ring, and if so, what the list of bridges should be. The trick is how this information is determined. How does the host find the source route? Notice this key distinction with other IEEE 802 approaches. In IEEE 802.5, the *hosts* must learn. In the other approaches, the *bridges* must learn.

The hosts learn much the same way that our ancestors learned about the great unknown wilderness: they send out scouts. In IEEE 802.5 source route LANs, these scouts are called discovery packets. A discovery packet is sent out, and each bridge forwards it. This might cause an endless stream of broadcast packets being sent around and around, because the source routing approach allows redundant paths. It is not limited to a tree configuration. The solution to this potential problem is for each bridge to include its address in a growing list of bridges along a path until it notes that its address is already included in the list, at which time the bridge simply discards the packet.

The net effect is that some number of discovery packets get through to the desired distinction host. The host responds to each including the accumulated list of bridges, thus confirming the source route. The originating host can select from these returned alternatives, usually selecting the one that is returned first because it is the shortest delay path. One or more alternate source routes may also be kept by the host in the event of a subsequent failure along the primary path.

In addition to finding the desired source route across a set of bridges, the discovery packet also determines the maximum packet size that can be handled along each source route path. The originating host sets a field in the initial discovery packet to a known, maximum value. Each subsequent bridge then decreases this value as required to get across the next ring along the path. The net effect is that its final value when reaching the destination host is the maximum packet size that can be handled along the entire path.

It is interesting to note that the IEEE 802.5 source routing and its discovery packets provide two key pieces of information: what is the path, and how large can the packets be? This is the same set of concerns handled by internet protocols at the network layer in alternative protocol approaches. The difference is that internet protocols make this set of concerns transparent to the host, with the network routers handling these chores. These are fundamentally different architectural approaches to networking.

The IEEE 802.5 LAN differs from other IEEE LANs in almost every conceivable approach, ranging from whether one should transmit the most- or least-significant bit first, to differences in bridging, connection versus connectionless operation, and internetworking.

IEEE 802.5 token ring network operation requires that each node know the address of its upstream neighbor — the node from which it receives packets and tokens. This information is needed for recovery from a damaged cable segment when a node suddenly begins to receive nothing. Dead silence is encountered on the input circuit of the node. As a consequence, it sends out a beacon control packet that includes the upstream neighbor address. Network management is able to determine the addresses of the nodes at each end of the defective cable segment. Service personnel can go to the wire closet to patch out the defective portion of the wiring system.

The final portion of the IEEE 802.5 packet is the frame status field that contains information from nodes other than the source. This information includes the following messages:

1. **Address recognized** — A node realizes a packet is addressed to it.
2. **Packet copied** — A node was able to copy the packet.
3. **Error noted** — A node detected an error such as a CRC problem.

These fields date back to early token-ring developments, and their use has evolved over time. While they provide some useful features, they also require that every packet be processed in real-time by the interface unit so these bits can be set at the end of each packet.

The first of these flags, the address-recognized flag, indicates that a node saw a packet addressed to it. The second flag indicates whether the node was able to copy it. Some early token rings used this returned information in determining if a retransmission would be pointless (the desired node is apparently not on the network) or if retransmission should be delayed (the node is out of buffers and cannot copy it). These flags have taken on quite different uses as designs evolved. For example, the address-recognized flag is used to detect duplicate addresses on the LAN when a node is about to set the flag and finds it already set. A major use of the address-recognized flag is to allow each node to know its upstream neighbor's address. Periodically the controlling node on the LAN (the active monitor) sends out a loop poll with a broadcast destination address. Its nearest downstream neighbor sees that the packet is addressed to it (the broadcast address) and sets this flag. Every other node sees that it is addressed to it as well, but the flag has already been set. Additional loop poll packets are sent (one per node on the LAN) until the cycle is completed. Every node then knows the address of its upstream neighbor.

The copied flag indicates if the packet was read (but not necessarily by the actual destination node). If two or more token rings are interconnected by bridges, the bridge will set the copied flag.

The error-indication flag is useful in isolating where errors are being introduced. Every node checks each packet for errors, including the CRC error check of the packet. If any error is detected, the node then checks to see if the error-recognized flag is already set. If not, it is the first node to see this problem. It sets the flag and increments a counter, which is later sent to network management. An unusually large value in this count field indicates that the errors are being introduced on the upstream cable segment. It can be patched out to restore the integrity of the ring and diagnosed off-line.

The IEEE 802.5 standard has been adopted as ISO 8802-5, with amendments to cover both 4 and 16 Mbps operation, MAC sublayer enhancement, management, and source routing.

## The ANSI Fiber Distributed Data Interface LAN

The ANSI Fiber Distributed Data Interface is a 100 Mbps, fiber-optic, token-passing ring. Similar to IEEE 802 LANs in many ways, FDDI was developed under the auspices of ANSI because it initially appeared to be a different application, acting more like an I/O bus than a LAN. In addition, an agreement was in effect that ANSI would be responsible for development of such standards when the data rate exceeded 20 Mbps. Fortunately, the two groups have worked closely together, and the FDDI standard appears as a normal extension of the IEEE 802 LANs.

FDDI builds on the token-passing bus and token-passing ring experience and attempts to draw the best of both. For example, it has adopted completely distributed, timer-based recovery mechanisms similar to those of the 802.4 token bus. In addition, it has also adopted many of the indicator flags of the 802.5 token ring.

FDDI provides a dual ring (see Figure 2-25) in which nodes (called stations) can be attached either to both rings or only one ring. The second ring is normally used only for fault recovery purposes. The nodes may be either concentrators or directly attached computers, both of which are called dual attached stations (DAS). Other devices called single attached stations (SAS) may attach to the concentrator. The devices that attach to an FDDI network are typically bridges, routers, large-scale computers, and high-performance workstations. Other devices are normally attached to smaller networks, which in turn are attached to the FDDI network by means of bridges and routers. The FDDI network serves as a backbone for such users.

The dual ring provides the capability to divert traffic back around the second ring whenever the direct path between two nodes has been cut. This

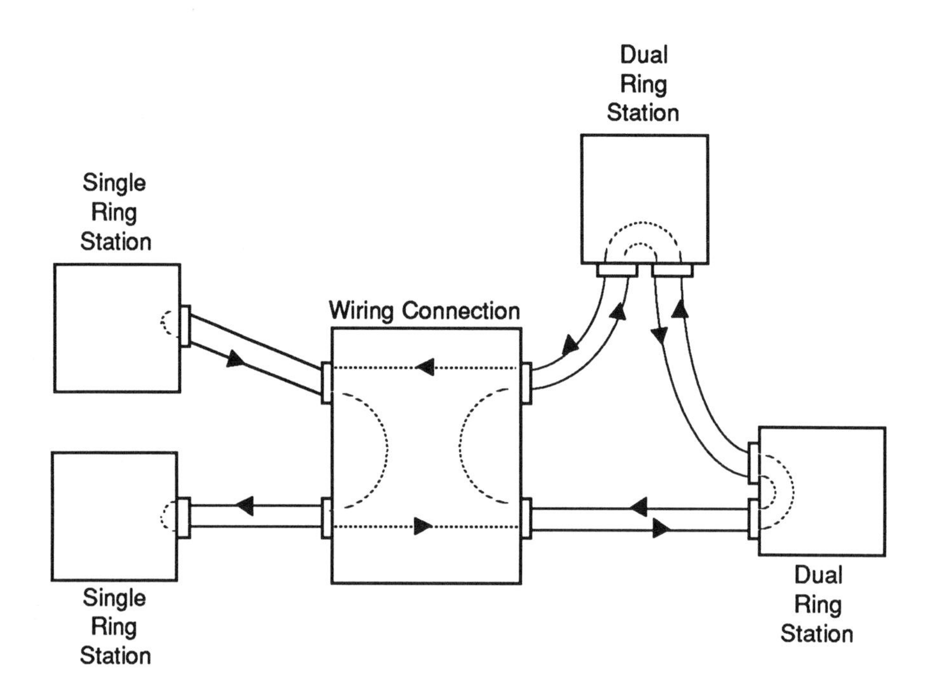


*Illustration courtesy of Learning Group International*

**FIGURE 2-25** FDDI utilizes both single- and dual-ring configurations.

happens when a node detects that it is suddenly not receiving any signal from its upstream neighbor. When a node detects this problem, it addresses a special control packet to its upstream neighbor, and then each of these nodes performs a wrap, diverting traffic to the secondary ring to travel between the two otherwise isolated nodes.

Use of the secondary or recovery ring affects the numbers that one associates with FDDI. For example, a baseline performance has been defined that limits an FDDI ring to a maximum of 1,000 attachments and 200 Km total circumference. When each node is a DAS, it counts twice, thereby limiting the design to 500 DAS nodes on the ring. Similarly, when the signals have to wrap back around the entire length of cable, it limits the overall circumference to 100 Km. It should be noted that these are not hard and fast limits on FDDI. They simply apply to this defined performance baseline.

Other numbers that apply to FDDI are based on the physical limits of the system. One of the most important is the maximum distance (2 Km) between nodes. Each node provides a repeater function, regenerating the signal. It is possible to exceed this limitation if single-mode fiber is used instead of the normal multi-mode fiber. Another FDDI constraint based on physical and electronic limits is the maximum packet size of 4,500 bytes, which is due to accumulated timing jitter. Timing is performed differently in FDDI and IEEE 802.5 token rings, resulting in different limitations. In the 802.5 approach, the timing method limits the number of nodes around the ring, with the maximum packet size not being specified by the standard but instead being limited by the buffering capability on the interface card.

The FDDI LAN supports 100 Mbps traffic, but it encodes this into 125 Mbps for transmission based on a 4 bit/5 bit (4B/5B) mapping. Surprisingly, this move was made so that light sources do not have to turn on and off so rapidly. At first glance, this seems to be backwards, but consider the alternatives. If FDDI attempted to encode its data using Manchester encoding as in IEEE 802.3 and 802.5, every bit would require an on/off light transition. Instead, FDDI uses NRZI encoding, thus selecting the appropriate five-bit coding to contain a desired number of ones and zeros. This ensures an adequate number of transitions for clock recovery. Some of the other extra five-bit patterns are used to represent non-data symbols to serve in start and end delimiters.

The FDDI packet or frame shown in Figure 2-26 is similar to those of IEEE 802 LANs, having the same addressing size and structure. It has a frame control field that distinguishes between network management (called station management in FDDI), token, and user data frames (called logical link control frames). The packet ends with the frame status flags much like those of IEEE 802.5.

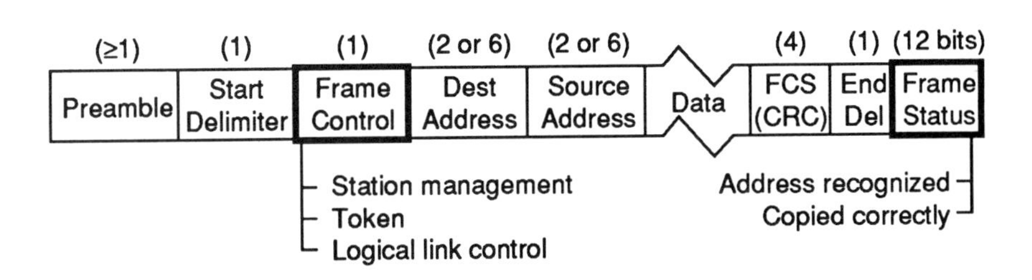


*Illustration courtesy of Learning Group International*

**FIGURE 2-26** FDDI frame format.

One distinguishing characteristic of FDDI is that it has control functions completely distributed across the nodes. In particular, it does not have an active monitor, as does IEEE 802.5. Instead, its recovery mechanisms are patterned after those of the IEEE 802.4 token-passing bus. The exception is that FDDI does not require the complex mechanisms of the token bus to control the token-passing sequence. Any node may be the first to notice that the token has been lost and therefore initiate the recovery operation.

The discovery that a token has been lost is based on timers. These timers are an important aspect of FDDI, since in addition to the recovery mechanisms, priority and guaranteed network access are also based on timers. A typical FDDI timer diagram is shown in Figure 2-27. The horizontal axis represents elapsed time, and the vertical axis represents the timer value at any given instant of the elapsed time. The circle in the center of the diagram represents the arrival of the token, approximately 3.5 milliseconds (ms) after it was last received. The timer has dropped from 5 ms to about 1.5 ms at this point. In a very simple approach to FDDI, the node could then hold the token, sending one or more packets, for a maximum of the remaining 1.5 ms. Then it would have to pass the token along.

Unfortunately things are not quite that simple. First, there is a form of data in FDDI called synchronous data that can be sent whenever the token is received, regardless of how little time remains on the timer. It is called synchronous because something is known about its timing, i.e., the worst case delay before a node will be able to send it. Secondly, FDDI implements priorities that may limit a node's ability to send non-synchronous (i.e., asynchronous) data when the remaining value of the timer is less than a preset value. Several such preset values may be established, creating a multilevel priority scheme.

FDDI uses the token rotation time as a measure of how busy the network is, just as Ethernet uses the number of collisions for such an indication. Under heavy load, both attempt to achieve the same objective, namely to keep some traffic off the network for awhile. In FDDI, it is the lower priority traffic that is not allowed to use the network, while in Ethernet, it is whatever node happened to have the collisions.

FDDI is being extended in an upwardly compatible manner to FDDI-II that will support isochronous transmission, i.e., the capability to ensure periodic access to the network. Isochronous transmission involves access every 125 microseconds, which corresponds to the 8,000 sample per second rate of

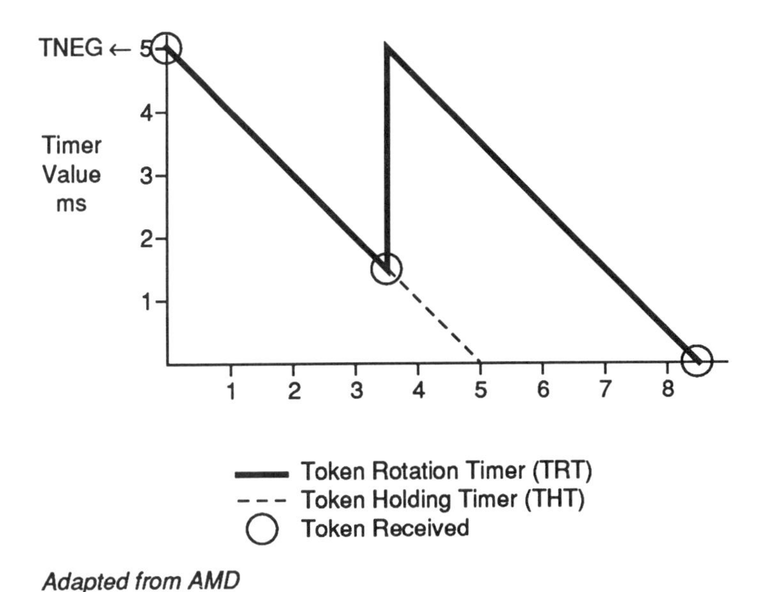


*Illustration courtesy of Learning Group International*

**FIGURE 2-27** FDDI timer values.

digitized speech. The ANSI standard for FDDI has been adopted as ISO 9314-3, with an amendment being developed to cover FDDI-II.

### Summary and Conclusions

The IEEE 802 and the ANSI FDDI LANs represent local area networks that are part of OSI. This section looked at the physical layer and the MAC sublayer components of such LANs. The next section will investigate the data link layer component of local area networks. It should not be a surprise to learn that there is once again more than one option.

## THE OSI DATA LINK LAYER

The data link layer of OSI is concerned with communications between any two directly connected computers. These communications are across a physical layer link or some set of cascaded physical layer links. One part of the physical path may consist of twisted-pair wiring with a connection to coaxial cable using a balun (balanced-unbalanced) device, and then through a repeater to a fiber-optic link that is attached to another computer. The two computers may be end systems (hosts) with a communications circuit between them, two adjacent packet switches, two hosts on a local area network, or a host-to-packet switch communication. All of these are candidate situations for a data link protocol.

The data link layer protocol should add value to the delivery capabilities of the basic physical circuit. This stems from the need to improve the communications quality of a voice-grade telephone channel to make it acceptable for data communications. Errors are often introduced on the physical circuit, with an average bit error rate of one bad bit in every 100,000 bits transmitted. For a 1,000 bit packet size, approximately one of every 100 packets will be in error. This clearly requires some method of error detection and recovery. Retransmissions based on acknowledgment (ACK) timeouts is the most common method. Any protocol that uses ACKs and retransmissions may introduce duplicate packets, leading to the need for sequence numbers. Finally, flow control is typically needed so that the user is assured that good packets, once delivered, have buffer space to be kept. This leads to the classical reliable, sequenced, flow-controlled delivery (connection) protocol that is so prevalent in OSI.

Most data link protocols are indeed connection-oriented, and therefore provide reliable, sequenced delivery. However, local area networks frequently use connectionless data link protocols. The LAN examples are characterized by the IEEE standard 802.2 type 1, which provides neither reliability nor sequenced delivery. The strong error checking of the LAN ensures that bad data are almost never delivered, but there is no error recovery when bad packets are detected. The IEEE 802.2 also provides a type 2, connection-oriented data link protocol that is optional. Each IEEE 802.2 implementation must include support for connectionless data link control and may also provide support for connection-oriented controls.

## OSI Reference Model Definition of the Data Link Layer

Developers of the OSI Reference Model clearly had existing data link protocols such as high-level data link control (HDLC) in mind when they drew up the top level requirements for the data link layer. However, they also envisioned a need to go beyond current HDLC capabilities at the data link layer. The services listed for the data link layer were the following:

- Provide data link connections:
  Connection endpoint identifiers.
  Sequencing.
  Flow control.
  Error notification (when non-recoverable).
- Provide quality of service (QOS) selection (optional).
- Provide data link service data units.

The services of the OSI Reference Model always lead to the service definition in the documents that eventually provide a specification for implementation. The data link service definition is contained in CCITT recommendation X.212 and ISO 8886.

The OSI Reference Model specifies several functions as a means to provide the required services. The functions listed for the data link layer are as follows:

- Provide data link connections:
  Connection establishment and release.
  Sequence control.
  Error detection.
  Error recovery.
  Flow control.
- Provide an SDU-to-PDU mapping.
- Provide identification and parameter exchange.
- Provide splitting across two or more physical links.
- Provide data link layer management.

The functions listed in the OSI Reference Model usually lead to the protocol specification for the layer. This has not been done, at least at the time this book is being written. The functions are intended to provide the desired services, and the connection-oriented services and functions follow quite closely. There is also a service requirement to support SDUs, as well as a function to map between SDUs and PDUs. From that point on, the relationship between services and functions is much less obvious. The functions of identification and parameter exchange, splitting across two or more physical links, and layer management do not relate directly to the services. These functions are a combination of ways to provide the desired services (e.g., splitting to obtain higher throughput) and network management. The QOS service is related to issues such as obtaining higher throughput.

One of the best ways to learn about protocols is to look at actual examples. HDLC is an example of a set of related protocols built around the general principles of the OSI Reference Model's data link layer.

## HDLC as an Example Data Link Layer Protocol

Before getting into the detailed operation of the HDLC protocol, it is worthwhile to provide some additional context for its usage. It began with an emphasis on polling environments and has evolved to support point-to-point needs as well.

In polling networks, one node is designated as the master (or primary) while the other nodes are slaves (or secondaries). This configuration has been around for decades and will continue as long as it serves a purpose in existing systems, extensions to those systems, or replications of such systems. However, most of our attention will be on point-to-point data link protocols.

The data link protocol is somewhat unique in having to find the beginning and end of packets, or frames as they are often called in data link layer discussions. At other protocol layers, there is nothing before the beginning byte of the packet to obscure the matter, and the length is often passed with the packet. The data link protocol has this unique problem because it is utilizing a bit serial transmission technique. No one knows in advance how long the packet is. The trick is how to indicate the end of a packet when one has to be able to transmit any possible pattern of ones and zeros in the data portion of the packet.

The approach to handling arbitrary bit patterns in the data stream is to modify the bit pattern to breakup any accidental occurrences of a special flag pattern that will terminate the stream. In the HDLC protocol, the flag pattern is 01111110. If this pattern appears in the packet itself, it is broken up by the following algorithm. Upon transmission, the sender looks for strings of binary ones in the packet. If it finds five ones in a row, it inserts a zero. The receiver does the inverse. It looks for five ones in a row and discards a zero if found. Only the real flag pattern will not have a zero after five ones.

LANs have yet another solution to this problem. LAN designers have used encoding schemes for binary ones and zeros that also include other non-data symbols. These non-data symbols can be used to indicate special cases such as the end of a packet. These non-data symbols are called encode violations.

Error-control mechanisms provide reliable delivery service. The techniques for providing reliable delivery may be either retransmission or forward error correction, but it is almost always by means of a positive-acknowledgement retransmission protocol. When a packet is received, its error check field is confirmed. If not, the packet is discarded. If it is received correctly, it is acknowledged. If no ACK is received within a timeout period, the sender of the packet will retransmit it.

As previously noted, the sender will retransmit a packet if an ACK is not received within a timeout period. But what if it is the ACK that gets lost, not the original packet? In this circumstance, two copies of the packet are delivered. Sequence numbers are needed to detect this problem. This is packet number one. The next is packet number two, and so forth.

To manage the lifetime of sequence numbers, a window mechanism is used. At any given time, only a subset of the possible sequence numbers are allowed to be sent. Therefore, there should never be any confusion, even if sequence numbers are later reused.

ACKs need to be associated with the specific packets being acknowledged. Therefore, one includes a sequence number with ACKs, as well as with data packets. The logical choice might be that ACK number 5 acknowledges packet number 5. This is sometimes done, but more often than not, the ACK number is the next expected packet sequence number. This allows an ACK number to be returned, even when no packets have been received. This capability is needed when ACKs are piggybacked on normal traffic.

Associated with the sequence control mechanisms are the flow-control mechanisms. While they build on a common framework, the intent of flow control is to make sure that the sender does not transmit more rapidly than the receiver can accept. This typically relates to buffering at the receiving end. Occasionally, the receiver has to indicate that it can no longer accept more packets. Do not send anything more until it informs that it can accept more packets. Enough basics have been covered to get into the actual HDLC protocol.

The HDLC protocol started out to be a modern replacement for older data link protocols such as bisync. However, HDLC has evolved into a family of data link protocols, covering everything from polled terminals to local area networks and personal computers to mainframes via modems. The basic HDLC specifications predate OSI, and therefore are not in the usual service definition and protocol specification form, although CCITT did introduce a data link service definition in the 1988 Blue Books (CCITT X.212). It is also available as ISO 8886. There is no CCITT or ISO protocol specification. The original ISO documents defining HDLC are ISO 3309 High-level Data Link Control Frame Structure, ISO 4335 Consolidation of Elements of Procedure, and ISO 7809 Consolidation of Classes of Procedure.

As expected from its name, the first of these specifications defines the frame structure, including the flag, zero insertion, address structure and usage, the control field, the information field, and the frame check sequence. The content of the second document is not so apparent from its rather strange name. The elements include the different primary/secondary station configurations, the modes of operation (discussed later in this section), and the command/response set. The third document defines the various meaningful groupings of modes of operation, subsets of the command/response set, and configurations that are then implemented.

Three basic forms of HDLC correspond to the meaningful combinations of polled versus non-polled and master/slave versus peer-to-peer. These three combinations and their official HDLC names are

**Polled, primary/secondary** — normal response mode.
**Non-polled, primary/secondary** — asynchronous response mode.
**Non-polled, peer-to-peer** — asynchronous balanced mode.

The polled, primary/secondary mode is called normal response mode because such polling was the normal way of doing business in the mid-1970s when this protocol was standardized.

The non-polled, primary/secondary mode is called asynchronous response mode because the secondary can transmit without having to wait for a poll. The transmission of a packet from the secondary to the primary is asynchronous because there is no predetermined time that it will be sent. Used in the same sense as asynchronous characters, here it applies to packets.

The non-polled, peer-to-peer mode is called asynchronous balanced mode because it has the asynchronous characteristics with respect to sending packets and balanced control (i.e., neither end is the absolute primary, nor is it the secondary). Both ends share these two roles. It is sometimes called a combined station.

An HDLC packet is framed with multiple occurrences of a special bit pattern called the flag, which is 01111110. When one wants to send an HDLC packet, it is preceded by a few flags. The first flag is usually not recognized because the receiver takes a few bit times to recognize that something new is coming in and to recover clock synchronization. Once in-coming bits are reliably detected, the receiver starts to search for the flag pattern. The second flag may then be detected. To verify that it is not merely a random occurrence of the bit pattern, the receiver checks the next eight bits as well. It continues to do so, eight bits at a time, until it finds a non-flag pattern. This is assumed to be the start of the packet. The next flag pattern indicates that the end of the packet, including its CRC error check, has been received. Any accidental occurrence of the flag pattern in the packet itself is broken up by the transmitting hardware by inserting a binary zero after any string of five ones. These inserted zeros are removed at the receiving end. Only the real end symbol actually arrives at the receiver as 01111110. This framing of an HDLC packet is shown in Figure 2-28.

The figure showing the framing also indicates that once one knows the start and endpoints of an HDLC packet, one can find the relevant address,

---

- **Address identifies**
  Secondary if polled.
  Command/response if point-to-point.
- **Control identifies the type of PDU.**
- **CCITT Standard CRC is $X^{16} + X^{12} + X^5 + 1$.**

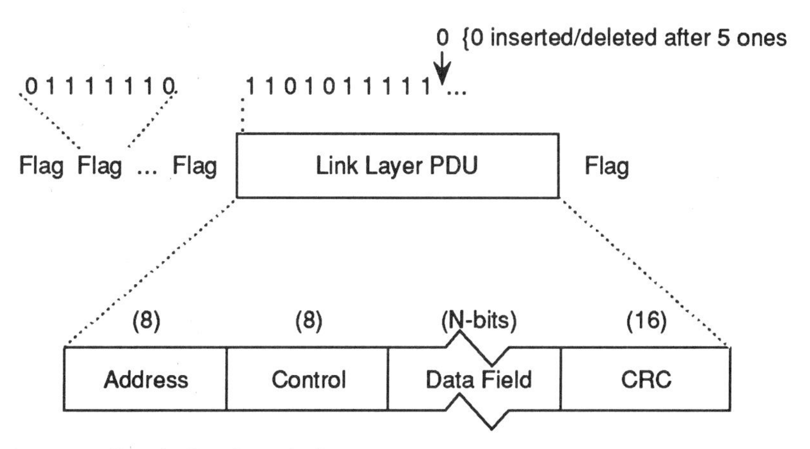


*Illustration courtesy of Learning Group International*

**FIGURE 2-28** ISO HDLC framing.

control, and error check portions. Of particular concern here is the control field, which is shown in greater detail in Figure 2-29.

Three types of packets are described in the following paragraphs.

Information frames convey user data. Each frame has a sequence number to ensure that all data are received, in order, and without duplicates. The sequence number space also provides a vehicle for the ACKs (the next expected sequence number). In an information frame, the sequence number and the ACK number relate to different directions of the data flow. The sequence number is the number assigned to this packet. In contrast, the ACK number is the sequence number that the other side next expects to receive.

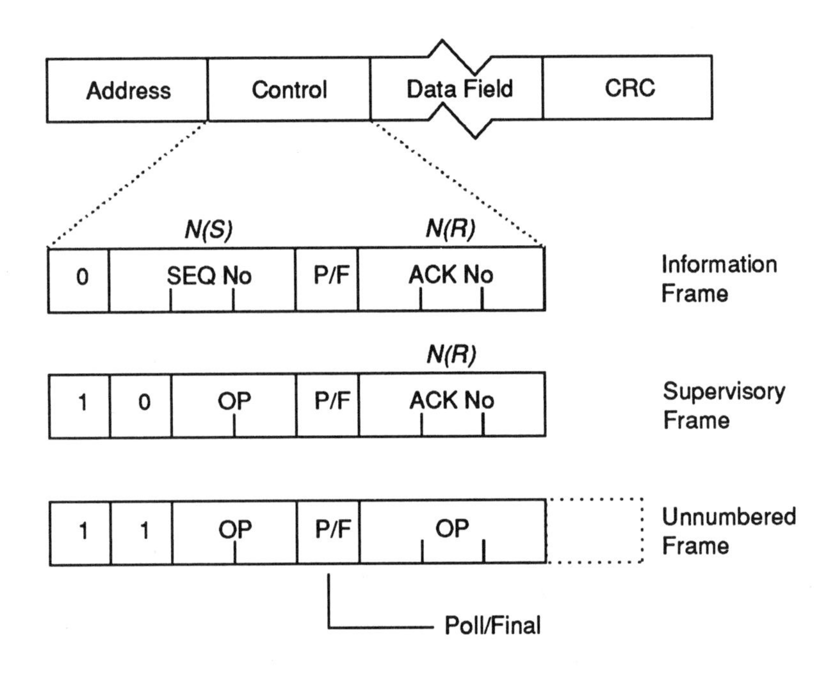


*Illustration courtesy of Learning Group International*

**FIGURE 2-29** HDLC control field uses.

Supervisory frames are used to convey ACKs (when there is no data to send) and flow-control signals. The flow control signals are as follows:

1. **Receiver ready** (RR) — More packets may be sent.
2. **Receiver not ready** (RNR) — More packets may not be sent until the message is received that it is all right to do so (with an RR).
3. **Reject** (Rej) — The packet number that was next expected was not sent. Go back and send it, and all that followed it. (Reject is not always available.)
4. **Selective reject** (SRej) — Go back and send just this one packet. (Selective reject is not always available.)

Unnumbered frames are used to control the initialization, fault recovery, and termination of the packet exchange. As used here, recovery refers to major problems such as erroneous commands. Normal bit errors are recovered by retransmissions. An example exchange of an unnumbered command and its corresponding unnumbered ACK is shown in Figure 2-30.

The unnumbered command, set asynchronous balanced mode, causes both ends of the link to become initialized and set to operate with this mode. The initialization consists of setting the sequence and next ACK numbers to zero. Note that the unnumbered commands and ACKs do not have sequence numbers. This is, of course, why they are called unnumbered.

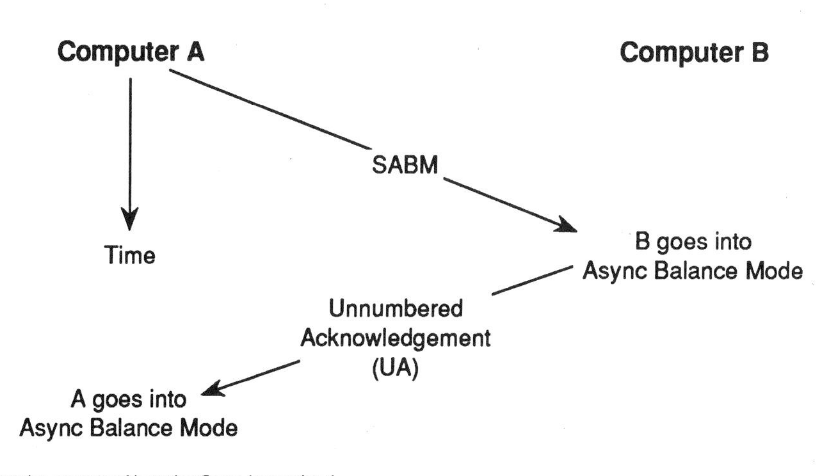


*Illustration courtesy of Learning Group International*

**FIGURE 2-30** Set asynchronous balanced mode (SABM).

The information frames are to be delivered exactly once, with one and only one copy of each packet being accepted by the receiver. Sequence numbers are provided in the information frames for this purpose. They are the only data link layer packets to contain sequence numbers, and therefore, to have this *exactly once* property. Note that supervisory and unnumbered packets do not cause problems if they are duplicated. Telling the sender twice to stop sending is no problem. Unlike information or unnumbered packets, however, supervisory packets do not have timeouts and retransmissions; they can be lost. If an RNR is lost, the other side later tries to send, and the RNR is sent back. The packet can be discarded because it will be retransmitted (but not until an RR is sent back). This does not work quite so neatly if an RR gets lost. Suppose that this RR is the one that will allow the other side to start sending after the last RNR. If the RR is lost, how will the other side get the message that it is okay to send? The implementations have to account for such what if conditions.

When an RR is received, there is a fixed upper boundary on how many packets can be sent before one has to wait for an ACK. This upper boundary is called a window. The window size is typically set to the value two, meaning that one can send two packets before waiting for an ACK to come back. The ACK provides a new (updated) left edge for the window, but the window size remains fixed at two. This is the default value for the window size. It is a system parameter, and to change it, one must recompile and link the software with that new parameter value.

Other system parameters include timer values and the maximum packet size. Higher layer protocols with similar features have much more adaptability, i.e., compatibility with change. That is because the higher layers must deal with a wider range of user needs and network environments. Meanwhile, at the data link layer, these are rather static values.

One remaining feature of the basic HDLC is the poll/final (P/F) flag. This control flag has a variety of meanings, depending on the mode of operation and the specific context . These uses include being a poll indicator, a status request, a checkpoint, and an end-of-sequence indicator. The latter interpretation is the one that provides a point of departure for future discussions of similar concepts, namely an end-of-record delimiter. A multi-packet poll message or response could be delimited by setting this flag on the last packet of the sequence. This concept and its relationship with the X.25 *more* flag and the transport protocol *end* flag will be explored in greater detail.

Many extensions to the basic HDLC form are possible:

1. **Exchange identification** (XID) — Method used by two nodes to provide information about themselves and their respective abilities to operate in certain modes.
2. **Unnumbered information** — The ability to send user data in unnumbered packets. This is especially useful in the connectionless data link layer variations used in LANs.
3. **Initialization** — Sets link control functions to an initial value.
4. **Unnumbered polling** — Requests that control information be returned.
5. **Extended addressing** — Multi-byte address fields that use a *more* bit in each extended byte except the last.
6. **Extended sequence numbers** — Use of seven-bit sequence (and ACK) numbers.
7. **Mode reset** — Resets sequence and ACK numbers.
8. **Test** — An echo function to test communication with another link entity.
9. **Request disconnect** — Request for a disconnect command.
10. **Longer** (32-bit) **CRC error check** — Use of a 32-bit cyclic redundancy check frame check sequence.

Various groupings of these optional extensions to HDLC have been given names and are widely used in selected areas. One example includes link access procedure balanced (LAPB) that is used as the data link layer in X.25. It is essentially the asynchronous balanced mode described in this chapter. Another variation is the link access procedure for the D channel of ISDN (LAPD). It uses a different addressing structure (see Figure 2-31). The address field is of the extended (two-byte) form. It conveys two levels of addressing: the service access point identifier and the terminal endpoint identifier. It also indicates if the content is a command or a response. This is the only information carried in the asynchronous balance mode address field, which rather wastefully uses eight bits to convey a Boolean piece of information. LAPD uses the asynchronous balanced mode, as does LAPB, but adds the XID, extended address, and extended control fields.

## IEEE 802.2 as an Example Data Link Layer Protocol

The IEEE has developed a variety of LAN standards, including CSMA/CD, token bus, and token ring. Within these categories there are many versions.

- **One variation of HDLC is link access procedure for the D channel (LAPD) of ISDN.**

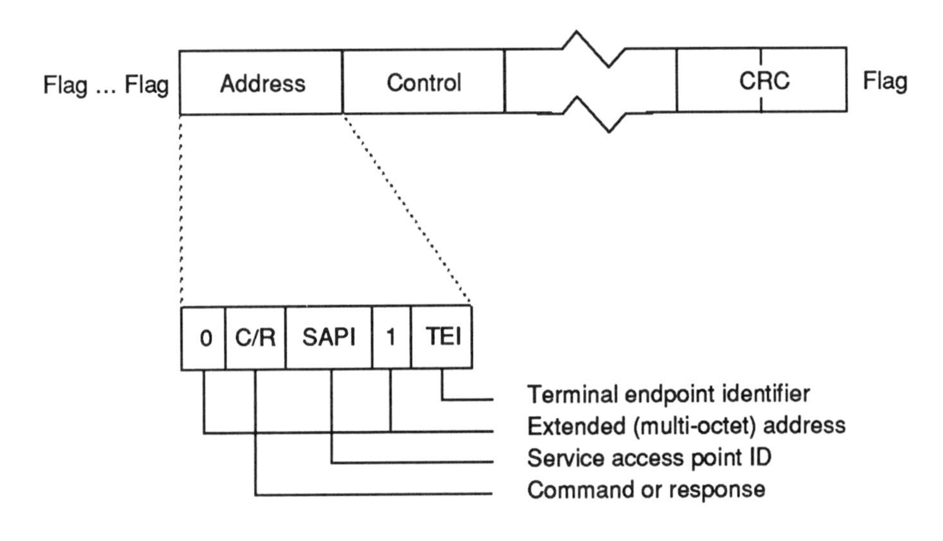


*Illustration courtesy of Learning Group International*

**FIGURE 2-31** Link access procedure for D channel (LAPD).

Many options and alternatives reflect the differing interests of DEC, IBM, and other companies. So wouldn't it be nice if there were a common protocol at the data link layer that would make these differences transparent to the user of the LAN? Why would one expect that to happen?

The companies and organizations that had differing views on what the LAN technology should provide also differed on what the data link layer or the logical link control sublayer should provide. Figure 2-32 shows the current situation, with three types of LLC.

The three types are rather unimaginatively called type 1, type 2, and type 3. Type 1 is connectionless and sometimes referred to as unacknowledged connectionless. It is the basic datagram or best-efforts service associated with pre-OSI LANs such as Ethernet. Type 2 is connection-oriented, providing the usual reliable, sequenced, flow-controlled delivery. Finally, type 3 is acknowledged connectionless. It has error recovery but none of the other connection-oriented properties.

Type 1, connectionless, is the approach preferred by companies and organizations that have an Ethernet heritage, including products from DEC, HP, Sun, and a variety of other vendors. Type 1 provides relatively little beyond what Ethernet provided, but it casts these minimal services into a proper OSI layering approach.

Type 2, connection-oriented, is the preferred approach of IBM in token-ring applications. It provides the virtual circuit services that IBM traditionally expects at the data link layer of its System Network Architecture. Color type 2 blue.

Type 3, acknowledged connectionless, is the preferred approach of a specialized group including the process-control industry. This group wants assurances that packets are being delivered without the overhead of heavy-duty connection-oriented approaches. In type 3, a packet is transmitted, and the sender waits for the ACK before sending the next packet. After a timeout when no ACK has been returned, the packet is retransmitted. Simple odd/even sequencing is sufficient to detect duplicates. None of the usual multi-bit sequence numbers and windows are required, nor is flow control.

The three types of LLC are provided by adapting a variation of HDLC to fit this need (see Figure 2-33). The address field of HDLC is extended and is divided into two fields: one for the destination and one for the source address in the form of service access points. Service access points (SAPs) are internal software addresses. The MAC sublayer address delivers the packet to the proper computer. Now it is the responsibility of the destination SAP (DSAP) and similar SAPs at each other layer to get the user data delivered all the way up to the application layer. The link layer SAP can be either an individual or

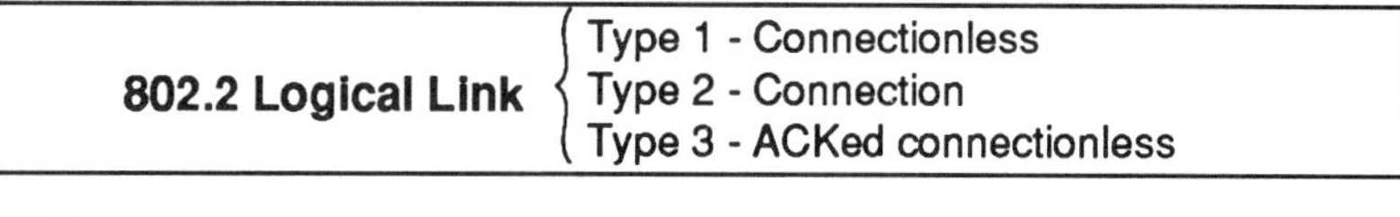


*Illustration courtesy of Learning Group International*

**FIGURE 2-32** IEEE 802 specification variations.

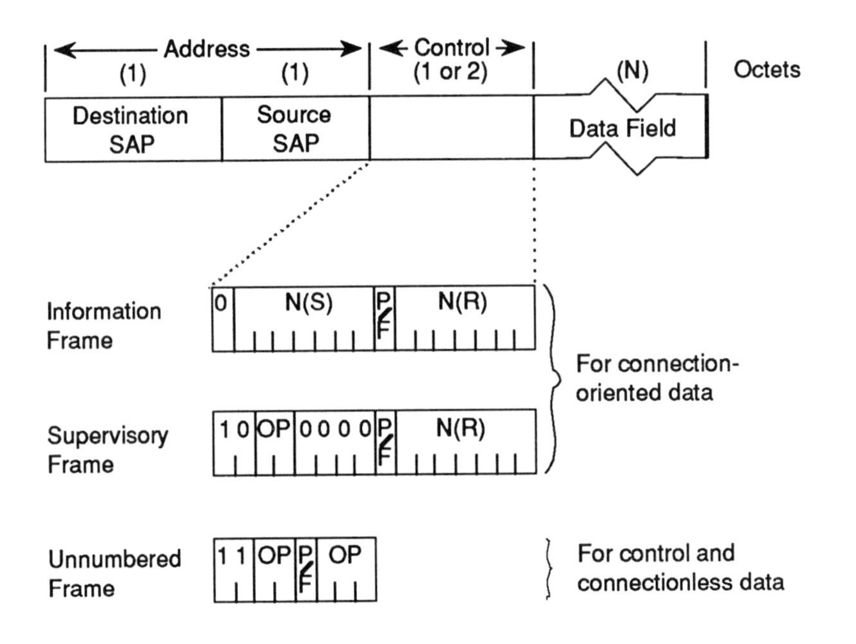


*Illustration courtesy of Learning Group International*

**FIGURE 2-33** Local area network logical link control.

a group, the latter including broadcast. This is modelled after the same two variations of addresses at the MAC sublayer. A broadcast software address (i.e., SAP) might be used to allow a node on the network to announce its presence to all protocols.

The two major forms of IEEE 802.2 data link protocols are type 1 and type 2 (i.e., connectionless and connection-oriented). They are shown along with class 1 and class 2, which IEEE has identified as the groupings to which implementations must conform. Class 1 is simply type 1 (connectionless). This is essentially what all IEEE 802.3 CSMA/CD and IEEE 802.4 token-bus systems use. Class 2 provides both type 1 (connectionless) and type 2 (connection-oriented) services and is the preferred approach of IBM 802.5 LANs. Since class 2 provides both connection and connectionless capabilities, it can interoperate with class 1. Thus, IBM can talk to DEC if it is willing to do so utilizing class 1.

The next logical question is how one host or end system determines which type (or class) is available for communication with another system? That question leads directly into the next topic, namely the exchange of identifying information between two or more nodes.

Figure 2-34 shows the specific commands and responses available for class 1 and class 2 nodes. XID is available to both classes and, therefore, can be used to determine the connection or connectionless operation of other nodes. The type 2 commands and responses are also shown in this figure, including establishing this mode of operation, determining flow control, and exchanging information. XID also includes the receive window size, as well as the mode of operation.

Another important class 1 capability is the exchange of test command/responses. This is a form of echo test, with the P/F flag used to correlate commands and their associated responses. The F-bit is set to the same value as the P-bit of the test command.

The connection-oriented operations of type 2 involve the OSI connection establishment handshake. During the handshake the parameter exchanges

---

- **Class 1 supports connectionless operation.**
- **Class 2 supports both connection and connectionless operation.**

|  | Type | Commands | | Responses | Format |
|---|---|---|---|---|---|
| Class 1 / Class 2 | Type 1 | UI | unnumbered information | — | U |
| | | XID | exchange identification | XID | |
| | | TEST | | TEST | |
| Class 2 | Type 2 | I | information | I | I |
| | | RR | receiver ready | RR | S |
| | | RNR | receiver not ready | RNR | |
| | | REJ | reject | REJ | |
| | | SABME | | UA (unnumbered ACK) | U |
| | | DISC | disconnect | DM (disconnected mode) | |
| | | | | FRMR (frame reject) | |

*Illustration courtesy of Learning Group International*

**FIGURE 2-34** LLC commands and responses.

include the local and remote link SAPs (LSAPs), as well as the desired service class such as priority (if supported in the LAN).

IEEE 802.2 logical link control is a special case of an HDLC-like data link protocol adopted for use in LANs. In the connectionless mode of operation, the LLC provides very few services, primarily conveying the internal software addresses (LSAPs) and the command/responses for XID and test. In the connection-oriented mode, essentially all the HDLC error, sequence, and flow-control properties are maintained. They provide interoperability between these two diverse modes or types of operation, Classes are identified, and all classes must include at least the type 1 (connectionless) operation.

## Summary and Conclusions

The data link layer operates between end systems and/or intermediate systems operating at the network layer or above. Intermediate systems such as repeaters at the physical layer and bridges at the MAC sublayer are not endpoints of a data link layer communications. They are transparent to the data link layer protocols.

The data link layer may provide either connection or connectionless service to the next layer (i.e., to the network layer). These alternatives will be considered in the next chapter.

# 3

# END-TO-END COMMUNICATIONS: THE NETWORK AND TRANSPORT LAYERS

Pre-OSI protocol stacks such as IBM's System Network Architecture (SNA) and DEC's DECnet matched OSI quite closely at the physical layer and the data link layer. However, this match did not carry over to the network and transport layers, at least partly due to difficulties in clearly separating the roles of the two layers. The functions required from the transport layer are significantly affected by the services provided by the network layer. This chapter discusses these two end-to-end layers, including relevant Open Systems Interconnection (OSI) Reference Model material and the protocols for each layer and sublayer.

## THE NETWORK LAYER

The principal purposes of the network layer are routing and relaying. However, to accomplish these requirements, the network layer must also provide several other capabilities. First, to route a packet the network switching elements must know the destination address, so addressing is a basic network issue. The addressing issue includes how to express addresses beyond a single network, i.e., internetwork addresses. Second, network switches and links may become overloaded as they attempt to provide routing and relaying services. Some form of congestion control is needed, in addition to the usual flow-control mechanisms. Congestion control and flow control differ in that congestion control applies to switches along the path, while flow control is between pairs of devices (end systems and/or switches). Finally, the delivery of some traffic may require expediting. This is an optional capability that is not provided by all networks.

The relay function at the network layer is in addition to possible relay functions at the physical layer (e.g., by repeater devices) and at the data link layer (e.g., by bridge devices). Bridges provide both routing and relaying at the media access control (MAC) sublayer, so these functions are not unique to the network layer. No MAC sublayer existed at the time OSI developers assigned this responsibility to the network layer.

## The OSI Reference Model Network Layer

The OSI Reference Model originally stated that the network layer was to provide connections between open systems, making the routing and relay functions transparent to the transport layer. This connection orientation has been broadened to include optional connectionless service.

The OSI Reference Model's definition of a *subnetwork* is generally what we refer to as a network (because of the ambiguity of whether the hosts (end systems) are part of the network). A subnetwork may be an X.25 network, a local area network (LAN), or a set of interconnected transmission facilities. The basic services provided by X.25 networks, LANs, and similar subnetworks differ, so the network layer may provide hop-by-hop (i.e., network-by-network) service enhancements to provide the desired OSI end-to-end network service.

The OSI Reference Model lists the services that are to be provided by the network layer. The connection-oriented services include

- Services related to connections:
  Establishment, maintenance, and release of network connections.
  Endpoint identifiers.
  Sequencing.
  Flow control.
  Error notification.
  Reset (reinitialization).
  Expedited data (independent of flow-control constraints).
- Addressing (unique identification of transport entities).
- Network service data unit (NSDU) transfer.
- Quality of service parameters (optional).

These services lead directly to similar services described in the OSI service definition for the network layer (Consultative Committee for International Telephone and Telegraph (CCITT) X.213 and International Standards Organization (ISO) 8348). However, the OSI network service definition also includes services above and beyond those from the OSI Reference Model. The principal example is the end-to-end delivery confirmation service that was added to X.213

and ISO 8348 to be consistent with X.25 services. Thus, the OSI service definition is the 1984 version of X.25.

The X.213 recommendation provides a set of service primitives for the establishment, use, and release of connections, as summarized in Table 3-1.

**Table 3-1** Connections primitive.

| Service | Primitive | Parameters |
|---|---|---|
| Connection Establishment | N-CONNECT request and indication | Called address, Calling address, Receipt confirmation select, Expedited data select, Quality of service, User data |
| | N-CONNECT response and confirmation | Responding address, Receipt confirmation select, Expedited data select, Quality of service, User data |
| Data transfer | N-DATA request and indication | User data |
| Receipt ACK (optional) | N-DATA-ACK request and indication | - |
| Expedited data transfer (optional) | N-DATA request and indication | User data (limited amount) |
| Reset | N-RESET request | Reason |
| | N-RESET indication | Reason Originator |
| | N-RESET response and confirmation | - |
| Connection release | N-DISCONNECT request | Disconnect reason User data Responding address |
| | N-DISCONNECT indication | Disconnect reason User data Responding address |

The connection is established by a confirmed exchange starting with an N-CONNECT request containing the listed parameters. All parameters are mandatory except for the optional user data. The parameters are described in the following paragraphs.

1. **Called address** — The address of the network service access point (NSAP) to which the connection is to be made.
2. **Calling address** — Address of the NSAP requesting the connection.
3. **Receipt confirmation** — Provides a limited form of end-to-end acknowledgment; an optional feature of the network service. Each implementer can decide whether to include this feature. If it is not provided by a network but is requested in the N-CONNECT request, the network will change it to *no use of receipt confirmation* on the indication. If the network provides this capability and the N-CONNECT request includes it, the responding N-CONNECT response can either accept it or change it to *no use of receipt confirmation.*
4. **Expedited data** — Also an optional service; the network may choose not to implement it. If it is requested in the N-CONNECT request, it can be denied by either the network provider or the other end system.
5. **Quality of service** (QOS) — The QOS negotiation is complex and includes subparameters such as the target value, the lowest acceptable quality, an available value (from the service provider), and the selected value. These subparameters apply to each listed parameter such as delay, throughput, and residual error rate. The QOS is further complicated because different default parameters can be assigned for different users.
6. **User data** — This refers to the user of the network service (NS), so it is called NS-user data. The amount of user data in the connection request is limited to a maximum of 128 octets. (Some networks cannot accept more than 16 or 32 octets in the N-CONNECT protocol data units.)

The connection establishment also involves the return of an N-CONNECT response and confirmation. The parameters associated with this returned information are listed below.

1. **Responding address** — The responding address should be exactly the same as the *called address* in the connection request.
2. **Expedited data** — If the connection request asked for the expedited data option, the response can be either *selected* or *not selected*, as discussed in the N-CONNECT request parameters. The response cannot ask for the expedited data option if the request did not ask for it.
3. **Quality of service** — The QOS indicated in the response cannot be greater than the connection request.

4. **User data** — NS-user data is usually limited to 128 octets, but in some implementations it is limited to a maximum of 16 or 32 octets.

As with other layers, the OSI Reference Model services are provided by a set of defined functions:

- Functions related to connections:
  - Establishment, maintenance, and release of network connections.
  - Sequencing.
  - Flow control.
  - Error detection and recovery.
  - Reset (reinitialization).
  - Expedited data (independent of flow-control constraints).
  - Network connection multiplexing (over a single data link).
- Functions related to NSDU transfer:
  - Routing and relaying.
  - Segmenting and blocking.
- Function related to quality of service (optional):
  - Service selection.
- Network layer management.

A close correlation exists between services and the functions that provide these services. In many instances, even the same wording is used. One example is sequencing, which is both a service and a function needed to provide that service. In other instances, additional detail is added in the functions, such as the need for segmenting and blocking to deliver service data units. In yet other instances, a function may appear with no corresponding service. Network management is the usual example. It does not relate to services, but it ensures the network is operating properly. These functions interface to a local network management application by means other than the seven-layer stack. This is normally pictured as an interface on the side of the layer rather than above or below it, as is the case for services.

OSI Reference Model functions lead to the protocol specification in the same way that services lead to the service definition. This is not the case for the network layer. The way in which services are provided is the business of the network provider. After all, these network providers are typically the post, telephone, and telegraph (PTT) utilities and others who vote on CCITT recommendations. These providers are not motivated to standardize the internal operations of a network because they already exist. Every PTT would have to change to the standard, so little is to be gained if they are standardized. Who cares if the internal operation of Transpac in France differs from that of Datapac in Canada or Tymnet and Telenet in the U.S.?

The document that most closely represents a network layer protocol specification is X.223 (ISO 8878). It is entitled *Use of X.25 to Provide the Connection-oriented Network Service*. It uses the number that would normally be assigned by CCITT. The X.2xx indicates that it is an OSI recommendation. The number 3 in X.223 indicates that it is a layer three recommendation, and the second number 2 normally indicates that it is a protocol specification. However, this is not the case in this instance.

The X.223 recommendation (see Table 3-2) includes the mappings from the X.213 service primitives to the X.25 packet layer protocol (PLP).

**Table 3-2** The mapping for the connection establishment phase.

| Connection-Oriented Service (CONS) | X.25 PLP |
|---|---|
| N-CONNECT request | Call request |
| N-CONNECT indication | Incoming call |
| N-CONNECT response | Call accepted |
| N-CONNECT confirmation | Call connected |
| Called address | Called DTE address |
| Calling address | Calling DTE address |
| Responding address | Called DTE address |
| Receipt confirmation select | General format identifier |
| Expedited data select | Expedited data negotiation facility (interrupt) |
| Quality of service | Throughput and delay facility negotiation |
| User data | Call and called user data field, plus fast select |

Care must be taken when reading the X.25 recommendation and the literature about X.25 because of terminology differences. X.25 remains something of a misfit in the OSI world and probably always will.

## The Network Sublayer Structure

While the X.213 network service definition provides an X.25 slant on the network layer, the OSI network layer may provide connectionless service as well. In addition, the X.213 service may be provided by either X.25 networks or other networks with suitable augmentation. For example, a non-X.25 network might not provide an adequate sequencing mechanism, in which case the augmentation software would build-in this additional capability.

The OSI network layer has been divided into three sublayers as shown in Figure 3-1. These sublayers are

1. Subnet Independent Convergent Protocol (SNICP).
2. Subnet Dependent Convergent Protocol (SNDCP).
3. Subnet Access Protocol (SNAP).

These rather verbose terms contain the words *subnet* and *protocol*, which apply to the subnet (network layer). The first two contain the word *convergent*, which means *to bring together into a common interpretation.* Each of these protocols brings the various forms of subnetworks into a common form, although the common form differs between the two protocols. SNICP makes all networks appear to be best-efforts connectionless networks, and SNDCP can make all networks appear to be X.25 networks.

SNICP, SNDCP, and SNAP are all sublayers and, therefore, are not needed in all OSI protocol stacks. The decision is whether to include them. An entire layer cannot be left out in that same manner without upsetting the protocol police, but sublayers may be omitted without any problem.

---

**Three network/internet sublayers have been identified:**
- **SubNet Independent Convergence Protocol.**
- **SubNet Dependent Convergence Protocol.**
- **SubNet Access Protocol.**

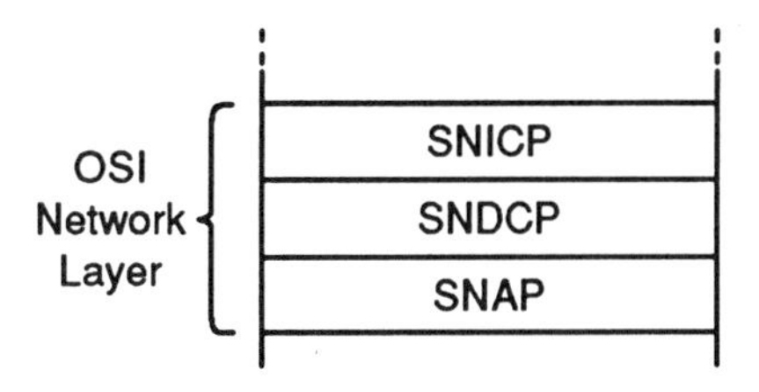


*Illustration courtesy of Learning Group International*

**FIGURE 3-1** The OSI internet sublayering.

Figure 3-2 shows how the SNICP can be bypassed or how the SNDCP can be used to augment a non-OSI network to provide the desired X.213 end-to-end service. In the example shown, only one network needed this augmentation. Figure 3-3 shows an alternate approach in which the SNICP is used over arbitrary subnetworks that may not provide OSI network service. Finally, SNAP is a subnetwork access protocol similar to X.25.

If all subnetworks implement X.25, neither SNICP nor SNDCP is required. If all subnetworks are Institute of Electrical and Electronics Engineers (IEEE) 802 LANs connected by bridges, SNICP, SNDCP, or SNAP is not required. Nothing is needed at the network layer. Although the entire network layer is removed, the protocol police ignore this apparent violation. Just keep a $20 bill next to the protocol permit in case the protocol police ask questions.

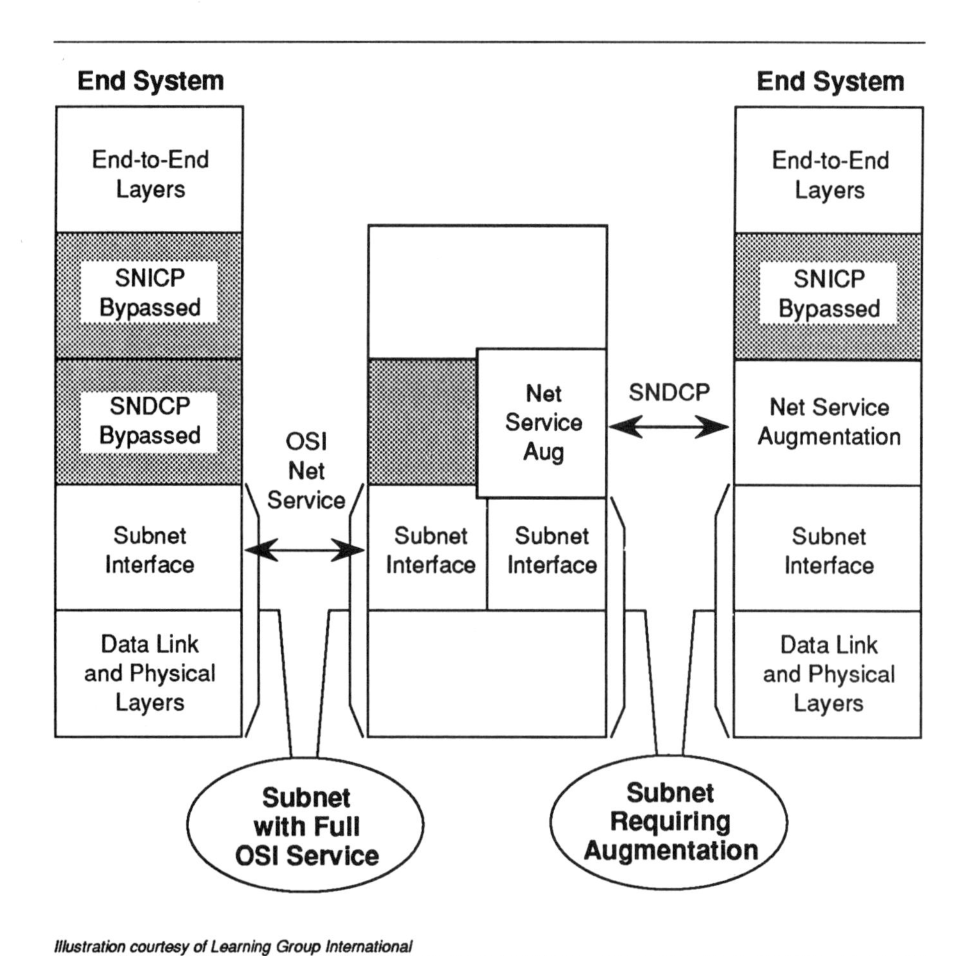


*Illustration courtesy of Learning Group International*

**FIGURE 3-2** The OSI Model of internetworking with subnet augmentation.

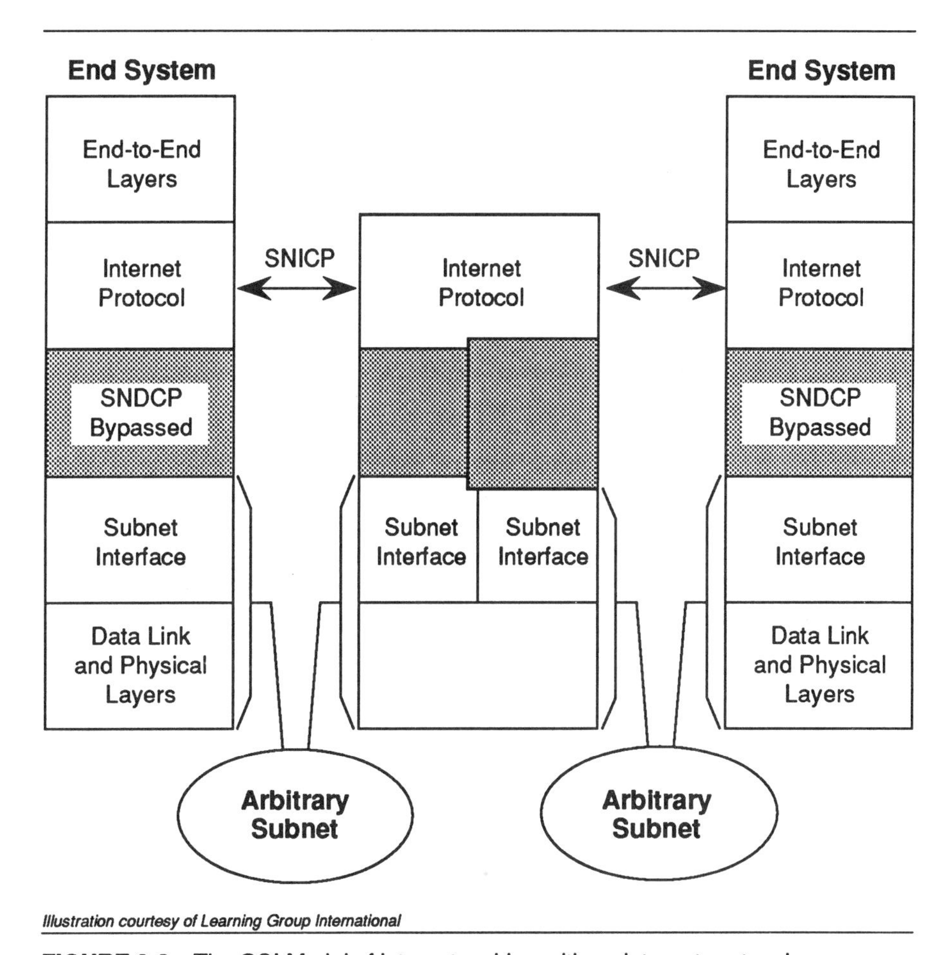


*Illustration courtesy of Learning Group International*

**FIGURE 3-3** The OSI Model of internetworking with an internet protocol.

## CCITT Recommendations X.25, X.75, and X.121

As previously described, X.25 is the model that OSI developers used to define the original network service. Associated with X.25 (an interface protocol to a packet-switching subnetwork) are X.75 (a way to interconnect two or more X.25 subnetworks) and X.121 (a way to express the network address of the other end system).

X.25 was developed as a host-to-network interface protocol for packet-switched networks. It was first included in the 1976 CCITT recommendations. It was imperative that some standard be introduced at that time because the next opportunity in the CCITT publication process would be four years later. It was obvious that many public packet-switching networks would be coming on line during that four-year interval. Unless a standard was defined, every network was expected to develop its own proprietary interface, and the opportunity for standardization might be lost. As a consequence, the 1976 X.25 recommendation was rushed through the standardization process. It has undergone many necessary changes since then.

Because of the nature of the X.25 development process and its creation a few years before the OSI Reference Model, it is not surprising that X.25 does not fit very well within the OSI Reference Model. Figure 3-4 indicates an overlap between the network and transport layers. This overlap accounts for end-to-end functions such as delivery confirmation, which is clearly not an interface matter between the host and a network.

The X.25 recommendation describes the X.25 interface as between data terminal equipment (DTE) and data circuit-terminating equipment (DCE). Technically, the interface is between DTE and data switching equipment (DSE), but CCITT continues to use the original terminology.

## *The Three Layers of X.25*

The X.25 interface is a network layer protocol, but it includes protocols at the data link and physical layers as well. Therefore, X.25 consists of three different protocol layers, with a choice of two variations at each of the two lower layers. At layer three, many variations have been built into the protocol as facilities that can be negotiated upon establishment of an X.25 connection. There are even variations in the way negotiations are carried out.

- **The X.25 standard does not map well onto the OSI Reference Model.**

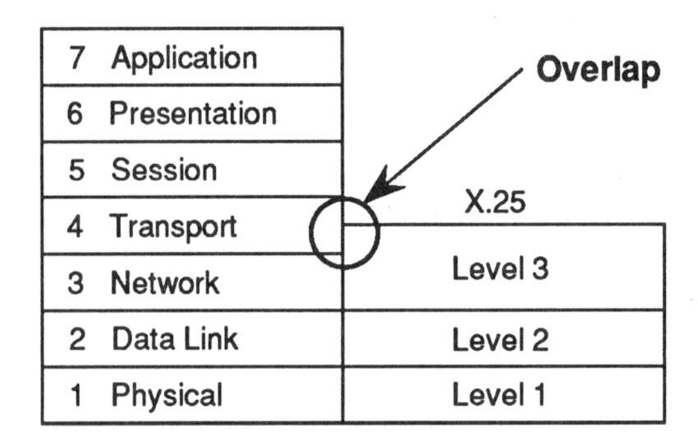


*Illustration courtesy of Learning Group International*

**FIGURE 3-4** X.25 and OSI Reference Model comparison.

The three layers of X.25 are shown in Figure 3-5. The physical layer contains either X.21 (a digital, synchronous communications capability) or $X.21_{bis}$ (which attempts to provide approximately the same capability over leased-line RS-232 circuits). $X.21_{bis}$ is considered an interim solution until full X.21 circuits are available.

The data link layer can be either link access procedure (LAP) or link access procedure balanced (LAPB). LAP was a mistake and should not be used in any new design. It was used with earlier implementations. LAP is based on the asynchronous response mode of high-level data link control (HDLC), which has operational problems including an unnecessarily complex initialization process and a potential deadlock condition. LAPB is used on all modern implementations of X.25 and uses the asynchronous balanced mode of HDLC.

At layer three, there are two choices in X.25 — permanent virtual circuits (PVC) and virtual calls (VC). (Virtual calls are switched virtual circuits.) Permanent virtual circuits are analogous to leased telephone lines, and virtual calls are analogous to direct-dial circuits. Just as with the analogs in the telephone world, the PVC and VC capabilities are administratively arranged and then requested as needed.

Notice that several PVCs and VCs can be multiplexed across the LAPB link-layer connection. The level-three PVCs and VCs use the error detection and recovery capabilities of the level-two LAPB, but they do not strictly rely on its other properties such as flow control. Each X.25 connection has its own flow-control mechanisms, so that no single (high-usage) connection will lock out all other connections.

## *Establishing an X.25 Connection*

When a PVC is used, all the characteristics of the channel are administratively determined and do not need to be initialized when a connection is first used. However, VCs (like their dial-up analog) must be initialized on each new connection. This requires control packets to establish the call between two computers whose addresses are included in the call request. (Actually, only the remote address is required.) The local address is optional because the packet switch knows what computer is attached at the other end of the access line. The call establishment also provides an opportunity to negotiate the specific characteristics of each call. These negotiated characteristics include the size of the sequence numbers, the maximum packet sizes to be transferred, the window size, and the party paying for the call. Such negotiated capabilities are called *facilities*. If a parameter is not negotiated, it will default to a predefined

**The X.25 interface layer has three component layers:**

- **X.25 Level 3: The packet level**
  Provides multiple data streams for host-to-host communications.
  Virtual calls (switched virtual circuits).
  Permanent virtual circuits.

- **X.25 Level 2: The link level**
  Provides reliable, sequenced delivery between the host and network.
  Link access procedure (LAP).
  LAP balanced (LAPB).

- **X.25 Level 1: The physical level**
  Provides a delivery mechanism.
  X.21 synchronous circuit switched.
  $X.21_{bis}$ (RS-232-based).

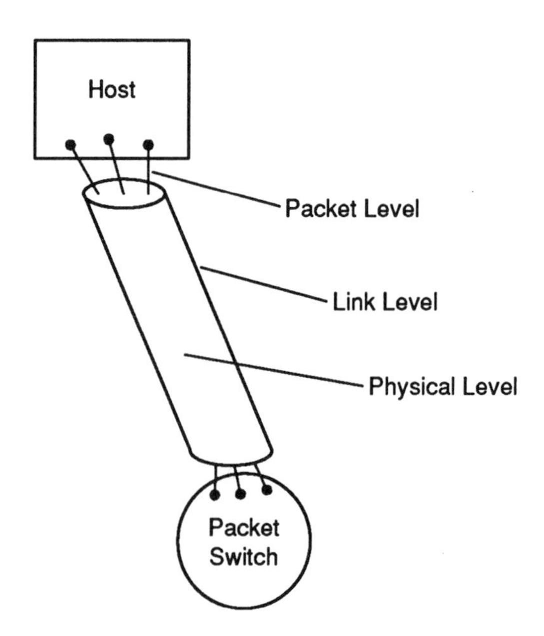


*Illustration courtesy of Learning Group International*

**FIGURE 3-5** X.25 interface components.

value. The default sequence number size is three bits, the default maximum packet size is 128 bytes, the default window size is 2 packets, and the default payee is the call originator. The negotiation explores a wide variety of values (requests), but both parties are willing to negotiate toward the default values (which everyone has to accept). A more detailed description of the X.25 facilities follows. Readers looking for an overview of X.25 may wish to skip over this detail.

Approximately 50 facilities can be used with X.25. These facilities are defined in CCITT recommendation X.2 and include both essential and optional mechanisms. Representative examples of these facilities follow.

- **One-way logical channel incoming facility** — Allows only incoming calls. Once established, the VCs can be used in both directions. The *one-way* applies only to who can establish the VC.
- **Closed user group facility** — Allows one to form communities on the X.25 network but places restrictions on establishing VCs.
- **Reverse charging facility** — Allows the equivalent of a collect call.
- **Maximum packet size negotiation facility** — Allows the negotiation of the maximum packet size for use on the VC. Allowable packet sizes are powers of two, from 16 to 4,096 bytes. The default is 128 bytes.
- **Window size negotiation facility** — Allows for larger window sizes to be negotiated up to seven for three-bit sequence numbers. The default window size is two.
- **Throughput class negotiation facility** — Provides a way to express the expected rate at which data are to be sent. This is not a binding negotiation, i.e., there is no guarantee that the agreed upon throughput can always be achieved. Throughput values range from 75 to 48,000 bits per second. The default is determined administratively.
- **D-bit modification facility** — Allows one to request the delivery confirmation option in which an acknowledgment (ACK) indicates delivery to the destination host. This facility is requested by setting the D-bit in the connection request packet, rather than being carried in the facilities field.
- **Extended packet numbering facility** — Allows one to negotiate to obtain 7-bit (rather than 3-bit) sequence numbers.
- **Call redirection facility** — Allows incoming calls to be rerouted to another DTE when the requested DTE is down.
- **Fast select facility** — Provides a form of transaction support in which the request can be conveyed in the call request and the response can be included with the immediate call clear.

- **Long address facility** — Allows the call request to indicate that the addresses are of the longer Integrated Services Digital Network (ISDN) format, rather than X.121 format.

This summary of X.25 facilities gives a glimpse of the wide variety of capabilities that have been added to X.25 over the years. Recall that the facilities are the items negotiated in an X.25 connection request and response.

---

- **The X.25 connection request includes facilities that are to be negotiated.**
- **These facilities include:**
  How big can the packets be?
  Who pays for the call?
  How large are the sequence numbers (3 or 7 bits)?
  How large is the window?
- **Negotiation always allows a response that is closer to the default value.**
- **Negotiations are always complete at the end of the connection request/acceptance.**

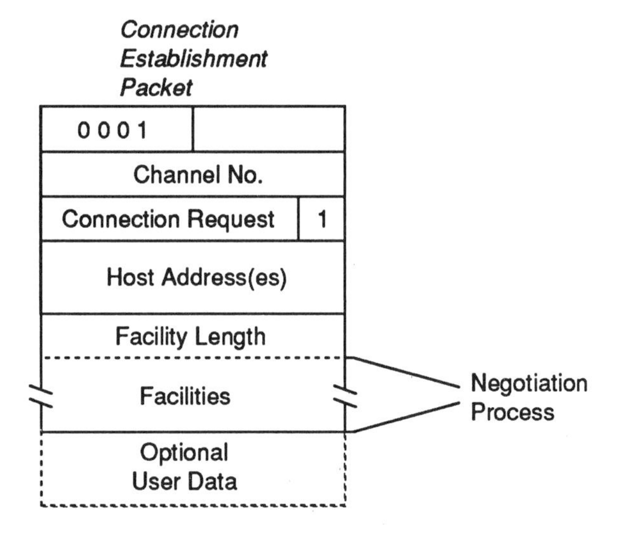


*Illustration courtesy of Learning Group International*

**FIGURE 3-6** X.25 connection request and facility negotiation.

A connection request packet is shown in Figure 3-6. It indicates some example facilities that are to be negotiated. The connection request packet identifies a channel number to be used in subsequent data packets on this connection. A minimal amount of user data also may be conveyed along with the connection request. The call establishment handshake is shown in Figure 3-7.

Note that the channel numbers are selected, not negotiated, during the handshake. Each end of the connection can select its own number to use. Clearly, this channel number does not have end-to-end significance. The initiating data terminal equipment selects the channel between it and the packet switch, and the packet switch at the other end selects the channel number between it and the receiving DTE. This selection process is managed as shown in Figure 3-8 to avoid (or minimize) a call collision in which both a DTE and a packet switch select the same number at the same end.

The channel number provides a shorthand method of referencing the connection. The connection is defined in the connection open request by the full addressee of the destination host, and optionally by the source host.

Both addresses can be variable in length because like telephone numbers, one only has to use area code extensions when going outside of one's area. The

- **X.25 calls (or virtual circuits) are examples of connections in OSI.**

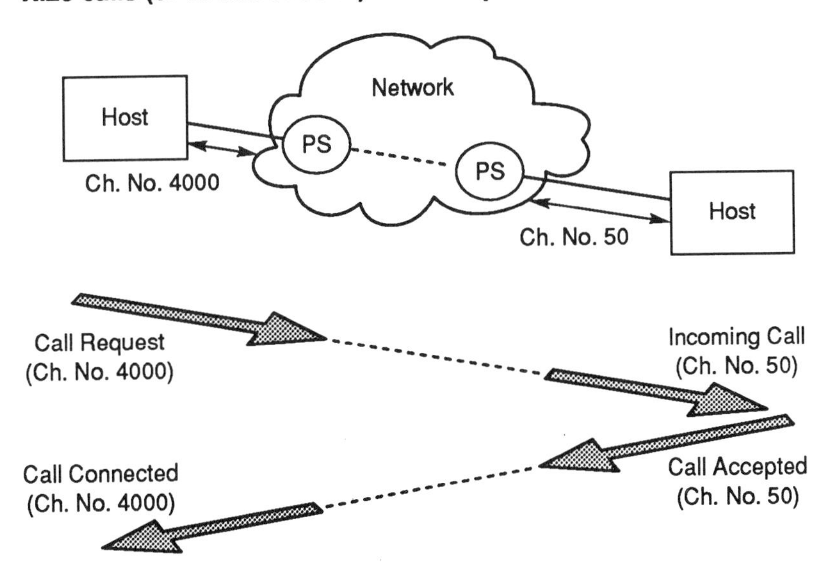


*Illustration courtesy of Learning Group International*

**FIGURE 3-7** X.25 call (virtual circuit) establishment.

- **LIC — lowest incoming channel.**
- **HOC — highest outgoing channel.**

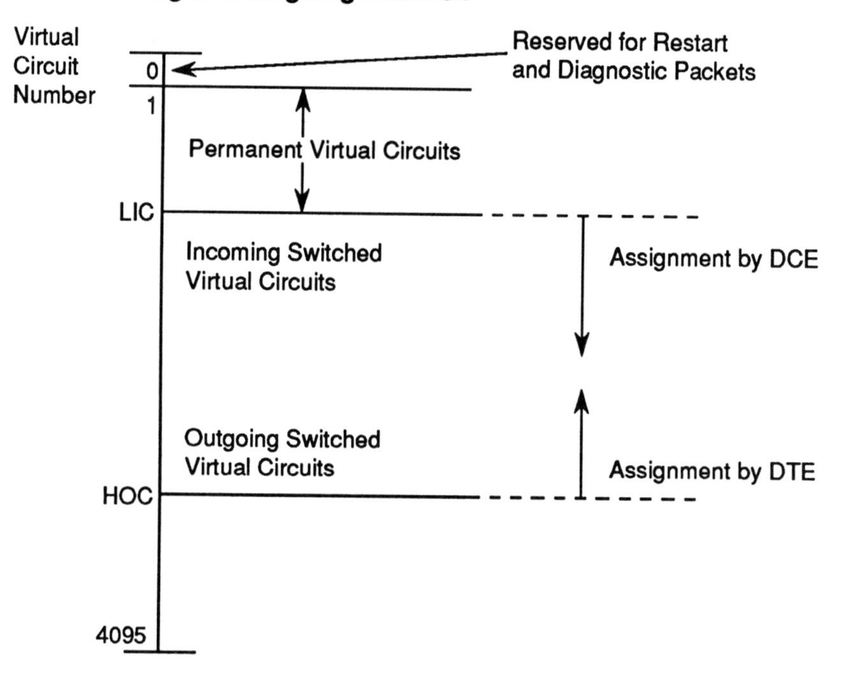


*Illustration courtesy of Learning Group International*

**FIGURE 3-8** Logical channel assignment on call establishment.

address format is defined as CCITT recommendation X.121 (see Figure 3-9). The country code for the U.S. is actually a range of values, with numbers 310 to 330 being set aside for U.S. networks. Note that country codes, network numbers, and the assigned host addresses are all decimal digits. Just as one dials decimal digits to place a phone call, so does the computer.

### *Utilizing an X.25 Connection*

Once a VC is established, data can be sent over the connection. Actually, a restricted amount of data can be sent with the connection request. But just as a telephone conversation does not start until the call setup has been verified, it would be unusual in a VC as well. An important exception is described in terms of fast select communications.

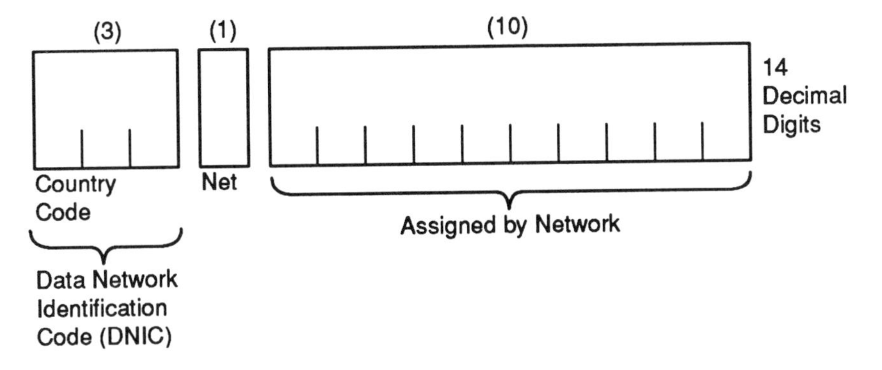


*Illustration courtesy of Learning Group International*

**FIGURE 3-9** X.121 addressing.

The data packet shown in Figure 3-10 contains only three bytes of control information in this form. (An extended 6-byte version can be negotiated.) One can see the similarity to HDLC in terms of the sequence number and ACK number fields. The M (more) flag replaces the poll/final flag of HDLC, but it has a similar use in marking the end of a group of packets. The D (delivery confirmation) flag and the Q (data qualifier) flag have been added.

Data to be sent over the connection may need to be segmented into packet-sized data units to be transmitted. However, a need exists to associate the data units as portions of a larger whole that the host wants to send. This is reflected in X.25's *more* flag, which indicates that more data units are coming until the last packet flag (which indicates *no more*).

The sending DTE is not the only network device that can use the X.25 more flag. The network (packet switches) also can use this capability, either to segment packets or to combine host-segmented packets. Suppose, as shown in Figure 3-11, that the sending host did not need to segment the transmission of a short file, but that its packet was segmented into two smaller packets before delivery to the destination host. This would not seem necessary in X.25 because a mutually agreed upon maximum packet size is negotiated in the facilities negotiation when the connection is established. However, such further segmentation is allowed in X.25. Alternatively, the network could combine the original packets that the host might have segmented. The network would then deliver one complete packet to the destination host. The net effect in all these cases is

- **Data packets are sent on the channel number (connection).**
- **ACK and sequence numbers are like those of HDLC.**
- **The D, M, and Q flags are described in the text.**

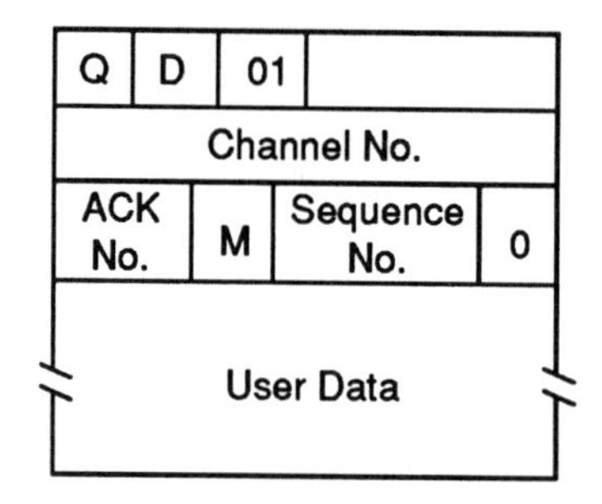


*Illustration courtesy of Learning Group International*

**FIGURE 3-10** X.25 data packets.

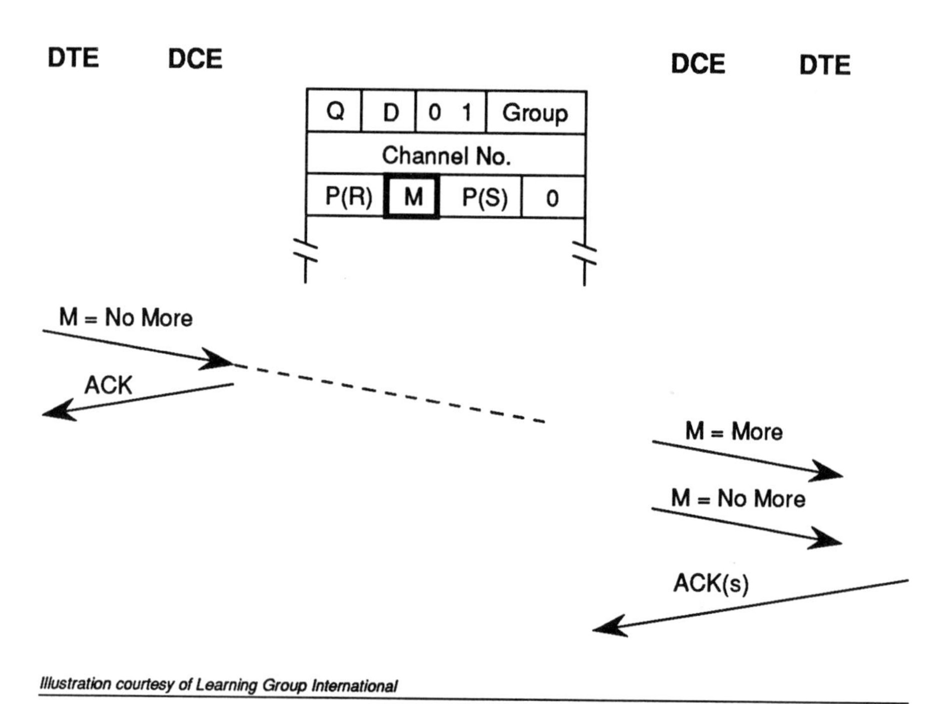


*Illustration courtesy of Learning Group International*

**FIGURE 3-11** Network segmentation.

the same, namely that the destination host receives a sequence of one or more packets that can be associated together as one logical unit.

The concern about segmentation and where it can be performed is due to the interaction of the more flag and another X.25 mechanism called *delivery confirmation.* The delivery confirmation mechanism provides a transmitting host with the option of asking that the returned ACK have end-to-end significance. In such cases it can require the transmitting host to indicate that the packet was delivered to the destination host. Otherwise, the ACK comes from the local packet switch and indicates that the packet was successfully received by the network. The latter is an interface protocol message, while the delivery confirmation overlaps the usual transport layer functions. Figure 3-12 shows a typical single-packet message example of delivery confirmation. It also shows the dilemma of sending packets by using both the *more* and the *delivery confirmation* mechanisms.

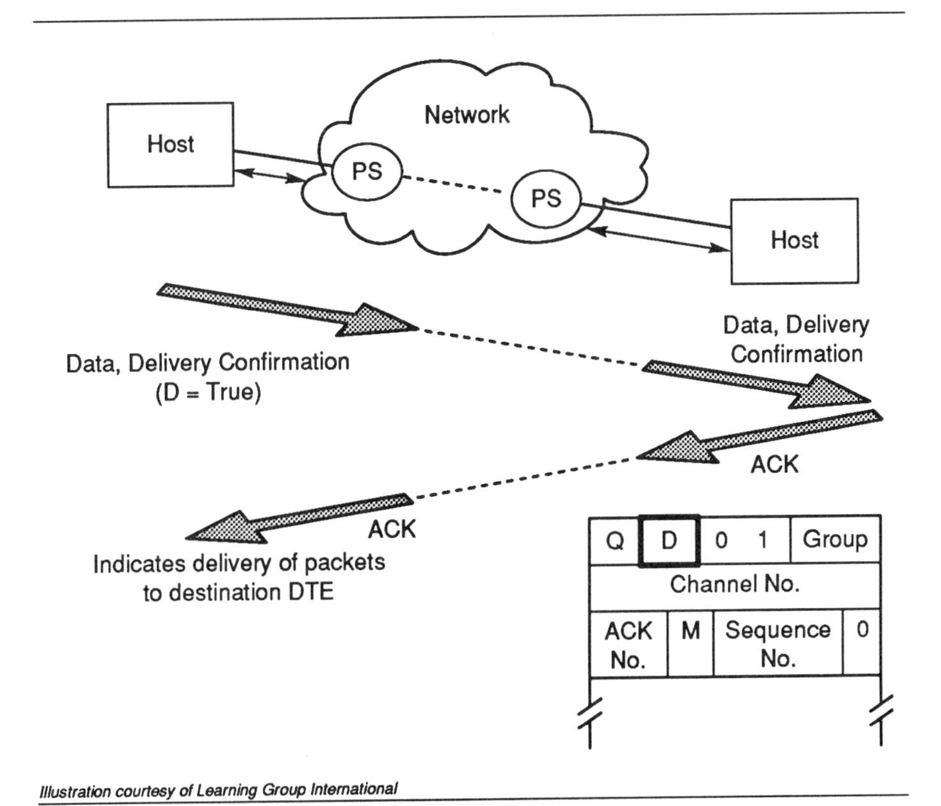


*Illustration courtesy of Learning Group International*

**FIGURE 3-12** X.25 delivery confirmation.

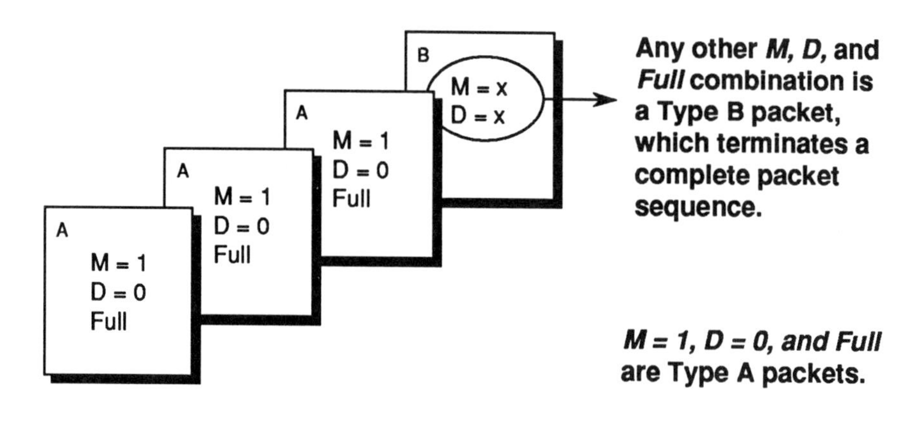


*Illustration courtesy of Learning Group International*

**FIGURE 3-13** Complete packet sequence.

A special set of circumstances exists under which both the more and the delivery confirmation mechanisms can be used; an example is illustrated in Figure 3-13. A group of packets can form a complete packet sequence, the end of which is clearly identified. In addition, intermediate groupings of packets (with the delivery confirmation flag set at the end of each of these smaller groupings) are shown in Figure 3-14. This allows assurance at these intermediate points that the data are being delivered to the destination host, while still allowing an unambiguous indication of the end of the complete data unit, e.g., a file. In X.25 terms, this complete data unit is called an M-bit sequence.

A third mechanism of X.25 is the data qualifier flag. As shown in Figure 3-15, this simple flag is merely going along for the ride as far as X.25 is concerned. If the transmitting host sets the flag, it is delivered to the destination as being set, and vice versa. X.25 is unaware of the significance of the setting, and no messy interactions occur between this flag and any other. If a packet is segmented, all the new smaller packets have the data qualifier set to *match* or *not match* that of the original packet. Similarly, packets of a more sequence could be combined. All packets of that sequence must have the same setting as the data qualifier or an error would be indicated.

The principal use of the data qualifier is in support of packet assembler/disassembler (PAD) devices that interface dumb terminals to X.25 networks. Hosts (OSI end systems) that communicate with terminals through use of the PAD must be able to read and write PAD parameters (by the X.29 protocol), as

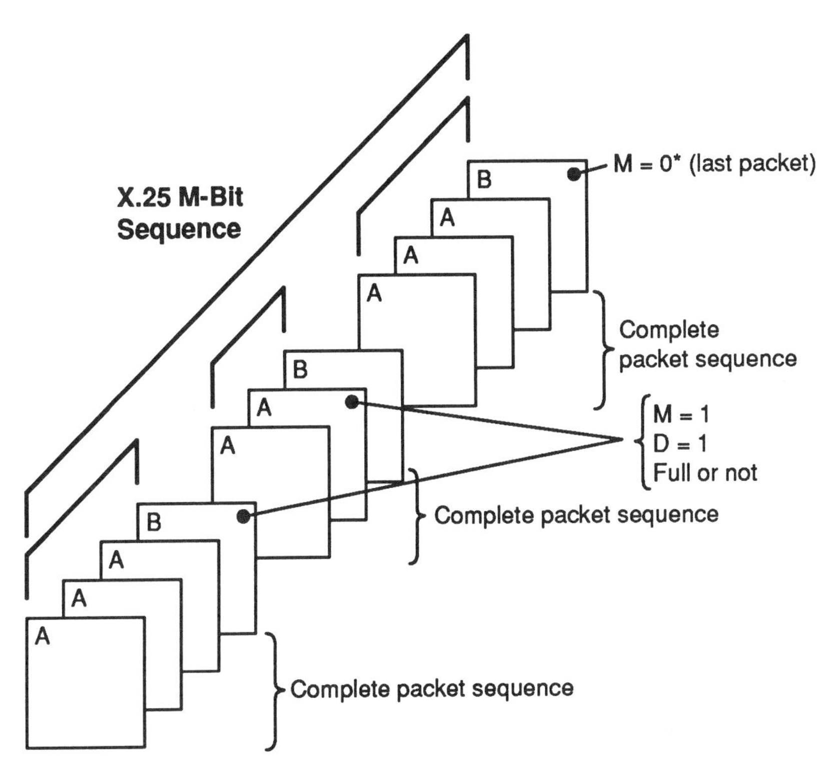


**FIGURE 3-14** X.25 M-bit sequence.

well as to read and write terminal traffic. The data qualifier is used to distinguish these two types of traffic between the host and PAD, as shown in Figure 3-16.

The data qualifier flag has no significance to the connection request packet, so it is borrowed for another purpose. On a connection request packet it is used as the so called *A-bit*, which indicates the type of address being conveyed in the packet. In addition to the X.121 address format, an extended format is also possible. The *A-bit* indicates which format is being used. If A = 0, the X.121 (short) address is being used. If A = 1, the ISDN E.164 (long) address is being used. The address length field for the short form is 4 bits, and for the long form it is 8 bits.

- **Delivered as sent.**
- **Neither interpreted nor changed by the net.**

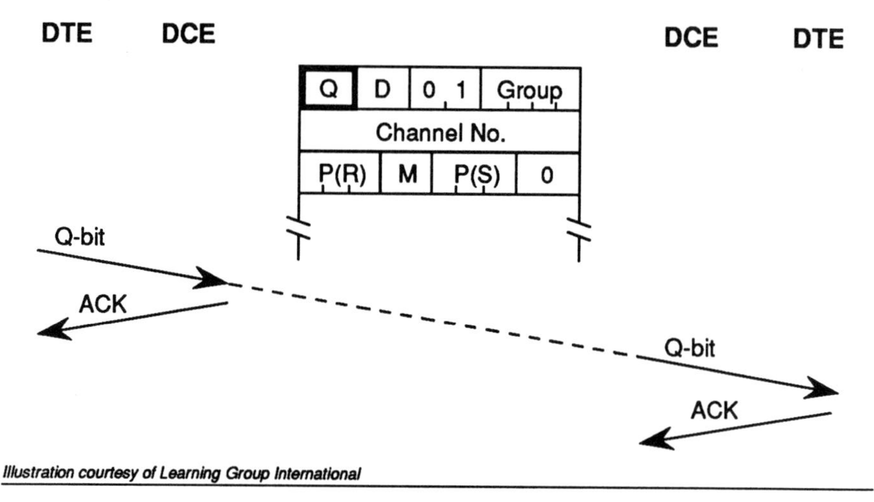


*Illustration courtesy of Learning Group International*

**FIGURE 3-15** The data qualifier flag.

- **X.29 gives an example usage of the Q-bit.**

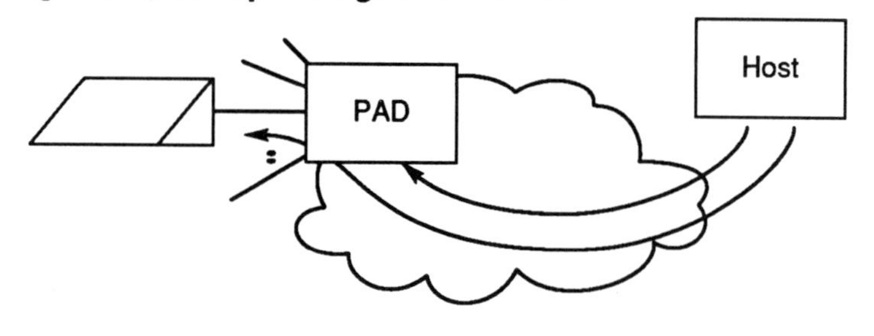


*Illustration courtesy of Learning Group International*

**FIGURE 3-16** The qualifier bit (Q-bit) used with a PAD.

## *Other X.25 Control Packet Mechanisms*

The above discussion covers the various flag bit mechanisms in the X.25 packet header. However, other control packets affect X.25 operations, including expedited data, fast select, reset, and restart.

*Expedited data* means exactly that. This data, which can be up to 32 bytes in length, is to be delivered as quickly as possible to the destination — perhaps overtaking ordinary data that has already been sent — to be processed as quickly as possible. The X.25 name for this capability is *interrupt*, presumably reflecting the processing situation when one arrives. This capability interrupts whatever is currently going on to process an exception message.

Because X.25 networks do not necessarily have internal priority mechanisms, all that can be guaranteed is that no subsequent normal data will overtake the expedited data. This is ensured simply by not sending any more normal data until the expedited data has received an ACK (on an end-to-end basis). Similarly, no subsequent expedited data packet can be sent on this connection until the ACK is received. Therefore, expedited data packets do not require sequence numbers and can be sent in the form of control packets. An expedited data packet and ACK exchange are shown in Figure 3-17.

The *fast select* variation was developed to support transactions over X.25. If one performed the usual call establishment and clearing packet exchanges of X.25 for each simple transaction exchange, the overhead would be quite large. A full exchange would be required to establish the call, followed by the one packet request/one packet response of the transaction, and then another full exchange to clear the call. Instead, fast select can be negotiated and operates as

- **Expedited data in X.25 is called *interrupt*.**
- **Interrupt is controlled by a full *handshake*.**

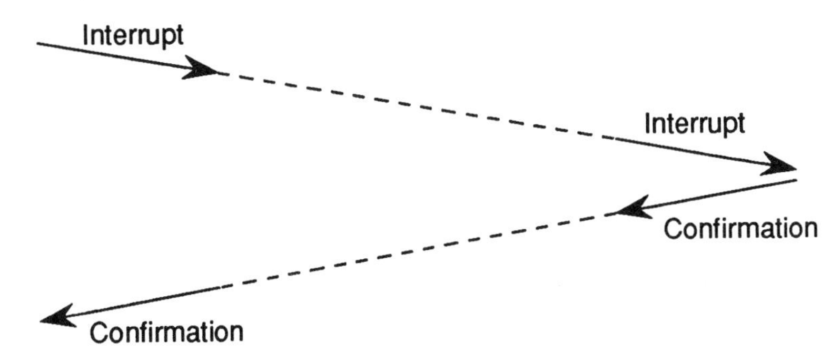


- **Up to 32 octets of data may be sent.**
- **Only one interrupt can be outstanding.**
- **No subsequent data can be sent until the confirmation is received.**

*Illustration courtesy of Learning Group International*

**FIGURE 3-17** Expedited data.

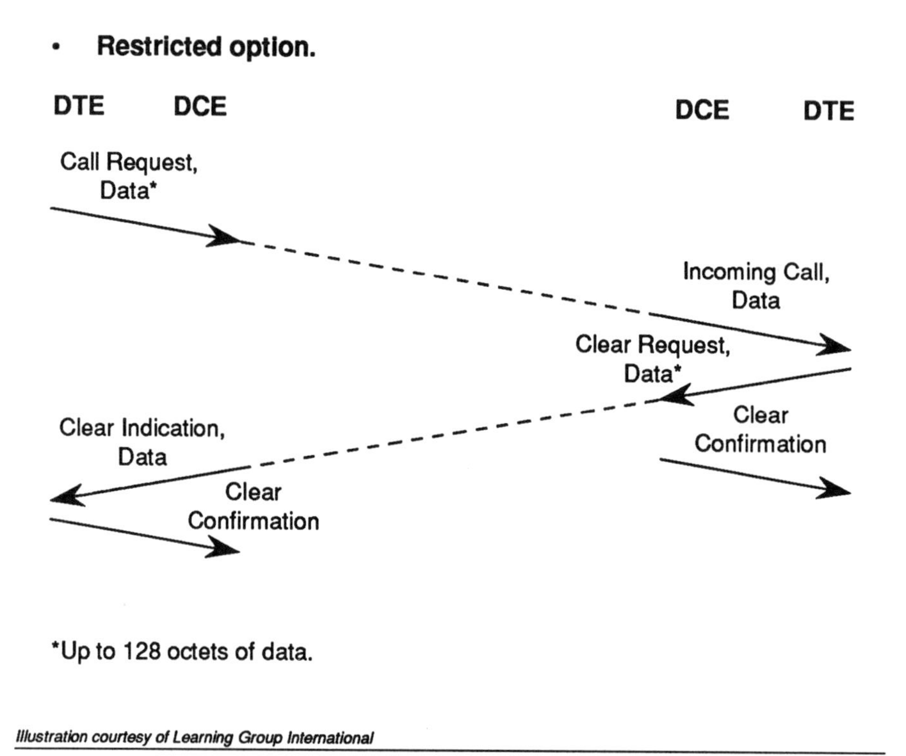


**FIGURE 3-18** Fast select operation.

shown in Figure 3-18. Up to 128 bytes can be sent in the request, and a maximum of 128 bytes can be returned in the response. The figure shows the restricted option, where the *once over* and *once back* is the only allowed communication. The unrestricted option differs in that the response does not clear the connection. It is simply a way to send more than the usual limited amount of user data with the connection request.

An X.25 connection is supposed to reliably deliver packets; but even so, some loss of packets may occur. *Error* or *fault* conditions may occur that will result in the loss of packets; a message indicates that such a condition has occurred. This is called the *reset* service. The effect is limited to a single connection, and its sequence and ACK numbers are reset to zero. Interrupt (expedited data) or normal data packets may be lost. The transport layer protocol is responsible for recovering from this packet loss. A typical DTE-initiated reset is shown in Figure 3-19. Reset also can be initiated by the network (i.e., the service provider); in that case it only appears to the DTEs as an indication.

Unlike *reset, restart* applies to all connections, i.e., both permanent virtual circuits and virtual calls. PVCs are reset, and VCs are cleared. A restart is performed for major fault recovery, such as the loss and recreation of a LAPB connection. It is also performed for the normal initialization of the X.25 (level three) connections when first bringing up a LAPB connection.

## *Characterization of X.25 Networks*

X.25 networks can be assigned a grade of A, B, or C, just like school grades. The issue of concern is how acceptable the X.25 network is in terms of two characteristics: (1) signalled errors such as resets, and (2) the undetected introduction of bit errors. If the network is acceptable in both categories, it gets a grade of A. If it is not acceptable on either count but presumably gets most of the data across, it gets a grade of C. To get a grade of B, the network must have an acceptable number of undetected errors, even though it does not have an acceptable number of signalled errors. The latter can be recovered by simple

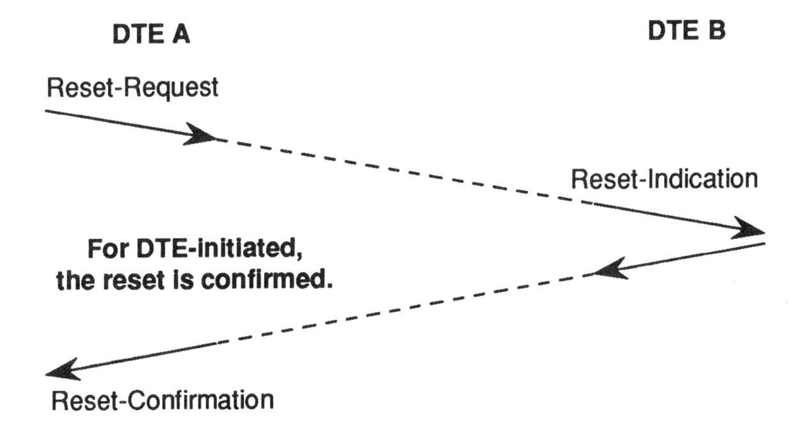


**FIGURE 3-19** X.25 reset.

transport protocols, while bit error detection and recovery involve more complicated error checks and retransmissions based on timers. The approach is based on the network either being completely acceptable or requiring a recovery mechanism from either type of error.

X.25 networks can be interconnected very simply because these networks provide the same virtual circuit service. The only requirements are that the interconnections also provide virtual circuit service and that the addresses allow the expression of the network and the host to which each connection is to be established. The format of X.121 addresses not only includes a network identifier, but also a country code. The combination <country> <network> <host> provides a globally unique name that is readily manageable because countries can allocate network numbers and networks can allocate host addresses. The network owners, e.g., the PTTs, would argue that there are other aspects of concern in X.75 such as collecting billing information for the use of their networks. This tariff information is carried in the utilities field of the X.75 packet, along with other X.75-specific fields such as transit network identification and a traffic class indicator. The relevant X.25 facilities also are copied into the utilities field, including *fast select* and *reverse charging*. The context of this X.75 protocol is shown in Figure 3-20.

# THE INTERNET PROTOCOL

The OSI internet protocol is functionally equivalent to the IP of the Transmission Control Protocol/Internet Protocol (TCP/IP) protocol suite that has been in use in government and commercial internetworks for over a decade. In addition, the OSI IP provides a few additional capabilities.

The basic purposes of the OSI IP protocol are the same as those of the TCP/IP internet protocol. They are to relieve the end systems (hosts) from having to know about (1) routing across the internet, (2) the maximum packet size that can be handled by all networks along the changing internet end-to-end path, and (3) the quality of service provided along each of the cascaded networks. All three of these matters are interrelated. If end systems do not have to know the route, then they cannot know how big the packets may be. This is especially true if the routes can change dynamically over time. All the end systems need to do is specify the ultimate destination and the desired quality of service (such as the relative concerns for delay, throughput, and the introduction of bit errors). The IP protocol handles these concerns (1) by providing dynamic alternate routing, (2) by segmenting protocol data units as required and reassembling them before

- **X.75 provides additional cascaded virtual circuits.**
- **The end-to-end service is still a virtual circuit.**

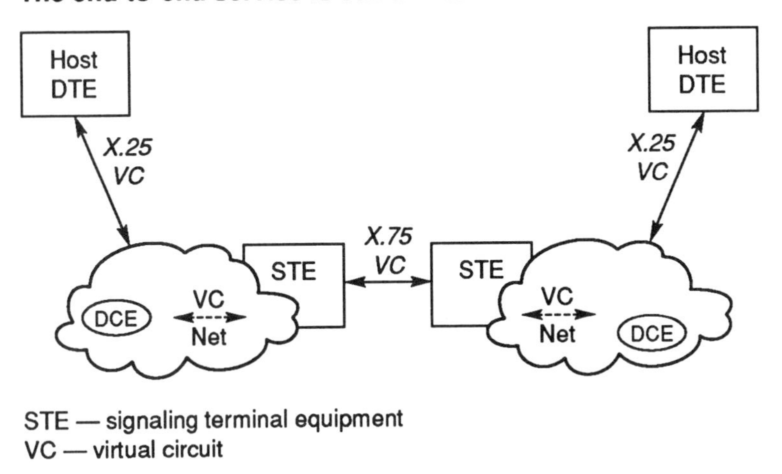


*Illustration courtesy of Learning Group International*

**FIGURE 3-20** X.25/X.75 cascaded virtual circuits.

delivery at the destination end system, and (3) by considering quality of service in its routing decisions.

The basic format of an OSI internet protocol data unit (IPDU) is shown in Figure 3-21. The bold outline portions of this PDU and the subsequent IP figures indicate the additions beyond the IP of TCP/IP, after which it is modelled. The user who is unfamiliar with the IP of TCP/IP may simply ignore the bold outlines. However, the reader familiar with TCP/IP can leap over entire paragraphs of this discussion by merely focusing on the differences.

The first byte (octet in OSI terminology) is a protocol identifier that indicates if the IP protocol is needed at all, and if so, if the segmentation part is included. This is followed by a header length field, which is the usual first byte in an OSI protocol header. The header length field is followed by a version number field, which is typical of a connectionless protocol. It must be carried in every PDU as opposed to being identified at connection establishment. The lifetime field that follows also is typical of many connectionless protocols. It establishes an upper limit on how long the PDU will remain in the internetwork before being discarded — presumably as being non-deliverable. A common need for the lifetime field is to discard PDUs that are caught in routing loops, bouncing back and forth between routers or around sequences of routers.

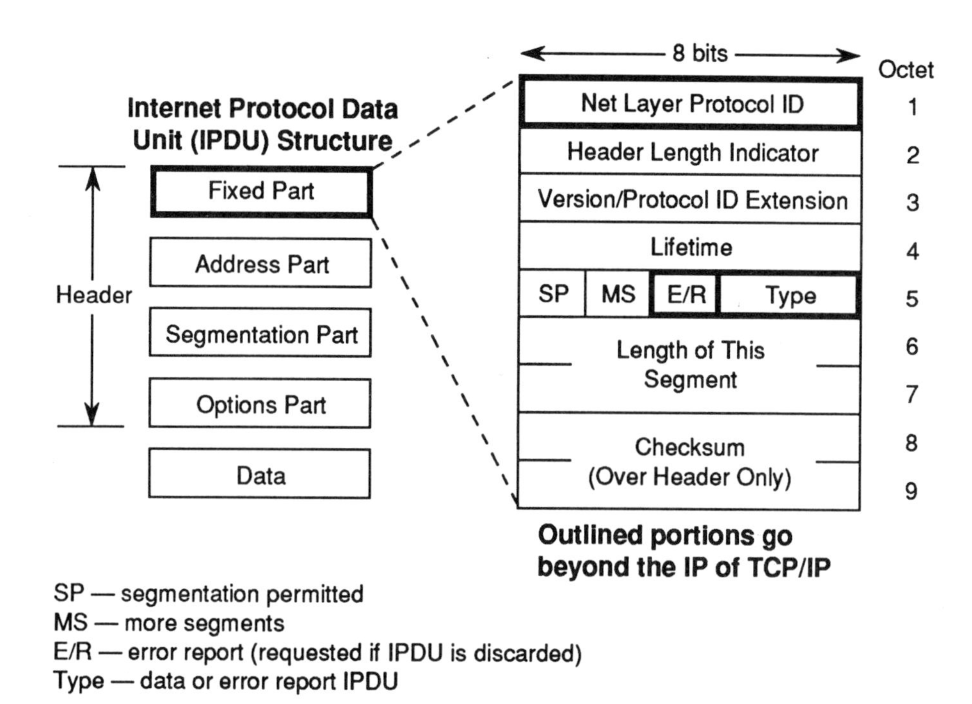


*Illustration courtesy of Learning Group International*

**FIGURE 3-21** ISO internet protocol.

The remaining fields specify if segmentation of the PDU is permitted, if more segments are coming, if error reports are desired, and the type of PDU and its length. The final field is an error check over the header fields only. The algorithm is the same one used by TP class 4, but only the protocol control information is checked by IP. Therefore, the computational overhead is minimized for IP.

Segmentation would normally be permitted, but it might not be in the special case of downloading a router. Its minimal boot load program would not have the full IP capability of reassembly. If segmentation is permitted, the *more segments* flag indicates if the current PDU is the last of a segmented sequence.

Figure 3-22 shows the variable-length address part of the IP header. It includes a length field and an address field for both the source and destination. This extensibility avoids the common problem with protocols that have not had an adequate size address field. The address field also includes the service access point fields for the source and destination. Reference identifiers such as those of connection-oriented protocols do not exist here because IP is a

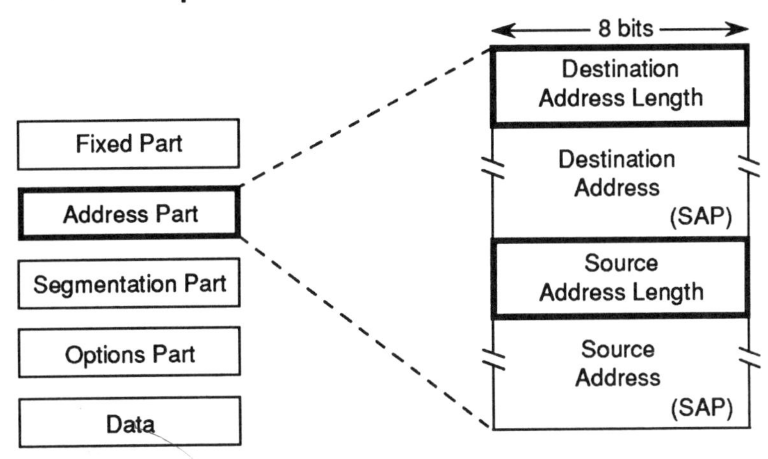


*Illustration courtesy of Learning Group International*

**FIGURE 3-22** The address part of the IP.

connectionless protocol. Some other fields of the protocol suite must sort out the multitude of requests and responses that are going to and from the SAPs.

Figure 3-23 shows the segmentation part, which is included only if segmentation is required. There are three important fields: an identifier that provides a common name for the segments of a segmented PDU, the location or offset from the beginning of the original data field where a particular segment fits, and the total length of the IPDU before segmentation. This is redundant because it is known how large the original unsegmented PDU was when the last segment was received. However, it is not known how large the reassembly buffer should be. Therefore, it is a useful piece of information to convey with each segment.

The final portion that an IP header may contain is the options part, as shown in Figure 3-24. These options are essentially the same as those of the TCP/IP protocols except that quality of service is an option in the OSI IP and is mandatory in each PDU in the IP of TCP/IP. Options can be identified by a type-length-value encoding. The end of the options field is determined by the overall header length field.

The IP protocol is rather unique in that the more one studies its bits and pieces, its mechanisms, and its implementations, the more one looses track of its fundamental intent. As previously stated, the IP protocol has three principal objectives. They are to relieve the end systems (hosts) from having to know

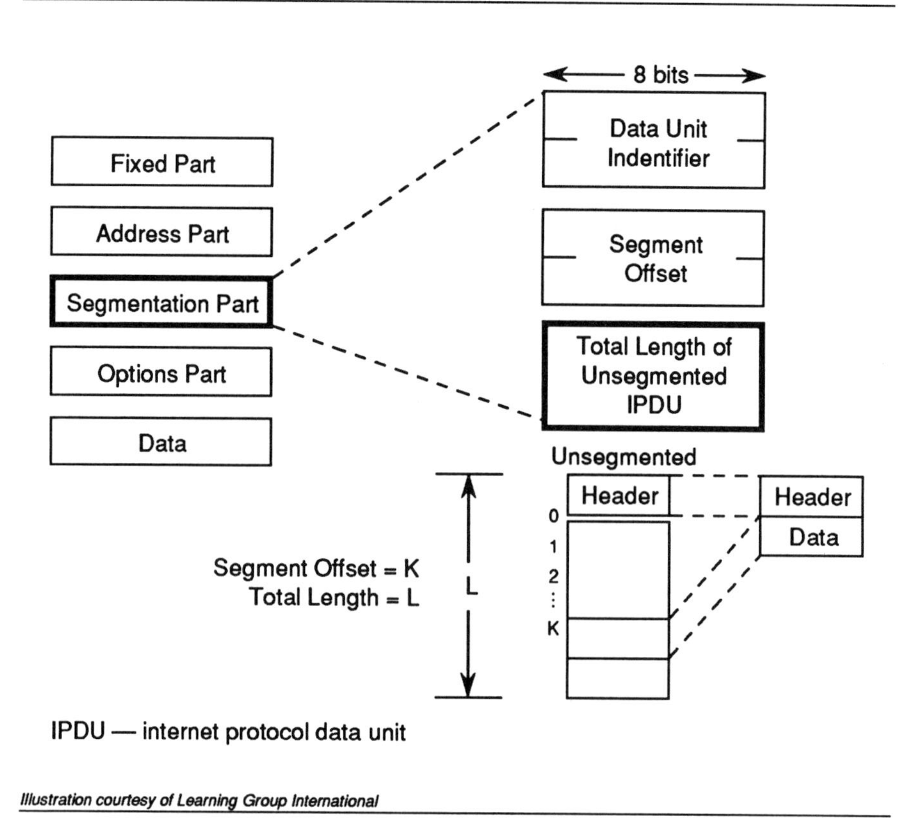


*Illustration courtesy of Learning Group International*

**FIGURE 3-23** The segmentation part of IP.

about (1) routing across the internet, (2) the maximum PDU size that can be handled by all networks along the possibly changing internet end-to-end path, and (3) the quality of service provided along each of the cascaded networks.

The first of these, the dynamic alternate routing, does not show up in the IP header mechanisms. It is implicit in that the destination address is specified in each IPDU. Each can be routed independently because there are no assurances of sequenced delivery. The second deals with segmentation, shows up in the IPDU header, and requires that the destination end system be capable of reassembling the segmented IPDU. Finally, QOS is an IP option.

## IP Routing

The internet protocol operates between intermediate systems, as well as between end systems and intermediate systems. In fact, these are separate protocols. The

**Example options:**

- **Source routing.**
- **Record route.**
- **Security.**
- **Quality of service (requested).**

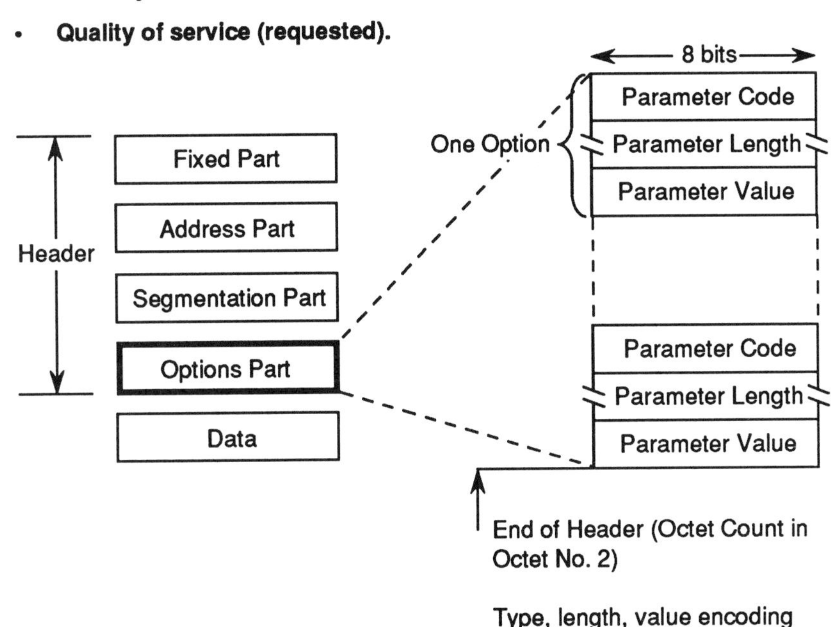


*Illustration courtesy of Learning Group International*

**FIGURE 3-24** The options part of IP.

end system–intermediate system (ES-IS) protocol is ISO 9542, and the intermediate system–intermediate system (IS-IS) protocol is ISO 10589. Both are routing exchange protocols for ISO 8473, connectionless network protocol (CLNP).

The intent is to provide dynamic, distributed routing that rapidly responds to changes such as outages in the internet topology. There are two primary approaches for such routing: distance vector and link state. The distance vector approach typically uses hop counts, i.e., the number of store and forward hops along the path. The best path is the one with the smallest hop count. This algorithm has been widely used, but it suffers from routing loops, slow convergence when changes occur, and disastrous failures when one router erroneously claims to be zero and hops away from everywhere. The link state approach (sometimes called shortest path first) avoids these problems and also provides support for routing selections based on a variety of metrics including

- Default established by routing administrators.
- Delay.
- Expense.
- Error.

Each IS builds a database for each of the above metrics.

The ES can influence the routing by including options in the IPDU including the desired quality of service, priority, and security. The ES also has the option to provide source routing, which is a list of network service access points along the path. Source routing can be either strict or loose. Strict source routing specifies the exact set of routers along the path, while loose source routing specifies a subset of the routers along the path.

Because of the large size of a global internet, it is structured into areas, domains, groups of domains (e.g., enterprises), and finally the world. These four hierarchical groupings each have their own routing exchanges. This is necessary for a number of reasons, including the need to keep the routing-table size manageable, to protect the overall internet from erroneous routing information, and to allow routing approach selections based on local considerations. The four levels of routing are

Level one — Relay between nodes in the same area.
Level two — Relay between different areas.
Level three — Relay between different domains.
Level four — Inter enterprise routing.

In each level, the routing mechanisms have the option to discard traffic under exception conditions such as severe congestion. This is a characteristic of connectionless protocols, which make no guarantees about reliable, sequenced, flow-controlled delivery, and therefore have the discard option that a connection-oriented protocol would not have.

Both the ES-IS and IS-IS exchanges include *Hello* packets that are broadcast when possible to allow other nodes to know of their presence. When broadcast capabilities do not exist, administrators must preconfigure the required paths for these Hello messages. One learns about the existence of a device by its Hello messages, but unfortunately, the devices do not say *Goodby* when they leave because leaving is usually due to some unexpected crash or outage. Therefore, timers are required to remove entries from which no recent Hello messages have been received.

ISs periodically exchange Hello messages and their entire routing tables. These tables are also sent when they are changed. The exchanges identify the routing metrics that are supported and their nearest neighbors.

The standardization of the routing algorithm for OSI internetworking was made available several years after the connectionless internet protocol itself. This was due to the problems that existed with earlier routing protocols. Fortunately, the standardized link state algorithm provides a much better routing approach.

### Network Layer Support to the Transport Layer

The OSI network layer provides differing services depending on the particular sublayers involved. If the network layer provides some assurances of reliable, sequenced, flow-controlled delivery, the transport layer can build directly on these services. Otherwise, the transport layer must provide these services on an end-to-end basis.

## THE TRANSPORT LAYER

Because the original OSI protocols were connection-oriented, it is no surprise that the major form of transport protocol is connection-oriented as well. The connectionless LAN logical link control and the internet protocols are about the only exceptions at this time. A connectionless form of OSI transport exists, but it is not currently used by higher-layer protocols.

### The OSI Connection-Oriented Transport Layer

The basic purpose of the connection-oriented transport layer is to provide end-to-end integrity of higher-level protocol packets. Like any other connection-oriented protocol, the distinguishing characteristic of a transport connection is that it provides reliable, sequenced, flow-controlled delivery, which requires that it maintain state information about the data transfers. This state information includes the current status of outstanding (unacknowledged) packets, the sequence number for the next transmission, the next expected sequence number for reception, and the current flow-control allocation.

The concept of end-to-end integrity of the data transfers includes assurances that no damaged PDUs are delivered and that no PDUs are lost, duplicated, or out of order. ACKs are delivered to indicate that PDUs have been successfully received. However, this ACK does not necessarily mean that the packet contents are safely stored on disk. Higher-level ACKs or recovery mechanisms are necessary when crash recovery is required. These higher-level mechanisms may also include checkpoint recovery and are the responsibility of the session and application layers.

Transport connections exist in three distinct phases: (1) connection establishment, (2) data transfer, and (3) connection release. Connection establishment consists of a full OSI handshake, with request, indication, response, and confirmation packets as shown in Figure 3-25. In Part a of the figure, a connection request is accepted, while in Part b it is refused by the responding user, and in Part c it is refused by the provider.

Figure 3-26 shows the data transfer phase, with normal data in Part a and expedited data in Part b. The usual ACKs are returned, but neither is confirmed by a full OSI handshake. The release of a connection is shown in Figure 3-27,

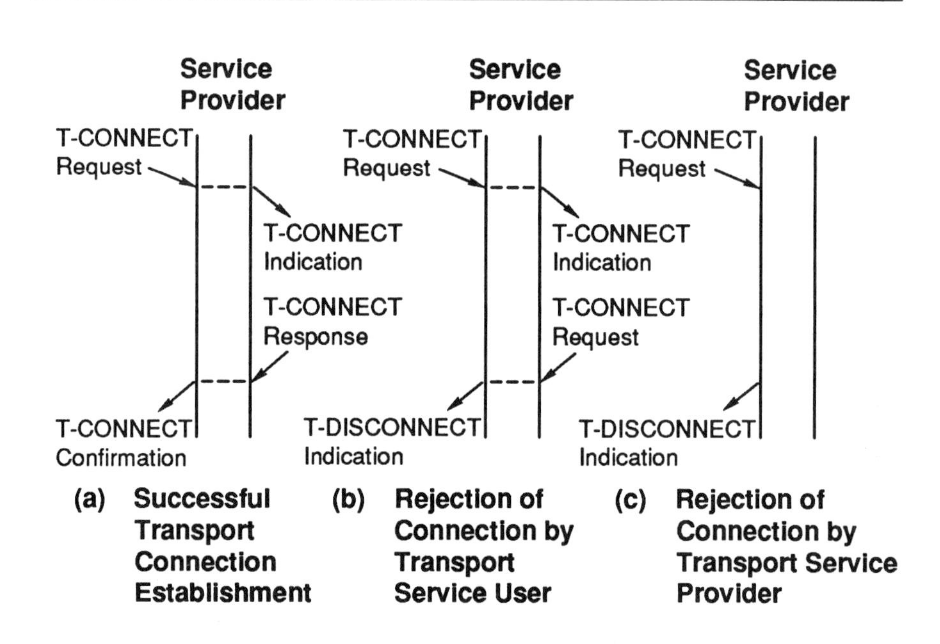


**FIGURE 3-25** Connection requests may be accepted or rejected.

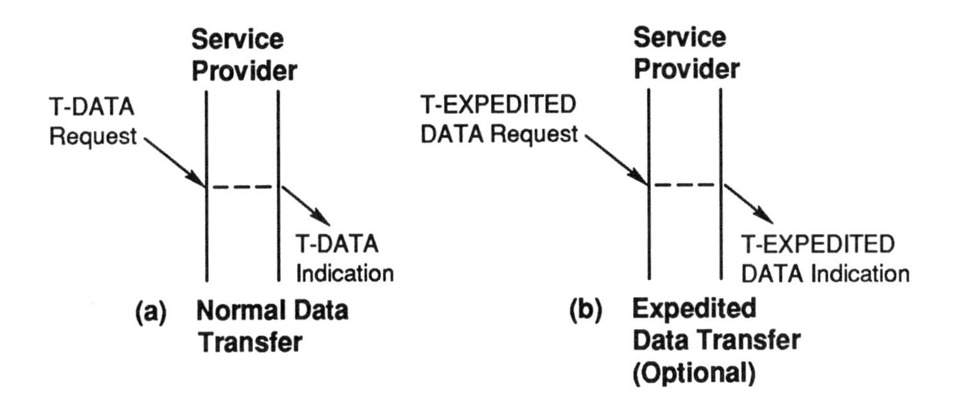


*Illustration courtesy of Learning Group International*

**FIGURE 3-26** Normal and expedited data transfers.

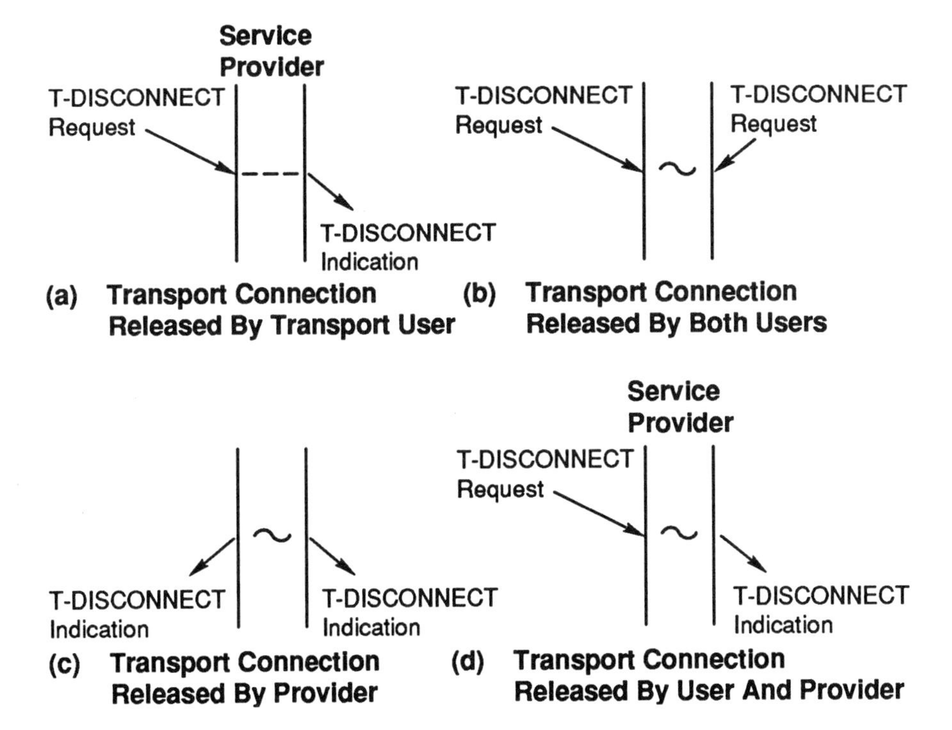


*Illustration courtesy of Learning Group International*

**FIGURE 3-27** Connection release may be due to any of several reasons.

which indicates four alternative release situations. The most common is shown in Part a in which the transport user initiates the release with a T-DISCONNECT request. In Part b both users send T-DISCONNECT requests at approximately the same time. In Part c the release is originated by the service provider, and in Part d it is performed simultaneously by both a user and the provider.

The transport connection establishment, use, and release can be represented in state machine form, as shown in Figure 3-28. The state machine starts in the idle state. When a T-CONNECT request is sent, it moves to the outgoing connection pending state. Upon receipt of a T-CONNECT confirmation, it moves to the data transfer ready state. Subsequent data transfers do

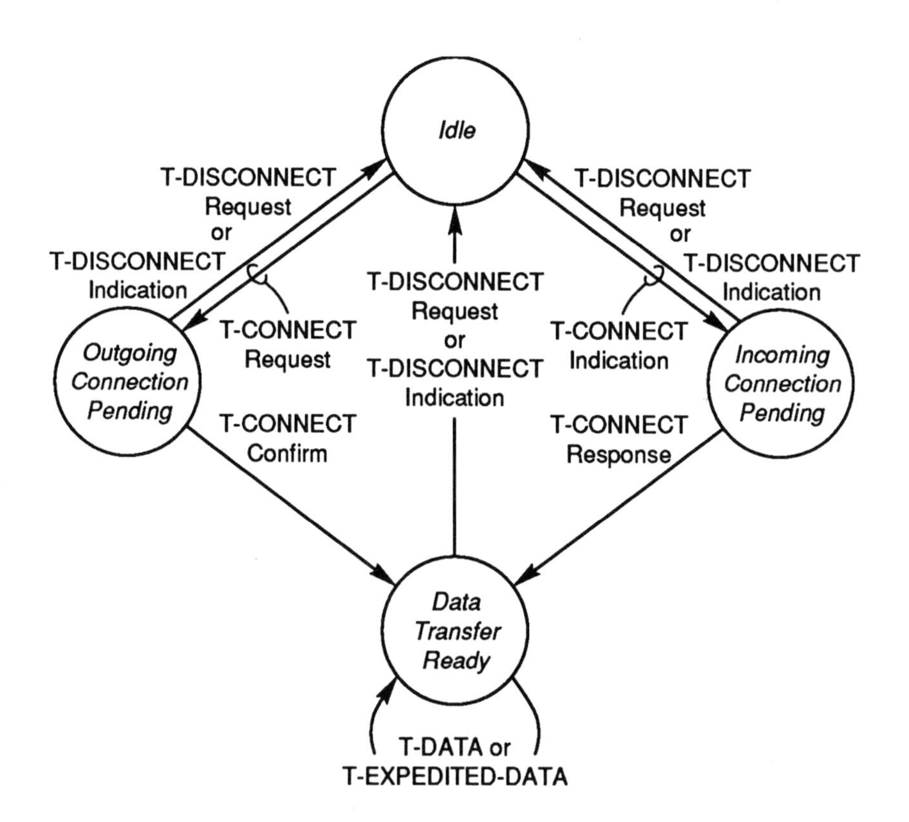


*Illustration courtesy of Learning Group International*

**FIGURE 3-28** Connection establishment, use, and release are governed by a protocol state machine.

not cause state changes. Releasing the connection and going back to the idle state can be accomplished by either the T-DISCONNECT request or indication. The line diagrams showing the flow of the request, indication, response, and confirmation, and the state diagrams are used at other protocol layers as well. The transport layer provides a set of service primitives for the establishment, use, and release of connections. These are summarized in Table 3-3.

**TABLE 3-3** Connection service primitives.

| Service | Primitive | Parameters |
|---|---|---|
| Connection Establishment | T-CONNECT request and indication | Called address<br>Calling address<br>Expedited data<br>Quality of service<br>User data |
| | T-CONNECT response and confirmation | Responding address<br>Expedited data<br>Quality of service<br>User data |
| Data transfer | T-DATA request and indication | User data |
| Expedited data transfer (optional) | T-DATA request and indication | User data |
| Connection release | T-DISCONNECT request | User data |
| | T-DISCONNECT indication | Disconnect reason<br>User data |

The connection is established by a confirmed exchange that begins with a T-CONNECT request containing the listed parameters. All these parameters are mandatory except for the optional user data:

1. **Called address** — The address of the transport service access point (TSAP) to which the connection is to be made.
2. **Calling address** — The address of the TSAP that requested the connection.
3. **Expedited data** — Although expedited data is an optional service, the connection request must specify whether to select for this service.

4. **Quality of service** — The QOS includes a lengthy list of performance parameters including connection establishment, release delay, throughput, transit delay, residual error rate, and various failure probabilities.
5. **User data** — User data refers to the user of the transport service (TS), so it is called TS-user data. User data in the connection request is limited to a maximum of 32 octets.

The connection establishment also involves the return of a T-CONNECT response and confirmation. The parameters associated with this returned information are listed below.

1. **Responding address** — As expected, the responding address should be exactly the same as the called address in the connection request. However, the OSI protocol is flexible enough to permit a different called address and responding address to allow for possible generic addresses at some time in the future.
2. **Expedited data** — If the connection request asked for the expedited data option, the response can be either *selected* or *not selected.* The response cannot ask for the expedited data option if the request did not ask for it.
3. **Quality of service** — The quality of service indicated in the response cannot be greater than that of the connection request.
4. **User data** — TS-user data, limited to a maximum of 32 octets.

As previously indicated, some of the transport services may actually be provided by the network or data link layers and simply passed through to the session layer. This means that the transport layer protocol does not always need its full complement of tools for error, sequence, and flow controls. The required set of tools is negotiated in terms of the class of protocol that is to be used. The two most common situations are the operation over X.25 networks and the operation over IP internetworks. These differences are shown in Figure 3-29. X.25 provides an interface and interconnection from the host to the packet switch. The ES-IS internet protocol provides the comparable interface and interconnection from the host to a router.

The OSI transport protocol defines a set of five protocol classes that provides approximately the same OSI transport layer service, but differs based on how the network layer services are involved. For example, a very light-

- **Two common forms of networking influence the work required by the transport protocol.**
- **Transport protocol a can often rely on the X.25 network for reliable, sequenced delivery of packets.**
  It has an easy job to do.
- **Transport protocol b cannot rely on the internet for other than best-efforts delivery.**
  It must work very hard.

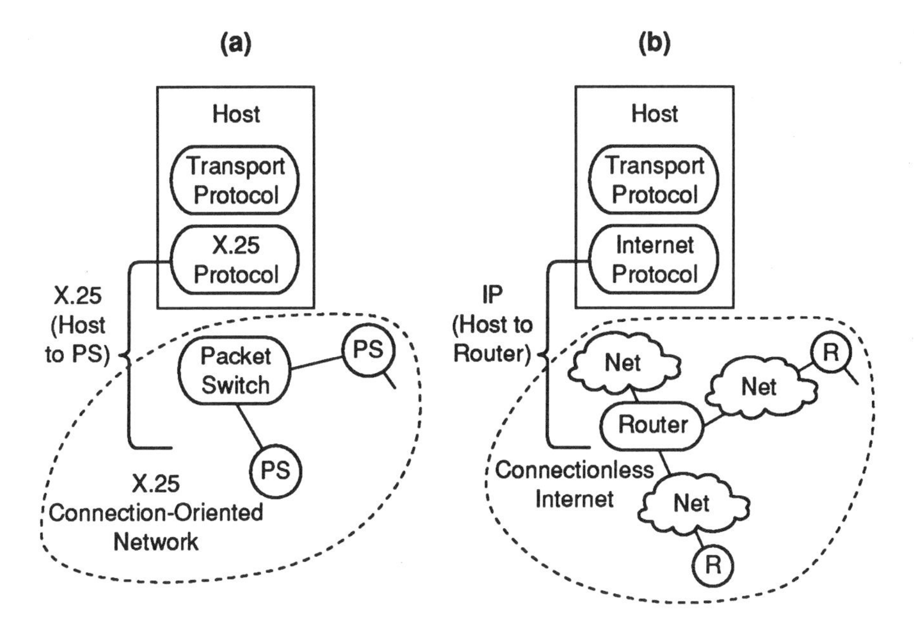


*Illustration courtesy of Learning Group International*

**FIGURE 3-29** Two common transport protocol situations.

weight set of transport protocol tools or mechanisms may be all that is required when an X.25 network provides acceptable integrity of the delivered data. At the other extreme, the network or cascaded set of networks may introduce errors, lost packets, or other forms of data integrity problems. In this latter case, the transport protocol mechanisms must be expanded to provide the required level of end-to-end data integrity.

- **Transport connection:**
  Gets to the appropriate utility program (addressing).
  Relies on the X.25 connection for reliable, sequenced delivery.
  Provides transport connection flow control.
  May provide additional recovery for lost packets.

- **X.25 connection:**
  Gets to the proper host computer.
  Builds on the LAPB reliable, sequenced delivery.

- **HDLC (LAPB) connection:**
  Provides reliable, sequenced delivery.

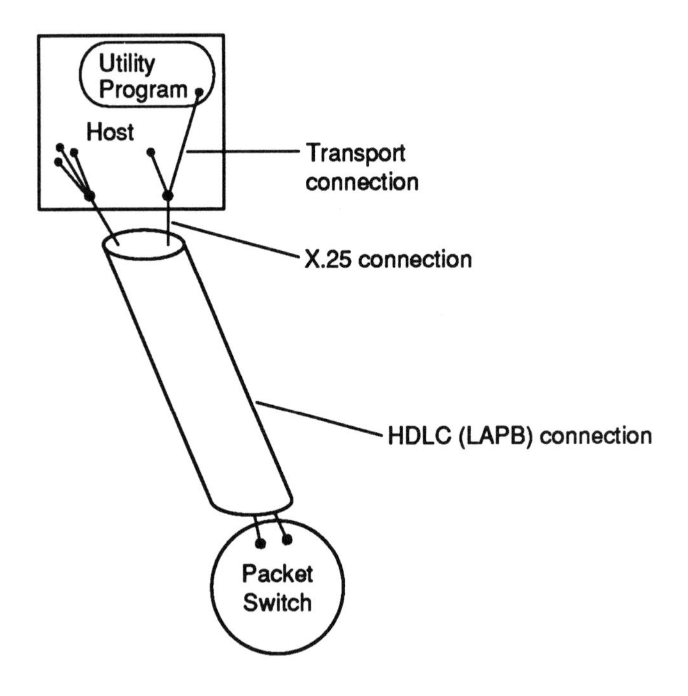


*Illustration courtesy of Learning Group International*

**FIGURE 3-30** The required transport protocol over an X.25 network.

The transport protocol may also differ in terms of its mechanisms based on whether or not a network connection is shared by several simultaneous transport connections. This is a form of multiplexing. In Figure 3-30 we actually see two levels of multiplexing because several transport connections are multiplexed onto one X.25 connection, and several X.25 network connections are multiplexed onto one data link connection. Each connection appears as a pipe or conduit over which data flows with a given level of integrity.

The use of multiplexing affects the choice of the transport protocol class. The combination of (1) adapting to differing levels of network service and (2) choosing whether or not to use multiplexing leads to the five different OSI classes of transport protocols (see Figure 3-31). In the U.S. networks are considered either type A (acceptable integrity) or type C (unacceptable integrity). This leads to the elimination of protocol classes 1 and 3 from consideration. The motivation is that a smaller number of classes will make interoperability more likely.

As shown in Figure 3-31, classes zero and 1 do not multiplex transport connections over an X.25 connection. Instead, there is a one-to-one correspondence between transport and network connections. Class zero is intended for X.400 electronic mail. Class 1 can be ignored, at least in North America and probably elsewhere.

Classes 2 and 3 multiplex two or more transport connections across one X.25 connection. Class 4 goes beyond this because there is no reason to limit

- **The network type determines the required level of transport service:**
  Type A — acceptable, low number of errors.
  Type B — errors occur, but host is not notified.
  Type C — errors occur without notification.

| | Network Type | | |
|---|---|---|---|
| | **Type A** | **Type B** | **Type C** |
| Single User per Network Connection | OSI TP Class 0 | OSI TP Class 1 | ---- |
| Multiple Users per Network Connection (Multiplexed) | OSI TP Class 2 | OSI TP Class 3 | OSI TP Class 4 |

*Illustration courtesy of Learning Group International*

**FIGURE 3-31** Candidate transport protocol classes.

net-works to X.25; they can be any form of network. In order to ensure interoperability, the National Institute of Standards and Technology has devised a strategy in which only transport protocol classes 2 and 4 would be used in the U.S. In addition, class zero (0) would be used for international X.400 electronic mail. The latter is mandated by CCITT for public X.400 systems.

The discussion here will focus on TP class 4, with a summary view of how classes zero and 2 can be derived from class 4. The protocol class to be used on any given connection is negotiated at the connection establishment. The negotiation rules are rather complicated and involve both the requested class and one or more alternate classes that can be defined in the connection request. For example, if the preferred and alternate classes are both zero, the combination is invalid for some unexplained reason. However, if both the preferred and alternate are class 2, then class 2 is clearly the only choice, which seems quite reasonable. If you then try the same logic on class 4 as the preferred and alternative classes, the options are either class 2 or class 4. In addition, any connection request that has the possibility of negotiating down to class zero cannot use multiplexing until after the completion of a class 2 or 4 resultant connection. It is similar to filling out your income tax forms: Do not rely on logic — just follow the rules.

All of the five classes of the OSI transport protocol, TP0 to TP4, are connection-oriented. As such, they require that a connection be established, and the connection establishment handshake provides the opportunity to negotiate certain options. In the examples, class 4 connections and the associated options are considered. A connection request PDU starts off the connection establishment process and contains the fields that are summarized in Figure 3-32.

The connection request PDU contains a SAP (although it is rather hidden in the parameters field) and a reference number. Both have end-to-end significance. The connection request PDU in the figure indicates that the originating end system has included a source reference number. The other end can select its own number to use, and it is shown in the connection request as simply zero, signifying that it is to be determined. There are also negotiated values such as the maximum PDU size (from 128 to 8192 octets in powers of 2) and the selection of the sequence number size (7 or 31 bits). In TP class 4, the error check is end-to-end, but it is optional and negotiated. However, the error check is mandatory on the class 4 connection request PDU. The window size is continuously variable, and the initial window size (the initial credit field) is included in the connection request packet. It indicates how

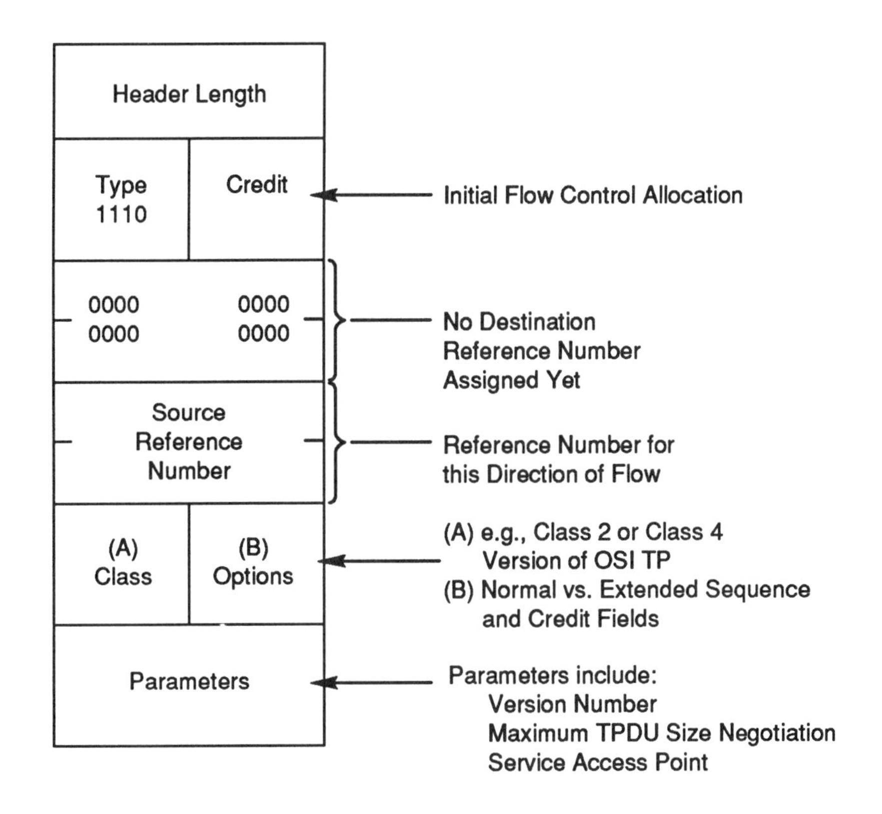


*Illustration courtesy of Learning Group International*

**FIGURE 3-32** A transport connection request.

many packets can be sent before having to wait for ACK to come back to slide the window forward.

Up to 32 bytes of optional user data can be in the connection request packet or the returned connection confirmation packet. Once the connection has been established, normal data packets can be exchanged with larger data fields. The formats of these data packets and their corresponding ACK packets are shown in Figures 3-33 and 3-34, respectively. These examples assume that the extended sequence numbers and error checks were negotiated when the connection was established, so the sequence number field and ACK number field will each be 31 bits in length, and the credit (window) field will be 8 bits in length.

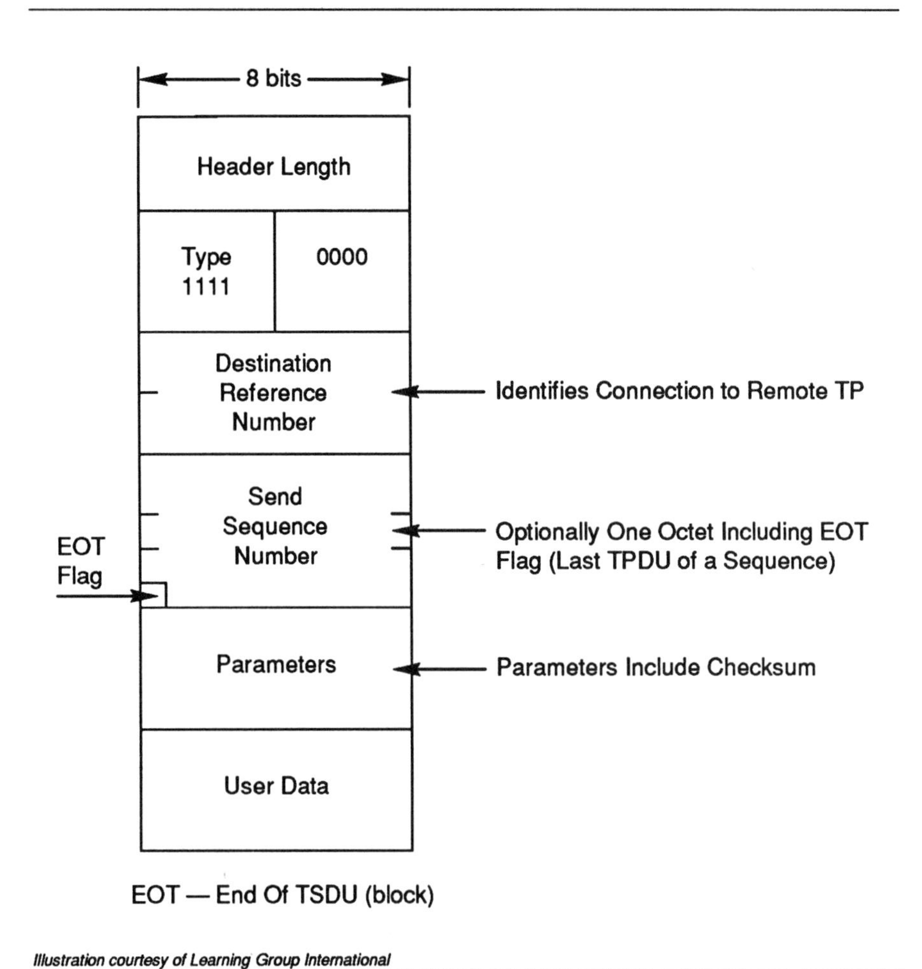


*Illustration courtesy of Learning Group International*

**FIGURE 3-33** A data TPDU.

Note that only the destination reference number is listed in each data and ACK format. These are the values that the receiving end selected for this connection. Therefore, the word destination must be interpreted in the context of the sending end system. Unlike earlier protocols that piggybacked the ACK number in data packets, a separate ACK packet is sent. The ACK approach is similar to the supervisory packet of data link protocols. The ACK provides the left edge of the window, and the credit field provides the window size (flow-control value). Indicating that the window size is zero is the equivalent of saying *stop sending*. However, the window should not be shrunk below any previously advertised size because that may cause packets sent by

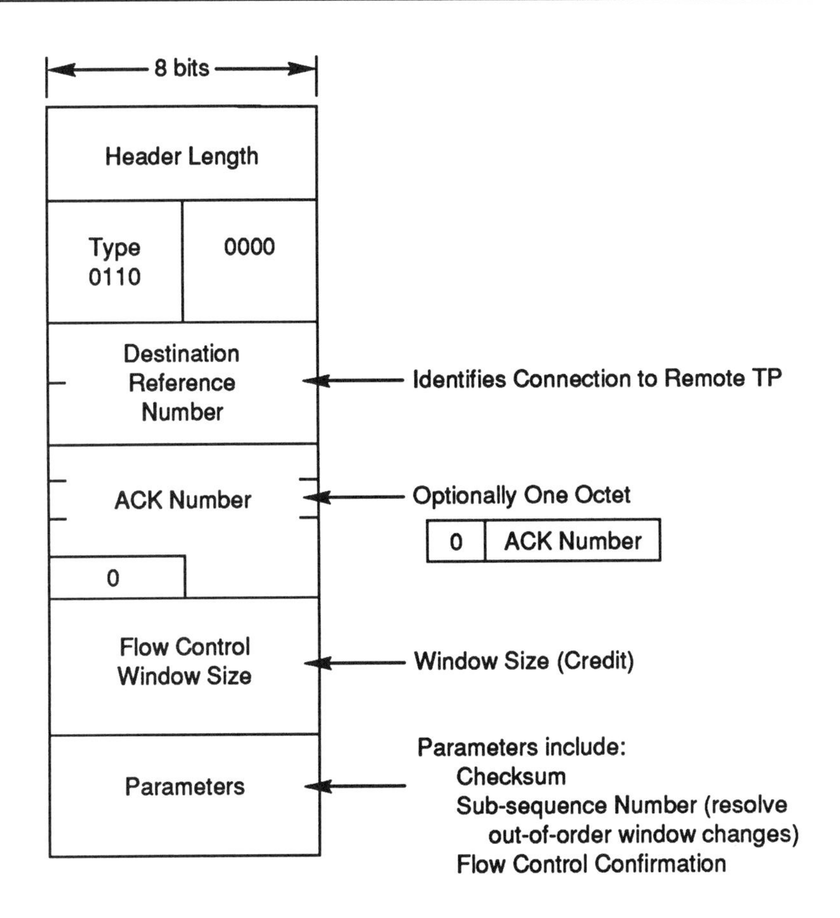


*Illustration courtesy of Learning Group International*

**FIGURE 3-34** TPDU ACK format.

the other party to be discarded, thus wasting communications resources. Because communications costs are more expensive than memory and processing cycles, this is not a good tradeoff.

Figure 3-32 showed the connection request packet. As previously described, a reference number is used by the other end in future packets to identify this connection. This is a shorthand form for the connection identifier. The negotiated fields include the protocol class (e.g., a request to run class 4), the sequence number size (e.g., request 31-bit sequence numbers), the use of error checks, the maximum transport PDU size, and the version number. The parameters field also includes a service access point. The SAP is a parameter because it may be implicit, i.e., if one always connects to a single service.

The data packet in the example uses the 31-bit sequence number and the optional error checks. The ACK packet of Figure 3-34 shows the next expected PDU sequence number and the credit (window) allocation carried as a 16-bit integer. Other parameters in the ACK packet include the checksum and two other interesting fields. The first is the sub-sequence number field. It allows one to put sequence numbers on ACKs. Suppose that you send an ACK with a credit field of 10, and then later send another ACK with a credit field of 20, thus attempting to increase the size of the window. The receiver may get them in either order not knowing which one to believe. The sub-sequence number resolves this problem because the ACK of 20 will have a higher sub-sequence number. The second of these fields is the flow-control confirmation field. It allows the two ends to reconcile their respective values for flow control in the same way the bank reconciles monthly statements of deposits and checks.

The transport protocol data unit (TPDU) has a field called end-of-TSDU (EOT) in which the name is modelled after the American Standard Code for

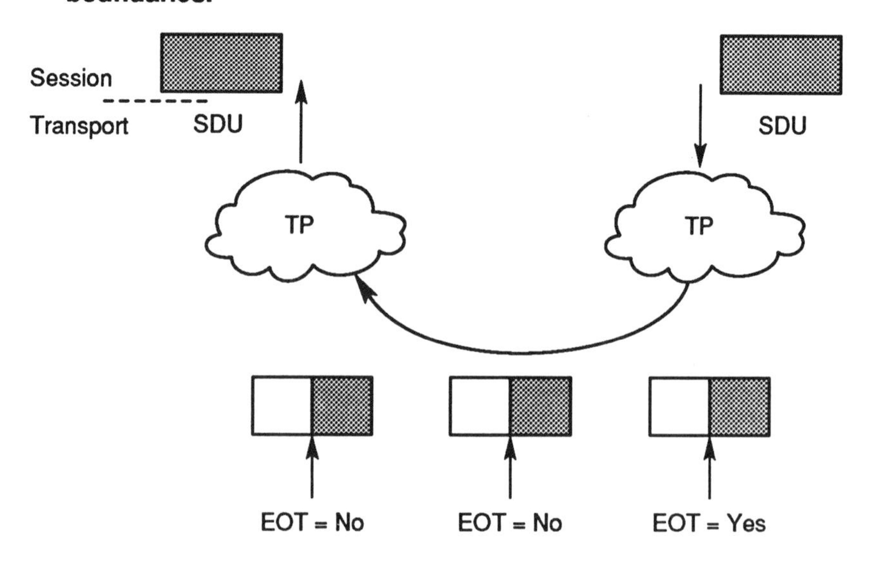


*Illustration courtesy of Learning Group International*

**FIGURE 3-35** Transport protocol handling of SDUs.

Information Interchange (ASCII) character of the same purpose. It is an end-of-record delimiter. The TP service is in terms of service data units, which are the data units (blocks) passed between the session layer and the transport layer. Figure 3-35 shows an SDU being received from the session layer, segmented into three PDUs for transmission, and then reassembled for delivery as the exact same SDU originally received. The EOT Boolean operation is used to indicate the last PDU of such a sequence.

Figure 3-36 illustrates the error check mechanism of TP class 4, including its algorithm for computation on transmission and reception. The error check consists of two one-byte checks. One is the modulo 255 sum of the bytes in the packet, and the second is the modulo 255 sum of the bytes multiplied by

**The Fletcher Checksum calculates X and Y (check octets) so that:**

- $\sum_{i=1}^{L} B_i = 0 \text{ MOD } 255.$
- $\sum_{i=1}^{L} (L - i + 1) B_i = 0 \text{ MOD } 255.$

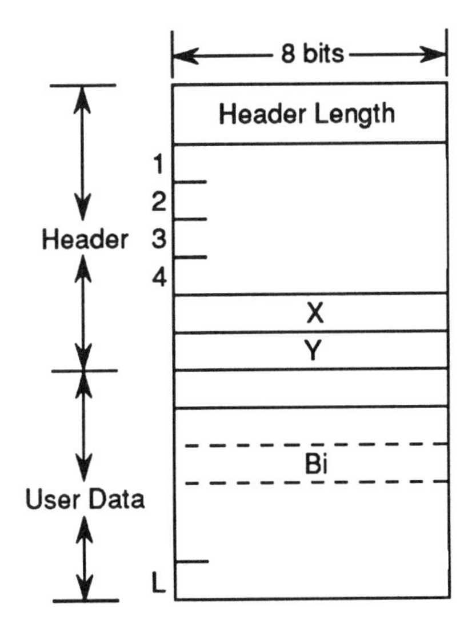


*Illustration courtesy of Learning Group International*

**FIGURE 3-36** Error checking for TPDUs.

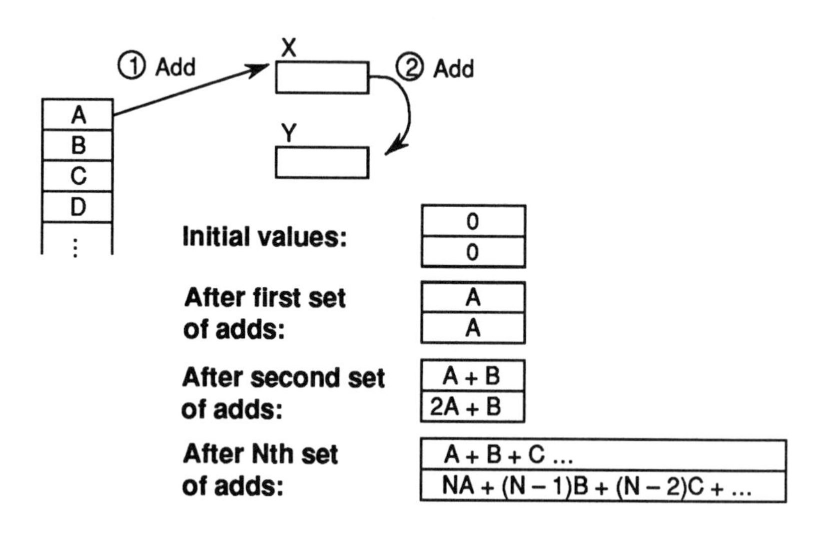


*Illustration courtesy of Learning Group International*

**FIGURE 3-37** A simplified example of the TP class 4 error check.

their relative location in the packet. This algorithm would detect swapped fields, e.g., if the first two bytes were exchanged in location with the second two bytes. The negative aspect of this error check is that it can be very demanding computationally, and the additional errors that it detects beyond those of simpler schemes are not likely to occur. Its direct implementation is shown in Figure 3-37, indicating that at least two additions are required per byte of the packet. Even with clever algorithms to expedite the computation, it is still slow when compared with earlier forms of error checking. This can be a major limitation when attempting to implement high throughput systems because the error check is often the major component of transport layer protocol processing.

Unlike most other reliable transmission protocols, the OSI TP does not piggyback the ACK on data PDUs. Instead, there is a more general way of piggybacking control information (see Figure 3-38). An ACK or other control PDU may be piggybacked with a data PDU if both are going to the same destination without having to be on the same transport connection. This seems like a good idea because processing time and communications overhead will be reduced due to the more general form of piggybacking. On the other hand, the resulting larger packet size may result in segmentation at the internet sublayer and may actually increase the processing time.

- **Transport protocol ACKs are not necessarily "piggybacked" on return traffic.**
- **An ACK PDU may be concatenated with data PDU to form a network service data unit.**

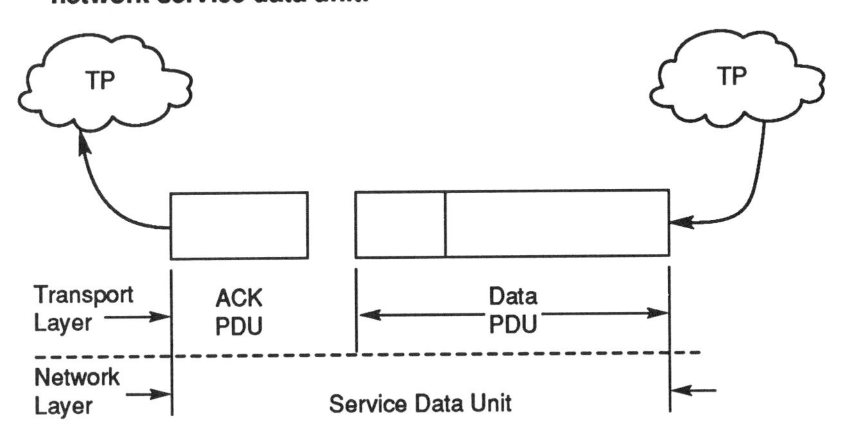


*Illustration courtesy of Learning Group International*

**FIGURE 3-38** Transport protocol ACKs.

TP class 4 has two forms of data transfer: normal data, as previously discussed, and expedited data, as shown in Figure 3-39. Expedited data is in the form of a special control packet. Unlike normal data, expedited data is not limited by flow control, although only one expedited data packet can be outstanding at any given time. After sending an expedited TPDU, the ACK must be received before sending another expedited data TPDU or any normal data packets. This ensures that no subsequent normal TPDU can get ahead of the expedited TPDU. The purpose of expedited data is not of concern to the transport layer. The task of the transport layer is to get it delivered as quickly as possible and to indicate that it is special data. It is then up to the higher-layer protocols to process it quickly and to accomplish whatever the sender had in mind based on the application context and protocols involved.

This discussion has focused on the TP class 4 protocol. Figure 3-40 compares the functions of this protocol with those of classes zero and 2 and indicates that class 4 has all the functions of the lesser classes. This may be somewhat misleading because it implies that the other classes should be obtained as direct subsets of class 4. This is not the case. Unfortunately, it is not that simple.

- **Only one expedited data unit can be outstanding.**

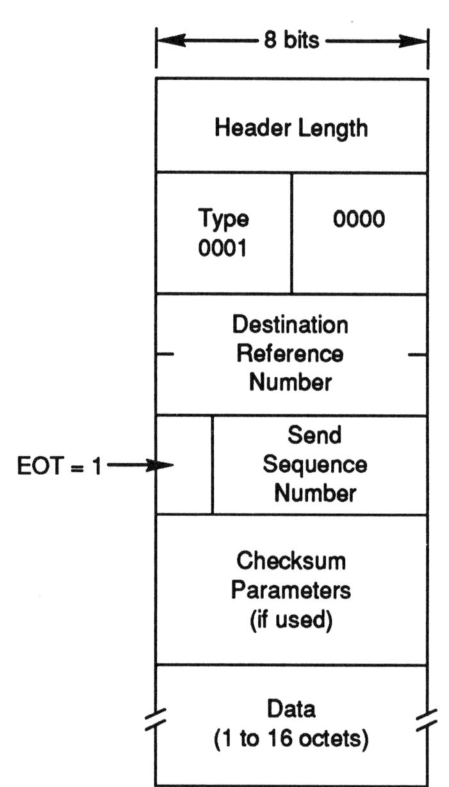


*Illustration courtesy of Learning Group International*

**FIGURE 3-39** Expedited data.

Class zero is one of the biggest exceptions in the subset concern, due to its origins and intended purpose. It was included because CCITT wanted it for the support of X.400 electronic messaging (electronic mail) and for backwards compatibility with the Telex system. Class zero differs because it does not send disconnect confirmation packets, does not use any flow control, and implicitly disconnects the transport connection when the X.25 connection is closed. Class zero also differs in its service definition. For example, it does not support any user data in its connection request packets. In spite of the minor differences of class zero, the five classes of OSI transport protocols differ primarily in the way they achieve a common delivery service.

| Function | Transport Protocol Class 0 | 1 | 2 | 3 | 4 |
|---|---|---|---|---|---|
| Connection Establishment | X | X | X | X | X |
| Option Negotiation | X | X | X | X | X |
| Connection Refusal | X | X | X | X | X |
| Transfer TPDUs | X | X | X | X | X |
| Handle Protocol Errors | X | X | X | X | X |
| Segmenting and Reassembly | X | X | X | X | X |
| Normal Release | | X | X | X | X |
| Expedited Data | | X | X | X | X |
| Sequence Numbering of TPDUs | | X | X | X | X |
| Extended Sequence Numbering | | | X | X | X |
| Multiplexing (e.g., over one X.25 Con.) | | | X | X | X |
| Explicit Flow Control | | | X | X | X |
| Reassignment After Failure | | X | | X | X |
| Retention Until ACK | | X | | X | X |
| Resynchronization | | X | | X | X |
| Frozen Reference Numbers | | X | | X | X |
| Error Checks (Checksum) | | | | | X |
| Retransmission on Timeout | | | | | X |
| Resequence TPDUs | | | | | X |
| Inactivity Control | | | | | X |
| Splitting and Recombining | | | | | X |

*Illustration courtesy of Learning Group International*

**FIGURE 3-40** Transport protocol functions.

## Connectionless Transport Protocols

Connectionless transport protocols are not nearly as common as connection-oriented protocols, but they are becoming increasingly used to support transparent user services. Many of these uses are transaction-oriented services in which one cannot always tolerate the overhead of opening a connection. The reliability and sequenced delivery assurances of the connection-oriented transport protocol are either not needed or provided by higher-level protocols such as a remote procedure call mechanism.

The services provided by the connectionless transport protocol are usually minimal, often being limited to multiplexing and demultiplexing. Error detection may be provided as an option, but error recovery is typically not provided.

The OSI connectionless transport service and protocol are defined in ISO 8072 and 8602 respectively. The fact that connectionless operation is foreign to OSI shows up in the numbering scheme, among other instances. In almost all other cases, the service definition and the protocol specification are consecutive integers. In the case of the connectionless transport, they have no such relationship. This is due in part to the variations that OSI considers between the transport and network layers.

Because any connectionless operation (including that of OSI) has no connection setup phase, the only primitives for the connectionless transport are UnitData.request and UnitData.indication. These correspond to sending and receiving data respectively. Each primitive has the following four parameters: source address, destination address, quality of service (an indication of error detection), and user data. The source and destination addresses include the specific host computer system and the internal software address to get to the connectionless transport service. Note that nothing is comparable to the reference identifier of the connection-oriented transport protocol.

The connectionless transport service is not expected to provide any form of reliable delivery (other than discarding bad PDUs), sequencing, or flow control. This is consistent with the concept of being connectionless. The OSI connectionless transport protocol may (optionally) include an error check. If an error check fails upon receipt of a PDU, the PDU is simply discarded. There is no retransmission at the transport layer in this case.

Because items such as the checksum are optional, the connectionless transport protocol header is encoded as a series of type-length-value sequences following a length indicator and a TPDU code field. The TPDU code field identifies the PDU as being connectionless. It replaces the PDU type and credit-field byte of the connection-oriented protocol. The resulting PDU structure is shown in Figure 3-41.

Note that there is no way in this transport protocol to segment an SDU into multiple TPDUs, i.e., there is nothing comparable with the EOT flag of the connection-oriented TP. However, segmentation can be performed at the internet sublayer.

## Summary and Conclusions

The end-to-end delivery mechanisms in OSI can be found at the internet sublayer of the network layer and at the transport layer. Being a sublayer, the IP protocol is optional. The transport layer is never optional, but it does come in several forms or classes with differing degrees of recovery properties. The particular class of transport protocol is selected based on the recovery mecha-

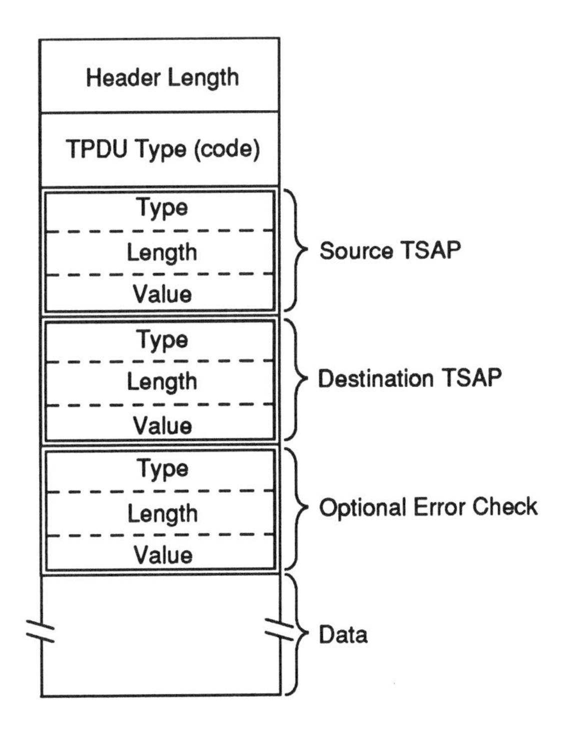


*Illustration courtesy of Learning Group International*

**FIGURE 3-41** OSI connectionless transport PDU.

nisms needed and on the amount of work already done by the network or data link layers.

This chapter has discussed methods for the delivery of bits and bytes of user data and upper-layer protocol control information. The principal concerns are with the integrity of the delivered bits and bytes. A very different set of concerns can be found with the upper-layer protocols, which are primarily involved with providing support to user applications such as file transfers and remote logins.

# 4

# THE OSI UPPER LAYERS

The upper three layers of the Open Systems Interconnection (OSI) Reference Model provide a number of different services to application programs. In contrast, the bottom four layers provide many different ways to get the same service, namely the delivery of data. Thus, the services and protocols of layers five through seven are quite different from those previously discussed.

## THE SESSION LAYER

The OSI session layer builds on the high-integrity, delivery platform provided by the transport layer, and therefore does not have to concern itself with lost or damaged protocol data units. It can assume that error recovery will be handled by the transport layer. However, the session layer can provide other forms of recovery such as processing and data transfer synchronization after a system crash. The session layer also provides primitive services that can be used to simplify network applications such as two-way alternate data flow. This allows a server to answer one request before receiving another from the same requestor. The session layer also provides a set of services developed specifically for the transmission of electronic messages but found to have a broader use.

The OSI session layer is documented in the usual two documents: a service definition and a protocol specification, which are named below.

| | | |
|---|---|---|
| Service Definition | ISO 8326 | CCITT X.215 |
| Protocol Specification | ISO 8327 | CCITT X.225 |

No previous protocol suite had anything quite like the OSI session layer. It came about as a merger of the European Computer Manufacturers Association (ECMA) session layer protocol and the Consultative Committee for International Telephone and Telegraph (CCITT) T.62 (Teletex) recommendation. As a consequence, it provides a set of services that on the surface seem quite reasonable, but in ways that are often rather convoluted, largely because of CCITT's desire for backwards compatibility with earlier messaging systems.

The session layer is primarily a general purpose *tool kit*. Looking at the tool set is comparable to walking into a hardware store. Few users need all the electrical, plumbing, painting, and other tools available. The same thing applies to the tool set provided by the session layer.

Some of the session layer tools are for modern computer applications, and others are for backwards compatibility with Teletex. In OSI terminology each of these tools is called a *functional unit*. The set of functional units is negotiated upon establishing a session layer connection. Even this negotiation is rather strange. Rather than have the initiator propose a set of functional units and the responder select from them, both suggest a set. The intersection of the sets is in effect for that particular connection. These functional units can then be propagated upward to the application programs with no further value added by the presentation or application layers. This led early OSI developers to question the need for the session layer. However, some application service elements do shield application processes from some of the complexity by packaging them in a more convenient form. One example is the reliable transfer service element, which will be described in Chapter 5.

As indicated above, the complete tool set is quite broad and may include more than one application would typically need. Some tools may not be needed at all on a particular computer. Therefore, the implementation might be a subset of the functional units. For example, early uses such as the Manufacturing Automation Protocol (MAP) and Technical and Office Protocol (TOP) have a very small subset of these tools.

The set of tools is also associated with a set of rules. The two-way alternate (half-duplex) tools ensure that only one end of a connection is allowed to talk at any given time. The tool enforces this rule. But as every good tax accountant knows, for every rule there is a way around it. An example exception in the session layer relates to the half-duplex rule. The ability to use this exception can be negotiated when a session connection is established. It is called *typed data*. If one negotiates the typed data functional unit, then there is a way to talk no matter whose turn it is.

The basic components of the OSI session layer are formulated in terms of these functional units. These functional units are organized into a *kernel* functional unit that must be supported and a set of negotiable functional units that are optional in each implementation.

## Session Layer Services

One of the session layer services is *dialogue management* or data-flow control. This is not flow control as previously discussed; instead it relates to the direction of the flow. Whose turn is it to talk? Once an application sends a request, it can be forced to wait for the response before issuing the next request. This is known as two-way alternate (TWA) communication. The functional units that are able to provide this TWA service resemble the tokens of a token-passing local area network. The other approach is to send consecutive requests without waiting for each response. This is known as two-way simultaneous (TWS) communication.

A second category of session services relates to how sessions are released. There are three variations. First, a session may be aborted by either the user (the application) or the provider (the session layer). In this case, data may be lost. Second, the session may be released in an orderly manner at the request of either side, in which case all data are transferred in both directions. This capability is provided by the kernel functional unit. Third, the ability to release the session may be based on ownership of a token. This is called *negotiated release*. Only the side that currently owns the token can release the session. The other side can request the token but does not necessarily get it. However, the other side can refuse the connection release if it has reason to do so.

A third category of session layer services is that of synchronization. There are two forms: the major sync point and the minor sync point. Both allow the sender to *mark* points in the message exchange with a *serial number*. They differ in terms of how these marked points affect the data exchange and how they are used. When a major synchronization point request is sent, no further protocol data units (PDUs) may be sent until confirmation of the synchronization has been received. In contrast, a minor synchronization request does not require a confirmation on every PDU. The application can continue to send minor sync points until it reaches the right edge of a window mechanism. The window size can be negotiated by the application layer. The session layer is not aware of (or involved with) this window mechanism. It is not intended to control flow but rather to avoid inefficient use of the network if some component is unable to sustain the data flow.

Major and minor synchronization points also differ in terms of their use as *rollback* points. The sender can never be required to rollback beyond the most recent confirmed major synchronization point. The confirmation implies that data up to that point are safely stored to whatever degree of safety is appropriate in a given transfer. A minor synchronization point does not have this restriction. Both major and minor synchronization points use a common (sequential) number scheme for the sync points. The initial value of the sync number can be negotiated when the session is established. The default is to start at number 1 and count to 999,998. (The value 999,999 is reserved, and the numbers do not wrap back to zero. Resynchronization is required if this maximum value is reached.)

The sync number is sent with the data request, and a confirmation number is returned indicating the last received sync number. For example, confirmation number 99 indicates that request sync number 99 and all prior sync numbers were received.

Synchronization numbers work well in TWA flow, but they could fail in TWS communication if both sides simultaneously attempt to use the next available sync number. Therefore, an addendum added a new session service called *symmetric synchronization.* It provides two independent sets of serial numbers — one for each direction of flow.

---

- **Synchronization and dialogue units.**

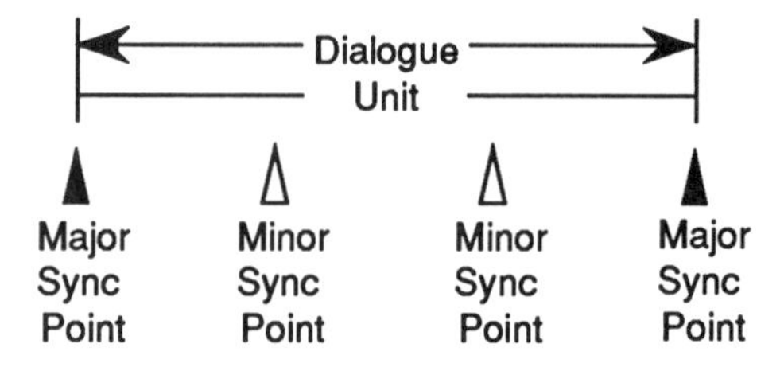


- **Example:**
  Numbered boxes represent files being transferred.

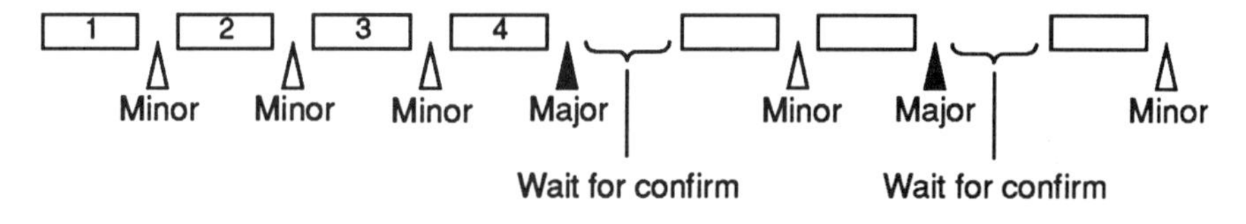


- **Resynchronization (recovery):**
  Can only go back to the last confirmed major sync.
  Can go back to any minor sync within the dialog unit.

*Illustration courtesy of Learning Group International*

**FIGURE 4-1** The dialogue unit provides well-defined recovery points.

Synchronization points are directly related to other session layer concepts, namely *dialogue units* and *activities*. An example of a dialogue unit is shown in Figure 4-1. It begins and ends with a major sync point and may have some internal minor sync points. As shown in the figure, the major sync points must be confirmed, and the flow of PDUs must stop until this confirmation is received. This delay may be required to get data safely stored on disk, to change the magnetic media that is receiving the data, or to obtain a new machine part in a factory example. Its use is quite general.

An activity is a further expansion of the dialogue unit, i.e., one or more consecutive dialogue units, prefaced with an *activity start* major sync point and terminated with an *activity end* major sync point, as seen in Figure 4-2. The rules associated with an activity state are that no data are to be sent until the activity start major sync point has been issued and that no data are to be sent after the activity end major sync point. However, if the functional unit called *capability data* has been negotiated, such data can be sent either before the activity start or after the activity end (see Figure 4-3).

Capability data are intended for control purposes. This data can be used to determine if both ends are *capable* of performing the activity. As indicated in this figure, a common relationship between the activity and the session is one-to-one. However, this is not required to be the case. Figure 4-4 indicates that several activities can sequentially use one session, or conversely, several consecutive sessions may be involved in one activity by interrupting and later resuming a single activity.

- **Activity and dialogue concepts.**

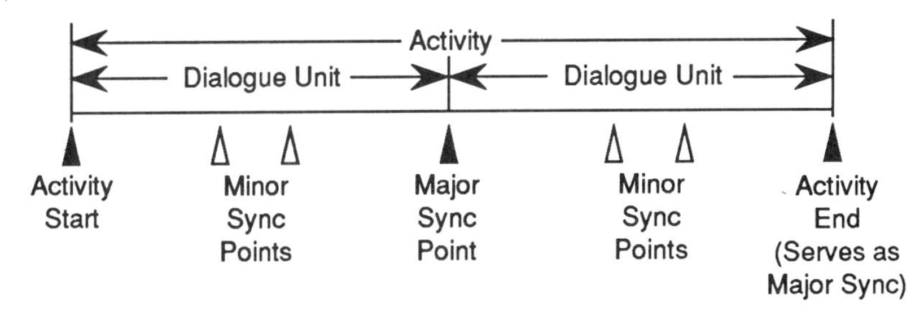


- **Example:**
  Transfer of one or more X.400 E-mail messages per activity.

*Illustration courtesy of Learning Group International*

**FIGURE 4-2** Activity management expands on the dialogue unit capabilities.

- **Capability data can be sent before or after an activity.**
  Intended for control purposes.
  Capability data transfers are ACKed.

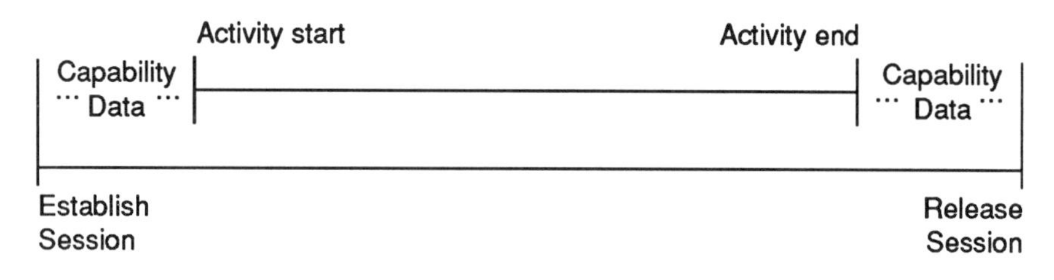


*Illustration courtesy of Learning Group International*

**FIGURE 4-3** Activities and capability data.

- **Several activities can sequentially utilize the same session connection.**

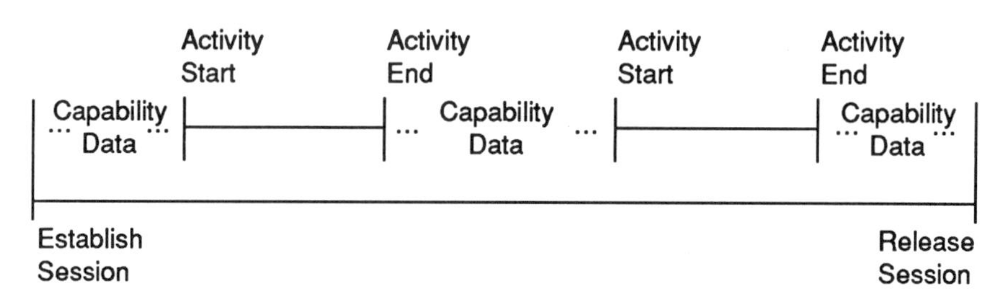


- **A single activity can span across several sequential sessions.**

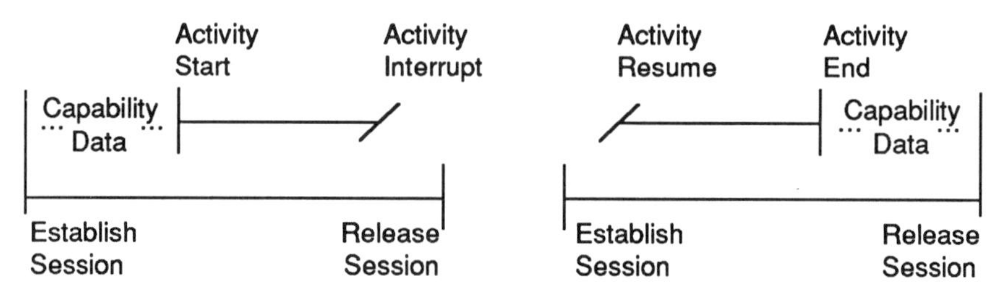


*Illustration courtesy of Learning Group International*

**FIGURE 4-4** Activities and session connections.

The remaining form of session layer service is the *exception reporting service.* As their name implies, exceptions are special events that need rapid attention. Exceptions can be from either the user (the application, the application layer, or the presentation layer) or the provider (the session layer itself). The exception reporting service is also a functional unit, but it is only applicable when the half-duplex functional unit has been negotiated.

## Token Controls

The tokens that are involved in a session layer must be examined before discussing the functional units in more detail. The use of tokens includes (1) two-way alternate communications, (2) negotiated release of a session, (3) minor synchronization, and (4) major/activity synchronization. The initial placement of the tokens for each of these operations is determined when the session is established. After that, the location of the tokens is controlled by three token-control primitives:

- **Please token request** — Asks for (but does not necessarily receive) one or more tokens.
- **Give token** — Passes one or more tokens.
- **Give control** — Passes all tokens.

The word *please* is intended to imply that it is a request, not a demand. The token need not be passed immediately. The *please request* and the *give token* primitives provide a complete request/response set, but the *give control* primitive also is included for backwards compatibility with earlier systems such as Teletex. In this case, all controls are passed in one unit.

## Functional Units

The functional units and the services are closely coupled because the functional units are the protocol mechanisms that provide the services. In this section, all the functional units are brought together for discussion and to describe the negotiation process that determines the functional units to be used on a given session.

The total set of functional units is shown in Figure 4-5. The kernel is *non-negotiable*, i.e., it is required in all implementations. It provides the basic session establishment and release (including abort) and the transfer of normal data. A description of he other functional units follows.

Negotiated release provides token control over the release of the session. Only the side that currently has this token can release the connection.

| Functional unit | Services |
|---|---|
| Kernel<br>(non-negotiable) | Session connection<br>Normal data transfer<br>Orderly release<br>User-Abort<br>Provider-Abort |
| Negotiated<br>release | Please tokens — *Token-controlled*<br>Give tokens — *connection release* |
| Half-duplex | Please tokens — *Two-way alternate*<br>Give tokens — *transfers* |
| Duplex | Duplex operation |
| Expedited data | Expedited data transfer (up to 14 octets) |
| Typed data | Data transfer not subject to token |
| Capability data<br>exchange | Data exchange outside of an activity |
| Minor synchronize | Minor synchronization point<br>Please tokens<br>Give tokens |
| Major synchronize | Major synchronization point<br>Please tokens<br>Give tokens |
| Resynchronize | Resynchronize to previous sync point |
| Exceptions | Provides exception reporting<br>User exception reporting |
| Activity management | Activity start<br>Activity interrupt<br>Activity resume<br>Activity discard<br>Activity end<br>Please tokens<br>Give tokens<br>Give control (all tokens) |

*Illustration courtesy of Learning Group International*

**FIGURE 4-5** Session layer functional units.

*Half-duplex* and *duplex* refer to the two-way alternate and two-way simultaneous dialogue controls as described earlier. TWA involves token controls. These two capabilities are mutually exclusive, but a given implementation can offer either.

*Expedited data* are usually relatively short in length and given special attention in delivery at the lower layers and in processing at the other end system. This special category of data was originally limited at the session layer to a maximum size of 14 bytes to fit within the expedited data length limitations at the transport and X.25 network layers. A subsequent amendment removes this restriction without indicating how this longer length data are to be handled at lower layers.

*Typed data* can be sent in a half-duplex mode without the need for a token. It is only a meaningful option if the half-duplex functional unit is also negotiated. The data are *typed* in the sense that it is unusual for this mode of operation.

*Capability data exchange* refers to the ability to send some data before or after the activity. It is only meaningful if the activity management functional unit also is negotiated. This data indicate if the two sides are capable of exchanging data during the subsequent or next activity.

*Minor* and *major synchronization* functional units provide the corresponding sync point capabilities. Either or both may be negotiated. Both are token controlled, and therefore include the *please* and *give* token primitives. Only major synchronization requires that the sender stop and wait for confirmation before sending more PDUs.

*Symmetric synchronization* was added as a functional unit in an addendum to provide separate sets of sync numbers for each direction of data flow.

The *resynchronize* functional unit allows the application to perform any of three functions. It can abandon the current dialogue and use the next serial number for subsequent needs. It can roll back to a previously confirmed sync point but no further than the last major sync point. And finally, it may reset the sync numbers to an arbitrary value. The resynchronized functional unit is only meaningful if one or more of the sync point functional units are negotiated.

The *exceptions* functional unit allows the user and provider to signal the existence of special events that need immediate attention. It is dependent upon negotiating the half-duplex functional unit.

*Activity management* is a very large functional unit that supports the general concept of an *activity*, i.e., a related set of PDU exchanges. While the idea of activities was initially limited to electronic mail exchanges, it has become a widely used tool. It is the only functional unit to include the *give control* (all tokens) primitive for backwards compatibility with Teletex. That further indicates its original intent to support electronic message communications.

In the past, the session layer functional units have been combined into subsets called the *basic combined subset* (BCS), the *basic synchronized subset* (BSS), and the *basic activity subset* (BAS). These subsets are strictly advisory, i.e., for those who implement OSI applications to consider for their uses. All require the kernel. The BCS adds either the half- or full-duplex functional unit. The BSS consists of the major, minor, and resync synchronization functional units, and the BAS consists of those functional units required for X.400 electronic messaging. The subsets are not negotiated as a group. Their separate functional unit components must be individually negotiated when desired.

In addition to negotiating the functional units, the session establishment also may negotiate the initial location of the token, the initial serial numbers for the synchronization points, and other such information. Representative examples of the 21 service primitives are given in greater detailed examples in the paragraphs and tables that follow.

The session layer service primitives are given names such as session connection, normal data transfer, minor synchronization, resynchronization, and orderly release. Each service primitive is associated with a set of table entries listing the service, the primitives, and the parameters.

## Normal Data Transfer

A simple example is that of data transfer once a session connection has been established. The normal data transfer primitive listing is provided in Table 4-1.

**TABLE 4-1** Normal data transfer primitive.

| Service | Primitives | Parameters |
|---|---|---|
| Normal data transfer | S_DATA request<br>S_DATA indication | SS-user data |

In the case of normal data transfer, there is no confirmation. The transport layer is assumed to deliver the data reliably.

## Session Connection Establishment

In contrast to the simple data transfer service, the session connection primitive is confirmed and has many more parameters, as shown in Table 4-2.

TABLE 4-2 Session connection primitive.

| Service | Primitives | Parameters |
|---|---|---|
| Session connection | S_CONNECT request | Session Connection ID |
| | S_CONNECT indication | Addresses, Result, |
| | S_CONNECT response | QOS, Session requirements |
| | S_CONNECT confirmation | Sync point S/N, Initial token assignment, User data |

The parameters list applies to all four primitives, although some of them may be null in one or more primitives. For example, do not expect the connection request to convey the result; the returned response/indication will do that. Some parameters are mandatory; others are conditional, based on user options, or not carried. The situation for each parameter is listed in Table 4-3 for the connection request and response.

TABLE 4-3 Parameters for connection request and response.

| Service | Primitives | Parameters |
|---|---|---|
| Session connection ID | User option | User option |
| Calling session address | Mandatory | Not carried |
| Called session address | Mandatory | Not carried |
| Responding session address | Not carried | Mandatory |
| Result | Not carried | Mandatory |
| Quality of service | Mandatory | Mandatory |
| Session requirements | Mandatory | Mandatory |
| Initial sync point S/N | Conditional | Conditional |
| Initial assignment of tokens | Conditional | Conditional |
| SS-user data | User option | User option |

The session connection identifier includes a reference number (up to 64 octets in length) that is selected by the session service users. Each user selects its own reference number and passes it to the other in the exchange. A common reference of up to 64 octets is shared by both parties, and a four-octet *additional reference* field exists.

The calling, called, and responding session addresses also are included in the connection establishment phase. The result is one of three possible outcomes:

accepted, rejected by the session service user, or rejected by the session service provider. The quality of service includes residual error rate, delay, throughput, priority, and security.

The session requirements are the functional units that are desired within the constraints of consistency, such as not requesting both the duplex and half-duplex functional units. Session service (SS) user session requirements (functional units) may be included in the response even if they were not included in the request. Those that were proposed in both are the ones that are selected.

The *initial* synchronization point serial number is a number in the range of zero to 999,998. It is a conditional parameter because it is only meaningful if synchronization services are requested. Similarly, the initial token assignment is only meaningful if token-controlled functional units are requested. For each token, the value in the request/indication may be requestor side, acceptor side, or acceptor choice. The value in the returned response/confirm is null unless the request/indication is set to *acceptor choice*, in which case the requestor or acceptor value is returned.

The SS-user data are optional and of unlimited length. This seems quite unusual because the amount of data sent in any other protocol connection request is limited.

## Minor Synchronization

The minor synchronization point primitive allows the sender to insert serially numbered synchronization points at desired places in the data transmission. The sender also controls whether these minor synchronization points will be confirmed. The minor synchronization point service primitive is described in Table 4-4 below.

**TABLE 4-4** Minor synchronization point service primitive.

| Service | Primitives | Parameters |
|---|---|---|
| Minor sync point | S_SYNC-MINOR request<br>S_SYNC-MINOR indication<br>S_SYNC-MINOR response<br>S_SYNC-MINOR confirmation | Type, Sync point<br>S/N, SS-user data |

As before, the parameters list applies to all four primitives, although some may be null in one or more primitives. The type parameter defines whether explicit confirmation is requested by the session service user. The synchronization point serial number was previously defined, and the session service user data are an unlimited number of octets of user data. The type and synchronization point serial number are mandatory in the request, and user data are optional to the user. The synchronization serial number is mandatory in the response, and user data are again optional.

### *Resynchronization*

The resynchronization primitive allows the sender to cause an orderly reestablishment of communications, typically after some significant fault has occurred. This is done by setting the connection endpoints to an agreed to state, including the synchronization point serial number and the location of the tokens. The primitives associated with this confirmed service are presented in Table 4-5.

**TABLE 4-5** Resynchronization primitive.

| Service | Primitives | Parameters |
|---|---|---|
| Resynchronization | S_RESYNCHRONIZE request | Resync type, |
| | S_RESYNCHRONIZE indication | Sync point S/N, |
| | S_RESYNCHRONIZE response | Token assignment, |
| | S_RESYNCHRONIZE confirmation | SS-user data |

Once again, the parameters list applies to all four primitives, although some may be null in one or more primitives. The resync type parameter is mandatory in the request and consists of one of three values: abandon, restart, or set. No synchronization point serial number is associated with *abandon* because the request is to abandon the communication. *Restart* and *set* differ in that *restart* cannot be requested at a synchronization point serial number smaller than a defined parameter. *Set* can be applied to any valid synchronization point serial number.

The token assignments in the request are one of three conditions: requestor side, acceptor side, or acceptor chooses. The value in the response is the same as that of the request, except when the acceptor is allowed to choose the token assignments. These three alternative values apply to each token type that is supported. The user data are an unlimited number of octets of optional user data.

As a final example, the orderly release service primitive is considered. Orderly release is always available because it is part of the kernel. It allows either party to release the connection without the loss of user data. The service primitive for orderly release is presented in Table 4-6 below.

**TABLE 4-6** Orderly release service primitive.

| Service | Primitives | Parameters |
|---|---|---|
| Orderly release | S_RELEASE request<br>S_RELEASE indication<br>S_RELEASE response<br>S_RELEASE confirmation | Result, SS-user data |

The *result* is only carried in the response/confirmation and indicates if the request is granted. The response is either *yes* or *no*, but the request can be refused only if the release token is in the possession of the receiving side and being used.

## Session Layer PDUs

The basic form of a session layer PDU is quite simple, being a type-length-value encoding. However, the actual PDUs that are exchanged can be quite complex due to the ways that multiple type-length-value encoding forms are combined. Fields are often both optional and variable in length. Therefore, each field is capable of self-identification, having a type field, a parameter length field, and the parameter value. Some protocol control information such as internet protocol (IP) options is encoded in this form. But in protocols such as IP, most protocol control information is in the form of fixed-length fields. This is not the case at the session layer where many fields are either optional or variable in length. Therefore, at the session layer all the header information is encoded this way. Figure 4-6 shows a simple type-length-value encoding in Part a and a more representative nested example in Part b. The initial field in each case is a *session PDU* (SPDU) identifier. The second field is the length of the overall protocol control information, which may have many nested fields as shown in Part b. The length indicator is usually one byte, supporting protocol header fields of up to 254 bytes in length. If that is not large enough, the value 255 indicates that the next two bytes are the 16-bit length field providing header lengths of over 65,000 bytes. That would certainly seem to be enough. Eventually, user data may be included, but it is of little concern from a protocol point of view.

The nested protocol control information shown in Part b of Figure 4-6 includes a *parameter group identifier* (PGI). An example PGI is the connection identifier, which consists of three parts: the calling session service user reference identifier that can be up to 64 bytes; a common reference (such as time) that can be up to 64 bytes; and additional reference information that may be up to 4 bytes. Each of these three parameters is encoded as *parameter identifiers* (PIs) in type-length-value form within the connection identifier PGI.

The session connection request also may include an optional PGI that conveys the protocols options, maximum transport service data unit (TSDU) size, version number, initial serial number, and initial token locations as PIs. This PGI is optional because default values may be acceptable to the user. Other PIs that are sent, but are not part of a PGI, are the session user requirements, the calling session service access point (SSAP) identifier, and the called SSAP identifier. This general format approach is rather straightforward when applied to session layer functions such as the connection request example. However, it becomes quite complicated (and the rules become complex) when applied to the Teletex functions of CCITT T.62.

If that isn't complicated enough, the session layer has complex rules to determine when SPDUs must, may, or may not be mapped directly to TSDUs. The X.225 specifications define three categories of SPDUs and a set of tables stating how they can be concatenated. Category zero SPDUs consist of the *give*

**(a) SPDUs have a common top-level format.**
In the simplest form, the parameters are encoded as a set of type-length-value entries.

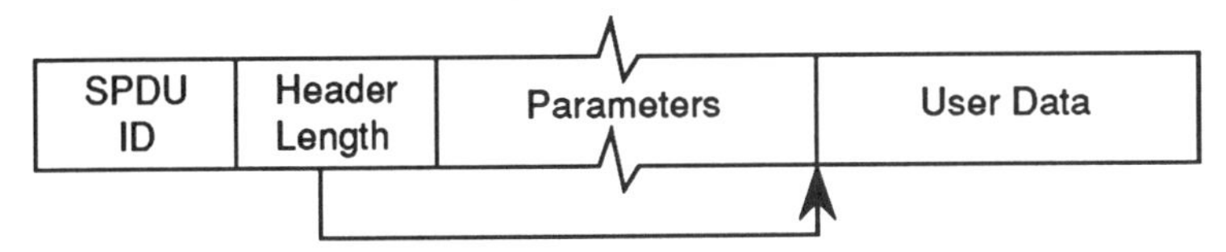


**(b) However, due to the variety of inputs (CCITT, ECMA, ISO, etc.), the session layer PDU formats have many ways of expressing the parameter list.**

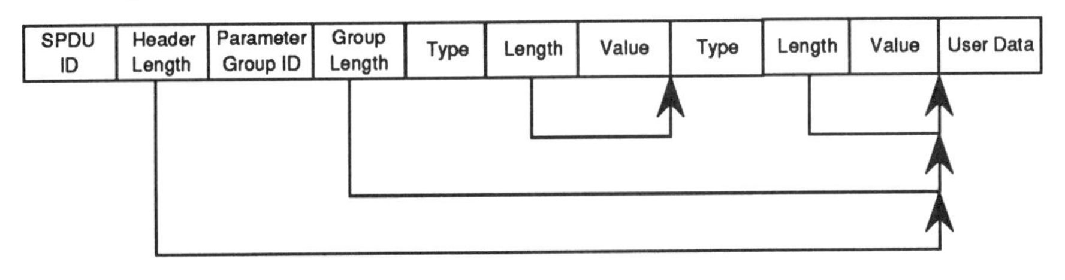


*Illustration courtesy of Learning Group International*

**FIGURE 4-6** Session PDU formats.

and *please* tokens. These SPDUs may be mapped one-to-one to TSDUs, or a single category zero SPDU may be concatenated with one or more category 2 SPDUs.

Category 1 SPDUs include a much larger set such as connect, disconnect, abort, expedited data, and typed data. Category 1 SPDUs must always be mapped one-to-one to TSDUs. Finally, category 2 SPDUs are never mapped one-to-one to TSDUs and must be concatenated with a single category zero SPDU and one or more category 2 SPDUs. These are concatenated in approximately two dozen defined sequences without any logical explanation of why only these sequences are allowed. One must play by the rules and not wonder why the rules are those stated.

As a further example of the encoding approach, the connection request has an *SPDU identifier* (SI). This is followed by the encoded values of the parameters. The connection identifier is a parameter made up of three pieces: the calling SS-user reference, the common reference, and additional reference information. Each of these three components has a type-length-value encoding within the group that is associated with the connection identifier.

The connection request also includes the determination of the tokens to be used and their initial positions. These are encoded as a single octet, with each of the four possible tokens being represented by a two-bit field containing either 00 (initiator's side), 01 (responder's side), 10 (responder's choice), or 11 (reserved). Tokens are relevant only if the related functional units are negotiated.

The functional units are encoded in a similar fashion, except that only a single bit is required for each. A two-octet field is used. Bit one corresponds to the half-duplex functional unit. To use bit one, set this bit to one; otherwise set it to zero. Bit two corresponds to the duplex functional unit. Pick one or the other. Bit three is the expedited data functional unit, which is proposed by setting the bit to a one or not proposed by setting the bit to zero. The same goes for minor and major synchronize (bits four and five), and so on through bit 11 that represents typed data. Bits 12 through 16 are reserved. The basic ideas of the session layer are straightforward, but the overall implementation can be overwhelming.

Some authors have described the session layer as *thin* with regard to its apparently limited and straightforward set of mechanisms. But its state tables and concatenation rules more than make up for its apparent simplicity. It can become a complex layer within the OSI protocols. On the other hand, many implementers do not provide all this capability anyway. The evolution of networking will sort this one out.

# THE PRESENTATION LAYER

Like the session layer, the presentation layer is primarily an invention of OSI. Presentation-like functions appear in earlier file transfer and remote login protocols, but without benefit of a separate layer.

The presentation layer is somewhat late in coming into place, and as a consequence, early OSI implementations (such as MAP/TOP) had a *null* implementation at this layer. The delay is partly due to a false start in development of this layer. Its very name reflects this false start. The original concept was *presentation of information* to the consumer (e.g., user at a terminal or a computer program). To make a screen of information *presentable* to the user requires conversion into the proper character set. The line lengths must be compatible, and the end of line conventions must be mapped to see the results. These same concepts applied to making data presentable to a computer program.

Then it was agreed that these terminal and program-specific mappings were the concerns of the application layer, e.g., as a part of the *virtual terminal* and *file transfer* protocols. This left the presentation layer concerned primarily with *data representation*. Examples of data representation differences include the internal representations of data within computers such as ones versus twos, complement integers, differing floating-point number representations, and byte ordering. These representation differences do indeed span across the range of application needs and provide a generic need for this layer.

Given that different computer systems have different internal representations of data, how can information be meaningfully transmitted between them without a loss of the intent? Some syntax is required to transfer the information while preserving its semantic content.

With the exception of the special case in which the two end systems have identical internal data representations, some transformations are clearly required. There are three possibilities for where and how these transformations could be done. First, the initiating end system could perform the transformations to match the internal representations of the other end system. Second, the opposite could be done. The associated system could perform the transformations. Neither of these approaches is satisfactory because large numbers of translations would be required — on the order of n-squared, where n is the number of end system types. A more satisfactory approach is to perform translations at each end to and from an intermediate form. This is not a new revelation. Terminals from different vendors have connected to computers of different vendors by this basic means for over two decades. The new revelation brought about by OSI was the generality with which this intermediate representation could be managed. In particular, the generalization was from one of extending from terminal characteristics to general data structures, including those of complex protocol data units such as those used by the application layer protocols.

## Abstract Syntax Notation and Transfer Syntax Negotiation

The new approach to describing application layer PDUs (APDUs) is by a technique similar to that of defining primitive data types, and subsequently complex data structures, in a programming language such as Pascal, C, or Ada. In OSI the data representation is in terms of *abstract syntax notation.one* (ASN.1), which is a notation for defining PDU structures. A PDU structure is an *abstract syntax* (AS). As its name implies, ASN.1 is the first of several possible notations for defining an abstract syntax.

Each APDU is defined as an abstract syntax. Using a notation that PDU(n) is defined by AS(n), for n = 1, 2, etc., the originating application layer protocol will notify its presentation layer of the set of AS(j), AS(k), etc. that it expects to use on an application layer association. Its presentation layer entity already knows about these ASs, as should the corresponding end system with which it intends to communicate. It is now up to the presentation layer to negotiate a *transfer syntax* (TS) that both end systems can use.

This negotiation will be in the following form: When the originator of the application layer association requests a set of ASs, the presentation layer determines the set of possible transfer syntaxes that could be used to provide encoding. For example, the originator's presentation layer connection request might include the following possible transfer syntaxes for each abstract syntax, i.e., for each PDU type.

PDU_type(1) = AS(1) with TS(a), TS(b), or TS(c)
PDU_type(2) = AS(2) with TS(a), or TS(d)
PDU_type(3) = AS(3) with TS(b), TS(d), or TS(e)

The associated end system might respond with the following negotiated values.

PDU_type(1) = AS(1) using TS(a)
PDU_type(2) = AS(2) using TS(d)
PDU_type(3) = AS(3) using TS(d)

Each AS(n) using TS(x) pair is called a presentation layer context. The combination of all such contexts is called a *defined context set* (i.e., the set of pairs that can be used). In the example, a single transfer syntax may be used for more than one abstract syntax. Also, it is possible that no common transfer syntax may be mutually acceptable. In this latter case, the association will not be able to interoperate. Assume that an acceptable defined context set is established. Unlike the negotiations at other layers, the presentation layer may continue to add to or delete contexts at any time. This is necessary at the presentation layer because it must be able to support a changing set of needs by the application layer.

Like negotiations at other layers, a default context exists if no negotiated defined context set exists.

## Sending Data Across the Association

After establishment of the association and its related connections of an end-to-end communication, the application programs can pass information units to each other. The application layer passes the identifier of the AS (APDU type) for each information unit that it sends to the presentation layer. The information unit becomes a presentation service data unit (PSDU), which is encoded in the local system's representation. It in turn may be sent as one or more presentation protocol data units, each of which will convey the presentation context (AS:TS pair) of the PSDU, of which it is a part.

## Services and Protocols of the Presentation Layer

There are two general categories of services that the presentation layer provides: pass-through services from the session layer and context management. These are defined in the following ISO (International Standards Organization) and CCITT documents.

| | | |
|---|---|---|
| Service Definition | ISO 8822 | CCITT X.216 |
| Protocol Specification | ISO 8823 | CCITT X.226 |

The presentation service primitives of ISO 8822 and CCITT X.216 are composed of a few new capabilities for handling the data structures of the application PDUs and the session layer services that are passed on without any value added to the application layer. While small in number, the presentation layer's own unique primitives provide a significant benefit to establishing OSI as a viable approach to multivendor internetworking.

The presentation service primitives are listed in ISO 8822 and CCITT X.216 in a manner shown below. They include the session layer pass-through services, as well as the added presentation layer services, as described in Table 4-7.

**TABLE 4-7** P-CONNECT primitive.

| Service Primitive | Parameters |
|---|---|
| P-CONNECT request and indication | Calling-presentation-address<br>Called-presentation-address<br>Presentation context definition list<br>Pres context def result list (indic only)<br>Default context name<br>Quality of service<br>Presentation requirements<br>Mode<br>Session requirements<br>Initial sync point S/N<br>Initial assignment of tokens<br>Session connection identifier<br>User data |
| P-CONNECT response and confirmation | Responding-presentation-address<br>Presentation context def result list<br>Default context result<br>Quality of service<br>Presentation requirements<br>Session requirements<br>Initial sync point S/N<br>Initial assignment of tokens<br>Session connection identifier<br>Result<br>User data |

These connection request and response parameters can be compared with those discussed for the session layer, and the similarities are apparent. As at the session layer, the request and response parameters can be considered in terms of mandatory, conditional, or user optional. See Table 4-8.

As indicated before, this list is similar in many ways to that of the session layer and includes many of the pass-through session services. The session connection identifier is one such example. There is no corresponding presentation connection identifier. However, there are presentation calling, called, and responding addresses in the connection establishment phase, just as there were session addresses. The *calling* and *called* presentation addresses are simply the presentation-selector values and the session-address values put together.

**TABLE 4-8** Request and response parameters.

| Parameter | Request | Response |
|---|---|---|
| Calling presentation address | Mandatory | Not carried |
| Called presentation address | Mandatory | Not carried |
| Responding presentation address | Not carried | Mandatory |
| Presentation context definition list | User option | Not carried |
| Pres context definition result list | Not carried | Conditional |
| Default context name | User option | Not carried |
| Default context result | Not carried | Conditional |
| Mode | Mandatory | Not carried |
| Presentation requirements | User option | User option |
| Session requirements | S-Mandatory | S-Mandatory |
| Quality of service | S-Mandatory | S-Mandatory |
| Initial sync point S/N | S-Conditional | S-Conditional |
| Initial assignment of tokens | S-Conditional | S-Conditional |
| Session connection ID | S-User option | S-User option |
| User data | User option | User option |
| Result | Not carried | Mandatory |

The result, like that of the session layer, has one of three possible outcomes: accepted, rejected by the presentation service user, or rejected by the presentation service provider. The quality of service includes residual error rate, delay, throughput, priority, and security; it is a direct pass-through of the session layer quality of service.

The parameter named *presentation context definition list* is used when the presentation user wishes to place one or more presentation contexts in the defined context set. Each entry consists of a presentation context identification and an abstract syntax name. The *presentation context definition result list* that is returned in the P-CONNECT response indicates the acceptance or rejection (by user or provider) for each of the presentation context definitions proposed in the P-CONNECT request.

The *default context name* and the *default context result* exchanges in the P-CONNECT request and response allow the presentation user to explicitly identify the abstract syntax supported by the default context. This is unusual because one normally expects the *default* values to be fixed, rather than user defined. If it is not included in the P-CONNECT service primitive, the default is a predefined context based on a prior (administrative) agreement.

The presentation layer has a service primitive called *mode* that is unlike anything described up to this point. The mode refers to a form of backwards compatibility with the 1984 CCITT recommendations for the X.410 reliable transfer service. If the mode is set, then the X.410-1984 mode is selected, and the P-CONNECT request service primitive cannot contain the presentation context definition list, default context name, or presentation requirements.

The presentation and session requirements are the functional units of the respective layers that are desired. The initial synchronization point serial number and token assignment are direct pass-throughs of the session layer services.

The presentation service user data are optional, but the layer must have presentation data values from presentation contexts proposed in the presentation context definition list parameter or in the default context.

Another presentation layer service primitive that is specific to this layer (as opposed to a pass-through service) is the P-ALTER-CONTEXT service. It is a confirmed service, allowing the presentation user to negotiate a modification to the defined context set at any time. This is the only example of a negotiation that can be performed at a time other than the connection opening. This service is associated with the context management functional unit of the presentation layer. The primitives as parameters are shown in Table 4-9.

**TABLE 4-9** P-ALTER-CONTEXT primitive.

| Service Primitive | Parameters |
|---|---|
| P-ALTER-CONTEXT request and indication | Presentation context addition list<br>Presentation context deletion list<br>User data<br>Presentation context addition result list (indication only) |
| P-ALTER-CONTEXT response and confirmation | Presentation context addition result list<br>Presentation context deletion result list<br>User data |

These parameters are much like those of the P-CONNECT request and response. The service is used to place one or more presentation contexts in the defined context set. Each entry consists of a *presentation context identification* and an *abstract syntax name*. Because context identifiers must be unique numbers and because they can be assigned by either end system, the connection initiator always uses odd numbers, and the other side uses even numbers.

The presentation context addition (and deletion) result list that is returned in the P-ALTER-CONTEXT response indicates the acceptance or rejection (by user or provider) for each of the presentation context definitions proposed in the P-ALTER-CONTEXT request. The absence of the result list parameter is considered to be acceptance of the proposed changes.

The parameters of the P-ALTER-CONTEXT service are related to the associated request and response primitives in a straightforward way. They are summarized in Table 4-10 for consistency with the other descriptions of service primitives.

**TABLE 4-10** Request and response parameters.

| Parameter | Request | Response |
|---|---|---|
| Presentation context addition list | User option | Not carried |
| Presentation context deletion list | User option | Not carried |
| Presentation context addition result list | Not carried | User option |
| Presentation context del'n result list | Not carried | User option |
| User data | User option | User option |

All other presentation layer services, including the connection release, abort, data transmissions of all types, token handling, synchronization, exception, and activity management, are identical to those of the session layer and are considered pass-through services.

The presentation layer protocols are grouped into useful units called functional units, just as those of the session layer were defined in terms of units by this same name. The name *functional unit* is common to all the upper layer protocols.

The functional units of the presentation layer include the kernel, which is always required and supports the establishment of a presentation connection, the transfer of data, and the release of the presentation connection. Another functional unit is called the *context management* functional unit. It is responsible for the addition and deletion of contexts from the defined context set. The only other presentation-specific functional unit is the *context restoration* functional unit that restores the proper context for recovery purposes such as the session layer resynchronize service.

The presentation layer protocol expands on the information available at the service interface. For example, in addition to the context definition parameters (*presentation context identifier* and *abstract syntax name*), the presentation protocol includes *transfer syntax*. In addition to the *abstract syntax name* for the default context, the presentation protocol includes *transfer syntax name*. When the P-CONNECT protocol exchange is initiated with a P-CONNECT request, the initiator includes a list of the names of the transfer syntaxes that the originator is capable of supporting. This allows the two ends to select the best mutually implemented transfer syntax for a given situation. If the request cannot be supported by the presentation layer protocol implementations at one or the other end system, the reason shall be returned as one of the following:

1. Reason not specified.
2. Abstract syntax not supported.
3. Proposed transfer syntax not supported.
4. Local limit on defined context set exceeded.

The protocol also supports a version number selection process. The initiating end system lists all versions of the presentation protocol that it can support in the P-CONNECT protocol exchange. The 1988 CCITT X.226 presentation protocol is version number 1.

The PDUs of the presentation layer are defined in terms of ASN.1. None of the box pictures of other protocol layers that show the various fields of the protocol headers (i.e., the protocol control information) are present. Instead, the definitions are of the form shown for the *connect presentation PDU*. This example is adapted from the 1988 CCITT X.226 recommendation.

```
CP-type ::= SET
{   [0] IMPLICIT Mode-selector
    [1] IMPLICIT SET
         COMPONENTS of Reliable-Transfer-APDUs.RTORQapdu }
              — Shall be used for X.410 mode only
    [2] IMPLICIT SEQUENCE
    [0] IMPLICIT Protocol-version
    [1] IMPLICIT Calling-presentation-selector
    [2] IMPLICIT Called-presentation-selector
    [4] IMPLICIT Presentation-context-definition-list
    [6] IMPLICIT Default-context-name
    [8] IMPLICIT Presentation-requirements
    [9] IMPLICIT User-session-requirements
    User-data
}
```

The *CP-type* is the *connect presentation* (P-CONNECT) protocol packet. It includes the X.410 backwards compatible option and the fields expected based upon the earlier discussion of the parameters to be negotiated. Recommendation X.216 gives no indication as to why the numbers of the sequence items are not consecutive integers. As indicated, the presentation layer relies heavily on the abstract syntax and transfer syntax documentation, which are included here.

| | | | |
|---|---|---|---|
| ASN.1 | ISO 8824 | CCITT X.208 \ | X.409 |
| Encoding Rules | ISO 8825 | CCITT X.209 / | |

The ISO and CCITT versions evolved along slightly different lines. ISO developed separate specifications for the two, while CCITT defined both in a single document, X.409, which is a part of X.400 electronic messaging. CCITT later developed two separate documents as well, as indicated.

## Abstract Syntax Notation.One

ASN.1 is a *notation* for describing abstract syntaxes where an AS is an *application layer PDU*. The APDU is a *syntax* because it has a format and a structure that describe it. It is an *abstract* description because it is independent of any particular implementation.

The description of an APDU in ASN.1 is similar to the definition of a data structure in a modern programming language. Primitives such as integers and Boolean operations are defined. From these primitives, more complex structures such as arrays (sequences) can be developed. Even more complex structures can be developed with mixed types such as integers and Boolean operations. The primitive types can be identified by a *tag* that consists of a class and an identifier. The class is one of the four types indicated below, with their respective encodings.

**00 = Universal Class** — Types defined within ASN.1
**01 = Application Class** — Types defined in OSI standards
**10 = Context-Specific Class** — The context defines the type
**11 = Private Class** — Types for use by a vendor

The concern will primarily be with the *universal class*. A brief list of some of its defined types is shown below.

Identifier 1: BOOLEAN
2: INTEGER
3: BITSTRING
4: OCTETSTRING
6: OBJECT IDENTIFIER
9: REAL
10: ENUMERATED
18: NumericString
19: PrintableString
22: IA5String (International Alphabet)
23: UTCTime
25: GraphicString
28: CharacterString

All of these types are primitives, as well as universal in their definition. Note that ASN.1 is case-sensitive. All of the above type names, like all other types, begin with a capital letter. Some types are expressed in all capital letters. These are built-in types.

In addition to the above listed primitive types, primitives can be *constructors* of any of the four classes mentioned earlier. The universal class constructors include the following identifiers.

Identifier 16: SEQUENCE and SEQUENCE OF
17: SET and SET OF

The constructor type SEQUENCE allows one to define an ordered list of data elements of arbitrary types. SEQUENCE OF is similar except that all the elements must be of the same type.

The constructor type SET differs from SEQUENCE in that a set does not require ordering. SET OF is similar but requires that all the data elements in the set be of the same type.

Another form of constructor that is primitive but does not have a tag assigned to it is CHOICE. It allows a selection from a list of different candidates of possibly differing types. The type of the resulting field depends on the choice that is made, which is why it does not have a specific type assigned to it.

The above primitives are of two forms: (1) the elements expected to be primitives, such as integers, and (2) constructors, from which more complex structures can be built. These more complex structures are called *constructed types* and include a variety of data structures such as records and protocol headers.

An example of ASN.1 helps understand what is going on. Consider a personnel record of the following form that has been adapted from CCITT X.208.

```
Name:
Job title:
Employee number:
DateOfHire
Name of spouse:
Number of children:

Child information
Name:
Date of birth:
.
.
.
Child information
Name:
Date of birth:
```

The ASN.1 description of this record structure follows. At this point, the structure is defined, but no content has been provided.

```
PersonnelRecord ::= [APPLICATION 0] IMPLICIT SET
{                         Name,
title                     [0] VisibleString,
number                    Employee number,
dateOfHire                [1] Date
nameOfSpouse              [2] Name
children                  [3] IMPLICIT SEQUENCE OF
                          ChildInformation }

ChildInformation ::= SET
      {                   Name,
      dateOfBirth         [0] Date}

Name ::= [APPLICATION 1] IMPLICIT SEQUENCE
{givenName                VisibleString,
 initial                  VisibleString,
 familyName               VisibleString}

EmployeeNumber ::= [APPLICATION 2] IMPLICIT INTEGER

Date ::= [APPLICATION 3] IMPLICIT VisibleString – YYYYMMDD
```

ASN.1 is a case-sensitive language. Type names such as *EmployeeNumber* begin with an upper case letter, as do module names. The second upper case letter (rather than spaces or other separators) is for readability. All other identifiers such as *familyName* begin with a lower case character, with the same concern for using capital letters rather than separators. Reserved words such as SET are entirely in upper case. These are considerably simplified examples, but they indicate the nature of the notation in defining data structures.

Current OSI developments dictate that all APDUs be defined using ASN.1. An application request to the presentation layer for a connection might be of the following form that has been taken from the context of X.400 electronic messaging. (The line numbers are used only for the sake of this description.)

```
 1.   PConnect ::= SET{
 2.   [0] IMPLICIT DataTransferSyntax,
 3.   [1] IMPLICIT pUserData SET{
 4.       checkpointSize [0] IMPLICIT INTEGER DEFAULT 0,
 5.       windowSize [1] IMPLICIT INTEGER DEFAULT 3,
 6.       dialogueMode [2] IMPLICIT INTEGER {monologue(0),
 7.       twa(1)} DEFAULT monologue,
 8.       [3] ConnectionData,
 9.       application protocol [4] IMPLICIT INTEGER
10.       {p1(1), p3(3)} DEFAULT p1}}
```

In line 1, the P-CONNECT is a SET, meaning that the order is not important and not all fields are necessarily of the same type. In line 2, the data transfer syntax is defined. On lines 3 through 7 the fields to be defined (and negotiated) for checkpointing, the synchronization window size, and the dialogue mode can be found. The defaults in each of these cases are no checkpointing, window of size 3, and the monologue mode. These options will be described in greater detail in Chapter 5, but essentially this means that the transfer will not require checkpoint/recovery. (The usual number would be every N data units, so the default of zero means that there is to be none.) Up to three minor sync points can be outstanding before having to wait, and only one side will be sending (i.e., a monologue). The final items are that there may be some data sent with the connection establishment and that the protocol may be either P1 or P3 as defined in X.400. The default is P1.

### *Transfer Syntax Encoding*

During the negotiation exchange at the presentation layer, a specific (concrete) transfer syntax is selected for each abstract syntax that is to be used. The key that relates a transfer syntax to an abstract syntax is the tag field, i.e., the class and identifier field. For example, an abstract syntax may have a tag of universal 2, which means INTEGER. This same universal 2 can be found in the transfer syntax as well, where it will also mean integer. However, in the transfer syntax, it will have a specific encoding, which it did not have in the abstract form.

The transfer syntax is expressed in type-length-value form. Note that the *type* is the *tag* that consists of the class and the identifier. In the INTEGER example, the class is universal and primitive, while the identifier is 2. This fits within the one-byte format shown in Figure 4-7. If an identifier value in excess of 30 is required, the extended format of Figure 4-8 is used. The length field is also extendible, providing an open-ended, network-wide mechanism for describing the data being transmitted.

## THE APPLICATION LAYER: OVERVIEW AND ARCHITECTURE

In many earlier protocol suites, the application protocols sat directly on top of the transport protocol. Such application protocols provided their own equiva-

- **Type-length-value encoding.**

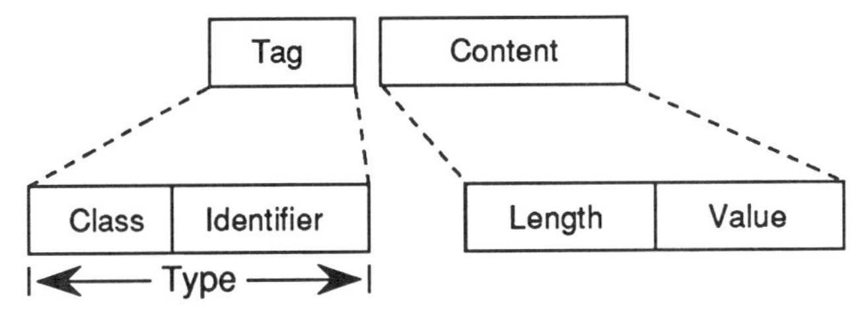


- **Example:**
  Class — Universal and Primitive.
  Identifier — 2.
  The content is then the length
  and value of the integer.

  } Represents an integer

*Illustration courtesy of Learning Group International*

**FIGURE 4-7** An example of encoded data.

lents of the session and presentation layer functionality, but only to the extent that they needed such services. Each application protocol developed its own set of mechanisms or borrowed part of a related protocol.

The OSI approach is to develop a set of common presentation and session layer services upon which the application layer can build. This approach is further extended to include commonly used application service elements as additional building blocks for application protocols.

The application layer has both similarities and differences with the presentation and session layers. The common application service elements are somewhat like functional units at these other layers, although they are configured in rather than negotiated. However, they are both optional from an implementation point of view. Not every system needs support for all possible applications.

The application layer protocols are large in number, functionality, and size. The layer is quite unique in this regard. However, it does reflect the same spirit of *one size fits all* that can be found in many OSI layers. If anybody needs a given service, it is available for all.

Even when OSI protocols have been developed from existing non-OSI protocols as a starting point, the end result is a much richer set of capabilities.

- **The tag format is either**
  For identifiers that can be represented by 5 bits.

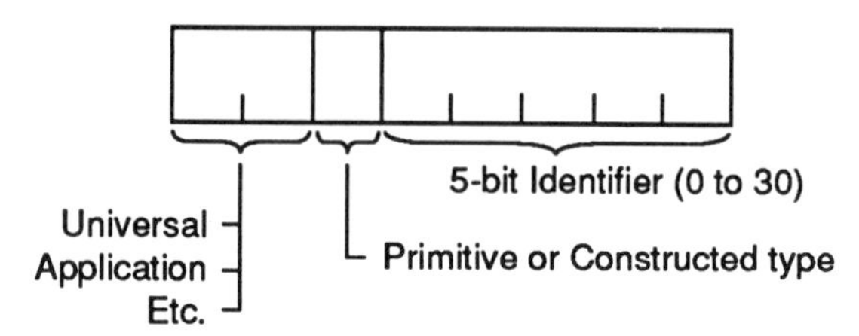


Or for larger identifiers (≥31).

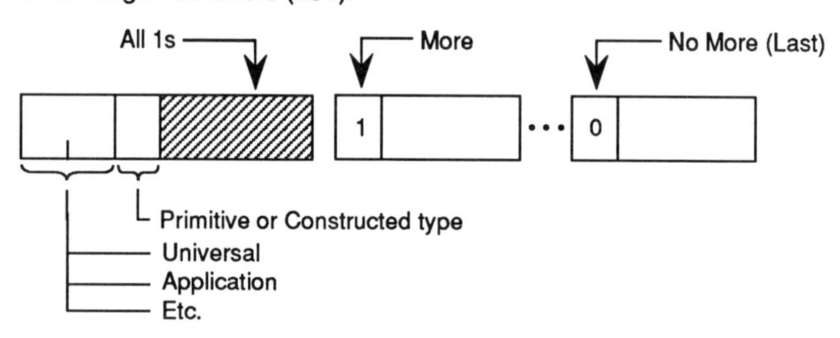


- **The length field can be extended in a similar manner.**

*Illustration courtesy of Learning Group International*

**FIGURE 4-8** The tag format.

While this richness can be quite attractive, remember that it is RAM memory and CPU cycles that are paying for it. This richness and extra complexity show up in the documentation, which includes the usual service definition and protocol specification but frequently also includes other documents that describe the operations of the application. The resulting documentation for a single application may exceed 400 pages in total size. The computer implementations are correspondingly large and processing intensive. Unlike some industry standard protocols of today, the word *simple* will not be found in the title of any OSI application protocol.

The architecture of the application layer differs considerably from that of layers six and below. Each of these lower layers is represented by one box in the typical layered protocol diagrams (such as that of Figure 4-9 which was adapted from the MAP/TOP 3.0 protocol suite). Each box provides a set of services, some of which can be negotiated at the time a connection is established. At the presentation and session layers, these negotiated services are in the form of functional units. At the transport and network layers, the negotiations are in terms of mechanisms (such as error checks to be performed) and parameters (such as the maximum packet size). Only a few actual services are negotiable at the transport and network layers, e.g., whether expedited data are needed and available.

In contrast, the application layer is pictured as having many boxes, with each providing a distinctly different form of application support with its own set of functional units and negotiations. Each application layer box will typically have a complexity of at least that of the presentation or session layer

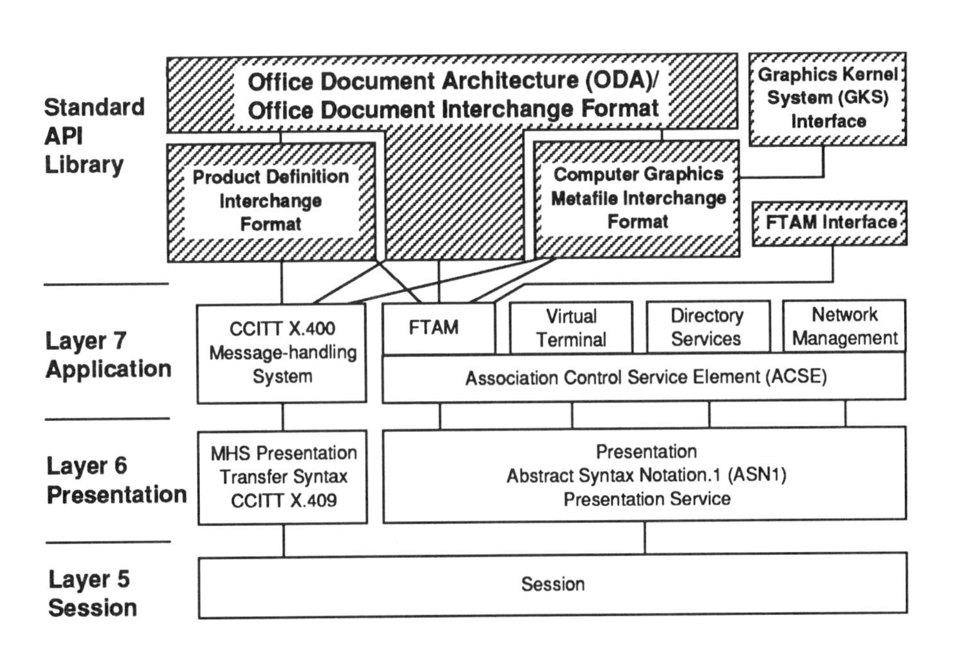


*Illustration courtesy of Learning Group International*

**FIGURE 4-9** MAP/TOP version 3.0.

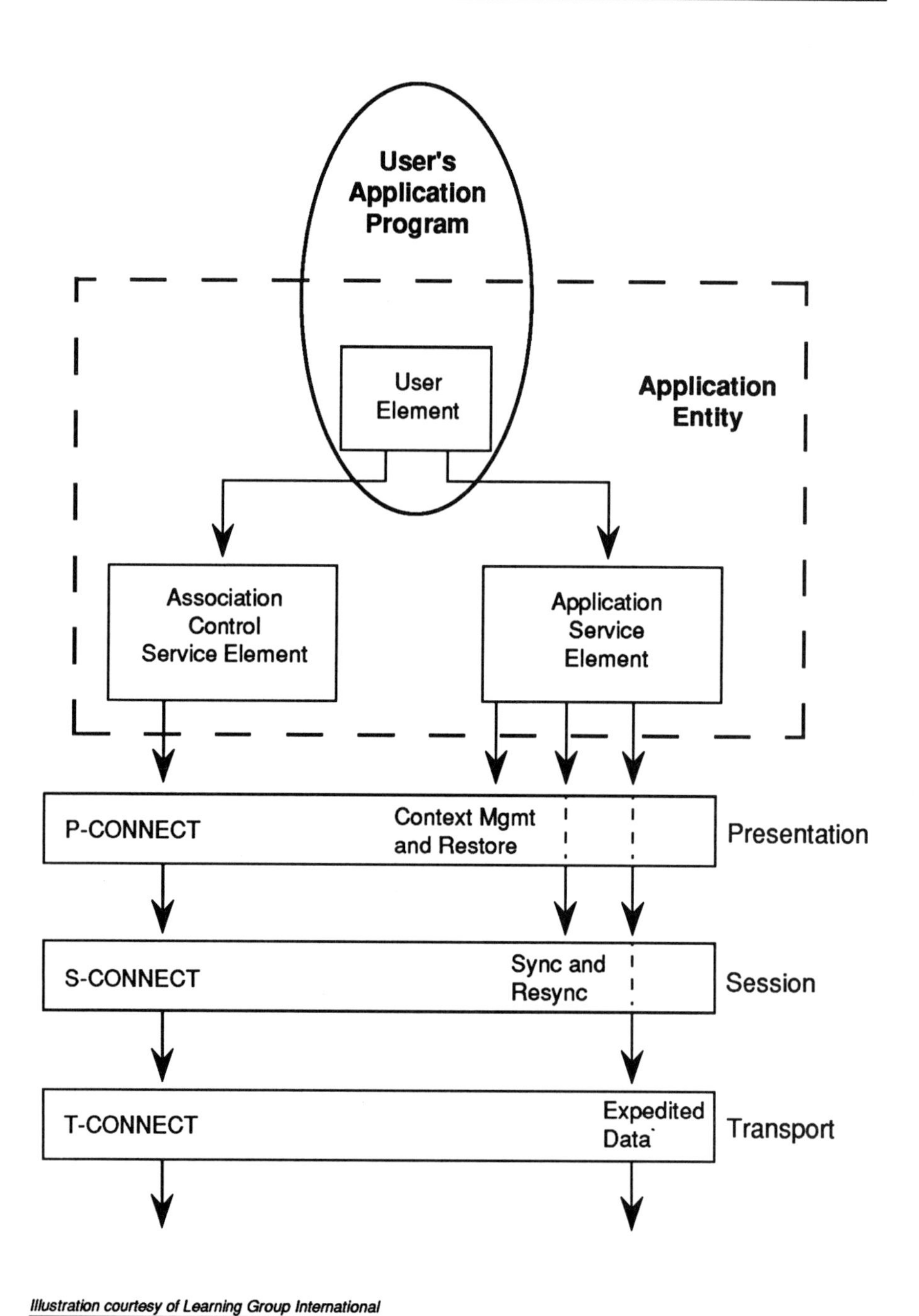


*Illustration courtesy of Learning Group International*

**FIGURE 4-10** The user element and application service elements make up the application entity.

boxes. Some will have a much greater complexity, while a few will have less. The application layer is the home of much networking software. This layer represents the end product of all the efforts of the lower layers.

The application layer provides support to user application programs that require networking capabilities. This support is in terms of both application-specific protocols (such as how to transfer files and how to perform transactions across a network) and utility routines that serve a number of needs (such as establishing application layer connections or *associations*). These application routines are called *application service elements* or ASEs. The ASEs are the building blocks of the application layer. They *hide* much of the detail and complexity of layers six and below from the user's application program. As shown in Figure 4-10, the user's program and the *user element* call upon two different service elements. One is used to perform the connection establishment (with all the required presentation, session, etc., which are options being negotiated). The second is a hypothetical ASE that uses the context management and context restoration services of the presentation layer, the synchronization and resynchronization services of the session layer, and the expedited data service of the transport layer.

These services are propagated upward to the application layer interface without further value added. The OSI rules say that an application cannot reach down to some lower layer (beyond the presentation layer) to obtain a service, but the rules do not require that each layer further enhance a given service. Figure 4-10 shows the actual layers where the services are being provided. The ASE shields the user's application from this detail.

The set of commonly used service elements were at one time grouped together into a *common application service element* (CASE) that was considered to be a sublayer of the application layer. The idea of making this a sublayer has changed, and CASE itself has been replaced by a set of service elements, each of which may be used in a given application. They provide a set of reusable modules that provide services needed by a number of applications. The existing general purpose service elements are included below.

1. **Association Control Service Element** (ACSE)
2. **Reliable Transfer Service Element** (RTSE)
3. **Remote Operations Service Element** (ROSE)
4. **Commitment, Concurrency, and Recovery** (CCR)

These service elements are discussed in detail in the next chapter, and therefore are only summarized here. ACSE provides the basic capabilities to establish and later release associations (application layer connections). RTSE provides reliable transfers of user data, where *reliable* refers to recovery from system or communication crashes. ROSE provides a form of remote procedure call, but one in which the transfers in both directions may be quite large. Finally, CCR provides a set of mechanisms to ensure that distributed operations are performed accurately, completely, and exactly once.

The relationship between the various service elements and an application process is shown in Figure 4-11. As mentioned previously, the glue that ties everything together is the user element (UE) that resides in the overlap region between the application process (which is outside of the OSI concern) and the OSI application entity. Figure 4-11 shows a generic set of application service elements: ASE a, b, and c, where a, b, and c could be any of several ASEs that can be made available to the user's application program. A more specific example (see Figure 4-12) includes the ROSE, RTSE, and ACSE service elements. In this hypothetical example, the application entity has been configured to allow the user element to access the services of both ROSE and

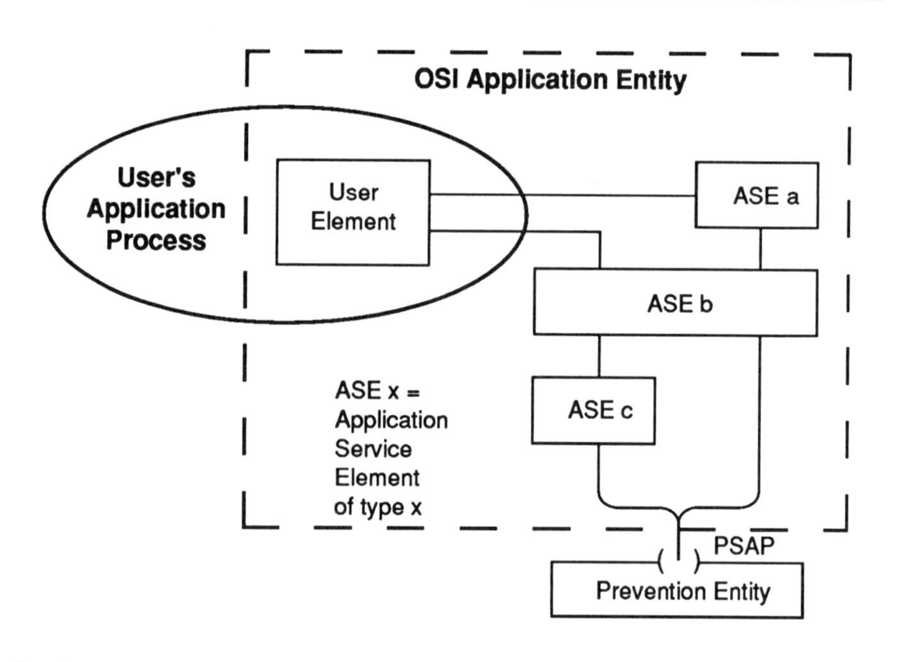


*Illustration courtesy of Learning Group International*

**FIGURE 4-11** The user element provides the *glue* to connect the user's application process and the OSI application entity.

RTSE. ROSE might be used for transaction-related operations (of any size), while the RTSE might be used for large transfers of data in a single direction. The RTSE sits between the user element and the ACSE, which establishes and releases the association. One of the rules involved in establishing the application entity is that if RTSE is included, only the RTSE can control the ACSE.

The application entity has a name or *title*. Information about a particular application entity can be obtained from the directory services using the title as a key. Implicit in the particular entity is the subset of the service elements that are used and their relationships.

Every application entity will use the ACSE because all applications use connection-oriented services. An application entity (and its application association) is related one-to-one to a presentation connection. This connection provides the pipe or conduit over which communications are established, with the syntax, dialogue control, delivery integrity, and other properties associated with OSI connections. The application layer association builds on this connection and provides a known semantics for the data exchange. The combina-

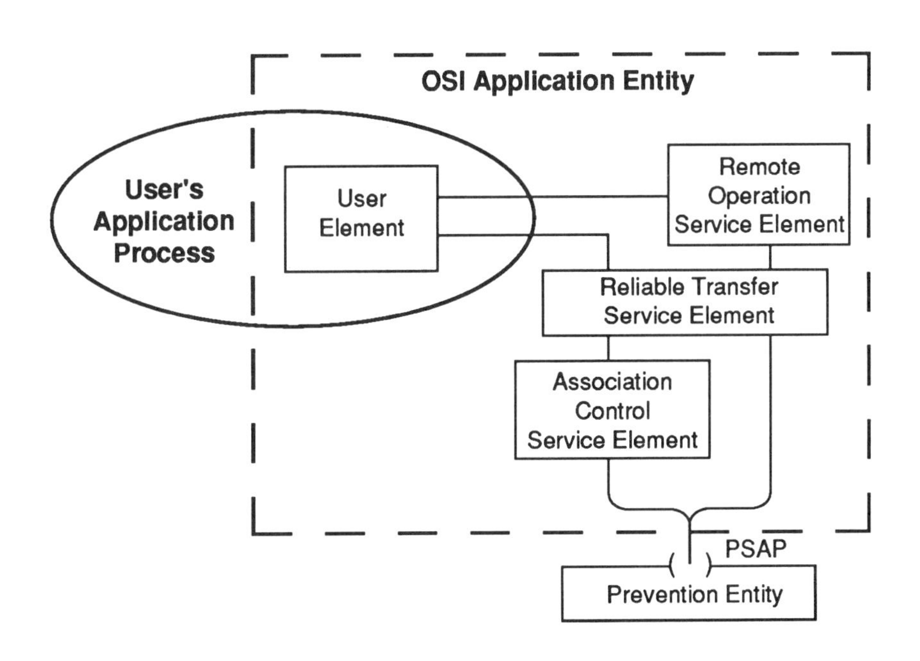


*Illustration courtesy of Learning Group International*

**FIGURE 4-12** A specific example of ASEs.

tion of this defined semantics and the agreed upon set of service elements is called an *application context.* It must be the same at both ends of a connection, and this is established when the association is made. A rudimentary form of negotiation is involved here. Although this is expected, in most implementations the proposal will be either completely accepted or entirely rejected.

All communications from the various service elements are conveyed across a common PSAP as shown in Figure 4-12. Multiplexing and demultiplexing is by means of differing presentation contexts.

# 5

# BASIC BUILDING BLOCKS AT THE APPLICATION LAYER

As indicated in the introduction to chapter 4, the application layer includes of a set of components called *service elements*. Some of these service elements are general utilities across a number of applications. These are the subject of this chapter. Utility service elements may or may not be used in a given application. They provide a set of reusable modules that provide services needed by a number of applications. The existing general purpose service elements include the following:

1. Association Control Service Element (ACSE).
2. Reliable Transfer Service Element (RTSE).
3. Remote Operations Service Element (ROSE).
4. Commitment, Concurrency, and Recovery (CCR).

Every application entity (AE) uses the ACSE because all applications use connection-oriented services. In addition, a user's application program (AP) may use one or more of the other utility application service elements (ASEs).

## ASSOCIATION CONTROL SERVICE ELEMENT

The association control service element provides the capabilities required to establish and release an association. Only the ACSE is allowed to invoke the service primitives to perform these functions. Therefore, it is a necessary part of every current (connection-oriented) application entity. ACSE is specified by the following International Standards Organization (ISO) and Consultative Committee for International Telephone and Telegraph (CCITT) documents.

| | | |
|---|---|---|
| Service definition | ISO 8649 | CCITT X.217 |
| Protocol Specification | ISO 8650 | CCITT X.227 |

The numbering scheme for these two sets of documents follows the familiar approach. The ISO service definition and protocol specification is designated by consecutive integers, while the CCITT versions are of the form X.2xy, where x is 1 for the service definition and 2 for the protocol specification, while y is the Open Systems Interconnection (OSI) layer. Because there are many layer-seven services and protocols, this is the last of the service/protocol recommendations that incorporates this convenient numbering scheme.

## An Overview of ACSE

The most important aspect of the ACSE is the set of parameters that are included with the establishment and release of an application association. We will look at these parameters in two passes. The first pass will focus on the especially important parameters, and the second pass will look at the entire set of parameters. This approach is due to the very large set of parameters involved when the association request must include application layer needs, presentation layer needs, and pass-through services from the session layer.

The particularly important parameters for the application association establishment request are as follows:

1. **Application context name** — The set of application service elements to be used.
2. **Presentation context definition list** — The set of presentation contexts required for communication.

The application context name (ASN.1 object identifier) is needed for a directory services request, as well as for ensuring that the two end systems have the same relationship between the service elements. In addition, the following minor parameters are optional for the *association establishment request:*

1. Calling and called application entity (AE) titles (i.e., identifiers).
2. Calling and called presentation service access points (PSAPs).
3. Session requirements, synchronization serial number, tokens, and session connection identifier.
4. User data (initialization data).

The association request ripples down through the other layers, producing lower layer (presentation and session) connections as required to support the application association. The transport connection may not be established and released on a one-to-one basis with application associations, but the presentation and session layer connections are.

The *association confirmation* contains the response to the association request and includes two principal parameters as indicated below.

1. **Application context name** — Typically the same as that requested, but can be a negotiated variation thereof.
2. **Result** — Acceptance or one of several forms of rejection, of the requested association. Rejection may be either permanent or transient and may be made by either the application or the service provider (i.e., the presentation layer).

The *association release request* provides an orderly release of the association with no loss of user data. It contains a reason code (normal, urgent, or user-defined) and optional user data. The association release confirmation also includes a result parameter and a reason code (normal, not finished, or user-defined). The corresponding presentation and session connections are released when the association is released. If the association establishment calls for the negotiated release service, the release request can be refused by the other party.

In addition, either entity may invoke an *association abort*, but any user data in transit will be lost. The association abort request is carried in presentation and session layer abort requests, which are in turn carried as transport layer expedited data when available.

## A Detailed Discussion of ACSE

The ACSE association service primitives are listed in ISO 8649 and CCITT X.217 in the manner shown below. They include the session layer pass-through services, as well as presentation layer and application layer services. The groupings shown in Table 5-1 separate out name and identifier issues, special concerns such as mode-of-operation and result information, and the carry-over of presentation and session parameters.

**TABLE 5-1** ACSE service primitives.

| Service primitive | Parameters |
|---|---|
| A-ASSOCIATE request and indication | Application context name<br>Calling AP title |

| | |
|---|---|
| | Calling AE qualifier<br>Calling AP invocation-identifier<br>Calling AE invocation-identifier<br>Called AP title<br>Called AE qualifier<br>Called AP invocation-identifier<br>Called AE invocation-identifier |
| | Mode |
| | Calling-presentation-address<br>Called-presentation-address<br>Presentation context definition list<br>Presentation context definition result list (indication only)<br>Default context name<br>Quality of service<br>Presentation requirements<br>Session requirements<br>Initial sync point S/N<br>Initial assignment of tokens<br>Session connection identifier |
| | User data |
| A-ASSOCIATE response and confirmation | Application context name<br>Responding AP title<br>Responding AE qualifier<br>Responding AP invocation-identifier<br>Responding AE invocation-identifier |
| | Result<br>Result source (confirmation only)<br>Diagnostic |
| | Responding-presentation-address<br>Presentation context definition result list<br>Default context result<br>Quality of service<br>Presentation requirements<br>Session requirements<br>Initial sync point S/N<br>Initial assignment of tokens<br>Session connection identifier |
| | User data |

These connection request and response parameters can be compared to those discussed for the presentation and session layers. As at those two layers, the request and response parameters are mandatory, conditional, or user-optional. The resulting list is discussed in four units: (1) new parameters added by the ACSE at the application layer, (2) previous parameters (with a few additions) treated as application layer parameters, (3) presentation layer carry-over parameters, and (4) session layer carry-over parameters. Table 5-2 shows parameters added by the application layer.

**TABLE 5-2** Parameters added by the application layer.

| Parameter | Request | Response |
|---|---|---|
| Application context name | Mandatory | Mandatory |
| Calling AP title | User-optional | Not carried |
| Calling AE qualifier | User-optional | Not carried |
| Calling AP invocation-identifier | User-optional | Not carried |
| Calling AE invocation-identifier | User-optional | Not carried |
| Called AP title | User-optional | Not carried |
| Called AE qualifier | User-optional | Not carried |
| Called AP invocation-identifier | User-optional | Not carried |
| Called AE invocation-identifier | User-optional | Not carried |
| Responding AP title | Not carried | User-optional |
| Responding AE qualifier | Not carried | User-optional |
| Responding AP invocation-identifier | Not carried | User-optional |
| Responding AE invocation-identifier | Not carried | User-optional |

None of the parameters above applies if the selected mode of operation is X.410-1984, which provides backwards compatibility with 1984 X.400 electronic messaging.

The parameters have the following meanings. The *application context name* identifies the application context proposed by the requestor. It can be accepted by the other end of the association by returning the same name as a parameter, or a different application context name may be returned. This latter situation results in an unusual form of negotiation, semantics, and rules that are user-specific (i.e., not standardized). The *calling AP title* identifies the requestor, and the *calling AE qualifier* identifies the particular application entity. The AP and AE *invocation-identifiers* are IDs assigned to this particular association. The same definitions apply for the *called* and *responding* versions of these parameters.

The next grouping of the A-ASSOCIATE parameters (see Table 5-3) includes several that appeared at the presentation or session layers. They are listed in the A-ASSOCIATE parameter list as if they were unique to the application layer.

**TABLE 5-3** A-ASSOCIATE parameters.

| Parameter | Request | Response |
|---|---|---|
| Mode | Mandatory | Not carried |
| Result | Not carried | Mandatory |
| Result source | Not carried | Mandatory |
| Diagnostic | Not carried | User-optional |
| User data | User-optional | User-optional |

The *mode* is the X.410-1984 backwards-compatibility mechanism mentioned previously. The value of the mode would otherwise be set to *normal.* The *result* field content may be provided by either the acceptor end of the association, the ACSE service provider, or the presentation layer service provider. The result values are *accepted, rejected (permanent),* or *rejected (transient).* The result source is one of the three possible sources listed before, i.e., the ACSE service user, the ACSE service provider, or the presentation service provider. If the result value is *accepted,* the source is the ACSE service user. The diagnostic parameter is used to provide additional information when the result is *rejected* (for either permanent or transient reasons.) If the diagnostic comes from the ACSE service provider, the defined codes include *no reason given* and *no common ACSE version.* If the diagnostic comes from the ACSE service user, it can have any of several values that indicate the application context name is not supported or a variety of *not recognized* indications on the calling or called parameter values. The *no reason given* indication is also possible.

The presentation and session layer parameters in Table 5-4 are also included in the A-ASSOCIATE request or response. Because they are identical to those discussed in the earlier sections on the presentation and session layers, they are not discussed here.

**TABLE 5-4** Presentation and session layer parameters.

| Parameter | Request | Response |
|---|---|---|
| Calling presentation address | P-Mandatory | Not carried |
| Called presentation address | P-Mandatory | Not carried |

| | | |
|---|---|---|
| Responding presentation address | Not carried | P-Mandatory |
| Presentation context definition list | P-User-optional | Not carried |
| Presentation context definition result list | Not carried | P-Conditional |
| Default context name | P-User-optional | Not carried |
| Default context result | Not carried | P-Conditional |
| Presentation requirements | P-User-optional | P-User-optional |
| Session requirements | S-Mandatory | S-Mandatory |
| Quality of service | S-Mandatory | S-Mandatory |
| Initial sync point S/N | S-Conditional | S-Conditional |
| Initial assignment of tokens | S-Conditional | S-Conditional |
| Session connection ID | S-User-optional | S-User-optional |

To this point, attention has been with the establishment of the association. A-ASSOCIATE is one of four ACSE service primitives, but it is by far the most complex. The entire set of ACSE service primitives is shown in Table 5-5.

**TABLE 5-5** ACSE service primitives.

| Service | Type | Usage |
|---|---|---|
| A-ASSOCIATE | Confirmed | Establish an association |
| A-RELEASE | Confirmed | Orderly release of association |
| A-ABORT | Non-confirmed | Abrupt user-initiated release |
| A-P-ABORT | Provider-initiated | Abrupt provider-initiated release |

The A-RELEASE service can be initiated by either application entity to cause the use of the association to be completed except when the negotiated release functional unit is selected. In this latter case, the release operation is based on ownership of the appropriate token, and therefore, it can be refused if initiated by the other entity. The parameters associated with the A-RELEASE service are shown in Table 5-6.

**TABLE 5-6** Parameters associated with the A-RELEASE service.

| Parameter | Request | Response |
|---|---|---|
| Result | User-optional | User-optional |
| User data | User-optional | User-optional |
| Result | Not carried | Mandatory |

Neither the *reason* nor the *user-data parameters* are included for the X.410-1984 mode. For normal mode, the reason parameter in the request may be normal, urgent, or user-defined. When used in the response, the reason parameter may be normal, not finished, or user-defined. The user data may be sent with either the request or the response or both. Its meaning depends on the particular application. Finally, the result parameter may take on either of two values: affirmative or negative.

The two forms of the abort service are combined in Table 5-7. In this table, there is no *response* column. It has been replaced by an indication column because in addition to the service user, the service provider can also provide this service.

**TABLE 5-7** Two forms of the abort service.

| Parameter | Request | Indication |
|---|---|---|
| A-ABORT | | |
| Abort source | Not carried | Mandatory |
| User information | User-optional | Conditional |
| A-P-ABORT | | |
| Provider reason | Not applicable | Mandatory |

The ACSE protocols relate directly to the services, with five basic protocol data units being defined. They are

1. A-ASSOCIATE request (AARQ),
2. A-ASSOCIATE response (AARE),
3. A-RELEASE request (RLRQ),
4. A-RELEASE response (RLRE), and
5. A-ABORT (ABRT).

In addition to the expected fields providing the required services, there are also fields in the association request and response conveying the protocol versions that can be supported. The request indicates all versions that can be supported, while the response selects one version from this set. Both the requesting and responding PDUs may also include optional implementation information, with the interpretation not subject to standardization.

# RELIABLE TRANSFER SERVICE ELEMENT

The RTSE is a generalized service that was derived from the 1984 version of CCITT's X.410 delivery mechanism for X.400 electronic messaging. The word *reliable* does not refer to recovering from damaged or lost packets. Rather it means that it has capabilities to recover from lost network connections and end-system crashes. RTSE builds on session layer synchronization services and hides much of their complexity from the other application service elements. These session services are used to ensure that data are safely stored (e.g., on disk) before sync points are confirmed. This provides a basis for checkpoint recovery of data transmission.

## A Summary of RTSE Operation

The flow of data units and minor syncs/confirmations is shown in Figure 5-1. The initial operation is *start activity* (a form of major sync), so the protocol must wait for confirmation. In this example, the start activity major sync has serial number 88 associated with it, as does its confirmation. After the confirmation has been received, the flow of data units and minor syncs may begin as

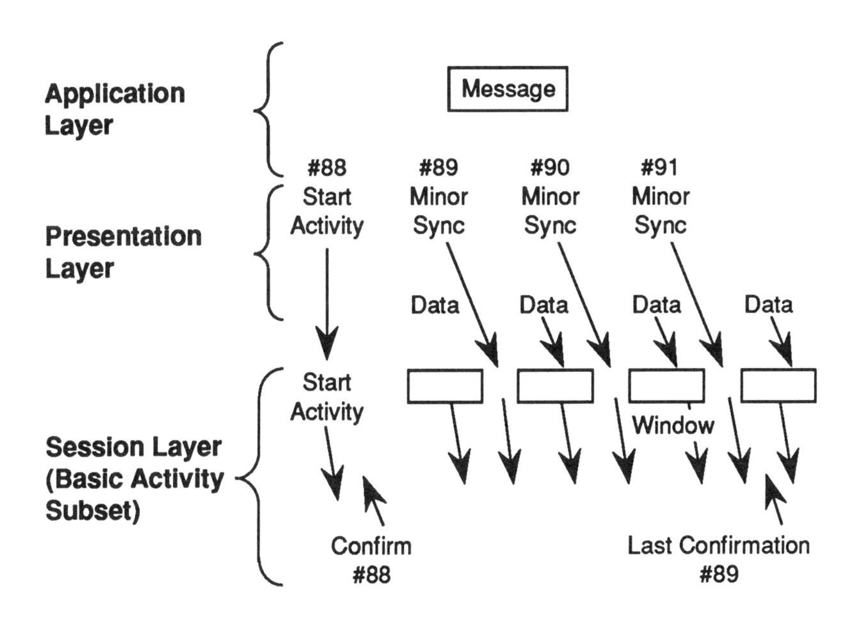


*Illustration courtesy of Learning Group International*

**FIGURE 5-1** The RTSE provides synchronization services to applicants.

long as they are within the window size negotiated when the association was established.

In this example, the window is size three. Minor syncs numbered 89, 90, and 91 are sent, utilizing the entire allocated window size. The figure shows that shortly after this, the confirmation for the first minor sync (i.e., number 89) arrives, allowing the window to slide forward one unit. With the timing as shown, the pipelining that is achieved by the window mechanism is operating in an ideal manner. Just as the right edge of the window is encountered, a confir-mation arrives, thus sliding the window to the right. If the window were much larger, an excessive number of data units would be sent (wasting network utilization) after a crash at the other end system.

When the RTSE is used in an application entity, it has sole responsibility for utilizing the ACSE and the presentation service for the formation of an association. Otherwise, the user element would typically call upon the ACSE to establish an association.

The association request includes the request for certain session layer functional units. For RTSE, these include half-duplex operation, exceptions, minor synchronize, and the activity set. A mandatory parameter in the association request called *initial-turn* determines if the initiator or the responder of the association will initially have the right to send an association protocol data unit. In some protocols, this is called the *first speaker*.

An additional mandatory parameter called *dialogue-mode* determines if (1) only the end system with the initial-turn can send (i.e., a monologue) or (2) if a two-way-alternate dialogue is to be used. In the latter case, turn management provides a token mechanism for control, with the associated *turn please* request for the token and the *turn give* response. Only the end system that currently owns the turn token can release the association. (All tokens involved are assigned to the end system that currently owns the turn. Therefore, the *give control* form of token passing is used.)

There also are optional parameters. One can determine if the mode of operation is to be normal RTSE operation or an X.410 (backwards compatibility) mode. Optional user data may also be sent with the association request.

Once the association has been established, data units can be sent. This flow was shown in Figure 5-1. Each transfer request has an associated minor sync point that is eventually confirmed. Not every minor sync point requires that the sender stop and wait for the confirmation, as is the case for a major sync point. Instead, some number of outstanding minor sync points are allowed; this number is called the *window*. Unlike data flow control, which is concerned with the receiver's ability to handle (i.e., buffer) additional data, the RTSE window is concerned with efficient utilization of the network.

An RTSE transfer is by means of an RT-TRANSFER request, but the rest of the confirmed handshake is quite unusual as shown in Part a of Figure 5-2. The confirmation is sent back by the receiving RTSE, but not by means of an RT-TRANSFER response from the RTSE user. Instead, it is sent back by the RTSE itself. The inherent logic is shown in the magnified view in Part b of the figure. The RTSE service is responsible for safe storage of the received data; therefore it is the transfer component that performs the equivalent of the RT-TRANSFER response.

When all the data have been sent and the minor sync points have all been confirmed, the RTSE issues a *presentation layer activity end request* to release the association and its related presentation and session layer connections.

The RTSE consists of the usual service definition and protocol specification and is defined in the following ISO and CCITT documents.

| | | |
|---|---|---|
| Model and service definition | ISO 9066-1 | CCITT X.218 |
| Protocol specification | ISO 9066-2 | CCITT X.228 |

The ISO document numbering has deviated from the usual convention of using consecutive integers for the service definition and protocol specifications; instead it makes these Parts 1 and 2 of ISO 9066. Perhaps ISO members felt that they were about to run out of numbers. However, this has actually become a fairly common practice, especially with application layer protocols that may have four or more volumes (parts) for a given standard. In addition, the CCITT numbering scheme recognizes the need for multiple services and protocols at layer seven; it simply uses the number eight for this one. So much for the simple numbering plan for these documents.

The RTSE uses the services of the ACSE to establish an association and then provides its reliable delivery to another application layer protocol. This is an example of the modularity and reuse within the application layer.

## A Detailed Description of RTSE

The RTSE takes upon itself the responsibility of managing the association establishment and release, although actual exchanges are made by ACSE. The RTSE protocol insists that it be in charge when it is included in an application

**RTSE Service Provider**

RT-TRANSFER
Request

RT-TRANSFER
Indication

RT-TRANSFER
Confirmation

**(a) The RTSE RT-TRANSFER**

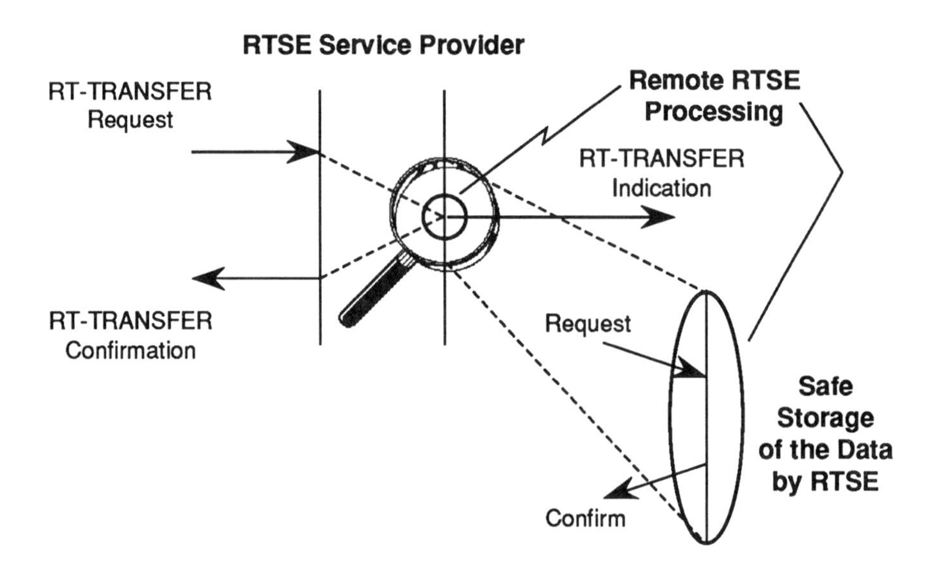


**(b) A closer look at RT-TRANSFER**

*Illustration courtesy of Learning Group International*

**FIGURE 5-2** The RT-TRANSFER primitive has an unusual method of confirmation.

entity. The user element does not have this option. The association establishment involves a large number of parameters as shown in Table 5-8.

**TABLE 5-8** Association establishment parameters.

| Service primitive | Parameters |
|---|---|
| RT-OPEN request and indication | Dialogue-mode<br>Initial-turn<br>Application-protocol<br><br>Application context name<br>Calling AP title<br>Calling AE qualifier<br>Calling AP invocation-identifier<br>Calling AE invocation-identifier<br>Called AP title<br>Called AE qualifier<br>Called AP invocation-identifier<br>Called AE invocation-identifier<br><br>Mode<br><br>Calling-presentation-address<br>Called-presentation-address<br>Presentation context definition list<br>Presentation context definition result list (indication only)<br>Default context name<br>Default context result (indication only)<br><br>User data |
| RT-OPEN response and confirmation | Application context name<br>Responding AP title<br>Responding AE qualifier<br>Responding AP invocation-identifier<br>Responding AE invocation-identifier<br>Result<br>Result source (in confirmation only)<br>Diagnostic<br><br>Responding-presentation-address<br>Presentation context definition list<br>Presentation context definition result list<br>Default presentation context name<br>Default presentation context result<br><br>User data |

Note: Quality of service, presentation requirements, and session parameters are not explicitly required in the service primitive.

Additional details on these parameters in the request and response primitives are listed in Table 5-9.

**TABLE 5-9** Request and response primitives.

| Parameter | Request | Response |
|---|---|---|
| Dialogue-mode | Mandatory | Not carried |
| Initial-turn | Mandatory | Not carried |
| Application-protocol (1) | User-optional | Not carried |
| Application context name (2) | Mandatory | Mandatory |
| Calling AP title (2) | User-optional | Not carried |
| Calling AE qualifier (2) | User-optional | Not carried |
| Calling AP invocation-identifier (2) | User-optional | Not carried |
| Calling AE invocation-identifier (2) | User-optional | Not carried |
| Called AP title (2) | User-optional | Not carried |
| Called AE qualifier (2) | User-optional | Not carried |
| Called AP invocation-identifier (2) | User-optional | Not carried |
| Called AE invocation-identifier (2) | User-optional | Not carried |
| Responding AP title (2) | Not carried | User-optional |
| Responding AE qualifier (2) | Not carried | User-optional |
| Responding AP invocation-ID (2) | Not carried | User-optional |
| Responding AE invocation-ID (2) | Not carried | User-optional |

(1) The application-protocol parameter applies only to the X.410-1984 mode.
(2) The calling, called, and responding parameters do not apply for the X.410-1984 mode.

The three new parameters introduced by RTSE have the following meanings. The *dialogue-mode* identifies which of the two alternatives (monologue or two-way alternate) is desired. The *initial turn* indicates which of the two RTSE users (association-initiator or association-responder) is to have the first turn. The *application-protocol parameter* designates the application protocol that will govern communications.

The next grouping of the RT-OPEN parameters (see Table 5-10) is limited to the three new parameters because the others have appeared at the presentation or session layers.

**TABLE 5-10** Three new parameters.

| Parameter | Request | Response |
|---|---|---|
| Dialogue-mode | Mandatory | Not carried |
| Initial-turn | Mandatory | Not carried |
| Application-protocol | User-optional | Not carried |

The RTSE services are summarized in Table 5-11. The table indicates their names, confirmation type, and use/purpose.

**TABLE 5-11** RTSE services.

| Service | Type | Use/purpose |
|---|---|---|
| RT-OPEN | Confirmed | Establish an association |
| RT-CLOSE | Confirmed | Orderly release of association |
| RT-TRANSFER | Confirmed | Transfer user data |
| RT-TURN-PLEASE | Non-confirmed | Request the *turn* |
| RT-TURN-GIVE | Non-confirmed | Give the *turn* to the other side |
| RT-U-ABORT | Non-confirmed | Abrupt user-initiated release |
| RT-P-ABORT | Provider-initiated | Abrupt provider-initiated release |

The RT-OPEN and RT-CLOSE services call upon the ACSE to perform these services. The RT-CLOSE is a special case of the orderly release of an association. The user may only request that the association be released (closed) if it possesses the turn and if there is no outstanding confirmation primitive. Recall that the RTSE operates in a window-based scheme in which some number of application protocol data units (APDUs) can be outstanding (nonconfirmed). All of these APDUs must be confirmed before the association can be released. Waiting for the last outstanding confirmation before releasing the association ensures an orderly release. The release cannot be rejected by the other end system. The RT-CLOSE request and response service primitives include two parameters: user data and a reason code.

Unlike the ACSE services, RTSE provides a data transfer service, RT-TRANSFER. This service enables the user possessing the *turn* to request the transfer of an application PDU over the association. It may continue to send other APDUs until it exhausts the defined window size. The parameters associated with the RT-TRANSFER service are shown in Table 5-12.

**TABLE 5-12** Parameters associated with the RT-TRANSFER service.

| Parameter | Request | Confirmation |
|---|---|---|
| APDU | Mandatory | Provider-optional |
| Transfer-time | Mandatory | Not carried |
| Result | Not carried | Mandatory |

The *transfer-time* parameter is the amount of time the RTSE has to deliver the APDU before declaring that it has been unsuccessful. The *result* parameter specifies the result of the transfer attempt as either positive (delivered and placed in safe storage) or negative. In some cases, the APDU may have been delivered and safely stored, but due to timing, the report may be negative. The window size and the amount of information sent between minor synchronization points are functions of the protocol machine and not parameters of the service.

The RT-TURN-PLEASE and RT-TURN-GIVE service primitives provide a mechanism that allows an RTSE user to request and eventually receive the *turn*, thus enabling one or more APDUs to be sent or the association to be released. The RT-TURN-PLEASE primitive conveys a priority that the other RTSE user can use to determine when to give up the turn. Priority zero is the highest priority; it is reserved for the association release operation. Surprisingly, this is also the default priority when none is explicitly stated. The RT-TURN-GIVE service primitive can only be invoked when that side has the turn with no outstanding, nonconfirmed transfer.

The ABORT service primitives are essentially the same as those discussed before. The abort operation can be initiated by either the user or the provider.

Several important RTSE parameters show up in the protocol specification but not in the service definition. These include the window size and the checkpoint size, which are fields of the RTSE OPEN REQUEST (RTORQ) PDU as shown in Table 5-13.

**TABLE 5-13** Fields of the RTSE OPEN REQUEST PDU.

| Field name | Presence based on |
|---|---|
| Checkpoint size | Protocol state machine |
| Window size | Protocol state machine |
| Dialogue mode | User-optional |
| Other miscellaneous | User and protocol state machine |

The checkpoint size parameter is negotiated between the two protocol state machines. A value is proposed in the request in terms of a multiple of 1K octets. The response can select some smaller multiple of 1K octets. If a checkpoint size is not included in the request, the responder can select it. A value of zero in the response indicates that the checkpoint will not be used. Therefore, in the case of checkpointing the default is a bit unusual.

The window-size parameter is also negotiated between the two protocol state machines. The window size is the maximum number of outstanding minor synchronization points before transfers must be stopped. The initiator can propose a value, and the responder can decrease it. If neither side proposes a value for the window-size parameter and a checkpoint is selected, the default window size is defined to be three.

The dialogue mode is not negotiated. The initiator can specify the dialogue-mode to be either monologue (one-way transfer) or two-way alternate. Two-way simultaneous is not supported by RTSE.

The recovery operations of RTSE are based on the use of the activity functions of the session layer. An activity can be interrupted, aborted, or resumed at a defined synchronization serial number. Because minor synchronization points are used (as opposed to major synchronization points), the recovery can be accomplished from any prior synchronization point (i.e., serial number).

RTSE provides a basic application-level capability to transfer large units of information in a controlled manner that allows checkpoint and recovery in case of end system or communications failure. It is a primary example of a generally useful application service element.

# REMOTE OPERATIONS SERVICE ELEMENT

The remote operations service element might initially be considered oriented toward request/response operations. However, it is more general and includes large-scale data transfers as well — such as electronic messaging.

## Introduction to ROSE

The primitive operations of ROSE are simple. A request is issued by means of the *invoke* operation. The response is either a result, a rejection, or an error report. This forms the basis for a remote procedure call (RPC) form of dialogue. However, ROSE is intended to be considerably more general than just an RPC mechanism, and it is also used by network management, message handling systems, and directory services. The invoke operation consists of

1. **An operation identifier** — What is to be done.
2. **An argument** — An arbitrarily complex structure passed to the other end system.
3. **An invocation identifier** — A unique identifier for this request.
4. **An invocation identifier** — Optionally linked to other invocations.

Each subsequent response is keyed to the invocation identifier to which it is responding, but it is not otherwise controlled in terms of possible asynchronous events. This is an application responsibility. The response may be the result of a successful operation with a result (of arbitrary complexity), an error identification, or a rejection (including a reason code).

The ROSE operation may have any of three levels of reliability. The most stringent is *exactly once*, in which the operation is performed one and only one time. Less stringent forms are *at least once* and *at most once*. An example of *exactly once* would be the debiting of a bank balance in a transaction. The account holder would certainly not want the *at least once* form to perform an operation multiple times. The *at least once* would be acceptable to the person whose account was receiving money, but it would not be acceptable to the bank. Some operations are quite useful under each of these three possible outcomes. Therefore, each service may be required under different circumstances.

As mentioned above, ROSE provides services to the more visible application layer protocols such as directory service and network management, and in turn, it can build upon the RTSE services. This is another example of the reuse of the service elements as was the case with 1988 X.400 electronic messaging. ROSE can operate with either the user element or another ASE (such as RTSE) managing the association control. These two alternatives are shown in Figure 5-3.

ROSE is defined in the following ISO and CCITT documents.

| | | |
|---|---|---|
| Model, notation, and service definition | ISO 9072-1 | CCITT X.219 |
| Protocol specification | ISO 9072-2 | CCITT X.229 |

The ISO change is also found here with the numbering of the service definitions and protocol specifications as *-1* and *-2* of a given number instead of consecutive integers. CCITT also changed its numbering system by going to numbers such as 9 instead of using the layer number. Both are simply running out of numbers. Networking is simply exploding in all aspects.

## Detailed Discussion of ROSE Service and Protocol

The basic model of ROSE is that of two *application entities* involved in an interactive request/reply form of operation. The request is sent from the *invoker*, and the response ID is returned from the *performer*. This is similar in many ways to the client/server model in other networking operations. The operation of ROSE can be categorized in several ways. First, the operation can be categorized on the basis of what the performer is expected to do to report its outcome. The response might be any of the following:

- Return a result reply (if successful) or an error response.
- No return is required if successful; otherwise, an error response is returned.
- Return a reply only in the case of success; no reply is expected for a failure.
- No return is expected for either a success or a failure.

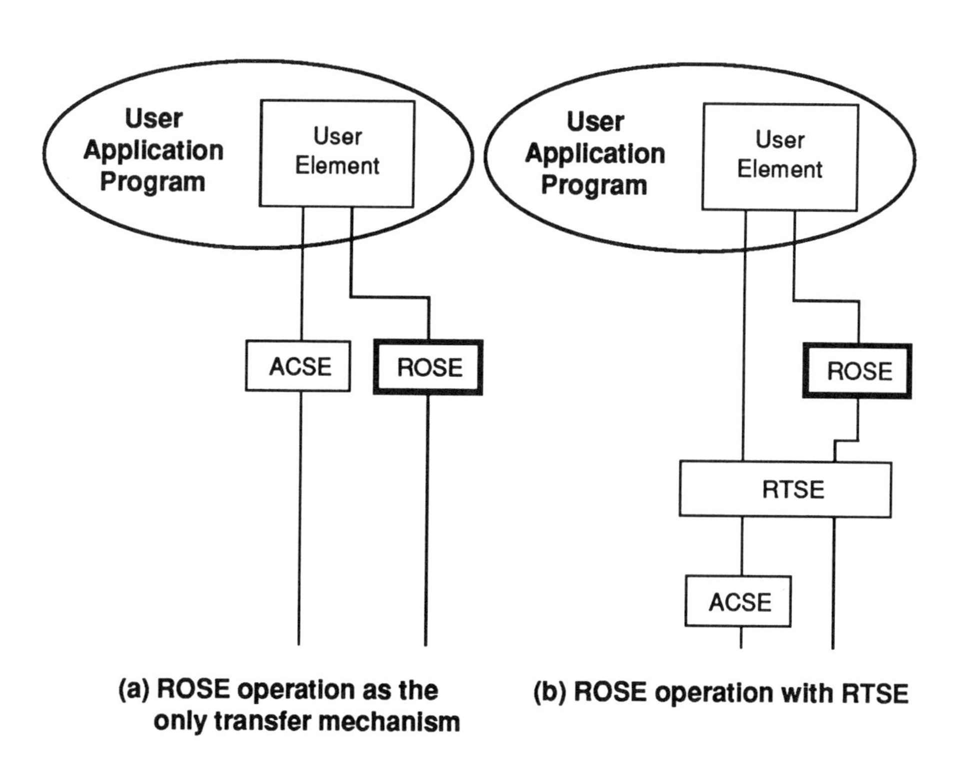


*Illustration courtesy of Learning Group International*

**FIGURE 5-3** ROSE can be configured in an application entity in several ways.

This variety of success/failure indications is typical of OSI applications. All possible needs seem to be included. The operations can also be categorized according to their need to wait for a response before proceeding. Borrowing terms from computer I/O operations, one can say a ROSE operation is *synchronous* if its reply must be obtained before the next operation can be performed. Its operation is *asynchronous* if this wait is not required. Synchronous operations must report either success or failure. In contrast, asynchronous operations may be of four classes: reporting success/failure, reporting failure only, reporting success only, or not requiring any report.

An important and rather complicated aspect of ROSE is its handling of *linked operations* in which a set of parent/child operations are conducted between two end systems. One end system invokes a parent operation to be processed on the other end system. The second end system can then invoke zero, one, or more child operations to be processed on the first system. Each child operation can then act as a parent to invoke further child operations in a recursive manner. See Figure 5-4, in which the *child of the child* is indicated as a grandchild.

While the invocation of the some networking functions such as the parent/child linked operations can be initiated by either end of a ROSE association, in other cases operations are not symmetrical and the two ends have specific names in this regard. The application entity that initiates a ROSE association is called the *association-initiating AE*, and the other application entity is called the *association-responding AE*. Only the association-initiating AE can release the association, but either side may invoke operations. The alternatives that ROSE supports are

Association class 1: Only the initiating entity can invoke operations.
Association class 2: Only the responding entity can invoke operations.
Association class 3: Both entities can invoke operations (the required class for linked operations).

ROSE is unique in providing what it calls an *operations-interface*. This operations-interface is between the user element and the ROSE service and is defined by the following four types of remote operations macros:

- BIND — Establishes the association and provides a type notation and a value notation for remote operations.

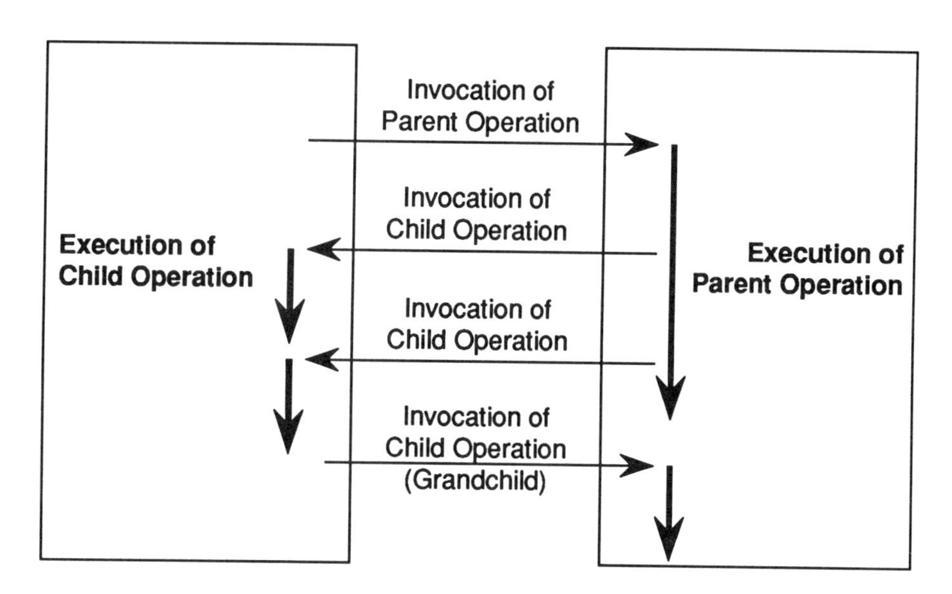


*Illustration courtesy of Learning Group International*

**FIGURE 5-4** ROSE provides linked operations between systems.

- OPERATION — Defines a set of allowed operations and user-data types to be exchanged.
- UNBIND — Releases the association and specifies the types for user data exchanged during the release phase.
- ERROR — Specifies the user-data types for negative reply situations.

The ROSE recommendation has five services, none of which have to do with the establishment and release of an association. Unlike RTSE, ROSE relies on some other component of the application entity to perform these operations. (Otherwise you could not mix ROSE and RTSE in the same application entity.) The five services that ROSE supports are

- RO-INVOKE — Request an operation to be performed.
- RO-RESULT — Return the positive reply of a successful operation.
- RO-ERROR — Return the negative reply of an unsuccessful operation.
- RO-REJECT-U — Reject when a user detects a problem.
- RO-REJECT-P — Reject when the provider detects a problem.

None of these services are confirmed. The RO-REJECT-P is provider-initiated. The parameters associated with this service are shown in Table 5-14.

The *operation-value parameter* is an identifier of the operation to be invoked and must be agreed upon by ROSE users. The values of this parameter are not provided in the ROSE standard. The operation-class parameter defines whether the operation is synchronous or asynchronous, and whether the reply is to be a result or error report (or if no reply is expected).

**TABLE 5-14** Parameters associated with RO-INVOKE service.

| Parameter name | Request | Indication |
|---|---|---|
| Operation-value | Mandatory | Mandatory |
| Operation-class | User-optional | Not carried |
| Argument | User-optional | Conditional |
| Invoke-ID | Mandatory | Mandatory |
| Linked-ID | User-optional | Conditional |
| Priority | User-optional | Not carried |

The *argument parameter* is the argument of the invoked operation. Its type must be mutually agreed upon by the ROSE users. The *invoke-ID parameter* is used to correlate the request and the subsequent response. This is especially needed in asynchronous operations. The *linked-ID parameter* is optional and only applies when a child operation is invoked.

The *priority parameter* defines the priority assigned to the application PDUs for this operation. The lower the number, the higher the priority. The priority of a reply should be given a higher priority, i.e., a lower number than the request.

Many RO-INVOKE parameters also apply to the RO-RESULT service primitive. These are shown in Table 5-15.

**TABLE 5-15** Parameters associated with the RO-RESULT service.

| Parameter name | Request | Indication |
|---|---|---|
| Operation-value | User-optional | Conditional |
| Result | User-optional | Conditional |
| Invoke-ID | Mandatory | Mandatory |
| Priority | User-optional | Not carried |

The *operation-value parameter* is an identifier of the operation that was successfully performed. The value is the same as that of the corresponding RO-INVOKE primitive. The *result parameter* is the result of a successful operation, expressed in a mutually agreed upon data type.

The *invoke-ID parameter* identifies the corresponding request and is the same as that received in the RO-INVOKE. The *priority parameter* defines the priority assigned to the application PDUs for this operation.

The RO-RESULT service is used when an operation is successful. Otherwise, an RO-ERROR or RO-REJECT primitive is used as a response. The parameters of these two services are summarized in Tables 5-16 and 5-17.

**TABLE 5-16** Parameters associated with the RO-ERROR service.

| Parameter name | Request | Indication |
|---|---|---|
| Error-value | Mandatory | Mandatory |
| Error-parameter | User-optional | Conditional |
| Invoke-ID | Mandatory | Mandatory |
| Priority | User-optional | Not carried |

The *error-value* and *error-parameter* entries are of a mutually agreed upon type. The error-value identifies the specific type of error, and the optional error-parameter provides additional information about the error. The *invoke-ID parameter* and the *priority parameter* are defined in the other service primitives.

**TABLE 5-17** Parameters associated with the RO-REJECT-U service.

| Parameter name | Request | Indication |
|---|---|---|
| Reject-reason | Mandatory | Mandatory |
| Invoke-ID | Mandatory | Mandatory |
| Priority | User-optional | Not carried |

The *reject-reason parameter* has several ROSE-defined categories and types of problems. The three basic categories of errors are (1) invoke problem, (2) return-result problem, and (3) return-error problem (see Table 5-18). Examples of the *invoke-problem* category include an unrecognized operation, a duplicate invocation, an improperly typed argument, and an unrecognized linked-ID. Examples of the *return-result problem* category include an unrecognized invocation, an unexpected result, and an improper result type. Finally, examples of the *return-error problem* category include an unrecognized invocation, an unexpected error response, and an improperly typed error report.

**TABLE 5-18** Parameters associated with the RO-REJECT-P service.

| Parameter name | Indication |
|---|---|
| Invoke-ID | ROSE service provider option |
| Returned-parameters | ROSE service provider option |
| Reject-reason | ROSE service provider option |

The *provider reject* service exists only in the form of an indication, and the parameters are solely at the option of the provider. The *invoke-ID* would be expected unless the provider were unable to obtain it from a ROSE service request or response. The *returned-parameters* are those of the rejected request or response. Finally, the only category of *reject-reason* is *general-problem*. Examples of the general-problem category include unrecognized, mistyped, and poorly structured APDUs.

ROSE provides a comprehensive remote operations or remote procedure call capability. In a subsequent chapter, it is used in a number of application-layer protocols, including X.400 electronic messaging and network management. Before getting into those applications, one more of the building block ASEs should be considered: the commitment, concurrency, and recovery protocol.

# COMMITMENT, CONCURRENCY, AND RECOVERY

CCR services are another service element within the application layer. Its name and acronym do not end in service element (SE) because CCR predates the appending of each such component with that phrase. CCR was originally considered an element of the common application service elements (CASE), which was viewed as a sublayer of the application layer. That is all history now. There is no CASE; there is no sublayer; but there is a CCR.

CCR provides the ability to perform distributed processing transactions such as updating multiple copies of a replicated data base and maintaining

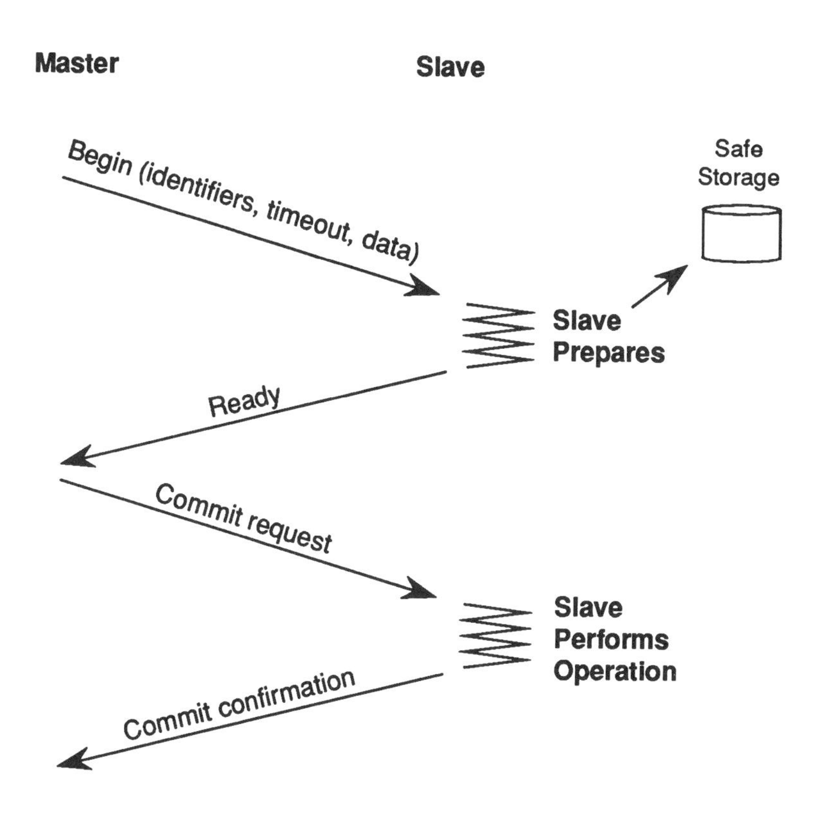


*Illustration courtesy of Learning Group International*

**FIGURE 5-5** CCR provides two-phase commit.

data integrity and consistency in spite of major outages (crashes) in communications or end systems. With CCR one system is always in control and attempting to perform operations on one (or more) other systems. The system that is in control for a given operation is called the master, the superior, or the initiator. The other system becomes the slave, subordinate, or responder.

## An Overview of the CCR Service Element

The basic mechanisms of CCR are shown in simplified form in Figure 5-5. The master system wants a change in a record in a slave system. The master issues

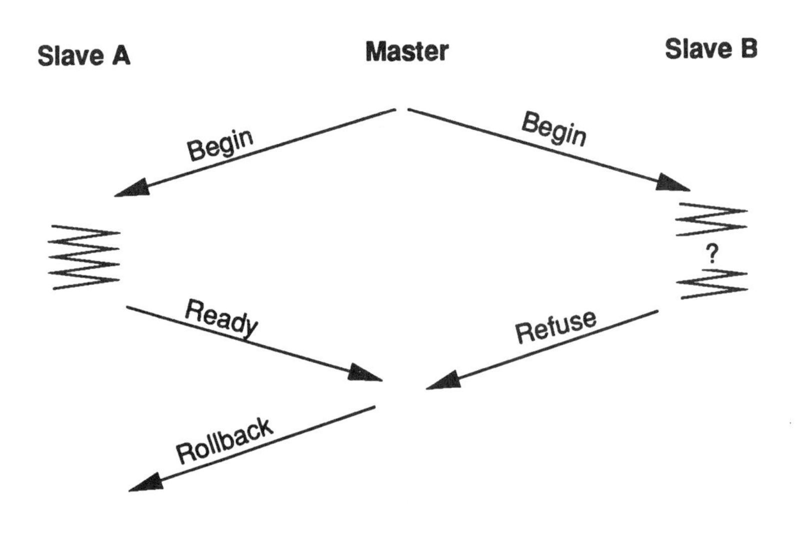


*Illustration courtesy of Learning Group International*

**FIGURE 5-6** Unless all slaves can perform request, none do so.

a BEGIN request, which includes a unique identifier, a timeout value, and application-specific data for the transaction. The slave responds to the BEGIN request by preparing the update but stopping short of actually making the change. All information required to make the change is safely stored on disk, and the record is locked to ensure that no one else attempts to read or write it. The slave then sends back a READY indication, completing the first phase of the two-phase commit process.

In this simple example with a single slave, the two-phase approach is overkill, but it does extend to multiple slaves. In the current example, the master has two options: (1) to order that the change be made by a COMMIT request or (2) to issue a ROLLBACK request to restore the slave to its original state. Figure 5-5 shows the former case, with the record being updated and then unlocked.

The reason the ROLLBACK request is needed is shown in Figure 5-6 in which a second slave has been included in the update process. Either both slaves should have their copies of the record updated or neither should be updated. Slave A performs as before, storing the required transaction information safely on disk and locking the record. However, slave B is unable to perform the update. Perhaps the entire file system in which the record resides is locked for some other reason. Slave B responds with a REFUSE indication.

The master must now cause slave A to release its lock on the record and discard the planned update information. The entire operation will be attempted again later.

The CCR services and mechanisms can be nested to form a tree structure in which a slave node at one level is a master at a lower level in the tree. The CCR delays its response until it has received a suitable response from the lower branches of the tree. In typical CCR applications, these are called *atomic action trees* because the operations of all trees and subtrees must succeed or all must be rolled back.

The BEGIN request maps onto a session layer major sync point request, and the ROLLBACK request maps onto a session layer resynchronize request. Both are confirmed operations.

The two examples above show the commitment aspect of CCR and at least one instance of the concurrency control, namely the locking of the record when preparing for an update. Recovery is yet another matter, and one that CCR shares with the application. For example, if slave A of Figure 5-6 crashes after sending its READY but before receiving the ROLLBACK request, the lack of a ROLLBACK confirmation indicates the need for recovery. CCR provides a RESTART capability that causes a session layer resynchronization. However, the application is expected to provide the remaining procedures for this recovery.

CCR provides a set of controls over what are called *atomic actions*. The usual example is one of a funds transfer in which the operation involves debiting one account and crediting another. The end result should be that either the entire operation or none at all has happened. The following is definitely not wanted: one account debited and the other not credited (or vice versa).

CCR is defined in the following ISO and CCITT documents:

| | | |
|---|---|---|
| Service definition | ISO 9804 | CCITT X.237 |
| Protocol specification | ISO 9805 | CCITT X.247 |

These two document numberings go back to when ISO was using consecutive integers, but the more recent CCITT numbering resorts to using 3 and 4 for the service and protocol because the last digit of the ROSE documents hits the limits of digit-based numbering at 9.

## A Detailed Discussion of CCR Service Primitives

The CCR service primitives were discussed in the preceding section in terms of their use in simple application scenarios. Now the discussion will center on their characteristics with regard to which party issues them, whether they are confirmed, what presentation services are used to provide them, and what parameters they use.

Table 5-19 shows the complete list of CCR service primitives, which side (master or slave) issues them, and whether they are confirmed. Lower-layer confirmations may occur in some cases, e.g. because the C-BEGIN maps into a major synchronization point.

**TABLE 5-19** CCR service primitives.

| CCR Service Primitive | Issued By | Confirmed? |
|---|---|---|
| C-BEGIN | Master | No |
| C-PREPARE | Master | No |
| C-READY | Slave | No |
| C-REFUSE | Slave | No |
| C-COMMIT | Master | Yes |
| C-ROLLBACK | Master | Yes |
| C-RESTART | Master or Slave | Yes |

Each of the CCR service primitives maps into a presentation service and subsequently into a session layer service where the actual mechanisms exist. The principal mechanisms are the major synchronization checkpoints and the resyn-chronization services. In the case of C-REFUSE and C-ROLL-BACK, the resynchronization is of the form that abandons the processing. In the C-RESTART, the resynchronization is of the restart form. Table 5-20 lists the principal mechanisms of commitment, concurrency, and recovery.

**TABLE 5-20** Principal mechanisms of CCR.

| CCR Service Primitive | Presentation Service |
|---|---|
| C-BEGIN | P-SYNC-MAJOR |
| C-PREPARE | P-TYPED-DATA |
| C-READY | P-TYPED-DATA |
| C-REFUSE | P-RESYNCHRONIZE (Abandon) |

| | |
|---|---|
| C-COMMIT | P-SYNC-MAJOR |
| C-ROLLBACK | P-RESYNCHRONIZE (Abandon) |
| C-RESTART | P-RESYNCHRONIZE (Restart) |

Only the C-BEGIN and C-RESTART service primitives have parameters. The parameters associated with the C-BEGIN command include

1. **Atomic action identifier** — The unambiguous identification of the application entity title of the master and the action to be performed.
2. **Branch identifier** — The unambiguous identification of the application entity title of the master and the branch of the atomic action tree.
3. **Atomic action timer** — A signed integer N indicating that the master intends to rollback after 2**N seconds if the action is not completed.
4. **User data** — Data from the application using CCR.

The parameters associated with the C-RESTART include

1. **Atomic action identifier** — Same as for the C-BEGIN.
2. **Branch identifier** — Same as for the C-BEGIN.
3. **Restart timer** — A time value, expressed like the atomic action timer, after which the master intends to release the association and try again later (restart).
4. **Resumption point** — The action to be taken (C-COMMIT or C-ROLLBACK) if the master has not issued the command prior to a crash.

None of the other CCR service primitives convey parameters, although the user data of a C-REFUSE is expected to carry diagnostic information about the refusal.

## Summary and Conclusions

The session and presentation layers provide their sets of *building blocks* called functional units, which can be negotiated as needed. Early application protocols built upon these services, but application developers found additional common needs related to groupings of these session and presentation functional units into useful procedures. This led to the development of yet another kind of building block at the application layer, namely the service elements such as ACSE, RTSE, ROSE, and CCR. In some cases they have evolved from applications such as X.400 electronic messaging, which initially developed portions of the RTSE and ROSE capabilities into X.400. Because the presentation service was still being defined at that time, the 1984 X.400 operated directly above the session layer. Now, with the standardization of the presentation layer and with the development of RTSE and ROSE, the 1988 X.400 builds on these standard building blocks.

# 6 APPLICATION PACKAGES

The ultimate benefits of Open Systems Interconnection (OSI) are twofold: (1) the multi-vendor interoperability and (2) the rich set of network application protocols that go beyond that typically available in either proprietary or industry-standard protocol suites. This richness comes about from the standardization process, which builds upon current practice and includes almost everything that anyone could possibly want in the spirit of consensus.

The principal application protocol packages that are available today (as International Standards) and that are on the near-term edge of availability (as Draft International Standards) are discussed in this chapter.

## ELECTRONIC MESSAGE-HANDLING SYSTEMS

The most widely used network application package in OSI, like any other protocol stack, is electronic mail. It is known in OSI as the message-handling system (MHS) and is defined in a series of CCITT recommendations, which are collectively known as X.400. The International Standards Organization (ISO) has a comparable system called MOTIS (Message-Oriented Text Interchange System). The two have been merged in the 1988 version of X.400 and ISO 10021. They provide a capable means for the exchange of multimedia information, i.e., message documents containing a mixture of text, graphics, images, and digitized speech.

X.400 is based on four components: (1) the user agent (UA), (2) the message transfer agent (MTA), (3) the message store (MS), and (4) the access unit (AU). These components are organized into an overall system as shown in the model of Figure 6-1. The model portrays three different levels of communication: the user-user text, the user-agent control information, and the message transfer control information. These three levels are also shown in

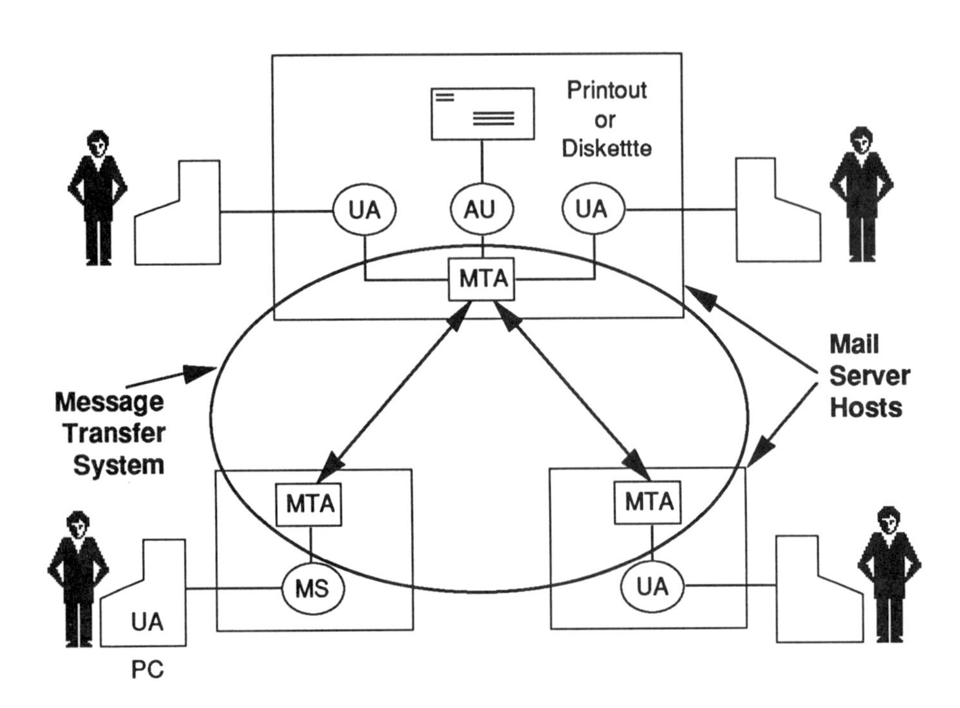


*Illustration courtesy of Learning Group International*

**FIGURE 6-1** The message handling system (MHS) model.

Figure 6-2, which demonstrates the body part, the header, and the envelope as the relevant information for these three levels.

The body parts are of concern to end users, but they are typically conveyed transparently by the MHS. The header contains the UA information such as the recipient(s), and the envelope conveys the control information required for delivery across the electronic postal system.

The user agent is the portion of the message system that supports the user in the generation of messages. It does not include a text editor and file system, although they are assumed to exist. They are not the subject of MHS standardization. The UA provides a standardized way of stating the recipient(s) of the message, the sender, the subject, the *carbon copy* and *blind carbon copy* recipients, and other such information as is typical in interoffice memoranda. A more detailed list of UA protocol elements are indicated in the list that follows. These are the elements of the so-called P2 protocol. The UA distinguishes between this control information and the *body part* that is the actual text of the message.

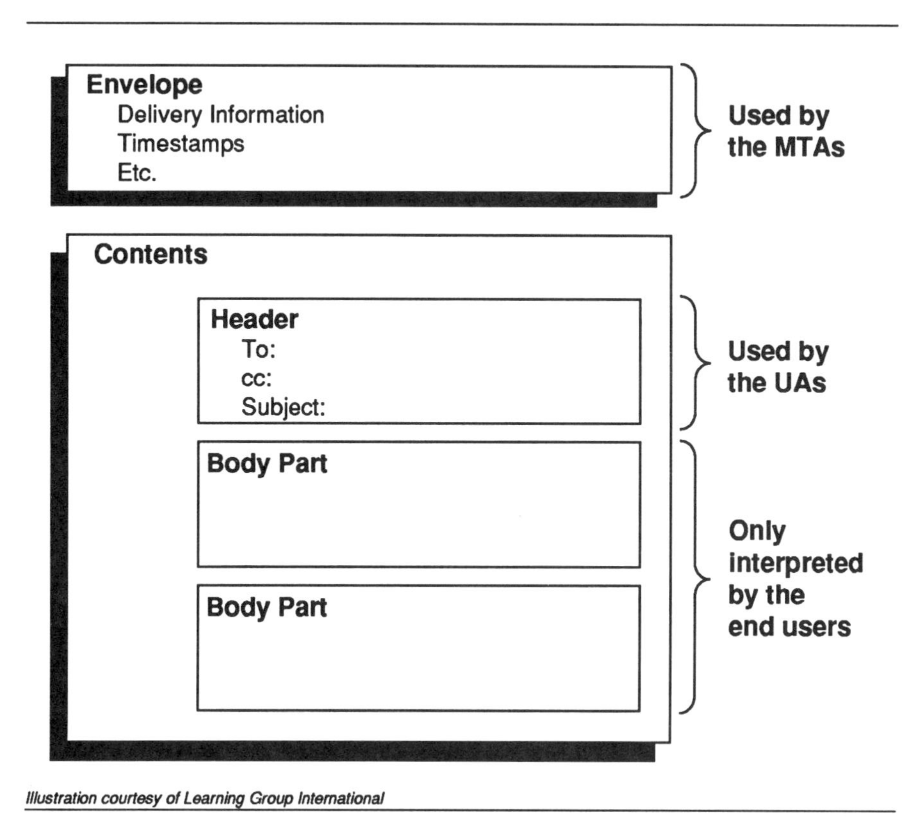


*Illustration courtesy of Learning Group International*

**FIGURE 6-2** The X.400 message structure consists of three main parts.

The UA P2 protocol includes

- Message identifier.
- Originator address.
- Recipient addresses:
  Primary recipients.
  Copy recipients.
  Blind copy recipients.
- Subject.
- Reference information:
  Other message to which this is a reply.
  Message(s) obsoleted by this message.
  Cross-referenced messages.
- Miscellaneous control information:
  Expiration date.

Importance.
Sensitivity.

The message transfer agent serves in the role of the post office. There may be many such MTAs, and a message may be sent through several along its path to the recipient(s). An MTA may simply forward the message, or it may copy it for a local recipient as well as forwarding it on. The MTA interprets the envelope portion of the message, paying no attention to the contents (i.e., header and body parts). This is consistent with its role as the electronic post office. It operates with a set of elements defined in the P1 protocol, which are shown below. In several instances the names of these control elements are similar to those of the P2 protocol. The differences are noted for each element.

The P1 protocol includes

- Message identifier (for this transmission attempt).
- Originator address (may differ from the P2 originator, e.g., if submitted on someone else's behalf).
- Type of content.
- Priority.
- Delivery time.
- List of recipients (includes flags to indicate special controls such as confirmed delivery).
- Trace information.

The P1 protocol handles at least three types of messages: (1) user messages, (2) delivery reports, and (3) probe messages. These were defined in the 1984 CCITT recommendations. The first two are to be expected, namely user-to-user messages and reports of the success or failure of their delivery. The third is a hack, which is used to determine if a message of a given type to a given destination can be delivered. Future directory services will provide a more elegant solution to this need.

The 1988 X.400 recommendations extended the P1 protocol into what it called the P21 protocol, which includes security mechanisms, message stores, and extensibility mechanisms. The message stores that were added in 1988 were needed because in the 1984 version of X.400, the MTAs would hold onto a message for a period of time, such as a few days and return it to the sender if it could not be delivered within that time. If the user did not happen to login to read the electronic mail, it would be sent back. This was a problem because people often go on vacation or business trips during which time they are out of contact with the electronic mail system. In the 1988 version of X.400, the message store was added. An MTA could now include an MS facility, which would provide longer-term storage for undelivered mail.

The 1988 version of X.400 also added a link between the worlds of electronic mail and the paper-oriented postal system. The latter is often called *snail mail* by the electronic community because of its slower pace. However, it does seem desirable to be able to include someone as a recipient, even if that person does not have an electronic mail account. The link between the two worlds is called an access unit. The AU provides the capability either to print out the message or to have it written to a floppy disk, but in either case to have it delivered by the regular postal system.

The specification of X.400 involves several CCITT recommendations, i.e., several separate specifications. A few such as X.409 have become widely known outside the X.400 environment as part of the ASN.1 notation and the related basic encoding rules. In addition, CCITT's X.410 reliable transfer service eventually became the RTSE discussed in Chapter 5.

The separate recommendations of the X.400 series are described in Table 6-1. Most (but not all) have comparable parts within ISO 10021.

**TABLE 6-1** X.400 series recommendations.

| Number | Recommendation |
|---|---|
| X.400 | System and Service Overview |
| X.401 | Basic Service Elements and Optional User Facilities (1984 only) |
| X.402 | Overall Architecture |
| X.403 | Conformance Testing (1988 only) |
| X.407 | Abstract Service Definition Conventions |
| X.408 | Encoded Information Type Conversion Rules |
| X.409 | Presentation Transfer Syntax and Notation (1984 only, became ASN.1 and Basic Encoding Rules) |
| X.410 | Remote Operations and Reliable Transfer Server (1984, only became RTSE) |
| X.411 | Abstract Service Definition and Procedures (Message Transfer) |
| X.413 | Message Store Abstract Service (1988 only) |
| X.419 | Protocol Specifications (1988 only) |
| X.420 | Interpersonal Messaging System (User Agent) |
| X.430 | Access Protocols for Teletex Terminals (1984 only) |

The Consultative Committee for International Telephone and Telegraph has identified several protocols that are important within the X.400 message system. They are defined in the CCITT recommendations, but have nevertheless become known by a shorthand name such as P1, P2, and P3. The P1 protocol deals with the delivery of the message. This is the portion that involves the MTA postal systems. The 1988 version of this protocol is called P21. The P2 protocol defines the header and body portions, along with their formats and fields. The 1988 version of this protocol is called P22. The P3 protocol is a variation of the P1 MTA-MTA protocol and is intended for workstation-to-MTA transfers of messages. The P7 protocol is for access to the message store. These protocols control the internal operation within X.400 for the creation and exchange of messages.

Stepping back from the internal details of X.400 for a moment, one can see the promise of X.400 as a worldwide computer-based messaging system as ubiquitous as today's voice telephone system. It will provide a wide range of communications capabilities, with the convenience of electronic mail and the flexibility of multimedia document communications.

Several pieces are needed to make this happen. First, X.400 services must become available from the post, telephone, and telegraph. This is definitely happening. Second, vendors must develop gateways to proprietary E-mail systems. This too is happening. In fact, X.400 is rapidly becoming the intermediate form for transferring electronic mail from any vendor's system to any other vendor's system. Finally, standard application program interfaces (APIs) are being developed to X.400 systems, providing the basis for the general purpose use of this deferred delivery capability, regardless of the nature of the body parts of the messages.

The X.400 API is being developed by the X.400 Application Program Interface Association, a consortium of two dozen vendors of the E-mail and gateway industry. They have developed a gateway API and an application API. Along with X/Open Company, Ltd., they also have developed APIs for the X.500 directory service and object management.

The gateway API divides the software between a proprietary E-mail system and an X.400 gateway implementation. The API provides input and output queues between these two modules, which could be provided by different vendors.

The application API is the boundary between the UA and the MTA, or between the UA and the MS. It defines the services that the mail system provides to applications. It provides a submission queue and either a delivery queue or a retrieval queue (as an implementation option).

The object management API supports the creation, examination, modification, and deletion of X.400 objects, i.e., complex data structures associated with X.400 E-mail. It does not require the application to have to deal with the encoding rules associated with ASN.1 defined objects or the delivery protocols such as P1, P2, and P3 of X.400.

# DIRECTORY SERVICES

Directory services provide a convenient way of finding information about the availability and location of people and computing resources across the network. This information is typically needed in order to deliver electronic mail messages and to map from user provided names to network addresses.

The general needs for and workings of a directory service are described, and then the specific models and operations of X.500 are defined. Finally, a listing of X.500 directory service specifications is provided, including both CCITT and ISO documents.

## Introduction to X.500 Directory Services

A basic purpose of the directory server is to provide a network-wide (eventually worldwide) capability to express a request in terms of a user-friendly, globally unique name and to have this name mapped into a particular network-specific address that can be used for its delivery.

The X.500 directory service provides a wide variety of information in addition to name and address mappings. It can be used to find addresses associated with people's names, in addition to computer names. It allows one to search for partial matches and then to select the desired response from the two or more responses that are obtained. X.500 is still in the process of development, but it is expected to provide both *white page* and *yellow page* services. It also provides a distributed form of service in which an agent system may contain the information that has been requested, will be able to contact another agent transparently, or will refer the requester to another agent.

When an application program (such as an X.400 user agent) needs access to the X.500 directory service, it contacts an X.500 directory user agent (DUA) and requests the desired information. The DUA will contact a local directory system agent (DSA) to attempt to find the information. The requested information may be available at that DSA and typically would be if the request is for a mapping to another local computer resource. However, if the information is not available at the local DSA, it can contact another DSA to attempt to find it. This chaining of attempts may go on for a number of levels before the information is found or cannot be located. The chained operations may be using the hierarchical tree structure (such as up to the root DSA node and back down on some other path) or any of the DSAs may be able to take a shortcut across the tree if the DSA that has the information is known.

In the chained approach, the desired information is returned transparently. This is not always the case. A DSA may return a reference to another DSA rather than transparently checking. The DUA must now make the request to this referred DSA, which may send back yet another referral. Having both the chained (transparent) and referral schemes available is a typical side effect of the standardization process. Compromise often results in multiple ways to do the same thing.

The above examples of finding a network address associated with a user or computer name is a *white pages* use of the X.500 directory server. Searches that can be requested are more like *yellow page* look ups. This can be requested for all entries that meet any arbitrary filtering of the X.500 data base. The X.500 system can contain different types of data in addition to address mappings. Therefore, administrative and security constraints exist on the allowed accesses.

In order to protect the contents of the stored data, the developers of X.500 will include many security features, including authentication, access control, confidentiality, and electronic signatures (using public key technology).

## Specific X.500 Models and Operations

The intent of this section is to dig a level deeper into the detailed operations of the X.500 directory service. The basic concepts will remain those discussed in the previous section.

X.500 provides a naming convention that is hierarchical in structure. This ensures global uniqueness because each portion of the name need only be unique within the bounds of that subtree of the directory system. This local uniqueness is the responsibility of the management of the subtree organization.

A global name of a person might be represented in the following form:

[country] [organization] [organizational unit] [personal name]

The international organizations (e.g., CCITT and ISO) would ensure that the country designations are unique. Then within each country, it is that country's responsibility to ensure that the organizations have unique designations. These organizations in turn are required to ensure that their organizational units are uniquely identified, and similarly, the organizational units are responsible for uniquely identifying people within them.

This hierarchical naming convention leads to a tree-naming structure called the directory information tree. The root node is associated with CCITT/ISO. The second level represents the various countries and so on down through the organizations to the individual people.

The total set of information maintained by the X.500 directory service is called the directory information base. It consists of information in the form of an *entry* for each known *object* in the system. These terms are intentionally general in the abstract definition, but as an example, the object might be a person, and the entry might represent all known information about that person including the appropriate X.400 E-mail address, postal address, and phone number. The *entry* is a set of attributes expressed in type:value pairs. The types are in ASN.1-defined object identifiers and therefore are standardized.

The name of an object, and therefore of its entry, is determined by its location in the directory information tree. As discussed before, the top node of the tree is, of course, the root; the next level represents the country; etc. Each node in the tree (e.g., at the country level) is responsible for assigning a unique relative distinguished name to each child node. The distinguished name is a globally unique name consisting of the path from the root to the node of concern.

A directory user requests an access based on a purported name that contains the desired type:value pair attributes at each applicable node of the hierarchical name construct. For example, the user might request a search of the entire world's directory for the person named Tom Jones. Alternatively, the user might limit the search to the U.K. or to a particular organization within the U.K.

The ways that a user can access the X.500 system are considered in its abstract services, which are implemented in the X.500 directory access protocol. These access methods include the following:

The user can issue a read request, which is like a *white pages* inquiry. A specific (i.e., single) name is of concern. The X.500 system returns the desired values or alternately an indication that the information did or did not exist there (called a *compare* operation).

The user can issue a search request, which is like a *yellow pages* inquiry. The search looks for entries that match a specified pattern of attributes called a *filter*. The returned result is the set of matches.

The third and final form of the user request may be to modify an entry. The user may change the attributes of the entry if authorized to do so.

The X.500 directory service contents are of specific types with predefined formats. X.500 provides a defined set of *schemas*, which are rules to ensure the structural (format) integrity, e.g., telephone numbers of U.S. entries in the format (xxx) xxx xxxx, where "x" represents a decimal digit.

The distributed operations of the X.500 directory service are defined in a directory system protocol that includes the user and server agents as described before. It also calls out the remote operations (ROSE) OSI application protocol for request/responses when utilizing the directory service.

Because the X.500 directory service may contain many different kinds of information about objects (e.g., users), security controls are needed over the read, search, and modify operations. Security is still an evolving aspect of X.500, but initially one fundamental security property has been addressed. This is the matter of user authentication. When a user has been identified and authenticated, he/she can be held accountable for subsequent access attempts, and access controls can be enforced based on his/her authorization. X.500 identifies two different forms of authentication: *weak authentication* that is represented by passwords and *strong authentication* that is represented by public key certificates. A certificate provides a non-forgettable identification and copy of the user's public key. Subsequent aspects of the authentication dialog rely on the user knowing, but not divulging, a personal matching private key.

## CCITT and OSI X.500 Standards

Like X.400, the X.500 specifications are defined in a series of CCITT and ISO documents. These include overview and concept-of-operation documents, as well as those that define the models of the system. The current set of X.500 and ISO 9594 documents are listed in Table 6-2.

**TABLE 6-2** Current X.500 and ISO 9594 specifications.

| Number | Specification |
|---|---|
| X.500/ISO 9594-1 | Overview of Concepts, Models, and Service |
| X.501/ISO 9594-2 | Models (naming model, abstract information model, and functional model) |
| X.511/ISO 9594-3 | Abstract Service Definition |
| X.518/ISO 9594-4 | Procedures for Distributed Operation |
| X.519/ISO 9594-5 | Protocol Specifications |
| X.520/ISO 9594-6 | Selected Attribute Types |
| X.521/ISO 9594-7 | Selected Object Classes |
| X.509/ISO 9594-8 | Authentication Framework |

Since these documents may be revised periodically, e.g., the four-year cycle of CCITT, an implementer should always be certain of which version he/she is expected to implement.

# FILE TRANSFER, ACCESS, AND MANAGEMENT

Users of networked systems frequently want to perform operations on remote files. One common operation of this type is to read a file. The user wants to obtain a local copy of a file that resides on some remote server, mainframe, bulletin board, or other network resource. In the personal computer environment, these transfers are often accomplished by using primitive file transfer protocols such as XMODEM or Kermit. In the TCP/IP community, the file transfer protocol (FTP) would typically be used. Similar capabilities also exist in vendor-specific protocols such as the directory access protocol of DECnet.

It is not uncommon for a given implementation to use several file access and transfer protocols. A typical diskless workstation in the TCP/IP environment will use the trivial file transfer protocol (TFTP) as part of its boot-loading file transfers, network file system for transparent access to files stored on a server, the UNIX remote copy capability to copy files within the UNIX community, FTP to copy files to and from other systems, and perhaps Kermit for transfers to and from other TCP/IP systems. There are many possibilities and many different approaches that one may have to implement. Part of what OSI is attempting to do is to provide a *one size fits all* solution to these many different needs. That is difficult to do because one protocol may have to be very small to fit into a boot ROM while another must provide both extensive and general capabilities. But nobody said that OSI was going to be easy!

In addition to reading (copying) a file, the user often wants to write files from one computer to another across the network. These same protocols provide the *write* capability. Users often need directories to determine the path name of a file or to change the name, access constraints, or other properties of their files. Not all file transfer protocols provide complete capabilities in these regards. Users also may want to move files between differing computing environments, such as between DEC and IBM. Here again, not all file transfer protocols provide all the desired data conversions. Users may want to access individual records of a file rather than transfer the entire file. Few of the above mentioned protocols address this need. The intent of the OSI file-handling protocol is to provide all these user needs, including some that users may not realize that they need!

This OSI file-handling protocol is file transfer, access, and management (FTAM, pronounced f-tam). This protocol lives up to its name. It can be used to transfer an entire file, to access individual records within a file, or to manage the file attributes such as its name and access permissions. There are numerous difficulties in performing such operations across diverse file systems, but that is the job taken on by FTAM. It must address the problems of handling different file and directory structures (e.g., flat and hierarchical).

The discussion of FTAM will consider its conceptual (long-term) and implementation (short-term) issues. These include the model of a virtual filestore, the model associated with files within the virtual filestore, constraint sets and document types to represent current implementations of filestores/ files, the FTAM file services and protocol, the functional units that can be negotiated, the currently implemented *profiles*, and the two major approaches taken in current implementations: the separate and integrated implementations.

## The Virtual Filestore

A key aspect of FTAM is the virtual filestore, which provides a common, standardized, external appearance for all network file systems. As in other uses of the term, *virtual* means that it can be seen, but it does not really exist in that form. The user of the remote file system *sees* a standardized method of transferring files, accessing records, and managing the file attributes, even though that is not the way the file is actually handled at the host. This concept is demonstrated in Figure 6-3.

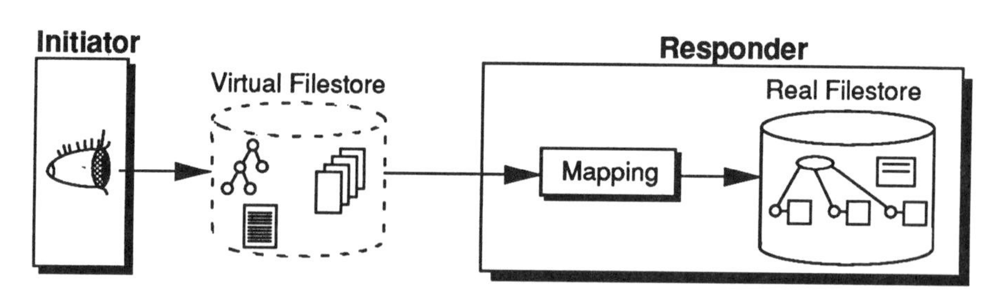


*Illustration courtesy of Learning Group International*

**Figure 6-3** The virtual filestore provides a common view of different file systems.

The virtual (and real) filestore can be considered a file server. It has an associated directory structure and a file system that supports one or more file structures. Each file has a number of attributes such as those listed below.

File name
Date and time of creation
Date and time of last access
Identity of the owner
Identity of last reader
Identity of last content or attribute modifier
Content type
File size

There also may be attributes associated with the permitted access actions, including the following attributes.

Read
Insert
Replace
Extend root data unit
Erase
Read attribute
Change attribute
Delete file

For each attribute, a mapping exists between the externally visible virtual filestore and the internal filestore. Similarly, an externally visible model of the file content exists, including its structure. This does not mean that FTAM is intended to provide structure (such as a record access orientation) when none exists in the basic file. The intent is that FTAM should be able to express structure-related access requests and to map these requests into specific files as appropriate.

The general structure of a file is shown in Figure 6-4. The concept is that a file can be represented in a hierarchical or tree structure with a root node, intermediate nodes, and leaf nodes. Each node has a data unit associated with it. Any subtree is called a file access data unit (FADU) and is an accessible unit of

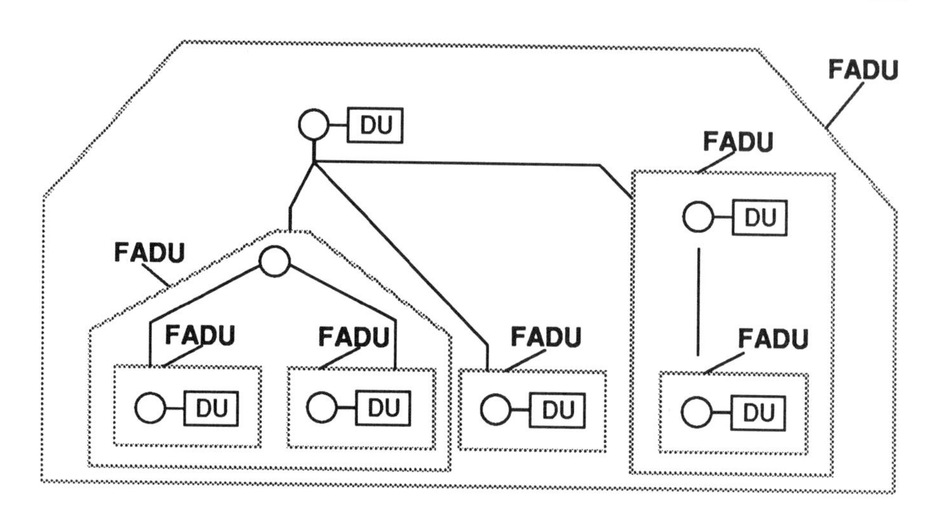


*Illustration courtesy of Learning Group International*

**FIGURE 6-4** The general file structure is hierarchical.

information within the tree. The entire tree is an FADU, as is any individual leaf node. These are the most common FADUs in today's file systems.

Common file structures that need support from FTAM are shown in Figure 6-5. In the first case, the file consists of a single data unit, which is a byte string associated with the root node. It is called an *unstructured file* because it lacks any hierarchical structure. A UNIX file is a typical example. In the second case, the file consists of data units at the leaf nodes only in a two-level hierarchy. It is called a *flat sequential file* and consists of numbered blocks or records. One can access block or record #N in the sequence of blocks or records. The concept of *flat* concerns its lack of depth in a hierarchical sense.

The third and final example in the figure is a *named sequential file*. This structure is similar to that of the flat sequential file, but the access is by means of a search key or name instead of by block or record number.

The unstructured, flat sequential, and named sequential structures comprise different *constraint sets* because each has different constraints for accessing information. In the case of the unstructured file, data can be accessed only as a sequence of bytes. Only the root node exists and has data associated with it. Allowed operations include read, replace, extend, and erase (the entire file).

The flat sequential file consists of a two-level hierarchy with a sequence of blocks or records, which can be accessed by block or record number. No data are associated with the root node. Operations include random access to blocks or

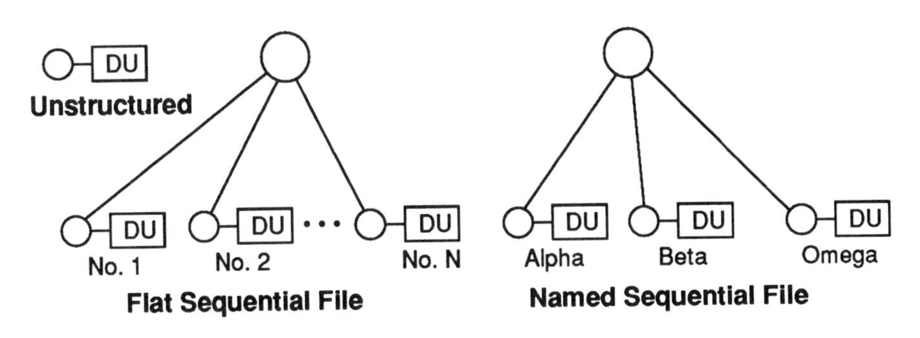


*Illustration courtesy of Learning Group International*

**FIGURE 6-5** Common file structures are a subset of the hierarchical structure.

records for reading, the addition of new blocks or records at the end, and the ability to erase the entire file (but not individual records).

For the named sequential file structure, access requires a search key or name. The differences between this scheme and the others is the difference in abilities to access portions of the information for read, write, or replace. For example, new FADUs can be inserted within the sequence and can modify or erase individual FADUs.

Because the different file structures have differing access rules, the *constraint sets* involve not only structural differences but also access differences.

An aspect of the file content that is related to the constraint set is the *document type* of FTAM. Two files are of the same document type if they have the same constraint set, the same data type (text or binary), and the same transfer syntax. FTAM has several defined document types including

FTAM-1 Unstructured text file.
FTAM-2 Sequential flat text file.
FTAM-3 Unstructured binary file.
FTAM-4 Sequential flat binary file.

The concept of a document type is an important aspect of FTAM, and additional uses will be revealed when FTAM *profiles* are examined.

## Services and Protocol

Like any other proper OSI protocol, FTAM has separate documents to define its services and its protocols. As is always the case, the services document defines what is to be provided, and the protocol document defines how it is to be provided.

Like other upper-layer OSI services, FTAM services are defined in terms of functional units, but unlike most other layers, FTAM also is defined in terms of *service classes*. These service classes are groupings of functional units that are useful.

The FTAM functional unit consists of less than a dozen negotiable capabilities, along with the usual kernel capability that is mandatory. As with the functional units at other upper layers, functional units must be implemented in their entirety and not just partially. The functional units are described as follows.

1. The *kernel* functional unit capability provides only the most basic FTAM services, including the establishment and release of the association and the selection regime.
2. The *read* functional unit capability opens files and transfers data to the initiator.
3. The *write* functional unit capability opens files and transfers data from the initiator.
4. The *access* functional unit capability allows an FADU to be located and manipulated.
5. The *limited management* functional unit capability allows the creation and deletion of files and read access to file attributes.
6. The *enhanced management* functional unit capability goes beyond the limited management to include write access to file attributes.
7. The *locking* functional unit capability provides concurrency locks on selected FADUs.
8. The *recovery* functional unit capability allows the initiator to recreate a previously open regime.
9. The *restart* functional unit capability supports the subsequent resumption of a file transfer at a restart point.

In addition to the functional units described above, FTAM provides *service classes* that are groupings of functional units into useful subsets for file transfers, file access, file management, file transfer and management, file transfer and access, and unconstrained operations. The relationship between service classes and functional units is shown in Figure 6-6. All of the service classes use the kernel functional unit. At least one other functional unit is required for any useful file transfer, access, or management operations.

M = Mandatory
O = Optional
Blank = Not Applicable

| Functional Units | File Transfer | File Access | File Management | File Transfer & Management | File Transfer & Access | Unconstrained |
|---|---|---|---|---|---|---|
| | | | **Service Classes** | | | |
| Kernel | M | M | M | M | M | M |
| Read | M | M | | M | M | O |
| Write | or M | M | | or M | M | O |
| File Access | | M | | | M | O |
| Limited File Mgmt | O | O | M | O | O | O |
| Enhanced File Mgmt | O | O | O | O | O | O |
| Locking | | O | | | O | O |
| Recovery | O | O | | O | O | O |
| Restart | O | O | | O | O | O |
| Grouping | M | O | M | M | M | O |

*Illustration courtesy of Learning Group International*

**FIGURE 6-6** Service classes include groupings of functional units.

FTAM services provide two optional forms of recovery. The FTAM level of service can be selected as either *reliable service* or *user-correctable service*. The reliable service implies that the system will keep enough context to be able to recover from major problems. This overhead may be eliminated by allowing the user to handle rare events.

## FTAM Regimes

FTAM has a set of file service *regimes* that are well-defined states of the file system. These states or regimes limit the set of valid commands that can be issued. A file cannot be read until it has been opened. A file cannot be opened until it has been selected. A file cannot be selected until FTAM is initialized. These nested states or regimes are shown in Figure 6-7. Because they are nested, one must exit each regime in its hierarchical order from the inside out, with the exception of an abort operation that exits from the FTAM association at once.

The outermost regime is called the *association regime*. It establishes the association and the related accounting for the network usage. It also provides filestore management capabilities, so that attributes can be accessed and manipulated at the remote filestore. The F-INITIALIZE primitive causes the association to begin and conveys information about the initiator (its application-entity title) and the set of functional units that it would like to use. They are negotiated during the association establishment *handshake*. This operation also contains information about the user associated with the request, including a user ID, account number, and password.

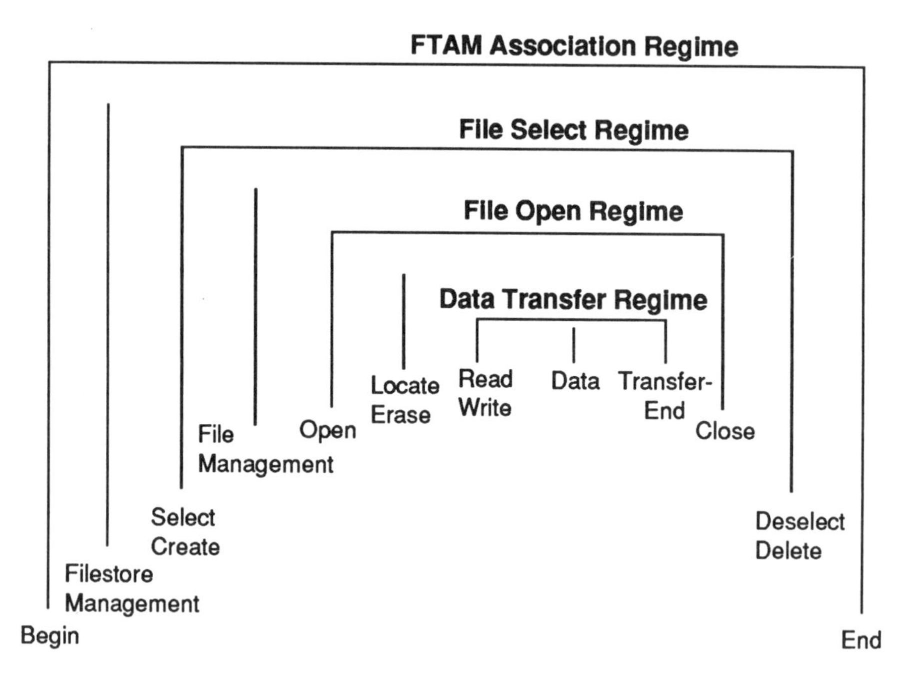


*Illustration courtesy of Learning Group International*

**FIGURE 6-7** FTAM services are meaningful within states, called *regimes*.

The next of the nested regimes is the *select regime*. It allows one to identify the particular file to be accessed by providing its name. This may be a new file that utilizes the F-CREATE primitive, or one that already exists in the filestore that uses the F-SELECT primitive. The attributes of the selected file can be manipulated by utilizing the primitives F-READ-ATTRIBUTE and F-CHANGE-ATTRIBUTE. However, the content of the file cannot be accessed without proceeding to the next of the nested regimes.

In order to read, write, or erase the contents of the selected file, it must be opened. This is performed by the F-OPEN primitive, which moves FTAM to the *file open regime*. An FADU can then be identified (located) and subsequently read, written, or erased. The data units that are read or written will often have the same abstract syntax, but this is not required by FTAM. The data type information associated with the file is determined when the file is opened using a *contents type* parameter in the F-OPEN primitive.

The read or write operations are the next of the nested regimes. This is called the *data transfer regime*. Any FADU may be read or written, where the FADU is often at a leaf node in the structure, but may be any subtree or the entire tree.

To exit in a normal manner, nested regimes are ended from the inside out. First, the data transfer is ended with F-TRANSFER-END. Then the file is closed with the F-CLOSE primitive, and the selected file, F-DESELECT, is used to save the file or F-DELETE is used to erase the file. Finally, the association is closed with F-TERMINATE or aborted with F-ABORT. Any of the regimes may be repeated in a serial manner, e.g., a second file may be selected after the first has been deselected within the same association.

FTAM provides a rich set of capabilities that can be used to map existing and future file systems into a virtual representation of the attributes and contents of these files. Because FTAM was developed to support the file and operating systems of the future, it includes some extensive features that are not necessarily implementable in today's systems. The elaborate concurrency and recovery mechanisms are examples of this *design for the future* approach.

If FTAM is to be used with today's systems, some subset of FTAM is required. Rather than have each vendor select its own subset, implementer groups have defined these *profiles* or *functional standards*.

## FTAM Profiles and Other Implementation Issues

Various subsets of FTAM have been identified to match the capabilities of current systems and to ensure that different implementers have a common subset specification. These subsets are called *implementation profiles* or *functional standards*. They include the defined subset of the specification, the specific options that are to be implemented, and any other implementation restrictions or agreements that apply. The principal source of these implementation profiles in the U.S. is the National Institute of Standards and Technology (NIST). The current profiles are described in the paragraphs that follow.

The simple file transfer profile provides a basic capability to operate with a file that is represented as a root node and a single, unstructured data unit. One can read the entire file, write it (extend or replace its content), and perform minor file management functions such as reading its attributes and deleting the file.

The positional file transfer profile is upward-compatible with the simple file transfer profile, and it provides the transfer of flat files as well. Document types FTAM-1 (unstructured text), FTAM-2 (sequential flat text), and FTAM-3 (unstructured binary) are supported.

The positional file access profile adds read/write access capability at the FADU level, supporting unstructured, flat text, and binary data. It also allows one to erase a selected FADU or to lock a selected FADU. Optionally, recovery and restart capabilities may be available.

The file management profile is to be implemented along with one of the other file transfer or access profiles, and it adds the capabilities of creating and deleting files, as well as reading and changing file attributes.

The Filestore Management Profile was still in development at the time this was written and hence has not stabilized. The intended capabilities include manipulations on directories.

The NIST implementation profiles are identified by the designations shown in the following listing.

T1 — Simple file transfer
T2 — Positional file transfer
T3 — Full file transfer
A1 — Simple file access
A2 — Full file access
M1 — Management

An FTAM implementer would expect the implementation to run at layer seven of an OSI stack, and to receive the composite services of the lower layer protocols. In particular, FTAM expects to be supported by the kernel at the presentation layer and optionally by its context management functional unit. Similarly, FTAM can operate with only the kernel functional unit at the session layer, but it can optionally take advantage of the minor synchronization and resynchronize functional units. Any of the connection-oriented, transport-layer protocols would be adequate, but one would expect that either class 2 or 4 would be used in practice.

### FTAM Standards

Reflecting its complexity, the FTAM specifications consist of five separate documents. These documents are five numbered parts of the ISO 8571 International Standard. These five parts are

Part 1 — General Approach.
Part 2 — The Virtual Filestore.
Part 3 — FTAM Service Definition.
Part 4 — FTAM Protocol Specification.
Part 5 — Conformance Statement.

The general approach document provides an introductory overview of FTAM. It is unusual for OSI to provide a tutorial description as a part of its documentation. This would again seem to indicate the developers' awareness of the complexity of this protocol.

The second document in the series defines the virtual filestore. This also is a tutorial document. It is then followed by the usual service definition and protocol specification documents. Any proper OSI protocol has these two types of documents. Part five is a statement about conformance to the FTAM protocol. Conformance definitions cannot be found in older OSI protocols, but this will be very common in more recently developed standards.

An implementer of FTAM must have information about the detailed operation of the primitives, their parameters, and the ways in which they can be used. This information should be obtained from the specifications named above and from any subsequent addenda.

## VIRTUAL TERMINAL SERVICE

The virtual terminal service (VTS) is to OSI what TELNET is to TCP/IP and what CTERM is to DECnet, namely a way to use any terminal to access any host in the network. However, VTS goes well beyond the capabilities of these earlier systems. VTS is discussed in terms of (1) the objectives of VTS, (2) its basic concepts, (3) its services and protocol, and (4) the OSI standards for VTS.

## Background and Objectives

For many years the normal method of interactive access to computing was by means of *dumb terminals* and communication links. Even today, almost all computers support user access by this means, but almost all such hosts expect something different about the terminals to which it can communicate. One of the requirements on a VTS is to mediate these differences.

Today, one is not limited to the use of dumb terminals and mainframes. A growing numbers of PCs and workstations provide distributed computing. However, the need to access remote hosts across the network still exists. The VTS should provide this capability, thus providing an alternative to terminal emulation hardware/software packages.

The VTS requires terminal processing and protocol support software, and therefore it needs to reside in something *smart.* This can be a terminal support device such as a controller or concentrator, but it cannot be a simple multiplexer. In the case of PCs and workstations, the software would run on their internal processors. The VTS software needs to create a *virtual terminal.* That is, the host *sees* a familiar set of terminal characteristics. Similarly, a terminal sees what appears to be a host terminal handler with which it can work. The PCs and workstations provide a terminal-like user interface and map to the required representations of data and control for transmission across the network.

The basic objective of the VTS is quite simple: it provides a remote login capability to any host on the network from any device that provides a keyboard and display. Providing this capability can become quite complex, particularly when specialized features of some terminals such as color, reverse video, blinking, and multiple fonts are considered.

A secondary objective of the VTS is to provide a general purpose, character-oriented, communications capability between any two computers. This means the VTS is not limited to the support of terminal access to computers, although that is by far its major use.

## Basic Concepts of the VTS

It is sometimes easiest to describe something in terms of what it is not. The VTS is not just another way of parameterizing terminal characteristics the way the *triple X* (X.28/X.3/X.29) terminal access protocols of CCITT operate. In the CCITT approach, a packet assembler/disassembler (PAD) provides a terminal controller function. The PAD implements a parameter-based form of terminal control. The X.3 recommendation defines a set of parameters that describe the terminal behavior, and X.29 defines how a host computer can read and write these parameters. Numbers can be assigned to the terminal's data rate, to the number of padding characters required after a line feed, and to the line length. Other such numbers can be used to define if character echoing is to be done at the PAD and when the PAD is to send the characters that it has been assembling into a packet.

Unlike the PAD approach that uses numerical parameters to define terminal characteristics, the VTS uses abstract objects as its parameters. This is sometimes referred to as the *object model* of the terminal device. Examples of these abstract objects include a virtual keyboard, a virtual screen, a virtual cursor, and virtual control objects such as indicators and *bell* signals. Abstract operations at the virtual terminal include character delete, clear the screen, move the cursor to the home position, and send a break signal.

One of the fundamental abstractions of the VTS is its conceptual communications area (CCA). As shown in Figure 6-8, the CCA consists of three forms of abstract objects: the display object, the control object, and the device object.

## The Display Object

The display object is the abstraction that models the keyboard and screen of a terminal. The screen is considered either one, two, or three dimensional. A one-dimensional display is a single line. Its character string is called an *X-array*. A two-dimensional display is the familiar page of text, usually 24 lines of up to 80 characters each. The two-dimensional display is called a *Y-array*. Finally, a three-dimensional display is a set of pages, called a *Z-array*.

The content of each display is made up of characters. Each such character appears at a *character box graphic element*. The primary attribute associated with each such element is the value of the character, e.g., it might be the letter "A." Secondary attributes include its font, foreground and background colors, and emphasis (e.g., being shown in reverse video). The character value or its secondary attributes may be independently changed. The character and its attributes is called an *atomic element of a repertoire* in VTS terminology.

The display object has the abstract concept of a *current position*, or *display pointer*, which typically refers to a cursor location. The location of the virtual display pointer can be changed on the virtual screen.

Changing the character values, attributes, and display pointer location can be accomplished by either end of the communications. For example, the user may type new entries at the keyboard and have them displayed, or the computer may generate output to the display. Writing to the display may be synchronized so that only one or the other side can write at any given instant (called synchronous

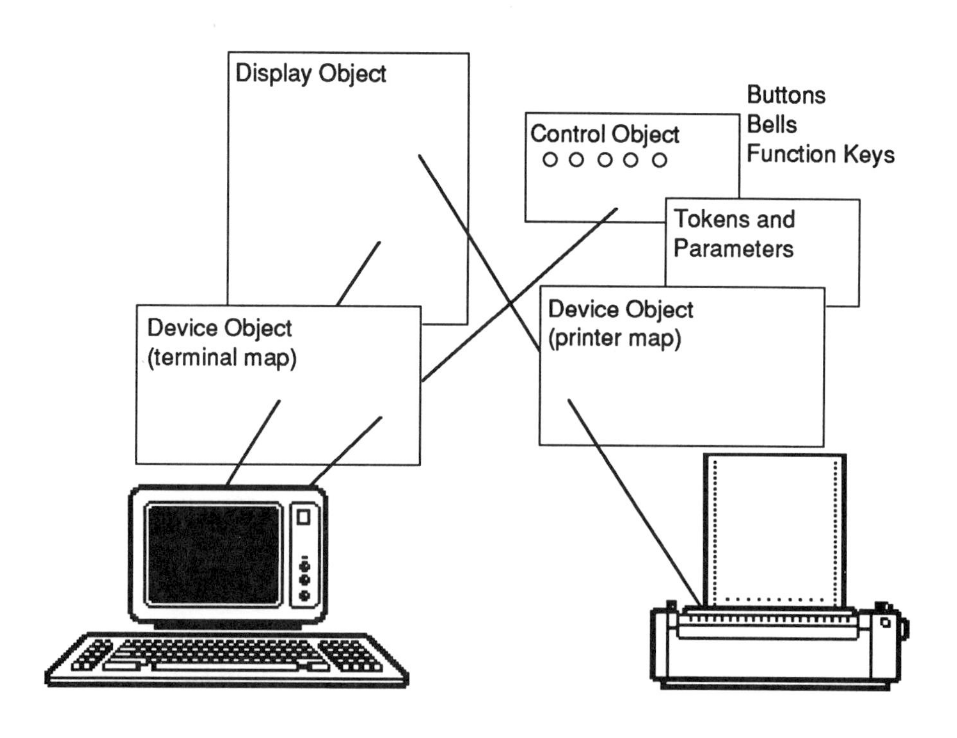


*Illustration courtesy of Learning Group International*

**FIGURE 6-8** Conceptual communications area.

or S-mode), or writing may be allowed at any time by either side (called asynchronous or A-mode). Separate controls are available for the keyboard and the display. This models several different terminal characteristics. If only the computer can write to the display at a given time, the user may not be allowed to use the keyboard. This is often referred to as *locking the keyboard.* If the user is allowed to enter characters at the keyboard, these characters may not be displayed, because the computer buffers them but does not write them at that time. This models the typical remote echo operation. If the user is allowed to enter characters and have them displayed at the same time that the computer is generating output, the two sources could interfere. This is the ultimate A-mode operation, where A seems to stand for anarchy. However, it would work quite well in a split-screen mode of operation.

A display object has a number of parameters associated with it. These include the display object name, access control (i.e., use of tokens), its X, Y, and Z dimensions, erasure capability, character sets, and types of emphasis (e.g., reverse video and color). A mapping is needed at both ends for these variations.

### *The Control Object*

The control object is the abstraction that models the special non-display functions of the terminals (such as the *bell* and function keys) and the various gadgets associated with PCs and workstations (such as a mouse or other point-and-select devices). The control object also includes other parameters such as the tokens associated with the control of the keyboard and writing to the display.

Like the display object, the control object can have write access controls in the form of tokens. Control objects also may have a *trigger* characteristic. The trigger comes into action when a given control object is updated, ensuring that all other pending updates are done at that time.

Control objects can have a number of parameters in addition to enabling or disabling its trigger characteristic. These parameters include whether it is subject to token-based access control, a priority relative to other control objects for update, the type of information in the control object, and its storage capacity.

### *The Device Object*

The device object is the part of VTS that models the characteristics of real devices. This is done to allow a mapping from the abstract display object to the actual physical screen, visual or audible indicators (LEDs or bells), and printers.

Associated with each device object is a control object. The meaning associated with the control object will be device-specific, but it might, for example, control whether the device is on-line or off-line.

The display object, control object, and device object make up the CCA and provide its conceptual communications area. Actually, there are two copies of this CCA, one at each end of the communications. They are often referred to as a *shared data structure* because they are intended to be two copies of the same information. Having a copy at each end is necessary because that is where the VTS operations (computations) are performed. It is the responsibility of the VTS protocol to ensure that the two copies are the same.

## VTS Operation: Services and Protocol

The VTS provides broad support for differing terminal types. This is desirable, but as a result, it contains much more than is needed for any specific terminal type. The solution is to provide multiple types of virtual terminals, which are referred to in VTS as *profiles*. A profile is an agreed upon, consistent set of virtual terminal parameters. Each profile has a name and can be requested when the association is established. (There also is a default profile.) The parameters of the profile may be negotiated to other values to tailor a profile further. A specific virtual terminal parameter set is called the *virtual terminal environment.*

The services primitives provided by the VTS service definition can be logically partitioned into three groups: (1) those involved in the establishment and release of the associations, (2) those that are *pass-through* session services to provide VT-REQUEST-TOKENS and VT-GIVE-TOKENS capabilities, and (3) those that are specific to virtual terminal needs. Only the latter group are of concern here.

In addition to VT-DATA, there are VT-DELIVER and VT-ACK-RECEIPT that are used with delivery control. There are three delivery-control options: (1) no delivery control, (2) simple delivery control, and (3) quarantine delivery control. The delivery control can be negotiated. The default is *no delivery control,* i.e., no ability to indicate when a delivery of data should be made.

Simple delivery control provides an ability to *push* the delivery and display, e.g., of a single character prompt when it is known that no further information will be sent. The use of the quarantine delivery control is more complex, but it might be used when either the entire screen image should appear or when nothing at all should appear.

If no delivery control was negotiated, these VT-DELIVER and VT-ACK-RECEIPT primitives cannot be used. If simple delivery control is negotiated, these primitives provide the ability to signal that delivery should be made, and optionally ACKed. If the quarantine delivery control was negotiated, then the deliver primitive would be required to deliver the information. The ACK is again optionally requested.

The negotiation mechanisms are supported by several primitives that include VT-START-NEG(otiation), VT-NEG-INVITE, VT-NEG-OFFER, VT-NEG-ACCEPT, VT-NEG-REJECT, and finally, VT-END-NEG. The *start* and *end* primitives bound the negotiation process. The *invite* and *offer* primitives allow one to give the other side the opportunity to propose parameter values or to propose such values. The *accept* and *reject* primitives provide responses to the offerings of the other side of the association.

The VT-SWITCH-PROFILE primitive may be used (if negotiated) to switch to a different profile without releasing the association. A final VTS service primitive is the VT-BREAK capability that causes any pending object updates to be discarded. It corresponds to what one typically expects to happen when they desperately hit the break key on the terminal keyboard.

The virtual terminal protocol provides a set of mechanisms that can support display and control objects. These include, as examples, the ability to modify the display object by commands to return the cursor to a home position, to move to the start of the next line, to move to the start of the next page, to erase a line or page, and to move to a specific cursor position. The control objects can be modified by controls over the on/off state and other parameters.

### VTS Standards

The ISO standards for the VTS are currently limited to the basic class, which includes scroll mode and page mode terminals. The VTS is defined in the usual two volume approach.

ISO 9040: Virtual Terminal Service — Basic Class
ISO 9041: Virtual Terminal Protocol — Basic Class

There also are two addenda, providing an extended facility set and additional functional units.

## TRANSACTION PROCESSING

Transaction processing (TP) is an evolving OSI application that is expected to be heavily used, particularly in financial and transportation industries. An example of a transaction is a credit card purchase approval. The store sends the transaction amount and credit card number across the network to the financial institution. An approval and an authorization code are returned, ending the transaction.

A more complicated example of a transaction is a funds transfer from one bank account to another. The controlling (master) computer for this transaction arranges for one account to be debited and then for this exact amount of money to be credited to the other account at a different bank. The transaction processing protocol must ensure that no possible failure mode will cause an inconsistent condition to exist, such as having debited the first account but not having credited the second account. The transaction is *atomic*, i.e., all the operations are performed or none are performed.

An even more complicated example of a transaction involves three or more parties, rather than just two. Imagine that your travel agent is arranging for your next business trip. This involves separate but inter-dependent transactions for a hotel accommodation, a rental car, a major airline, and a regional airline to get from a major hub to a small city. The funds transfer example was *atomic* in nature, and likewise the multi-party transaction should be performed in its entirety or not at all. It is not enough to have the airline flights and the rental car reservation handled properly if a hotel room reservation is not made at the destination city.

Transaction processing definitely involves networking, but it also requires additional recovery mechanisms beyond those of handling damaged packets, connection failures, and end system crashes during data transfers. The additional form of integrity control is one that meets the *acid test*, where ACID stands for atomicity, consistency, isolation, and durability. These four basic properties are briefly defined below.

1. **Atomicity**—Either all operations are performed or none are performed.
2. **Consistency**—Data are left in a proper condition so that no subsequent contradictory results will be obtained. This requires accuracy and correctness of the updates.
3. **Isolation** — Internal (partial) results are not visible from outside the transaction. No other program can read the intermediate results of the transaction processing.
4. **Durability**—The transaction result is not affected by failures.

The characteristics that are associated with transaction processing and the transaction processing protocols closely resemble those of the CCR protocol described in Chapter 5. One might expect that the CCR *building block* would be used to provide these support capabilities in transaction processing. While that would seem quite reasonable, it does not reflect the origins of the OSI transaction-processing standardization process. The transaction-processing protocol builds upon the IBM LU 6.2 transaction-processing protocol. On two separate occasions, the OSI protocol developers considered making the IBM LU 6.2 protocol an international standard for transaction processing, and on both occasions they decided not to do so. The reasons seem to be political and business-related rather than technical. The other representative organizations, many of which were competitors of IBM, did not want to provide IBM with such an easy way to proclaim compliance with OSI protocols. And they particularly did not want to do so in such a large and growing business area as transaction processing.

The net result is that OSI transaction processing is similar to LU 6.2, and applications written to use LU 6.2 can generally be ported to OSI transaction processing quite easily. The OSI transaction-processing protocol is expected to evolve well beyond the current capabilities of LU 6.2.

Like most upper layer OSI protocols, the transaction-processing protocol consists of functional units. The following functional units are available.

1. **Kernel functional unit** — Provides basic dialog and error control.
2. **Shared control functional unit** — Either party can invoke services.
3. **Polarized control functional unit** — Only one party can invoke most services.
4. **Handshake functional unit** — Used for synchronization.
5. **Commit functional unit** — Commit (or roll back) a transaction.
6. **Unchained functional unit** — Makes individual transactions disjoint.

Unlike most prior transaction processing protocols, the OSI transaction processing provides both chained and unchained forms of transactions. A chained mode of operation overlaps the beginning of one transaction with the ending of the previous one. For example, a *begin transaction* command can be piggybacked with a *commit* command that ends the previous transaction. If no additional transaction is to be made, the dialogue ends.

Like most application protocols, OSI transaction processing contains more features than are needed by all users, and subsets have been defined. These subsets are important because they provide the basis for conformance classes and allow smaller implementations, such as may be needed for PC applications. Three classes of transaction processing are defined below.

1. **Basic functional units** — The kernel and either the shared or the polarized control.
2. **Basic plus commit functional units** — Provides the chained mode.
3. **Basic plus commit and unchained functional units** — Provides the unchained mode of operation.

OSI transaction processing is defined by ISO 10026, which consists of three parts. ISO 10026-1, "Distributed Transaction Processing, Part 1: Model" defines the concepts of OSI transaction processing, including what transactions are, the structures involved, the recovery mechanisms, and the abstract service to be provided. The remaining parts of ISO 10026 are 10026-2, "Part 2: Service Definition," and 10026-3, "Part 3: Protocol Specification."

## OFFICE DOCUMENT ARCHITECTURE

The concepts of an Office Document Architecture date back to the origins of word processors, the many differences in their format controls, and the representation of the structure and contents of a document. Even when an on-line copy of a document could be moved from one system to another, e.g., by having compatible magnetic media or data communications, the document could not necessarily be printed, let alone modified on the second system. Standards were needed to represent the structure of the document, the component parts of the document, and the computer representation of the data and control characters.

Initially, two forms of document representations were of concern: (1) a formatted form in which the originator can determine the way that the document will appear to the recipient and (2) a processable form that is revisable by the recipient. Eventually, a third form called the *formatted processable form* was defined that combined these two original capabilities. This form contained all the information required to present the desired image of the document, as well as to revise and reformat it.

The OSI committees defined a *document architecture* and a *content architecture*. The document architecture defined the structure such as chapters, pages, frames, or blocks. The content architecture included three forms of the contents: characters, geometric graphics, and raster scan graphics. Clearly, there are some interrelationships between the document and content architectures, e.g., a form-feed character content affects the document structure. The rules for handling these relationships are known as the architecture interface.

There also was a need for defining the representation of document structure and content during communications between end systems. As would be expected, ASN.1 was used to develop an application for the interchange data elements. This representation became known as the office document interchange format.

CCITT has also been involved in document architectures and has defined document transfer, access, and management (DTAM) with a close correspondence in naming to the FTAM recommendations. DTAM is defined in the CCITT T.400 series, which begins with CCITT T.400, "Document Transfer, Access and Manipulation (DTAM) — General Introduction." Other documents in this series and their ISO equivalents include the following:

1. ISO 8613-1, CCITT T.411 Text and Office Systems-Office Document Architecture and Interchange Format, Part 1: Introduction and General Principles.
2. ISO 8613-2, CCITT T.412, Part 2: Document Structures.
3. Other miscellaneous recommendations up through Part 9.
4. T.431 Document Transfer, Access, and Management (DTAM), Introduction and General Principles.
5. T.432 Document Transfer, Access, and Management (DTAM), Service Definition.

6. T.433 Document Transfer, Access, and Management (DTAM), Protocol Specification.
7. T.441 Document Transfer, Access, and Management (DTAM), Operational Structure.

# ELECTRONIC DATA INTERCHANGE

Suppose your company or agency sent a purchase order on your own specific purchase form to a vendor who then rekeyed the information onto the vendor's forms. The subsequent invoices, credit adjustments, bills of lading, shipping documentation, payments, and other related documentation are all manually rekeyed onto customer- or vendor-specific multi-part forms, which are manually distributed across the appropriate organizations within the company or agency. All of the communications are by means of *snail mail* messages or at best by fax. Is this the way to run an organization and its procurements? It certainly isn't if you believe in Electronic Data Interchange (EDI).

## Motivation for EDI

EDI is intended to communicate purchase orders, invoices, and other procurement documents in a standard format and to use a standard X.400 electronic mail delivery mechanism. The advantages include reduced costs, e.g., the information does not need to be rekeyed manually, which also reduces rekey errors. This is important because estimates show that up to 70% of printed computer output is rekeyed in such procurements. In the automobile industry, the cost savings are estimated to cut $500 off the cost of each car produced. In another business area, one retailer reduced the total cost of each purchase from $50 to $15. A U.N.–sponsored study found that the cost of purchase and shipping paperwork averaged about 7% of the cost of the goods, considering that up to 200 paper forms are involved in some import/export operations.

The turnaround cycle is also substantially reduced as a consequence. One computer company found that the use of EDI cut the cycle time for an inventory system from over 30 days to only three days.

## Planning for EDI

A key aspect in the planning for EDI is an assessment of the nature of one's procurements. EDI is most beneficial for repetitive ordering, and as a consequence, it has become most widely used in automobile manufacturing, grocery industries, and merchandising. Large companies in these areas often require that their suppliers use EDI.

Fortunately, several factors have made EDI more readily available to small businesses. Almost all companies have at least PC computing capabilities, and affordable EDI software (e.g., $3,000 or less) has become available. There are also third-party providers of EDI document preparation and delivery services. The development of standards have also been a major factor in EDI usage. The American National Standards Institute (ANSI) X12 work has produced EDI standards for use in the U.S., and the X.400 standards have become widely available and relatively stable for use as a delivery vehicle for EDI documents. The existence of third-party network delivery vehicles and X.400 E-mail delivery provide options that may seem desirable, but they also present obstacles when one company wants to use X.400 and the other wants to use a third- party network. In addition, while X.400 is capable of multimedia transmission and should have no difficulty conveying business forms information, the user agent of X.400 is not particularly well suited for EDI forms. Current work on a new CCITT recommendation X.435, "Message Handling Systems: EDI Message System," will attempt to resolve X.400 and EDI differences.

EDI is expected to be included in the future Government OSI Protocol version 3, adding it to the government's "shopping list." In fact, the U.S. Government has become a major user of EDI already.

Initially EDI will not be involved in all phases of procurement. The first aspects will involve purchase orders and invoices. Then status information will be included, and eventually payment transfers will be part of EDI. Certain security and legal issues such as electronic signatures are needed in these areas. Some countries still require paper documents to satisfy legal requirements, and others only accept computer-generated documents when significant security measures have been taken.

## What Is EDI?

EDI comes in two forms: (1) vendor-specific (proprietary) mechanisms that are used by a few companies and (2) the standardized versions. The latter are of concern here, but the reader should be aware that not all uses of the acronym EDI refer to the standard.

The U.S. standardized version of EDI is defined by the ANSI standard X12. (The trade press often thinks that X12 is a typo and changes it to X.12, which makes it look like a CCITT standard.) The international variation of EDI is ISO 9735, EDI for Administrative, Commerce, and Transportation

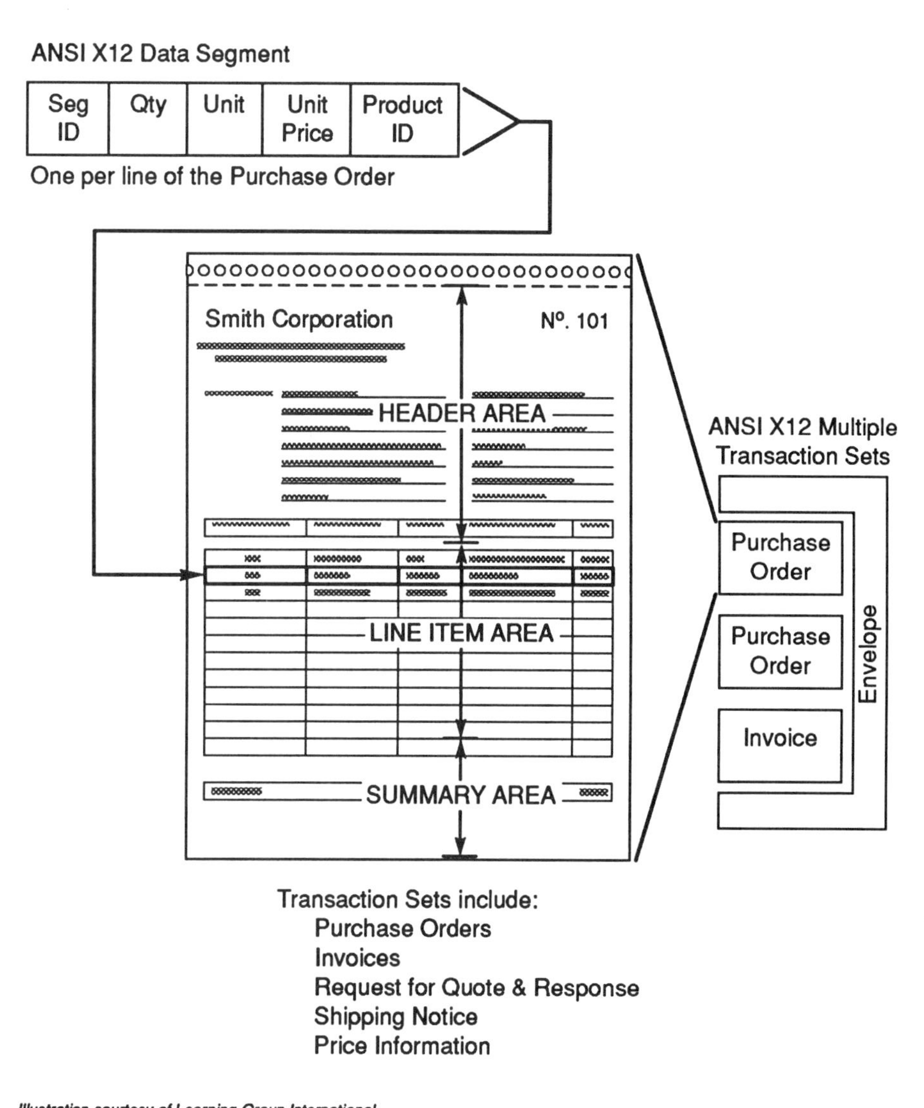


*Illustration courtesy of Learning Group International*

**FIGURE 6-9** EDI provides an electronic representation of purchase documents.

(EDIFACT). It is similar to ANSI X12, but it is not the same. The stated goal is that the two will *be compatible*. It is never clear what the word *compatible* really means, but presumably it means that one can convert from EDI to EDIFACT and vice versa. Such conversions are often possible between the vendor-specific forms of EDI and ANSI EDI as well.

EDI is modelled after the paper forms approach to business information. A single form is considered an X12 transaction set, as shown in Figure 6-9. Each line of a given form is expressed as an X12 data segment, which has fields for quantities, unit of measure, unit price, product identification number, etc. One or more transaction set(s), or electronic forms, can be placed in an X12 interchange envelope (header and trailer). Standardized transaction sets include purchase order, invoice, request for quote and response, shipping notice, price information, and change request forms.

The interchange envelope with its enclosed transaction set(s) is then delivered electronically. This delivery can be by means of proprietary network schemes, but X.400 electronic mail is the planned method of the future.

## Summary and Conclusions

OSI application protocols provide more than just standardization. They also provide a richness that goes beyond current industry-standard and proprietary networking applications. This richness comes about as the result of a conscious decision on the part of the standards makers to err on the side of providing too much and not too little. Issues such as memory, CPU limitations, and efficiency were not the driving forces, probably because the trends of the past decade have made memory and processing power more readily available.

In addition to the wealth of applications that OSI provides, many other protocols at the lower layers are now available. Some would say that there are too many! How can the interoperability of the applications be developed if the lower layers have so many alternatives in terms of connection versus connectionless, different classes of protocols, and implementations consisting of different sets of functional units? The answer at least partially lies in the definition of agreed upon subsets of OSI that implementers actually use. These are sometimes called *profiles* and are one of the issues considered in Chapter 7.

# 7

# OSI PROFILES: SPECIFICATION, IMPLEMENTATION, AND TESTING

Open Systems Interconnection (OSI) provides a rich set of possible capabilities at each of its seven layers and within multiple sublayers at many of these layers. This richness and diversity reflects the development process of OSI. Many different groups were involved, with different needs, different approaches and differing vested interests. As a consequence, not every vendor (or other implementer) has to implement every aspect of OSI. This means that different systems have not necessarily implemented the same subset of OSI. Therefore, the diversity of OSI protocols also presents a potential problem for OSI. Can vendor A's implementation of OSI necessarily interoperate with vendor B's implementation if they have not implemented the same subset?

This chapter observes that the solution to the problem of this overabundance of riches is to introduce subsets of the computer networking protocols called *profiles*. If everyone implements the same subset of OSI, interoperability should be much easier. However, agreement is still needed as to who defines this commonly accepted profile or subset and who tests to ensure that each implementer has indeed met the specification. This form of testing is called *conformance testing*. Even then, additional testing is required to informally demonstrate interoperability, just in case something was missed in the conformance testing.

This chapter is divided into seven sections. The first section describes the general concepts and concerns about profiles. The second and third sections describe the two major U.S. profiles: (1) the Government OSI Profile (GOSIP) and (2) the Manufacturing Automation Protocol (MAP) and Technical and Office Protocol (TOP) profiles, which are typically integrated into a single MAP/TOP profile. The fourth and fifth sections cover conformance and interoperability testing. The last two sections cover performance and functional testing.

# THE INTENT AND USE OF PROFILES

The abundance of riches of OSI is both a strength and a weakness. The currently perceived solution to this weakness is to develop subsets of OSI called profiles. These are also called functional standards, implementation agreements, and implementer specifications. Different groups may have adopted one or more of these terms to mean specific variations of this concept of a profile, but they are commonly considered synonymous.

The general idea of a profile is much the same as that of a person's profile. How does the hairline look? The forehead? The nose, lips, mouth, and chin? The profile of a protocol suite or stack answers the question: what does each layer and sublayer include? A given protocol, option, class, subset, or parameter is either inside or outside the profile.

At any given snapshot in time, some OSI protocols have reached International Standard status, while others are in earlier phases of the standardization process. The organization responsible for defining the profile may require protocols that are to be included reach a given status (such as the International Standard) before being included in the profile. This implies that profiles will evolve as new protocols reach the acceptable threshold in the standardization process. This can be seen in both the U.S. and the United Kingdom Government OSI Profiles (GOSIP), which differ in content but serve as the current set of OSI protocols for procurement by the respective governments.

Not all protocols are of concern to every community; they may be left out of a given profile for reasons of disinterest rather than their status along the standardization process. This implies that profiles may be industry-specific, as the MAP and TOP profiles are.

Different geographic regions of the world may have separate standardization bodies, each of which may be developing its own definition of what fits within an existing profile. This suggests that profiles may be specific to a given part of the world. The U.S. National Institute of Standards and Technology (NIST), the European Workshop for Open Systems (EWOS), and the OSI Asia-Oceania Workshop (AOW) all represent geographically separate profile standardization efforts.

Looking at the first principles of profiles, the intent was to reduce the number of variations of protocols to a manageable subset of all possible combinations. But what about the time variations (based on the evolution of protocol standardization), the industry-specific variations, and the global variations across the world? Has the problem of interoperability been solved for the long term for the multinational organization? This is where the more recent international standardized profile work of ISO comes into practice. Until such standards are in place, the more fragmented efforts of other industry and geographically separated groups must be dealt with. This is typical of the ever-changing aspects of industry-wide and worldwide computer networking.

As stated before, OSI has a rich set of capabilities, but not all need be implemented by any given vendor or application. The resulting variations and sources of incompatibility include the following possibilities.

Vendor or application protocol suites may differ based on the *options* that they require and have implemented. Examples of such options include: (1) X.25 implementation options such as expedited data (the X.25 interrupt facility) and delivery confirmation, and (2) security options in the Internet Protocol.

Implementations also may differ based upon the classes that are supported. Examples of the different classes can be found at the transport layer in which five different connection-oriented classes are identified, namely Classes zero (0) through 4. These classes differ based on two criteria: (1) whether a network connection is used (multiplexed) across two or more transport connections, and (2) the extent to which connection-oriented services (reliable, sequenced, flow-controlled delivery) are provided by the network layer rather than by transport layer mechanisms. In Class zero, almost all transport services are simple pass-throughs from the network layer, while in Class 4, almost all services are provided by the transport layer itself.

Not all implementations include all five classes. Typical implementations in the U.S. use Class zero (0) for handling X.400 messaging, Class 2 for multiplexed use over X.25 networks, and Class 4 for use over any arbitrary networks in an internetwork environment. Classes 1 and 3 are almost never implemented in the U.S. and are not expected to be found in profiles.

Protocol subsets exist at several application layer protocols, including the file transfer, access, and management (FTAM) protocols and the remote login, virtual terminal service (VTS) protocols. These subsets are sometimes referred to as application layer protocol profiles, which makes the term appear in a recursive form. Examples include specific file structures in FTAM and specific terminal types in VTS.

Implementations (and therefore profiles) may also differ in terms of the *parameters* that they include. These parameters are often closely related to the options of the protocols. For example, error and integrity checks may optionally be carried as parameters at the transport layer. Error checks might be done by means of a selected form of arithmetic check across the data and control information, while integrity checks might be done in the form of cryptographic checks across the data/control information using secret cryptographic keys. These variations provide many possibilities for increased protection functionality, but they have concomitant difficulties in interoperability.

The typical implementer of OSI is faced with a common problem independent of whether the protocols are being implemented within an operating system (as the producer) or within a network of workstations and hosts (as the consumer). In either case, there is a need to narrow the set of protocols to be implemented. The general flow of information is demonstrated in Table 7-1 below.

**TABLE 7-1** General flow of information.

| | | | | |
|---|---|---|---|---|
| OSI standards | → | Profiles<br>Functional standards<br>Implementation agreements | → | Procurement specs |

The procurement specifications are the *common glue* between the producer and the consumer of OSI products. The producer of OSI products should be producing what the consumer wants, needs, and will specify in a procurement. This is what the profile is all about! The profile defines the procurement specification. This is useful for both the producer and the consumer.

## THE GOVERNMENT OSI PROFILE

The single largest consumer of computers and computer networks is the federal government, with an annual procurement budget of more than $20 billion. Another $10 billion is expended by companies that need interoperability with government computers and networks. "A billion here and a billion there, and after awhile it adds up," a U.S. senator once said. Networking is big business, and GOSIP is leading the way. This profile defines the procurement specifications now and for the years to come.

This discussion considers GOSIP activity in the U.S., although a similar GOSIP activity exists in the U.K. and another in Canada (under the name COSAC). GOSIP is intended to provide interoperability across federal systems, although some states are also adopting it.

GOSIP was written by an interagency group and is now under the control of the GOSIP Advanced Requirements Group within the NIST. It is an evolving set of procurement documents, starting with GOSIP 1.0 that became effective in 1990. Subsequent GOSIP updates will occur at 18-month to two-year intervals.

GOSIP applies to procurement of new networks and major upgrades of existing networks, but not necessarily to every network procurement. If an agency is adding a few nodes to a non-OSI network, there is no requirement to convert the entire network to OSI. However, the move to OSI is viewed as a strategic investment by the government. Short-term gains are not the primary purpose for this move. Instead, the long-term benefits of OSI applications and multi-vendor interoperability are the principal motivations.

An immediate and total transition to OSI is not feasible due to a number of factors. There is a large installed base of IBM's System Network Architecture (SNA), DECnet, Transmission Control Protocol/Internet Protocol (TCP/IP), and Xerox Network Service (XNS) Protocol networks. OSI protocols are not yet complete in areas such as network management, internetwork routing, and directory services. And finally, a number of reservations have been expressed about an immediate move to OSI based on (1) the lack of additional functionality in current OSI implementations beyond that of TCP/IP and other protocols, (2) the relative expense and lack of demonstrated bug-free, robust operation of OSI protocols, (3) the relatively few vendors offering OSI implementations, and (4) the general uncertainty about using OSI protocols instead of TCP/IP and other protocols. These hesitations should be overcome as OSI protocols become more readily available, but a short-term chicken-and-egg phenomenon is involved. Which comes first: supply or demand?

One limitation of GOSIP is that it specifies only protocols that are full International Standards. This is good in that International Standard protocols are by definition well-established and solid. The other side of the coin is that non-standardized portions are missing from GOSIP and must be filled in by some other means. These filled in portions may be from implementer agreements or from vendor-specific enhancements.

The initial version of GOSIP is often called GOSIP 1.0, which indicates that subsequent versions are in various stages of development. Version 1.0 is specified in the NIST Federal Information Processing Standard (FIPS) Publication 146. It is limited to the 1984 X.400 electronic messaging and FTAM applications. At the lower layers, it includes the heavy duty Class 4 Transport Protocol, the connectionless Internet Protocol, X.25 for wide area networks, and the common IEEE (Institute of Electrical and Electronics Engineers) local area networks. These include Ethernet-like carrier sense multiple access (IEEE 802.3), token bus (802.4), and token ring (802.5) with connectionless logical link control (802.2, Class 1).

GOSIP 2.0 is specified in FIPS Pub 146-1. (It would have been easier to remember 146-2, but who's counting?) GOSIP 2.0 adds and requires the following protocols that were not available for version 1.0:

Virtual terminal service (Telnet and Forms profiles).
Office Document Architecture (ODA).
Integrated Services Digital Network (ISDN).
End System – Intermediate System (ES-IS) Protocol.

Version 2.0 also adds two optional services. Because these services are implementation options, they are not required for conformance with GOSIP version 2.0:

Connectionless Transport Service (CLTS).
Connection-Oriented Network Service (CONS).

Version 2.0 also adds a number of errata for version 1.0 implementations. These errata are summarized below. FIPS Pub 146-1 should be consulted for additional detail.

1. The more recent Stable Implementation Agreements have resulted in corrections, particularly at the application layer, that should be included in version 1.0 networks.
2. Messaging systems in version 1.0 were required to route based on a number of addressing fields including the *personal name*. Routing based on the name was deleted in version 2.0.

3. For alignment with current routing standards, the address structure of the network service access point for version 2.0 should be used instead of that of version 1.0.
4. The version 1.0 requirement for priority processing of connectionless internetwork packets has been deleted.
5. The version 1.0 security services and options have been revised.

In addition to version 2.0 changes and enhancements, further work is planned in GOSIP version 3.0 that will add more protocols as they become full International Standards. Protocols expected to be incorporated into GOSIP 3.0 include the following protocols:

X.500 directory services.
Class 2 Transport Protocol.
Computer Graphics Metafile (CGM).
Added virtual terminal service (X3, page, and scroll).
Message-handling system (MHS) extensions (1988 recommendations).
File transfer, access, and management (FTAM) extensions.
Fiber Distributed Data Interface (FDDI).
Network management.
Optional security enhancements.
Standard Generalized Mark-up Language (GML).
Manufacturing Message Specification (MMS).
Intra-domain dynamic routing.
Electronic Data Interchange (EDI).

Version 4.0 of GOSIP is expected to include the following:

Transaction processing.
Remote data base access.
Additional optional security enhancements.
Additional network management functions.
Inter-domain dynamic routing.

Presumably, extensions to GOSIP will be an ongoing process for well into the next century as OSI protocols continue to be developed and standardized. The GOSIP 2.0 specification comments on the evolution of the GOSIP series of specifications and indicates that the intent is for versions be upward-compatible. Later in the specification, this is referred to as a goal, but one that cannot necessarily be met in all cases. Some changes may not allow simple upward compatibility.

Implementers should be cautious of issues such as upward compatibility. They should also avoid misinterpretations of the GOSIP specifications that are commonly made, especially in some trade journals. GOSIP does NOT require that all networking systems be procured with OSI protocols. Entirely new systems and those with substantial increases in network functionality should conform to GOSIP, but minor extensions to existing networks certainly need not. This decision is left to each separate procurement agency. A waiver process gives such agencies some flexibility. However, because the stated objective of GOSIP is to guide a strategic investment by the government to obtain the interoperability and increased application-level functionality of OSI as quickly as possible, such waivers should not be taken lightly. Government officials may very well find an over-dependence on vendor-specific and other non-OSI networking approaches to be severely career limiting! In any case, enforcement of GOSIP is by the government agencies and not by NIST.

However, the emergence of GOSIP does not necessarily mean that the use of vendor-specific and industry-standard protocols will end. The GOSIP specification provides a definition of an end system that suggests the possibility of its including more than one computer. This is consistent with the definition of an end system in the original OSI Reference Model. Both OSI and the OSI Reference Model support the designation of an entire non-OSI network as a single end system, with a gateway between it and the OSI world.

A common misconception is that GOSIP will include a transition strategy from vendor-specific or industry-standard forms of networking to OSI networking. This is not the case. GOSIP specifies the procurement practices and not the transition from other protocols.

## THE MAP/TOP PROFILE

Probably one of the most important profiles is that of the Manufacturing Automation and Technical and Office Protocols, which are commonly considered together as MAP/TOP. They were actually developed before the term profile was used, but the concept was the same. A well-defined subset of evolving OSI standards was to be used to meet a specific user-community (functional) need. The driving force behind the development of MAP was General Motors.

The auto maker needed to introduce more technology and automation onto the manufacturing floor to remain competitive. However, GM was also finding that much of the cost of introducing new technologies such as robotics and numerical control machines was the need to rip out and replace previous communications hardware and software. As much as one-third of the replacement cost was due to this otherwise unnecessary change from one vendor's proprietary communications system to another proprietary approach. GM wanted a standard set of networking hardware and software (protocols) for use in the factory. This led to MAP.

A parallel activity to define the office equivalent of MAP (called TOP) was initiated by Boeing. MAP and TOP needed to be compatible because online equivalents of blueprints and other manufacturing documentation clearly had to be developed in the office and subsequently used in the factory. Thus, MAP and TOP were closely coordinated in their early forms and were officially synchronized with the introduction of version 3.0 of each. (MAP had previously reached versions 2.1 and 2.2, while TOP was at version 1.0.)

MAP version 2.1 was developed to provide minimal OSI application services to get on with the introduction of OSI onto the factory floor. It might be viewed as a calculated risk, or at least as a strategic investment (to borrow the GOSIP term). MAP 2.1 provided simple file transfers based on the draft proposal form of FTAM and electronic messaging based on the 1984 X.400 recommendations. Both FTAM and X.400 were expected to change, perhaps dramatically. The words *draft* and *proposal* imply change. When used together, as in the *OSI draft proposal stage of development*, one can guarantee change! As a consequence, version 2.1 MAP devices were not upward-compatible with version 3.0 MAP devices.

This lack of upward compatibility shook much of the MAP community, causing companies to adopt a more cautious *wait-and-see* attitude. Before this shock, the MAP/TOP user group meetings took on the appearance (to the author) of a religious revival meeting. Companies would announce they were joining the group and would be following the MAP/TOP way in future product offerings. This changed when the time-line associated with the standardization process became better known to the participants. Companies that had developed (or purchased) MAP 2.1 products and found them incompatible with MAP/TOP 3.0 products were much more cautious in their subsequent developments and purchases. Looking back on this phase of development, one finds that the best interests of all concerned were served by moving ahead as quickly as possible with OSI. However, those who jumped in without realizing the possible impact of protocol changes may have learned an expensive lesson. GOSIP has taken a far more cautious approach in this regard.

MAP also provided a pioneering effort in the development of a major variation of OSI called the Enhanced Performance Architecture (EPA) in which the network, through presentation layers and the association control service element of the application layer, were by-passed entirely. The application protocols operate directly upon the data link layer of the local area network by using an acknowledged connectionless service (called Class 3 in OSI). The direct by-passing of one or more OSI layers is considered heresy by many OSI purists. The OSI Reference Model states that while sublayers are optional, each layer must be included in every end system. EPA is more concerned with performance than the purist's approach. Its typical application is in the process control industry in which events must be acted upon quickly to avoid major breakdowns in closed-loop control systems or other time-critical processes involving the real-time flow of materials. In defense of the purist's position, past experiences have shown that bending the rules to meet

<table>
<tr><td rowspan="3">X.400<br>MHS<br>(1984)</td><td>FTAM</td><td>MMS</td><td>X.500 Dir Serv</td><td>Net Mgmt</td><td></td></tr>
<tr><td colspan="5">Association Control Service Element (ACSE)</td></tr>
<tr><td colspan="5">Presentation Protocol</td></tr>
<tr><td colspan="6">Session Protocol</td></tr>
<tr><td colspan="6">Transport Protocol Class 4 (Connection-Oriented)</td></tr>
<tr><td colspan="5">Internet Protocol<br>(Connectionless)</td><td rowspan="4">X.25</td></tr>
<tr><td colspan="5">IEEE 802.2 Logical Link Control Class 1 (Connectionless)</td></tr>
<tr><td colspan="2">IEEE 802.4<br>Broadband Token Bus</td><td colspan="3">IEEE 802.4<br>Carrierband Token Bus</td></tr>
<tr><td>5 Mbps</td><td>10 Mbps</td><td>10 Mbps</td><td colspan="2">5 Mbps</td></tr>
</table>

*Illustration courtesy of Learning Group International*

**FIGURE 7-1** Manufacturing Automation Protocol (MAP) profile.

performance needs often comes back to haunt developers when they want to go beyond the limits of their original plans, e.g., when they want to provide internetworking.

In addition to the EPA, the MAP/TOP profile includes some protocols that are not yet part of GOSIP. MAP/TOP has historically not been limited to protocols that have attained International Standards status. A snapshot of the MAP/TOP profile is shown in Figures 7-1 and 7-2.

# CONFORMANCE TESTING

Conformance testing demonstrates that a protocol suite implementation operates in accordance with the specification (such as GOSIP 1.0). Such tests should demonstrate that the implementation meets functional requirements (e.g., a protocol profile provides the specified electronic messaging and file

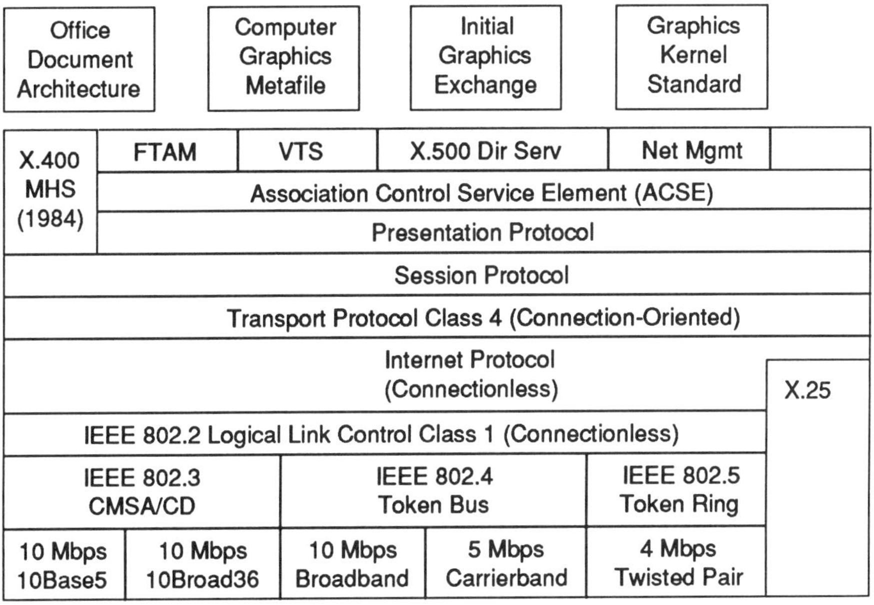

Office Document Architecture
Computer Graphics Metafile
Initial Graphics Exchange
Graphics Kernel Standard

X.400 MHS (1984)
FTAM
VTS
X.500 Dir Serv
Net Mgmt
Association Control Service Element (ACSE)
Presentation Protocol
Session Protocol
Transport Protocol Class 4 (Connection-Oriented)
Internet Protocol (Connectionless)
X.25
IEEE 802.2 Logical Link Control Class 1 (Connectionless)
IEEE 802.3 CMSA/CD
IEEE 802.4 Token Bus
IEEE 802.5 Token Ring
10 Mbps 10Base5
10 Mbps 10Broad36
10 Mbps Broadband
5 Mbps Carrierband
4 Mbps Twisted Pair

*Illustration courtesy of Learning Group International*

**FIGURE 7-2** Technical and Office Protocol (TOP) profile.

transfer capabilities), as well as the dynamic properties such as error, fault, or crash recovery.

Conformance testing is quite formal and may include test criteria from the specifications themselves, as well as positive test results. In the U.S. the major organization involved with conformance tests has been the Corporation for Open Systems (COS).

COS was formed in January, 1986, and differed from earlier organizations in the diversity of its member companies and government agencies. Its members include companies involved in computer hardware, software communications, engineering, semiconductor development, government, finance, and manufacturing. The original goals were to focus OSI development efforts, to introduce a sense of urgency in these developments, and to address a broader set of concerns than just MAP/TOP. Subsequently, the dominant COS objective became development of conformance tests for OSI products.

The conformance test process involves several steps. First, COS develops a COS stack specification as a subset of the OSI protocols. For example, the first COS stack that was developed in 1988 was for the bottom four layers and included Transport Protocol Class 4, connectionless internet, and IEEE 802.4, token bus. This portion of the MAP stack was chosen because of its availability from several vendors. The next step is the development of a set of test cases and a test facility. Vendor implementations can then be tested against the test suite; if they pass, they are awarded the *COS Mark.* The vendors can then use this COS Mark in promoting their products. It is similar to the *Good Housekeeping* Seal of Approval in that it provides customers with a degree of confidence that the product will work as advertised. Hewlett-Packard, Motorola, and Concord Communications were the first companies to receive the COS Mark based on this limited test suite in 1989.

Current conformance tests exist for 1984 X.400 and FTAM and are under development for other protocols. COS has been criticized for delays in getting conformance test suites in place, and for its reluctance to accept European-developed conformance test suites that were available. The harmonization of these multinational groups now seems to have been accomplished.

The intent of conformance testing is to substantiate a vendor's claim of being *conformant to* a protocol specification or profile. This testing can provide the *teeth* in a contractual arrangement calling for GOSIP 1.0 (or other) compliance. Vendors may use similar-sounding terms such as being *compliant with* the specifications. Caution is advised in procuring such products.

CCITT recommendations are being developed to address conformance testing. These are X.290 through X.294, which cover OSI conformance testing methodology and framework. These recommendations address applications testing, abstract test suite specifications, tree and tabular combined notation, test realization, test laboratories, and clients. Of these developing recommendations, only X.290 was available in the 1988 Blue Books. A footnote indicated that it was in an early stage of development and changes should be expected. That caveat applies to the summary statements that follow.

X.290 introduces a new notation, appending an asterisk (*) to OSI and Recommendation, based on the following definition taken from X.290:

> Systems need to be tested to determine if they conform to relevant OSI or related CCITT X-series or T-series (hereafter abbreviated to "OSI*") protocol Standard(s) or Recommendation(s) (hereafter abbreviated to "Recommendation(s)*").

The T-series has not been discussed; it refers to telematic (messaging) systems. The concern for such systems was limited to X.400 and X.500 protocols. The basic concern of X.290 is that test suites should be developed for each OSI* protocol recommendation for use by suppliers, implementers, users, administrators, and third-party testers. X.290 goes on to state that

> conformance testing involves testing both the capabilities and the behavior of an implementation and checking what is observed against the conformance requirements in the relevant Recommendation(s)* and against what the implementer states the implementation's capabilities are.

In the terminology of X.290, *capabilities* are the static requirements of the recommendations. These static tests include verifying the groupings of functional units and options into classes and the range of values that are supported by parameters. The static tests are a small portion of the conformance demonstration. The *behavior* refers to the dynamic aspects of the recommendations; it covers the larger portion of the recommendations such as message exchanges. The final part of the above quote refers to what the implementer states the implementation capabilities are. Here, the word *capability* is undoubtedly used in a different context than that of the static characteristics and probably refers to the statements concerning which options have been included in the implementation.

The general test approach of X.290 is that of a C-clamp tester setting on both sides of the implementation under test. The test descriptions are called *abstract testing* because they define the concept rather than the specific test plans and procedures.

In addition to the conformance testing specified in X.290, each of the more recent protocol recommendations includes a section on conformance. Although they tend to be brief, they cover (1) statement requirements, e.g., defining the application context for which conformance is claimed, (2) static requirements, e.g., the abstract syntax definition of application protocol data units, and (3) dynamic requirements, e.g., conformance to the elements of procedure and mappings. The service definitions do not include conformance sections.

## INTEROPERABILITY TESTING

Interoperability testing demonstrates that an implementation will operate successfully with other implementations of the same protocol suite, such as GOSIP 1.0. Unlike formal conformance tests, interoperability testing is considerably less formal. However, it is also very important. Studies have indicated that a major concern of potential OSI network buyers has been (and still is) the lack of demonstrated interoperability of different vendors' products. Proof of interoperability is required! Conformance testing by itself has not been an acceptable solution. While it may be considered necessary, it has not been sufficient to ensure interoperability in *real-world* applications.

In a procurement, the procuring agency must provide the specific interoperability test requirements. These requirements include the defined set of hardware/software components in the test, the planned test scenarios to be run between the various systems under test, and the criteria for failing or passing the test.

Interoperability is a concern of both the consumer and the producer. A producer of OSI protocols should be familiar with the various implementer agreements. In the U.S. the principal implementer agreements come from NIST, but there are also other regional groups including the European Workshop for Open Systems and OSI Asia-Oceania Workshop. These different groups realize that the ultimate desire is for worldwide interoperability; thus, recent efforts have been to develop ISO international standardized profiles.

While the international groups are important, the major influence within the U.S. is from the NIST workshop for implementers. It periodically updates its document series called the Stable Implementation Agreements (SIA) and Working Implementation Agreements (WIA).

The SIA and WIA documents have the exact same structure, and the idea is to move sections from the WIA to the SIA (but never vice versa). The SIA is published at the beginning of each year by NIST and represents the current status of agreed upon implementations.

NIST also developed an interoperability test vehicle known as OSInet for the testing and registration of announced products. Initial vendors involved in OSInet included IBM, DEC, Unisys, HP, Control Data, NCR, Xerox, Retix, Touch, and Wollongong. At the time this book was written, responsibility for OSInet was being transferred from NIST to COS. However, its basic objectives do not seem to have changed.

## PERFORMANCE TESTING

Performance testing is beyond the scope of existing protocol profiles and relates to a specific user need for network performance criteria such as those defined in the different quality-of-service parameters. These include delay, throughput, and residual bit-error rate.

The protocol specifications give no indication about the performance a protocol is to achieve because this performance is dependent upon the implementation trade-offs, the central processing unit and memory speed, and the network technology. Performance testing and specifications from which to perform these tests must be developed based on a specific end-user need.

## FUNCTIONAL TESTING

Functional testing demonstrates the extent to which a given protocol suite implementation actually meets a specific set of user needs. NIST has issued guidelines for MHS and FTAM applications from which functional testing specifications may be derived. Other such guidelines will be developed in the future. The generation of functional testing specifications is a task that is unique to each agency based on its specific needs.

## Summary and Conclusions

In spite of OSI's intention that computers from all vendors be interoperable through the use of common protocols, there are still many instances where this will not happen because of the diversity of approaches within OSI itself. The definition and use of profiles or functional standards help to ensure that interoperability will actually occur.

However, even with agreed upon profiles and the subsequent interoperability, it is possible that the multi-vendor quest still is lost. It may be lost because the multi-vendor network cannot be managed in a common way. Network management tools are needed from vendor X to manage vendor X's network, and network management tools are needed from vendor Y to manage its networks! What is needed is OSI network management. That is the subject of Chapter 8.

# 8

# OSI NETWORK MANAGEMENT

Network management means just that — specifically, how one manages a network. Like all management, network management involves many factors, but it is conceptually very simple. One knows what should be happening, monitors to see what is actually happening, and takes control action as necessary to bring the actual happenings into line with the expectations. The multiplicity of factors involved in management includes fixing things when they are broken, maintaining high performance and security, and accounting for the way resources are being used. The tricky part is to accomplish these simple goals across a network that spans an entire corporation or government agency. It is difficult enough on a departmental network.

## THE ROLE OF NETWORK MANAGEMENT

In a discussion of network management, the best place to start is with the end. What is the desired end result of network management? Specifically, what is the desired end result of Open Systems Interconnection (OSI) network management? The context of the questions will yield quite different answers.

The most obvious difference is that when one asks about OSI network management, one expects to get answers about managing OSI networks. This is by far the lesser distinction between the two questions. The more significant difference is in the scope of concern with OSI network management. OSI network management is concerned with the current network configuration, with faulty components, with the level of performance achieved by the network, with its security, and even with accounting for its use. These different parts of the network management problem, sometimes called functional areas, are shown in their application level positions in Figure 8-1. This figure also shows the management information base (MIB) that is used by each of these applications. Each network management application is described in the paragraphs that follow.

1. **Configuration management** — Maintaining an awareness of the physical and logical topology of the network, including the existence of components and their interconnectivity. This information could be used to generate a display of the network topology on a network management console. It also includes facilities for the setting of parameters, initializing and disabling of resources, reconfiguration,

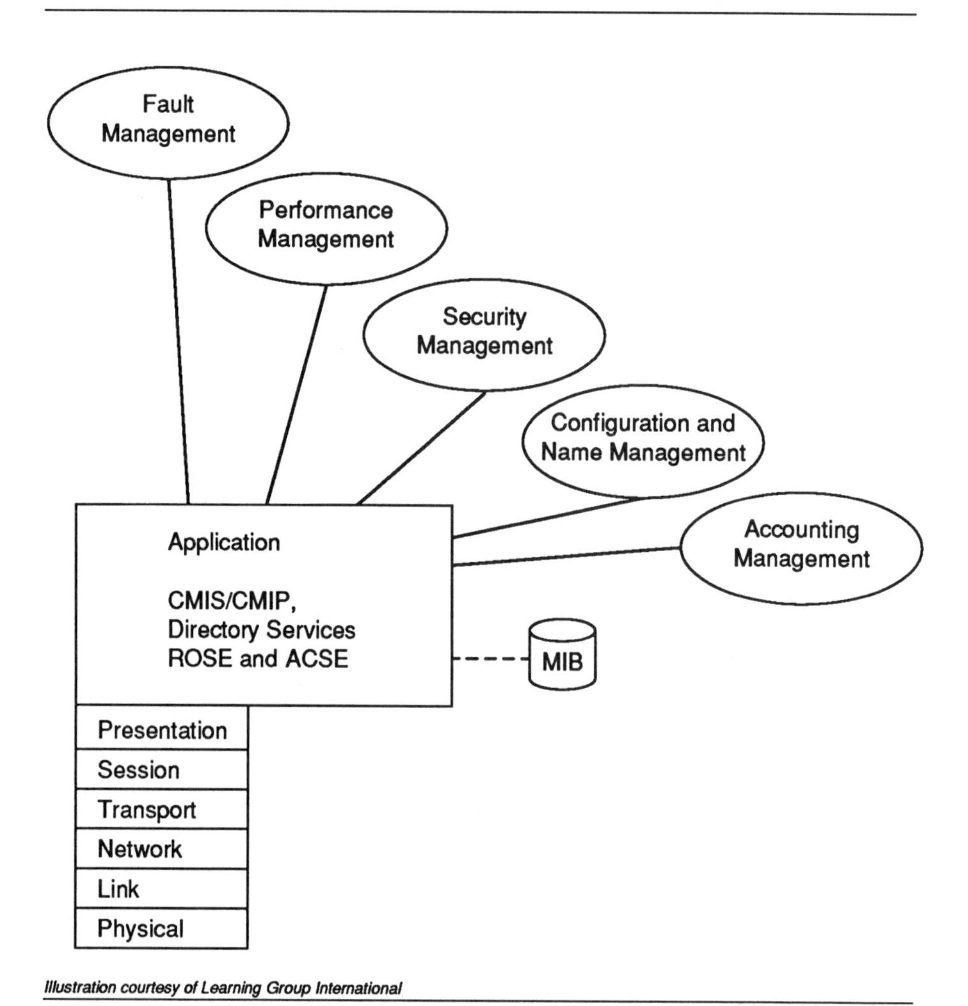


*Illustration courtesy of Learning Group International*

**FIGURE 8-1** OSI network management includes five major application components.

and collecting information about the state of the network components. Name management is sometimes also included in this functional area so that resources can be managed by convenient names rather than addresses. However, this function seems better allocated to the directory services.

2. **Fault management** — Maintaining an awareness of the current up/down status of each switching component and interconnection in the network and of the current activities with regard to restoring any faulty units. This information could be used with the topology map to indicate which portions of the network are functional, operating in a marginal manner, or down. Typical displays of this information would use color to indicate the fault status, e.g., green for components and interconnections that are fully functional, yellow for marginal operation, and red for failures. Fault management also provides logging of fault occurrences, guidance on how to diagnose the faults, what diagnostics should be run, and how to correlate the results of the diagnostics with subsequent repair actions.
3. **Performance management** — Maintaining an awareness of the current and previous performance of the network, including statistical parameters such as delay, throughput, availability, packets per second, bits per second, and number of retransmissions. This information would supplement the previous examples of displayed network status, providing additional insight into traffic loading or other factors affecting the observed network behavior. The statistics are frequently in terms of counts and running totals, the combination of which produces averages. For example, the total number of bits sent divided by the packet count gives the average packet length. By collecting data in these forms, the processing and data transmission overhead for the collection of performance data can be kept to a minimum and can ensure that it does not bias the observed network performance.
4. **Security management** — Maintaining an awareness of who is using the network and that access to resources is within authorized constraints based on the *need to know* of the authorized users. The network management display might provide alerts to the network manager when security events (e.g., an excessive number of failed login attempts at a network terminal server) are detected. An on-line audit data base would also be available for more detailed analysis. Security management also includes password procedure controls (e.g., enforcing periodic changes and access controls for network resources).

5. **Accounting management** — Maintaining an awareness of how and by whom network resources are being used. This information may be needed for statistical or billing purposes. It would not generally be displayed except in response to queries. Accounting management can also provide limits on the use of the network, its resources, and administrative mechanisms to set these limits.

The descriptions of each of the five major functional areas of network management begin with the words *maintaining an awareness of.* This repetition was intentional to emphasize the point that network management fundamentally intends to provide *insight*, not *numbers*. This insight can be amplified by the manner in which the information is displayed and made available to the network manager. These are important issues, independent of OSI versus non-OSI network management. The basic concern is that the network manager (person) is not necessarily a networking guru, system programmer, or other highly technical person. Network management tools need to take this into consideration; this is typically accomplished by heavy use of menu-driven user interfaces, icon-based invocation of capabilities, color coding, automatic alerts, and multiple window displays. As an example use of the multiple window capability, it is common to keep a window open that displays the overall network topology and status, even when more detailed work is being done in other windows.

The insight that is needed for network management comes through having sufficient information available to recognize and isolate problems. Although it may be summarized elsewhere, this requires that certain information be centralized in one place. This is typical of management in other forms within organizations. A department manager needs sufficient data upon which to base a decision. These data must be available in one place for analysis. The data may be in the form of summaries of lower-level data and may result in even more condensed management data being forwarded to the next higher level of management. The same need exists in network management.

With the exceptions of the highest- and lowest-level components in a management system, all components are both managers of lower-level entities and agents reporting to a higher-level manager. The terms *manager* and *agent* reflect these two roles. (Some network management systems use differing terminology, but all involve the same concepts.) The manager/agent structure is shown in Figure 8-2. One manager is shown in this figure with its monitoring and control of agents by means of the common management information

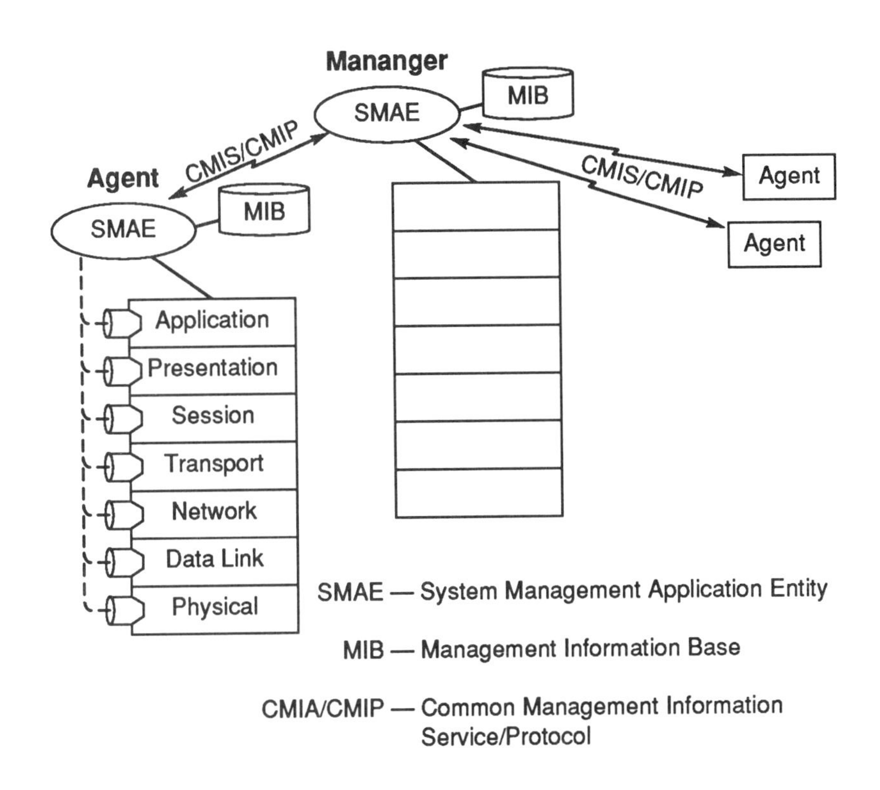


*Illustration courtesy of Learning Group International*

**FIGURE 8-2** Network management agents control their seven-layer stacks and report to the manager.

service (CMIS) and common management information protocol (CMIP). Each agent monitors and controls the seven OSI layers within its implementation, reporting back to the manager. The application layer components that are shown are the system management application entities (SMAEs).

The SMAE internal structure is shown in Figure 8-3. At the very top is a system management application service element (SMASE) that manages the collection of periodic status and performance information from the agents, sets the initialization and configuration parameters of the agent devices, and receives notifications of device exceptions such as a reboot. The SMAE uses the primitives such as M_Get and M_Set of the common management information service element (CMISE) to perform these operations with the agent.

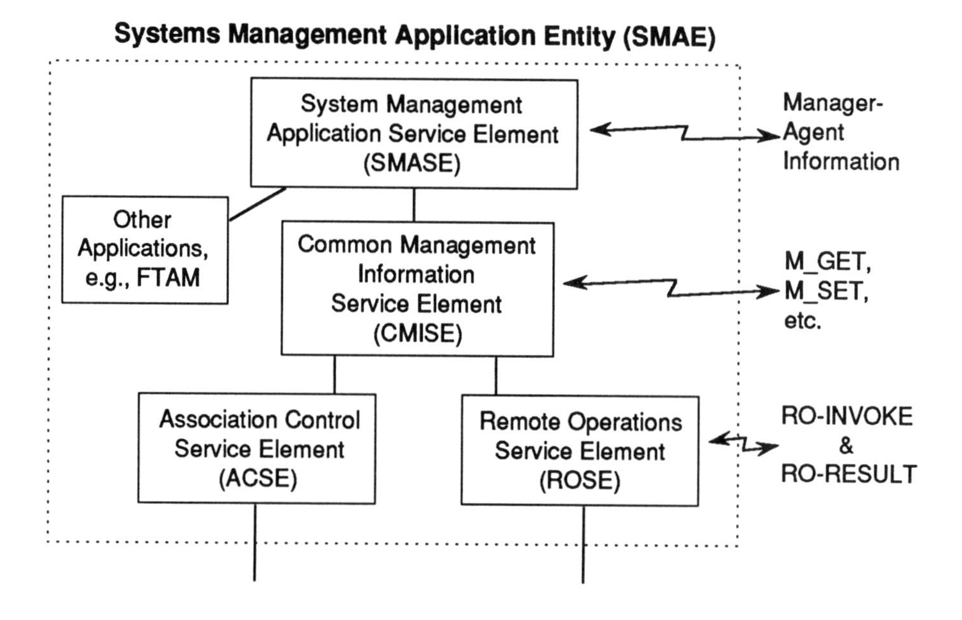


*Illustration courtesy of Learning Group International*

**FIGURE 8-3** Systems management involves several application layer service elements.

These primitives are in turn sent by means of the ROSE RO-INVOKE and RO-RESULT remote operations primitives. As indicated in Figure 8-3, the SMASE may also use the services of other applications such as file transfer, access, and management, e.g., to move large portions of information between managers and agents.

# NETWORK MANAGEMENT STANDARDS

Both the International Standards Organization (ISO) and the Consultative Committee for International Telephone and Telegraph (CCITT) have been active in the development and harmonization of network management standards. In OSI terminology, this is frequently referred to as *systems management.*

ISO considers the general management framework to be an extension of the OSI Reference Model. It is therefore numbered ISO 7498-4. CCITT considers it the introductory part of a new X.700 series of recommendations on network (system) management. Therefore, X.700 corresponds to ISO 7498-4. Both ISO and CCITT then provide a *system management overview.* This is ISO 10040 and CCITT X.701. At the time of writing, ISO 10040 was in the Draft International Standard stage of development, which usually indicates the final technical form of a standard. However, recent experience indicates that the draft stage is not necessarily as stable technically as has been the case in the past. Caution is still needed in building or buying network management products based on draft versions of standards.

The next documents in the sequence are OSI common management information service and protocol, which are ISO 9595/9596 and CCITT X.710/X.711. These two documents and their International Standard status are the basis for most of the OSI and OSI-like network management approaches that are currently available. Implementers have felt comfortable using them and, as a result, have filled in the missing pieces with interim approaches.

Portions of network management that have trailed behind include the ISO (DIS) 10165-1 to -4 series and the CCITT X.720 series, which cover the management informational model. Other portions in a similar status include the ISO (DIS) 10164-1 to -11 series and the CCITT X.730 series, which cover a wide variety of detailed functions such as object management, state management, relationship managment, alarms, events, and logs. These are discussed in the following paragraphs:

1. **Object management** — Creates, deletes, and manages values of object attributes and notifications of changes.
2. **State management** — Handles administrative, operational, and usage states, such as enabled/disabled, active, busy, locked/unlocked, and shut down (i.e., not accepting additional user).
3. **Relationship management** — Represents relationships between objects, including direct versus indirect and symmetric versus asymmetric.
4. **Alarms** — Specifies the alarm types and formats, including error report severity of indeterminate, critical, major, minor, and warning.
5. **Events** — Defines events that are to be reported and the event processor that is to receive each such event.
6. **Log management** — Assures that events are entered into a log.

Other functions (e.g., security audit trails, access controls, accounting meters, workload monitoring, test management, statistical analysis, and network time management) are also being developed.

# THE MANAGER/AGENT MODEL

A manager entity operates with a number of agent entities as seen in Figure 8-2. The manager has access to the network-wide MIB and coordinates with subsets of the MIB maintained in the agents using three basic capabilities. The manager must be able to read (or get) parameters of the agent such as its current retransmission timeout value and its packet handling count. The manager must also be able to write (or set) some parameters such as the retransmission timeout value. The manager would not be expected to write into parameters such as the packet-handling count except to reset it after it has been read. In addition, a network device must be able to notify the network manager of some events in an unsolicited manner. This is called an *event report*. For example, a network device might report that it has been rebooted by an event report. The three fundamental network management capabilities are

1. **Get** — To read a network device parameter value.
2. **Set** — To write a network device parameter value.
3. **Event_report** — To obtain an unsolicited indication of an event from a network device.

Two related additions in version 2 of CMIS/CMIP are the *Cancel_Get* and *Modified_Set*. The Cancel_Get operation is used to stop a lengthy Get operation that has been initiated. It is a confirmed operation. The Modified_Set operation is used to manage set-valued attributes and includes the ability to add or remove a value to a set-valued attribute. A *Set_To_Default* operation is also added, as the name implies, to set a value to a default.

In addition, OSI network management version 1 identifies three other network management primitives. They are

1. **Action** — A command from the network manager to the agent to perform some operation, e.g., to reboot.
2. **Create** — A command from the network manager to the agent to add a new entry into the agent's subset of the MIB, e.g., to add a new routing table entry.
3. **Delete** — A command from the network manager to the agent to delete an entry in the agent's subset of the MIB, e.g., to remove an entry from a routing table.

OSI provides all these primitives as confirmed operations, as well as optional unconfirmed set, action, and event_report primitives. In addition, OSI network management provides a variety of synchronization options including best efforts, ordered, and atomic execution. All of these primitives are ways of getting information between the MIB components in the manager and agents. Because all OSI network management operations involve connection-oriented services, primitives are also required to invoke the association control service element (ACSE). The following final subset of primitives include:

1. **Initialize** — Used in a confirmed manner to establish an association for use between CMISEs.
2. **Terminate** — Used in a confirmed manner to release an association between CMISEs.
3. **Abort** — Used in a unconfirmed manner to abruptly release an association between two CMISEs.

OSI network management uses the services of other application layer service elements for the actual communications between the distributed managers and agents. The basic form of this use of other service elements is shown in Figure 8-4.

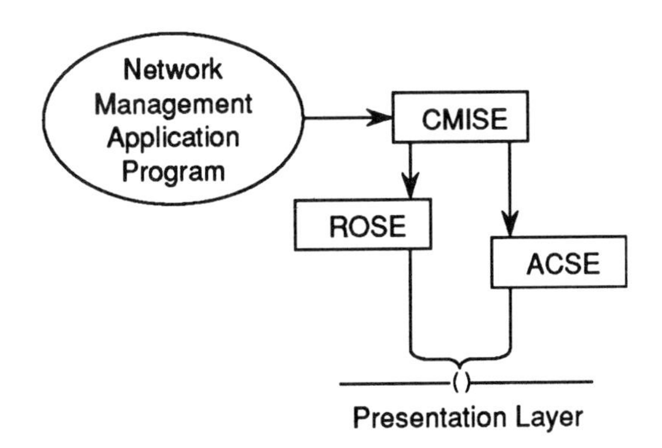


*Illustration courtesy of Learning Group International*

**FIGURE 8-4** OSI network management uses the services of ROSE and ACSE.

The common management information service elements call upon the ACSE for the establishment and release of the association. Otherwise, all requests and exchanges are by means of the remote operation service element, which provides a transaction mechanism for the get, set, action, event_report, create, and delete primitives. All of these transactions except event_report are initiated by the manager (initiator side) of the connection. The handling of the agent-initiated event_report required some modification in the ROSE protocols. Work is also underway to provide connectionless support for some network management transactions.

## MAINTAINING THE MANAGEMENT INFORMATION BASE

The key to network management is the ability to manage large amounts of the right kind of information. In OSI, this management information is called the management information base or MIB. The MIB includes all the data discussed, including the network configuration, fault status, performance data, security data, and accounting data. The nature of the information and its format are the subject of OSI. The tools to collect it from the network devices and to control parameters within the network devices are also the subject of OSI. However, the tools to manipulate the data for display to an operator are not the subject of OSI and include the use of existing relational data base management systems for access to the data based on structured queries. The information in the MIB includes the managed objects, their attributes, the operations they may perform, and the notifications they may provide.

The MIB parameters are defined as data structures using abstract syntax notation (ASN.1). Most of these data structures are quite simple, e.g., counts, running sums, and status information. However, it is still useful to have a precise and unambiguous definition of the MIB data, especially when multiple vendors are involved in the collection, dissemination, and processing of MIB data.

## IMPLEMENTATIONS OF OSI NETWORK MANAGEMENT

OSI network management implementations have been under development for some time by major computer and data communications companies. However, the lack of established standards and implementation agreements has severely limited product offerings to date. As with other protocols, the involvement by the U.S. National Institute of Standards and Technology (NIST) and by the European and Asian standards groups has been helpful, but they cannot make up for missing pieces in the network management puzzle.

Various vendors have attempted to fill this vacuum by providing OSI network management tools when available and by filling in the gaps with their own developments. These vendor products include HP's OpenView, AT&T's Accumaster, and Digital's Enterprise Management Architecture (EMA). IBM also has announced intentions to couple OSI into NetView, its proprietary network management umbrella product. In the past, IBM has integrated other network management systems into NetView by means of NetView/PC as shown in Figure 8-5. This is one option for the integration of OSI and IBM's System Network Architecture (SNA) forms of network management.

Vendors have developed international support for the OSI Network Management Forum, which has representatives from North American, European,

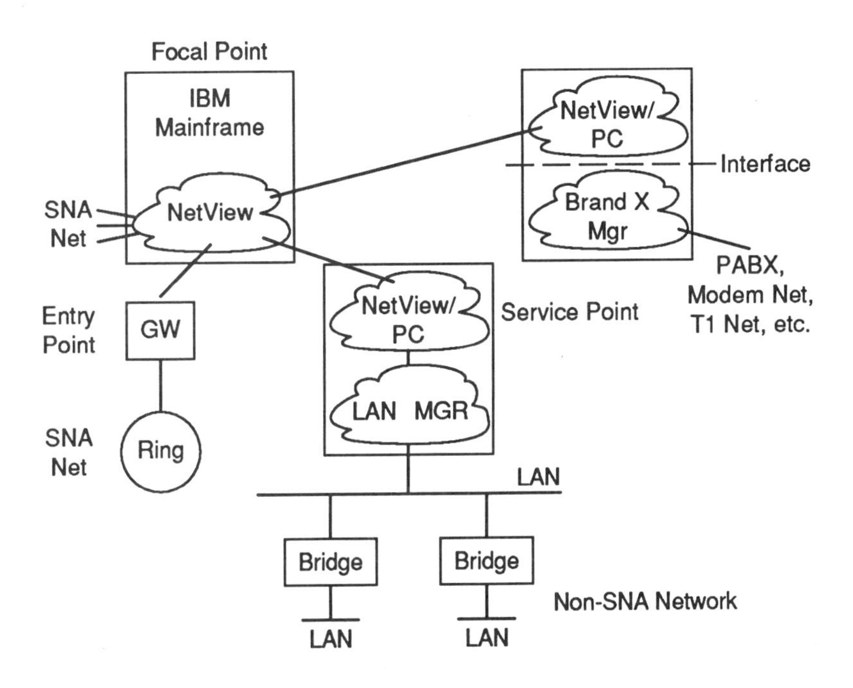


*Illustration courtesy of Learning Group International*

**FIGURE 8-5** Non-SNA networks may be managed from NetView using NetView/PC.

and Asian companies in over 16 countries. While they have over 100 member organizations, less than 20 percent of these are dues-paying, voting members.

A primary concern of the Forum is the development of an implementation profile for network management, along with a network management interface definition. This comes with a new set of jargon, including a protocol stack (the *p stack*), a set of network management messages, called the *m messages*, and the resultant *P+M interface* that combines the two.

Conformance tests for network management were needed but unavailable; thus, a set of such tests was produced. Because no organization was available to administer them, a self-certified approach was initially defined. These steps are indicative of the sense of urgency that the Forum has applied to getting OSI network management in place.

It is particularly interesting that the major vendors have banded together to produce an early version of an OSI standard network management system. Having proprietary control of the management of a customer's network can be a major marketing advantage to a computer or communications vendor. The vendors' agreement to work together to promote OSI network management in this early form must represent a mutual corporate awareness of the inevitability of OSI. Or maybe these corporations see a way to make revenue in this hotly contested business area. Only time will tell. In the meantime, if IBM, Digital, Unisys, HP, and other companies all want to make it happen, it probably will.

# EVOLUTION TO OSI NETWORK MANAGEMENT

Three dominant approaches to computer networking today cover the scale of networks that require sophisticated network management. Two of these are vendor-proprietary approaches, namely IBM's SNA and Digital's DECnet. The third is the industry-standard Transmission Control Protocol/Internet Protocol (TCP/IP) suite. All three have adopted plans for an evolution to OSI, including OSI network management.

The basis for most strategies for migration to OSI network management is in the use of those portions of OSI network management that are currently available and in providing interim solutions when OSI standards are not yet available. The MIB is the key to most strategies. If a network management system is built to use the OSI MIB, then the software support tools that humans and application programs use to operate with the MIB can be salvaged when the total OSI solution becomes available. These tools typically include relational data base management systems with extensive query and data manipulation capabilities.

The other key interface with the MIB is that of the devices being managed. This is where most of the alternative solutions differ. There are at least three fundamentally different approaches: (1) use an interim, non-OSI set of protocols between the MIB and the managed devices, (2) use the OSI CMIS/CMIP service and protocol, but operate over non-OSI transport and lower protocols, and (3) place an intermediate gateway between the CMIS/CMIP and non-OSI portions of the network. Each of these approaches is described in more detail in the paragraphs that follow.

The first approach, which uses non-OSI protocols between the MIB and the devices being managed, is best illustrated by the simple network management protocol (SNMP) of the TCP/IP community. SNMP provides a minimum (i.e., simple) set of mechanisms that can convey information between the MIB and the managed devices. These managed devices are typically non-OSI devices such as IP routers and local area network (LAN) bridges. The SNMP capability is to perform read and write operations on device parameters and to receive unsolicited event notices (called *traps*) from the devices. Typical operations of interest would be to read the number of discarded packets at a router due to congestion, to write a packet filtering criteria to a LAN bridge, and to receive an unsolicited trap indicating that a router has rebooted.

SNMP provides these capabilities by implementing a few basic primitives. One, called *Get*, reads a parameter value from the device, i.e., the device returns a *Get_Response*. Because the amount of data that can be sent in one response is limited, SNMP actually provides another variation of this command, namely *Get_Next*. A large amount of information, e.g., a complete routing table, can be read a piece at a time using the Get_Next command repetitively and receiving a Get_Response for each.

The write capability of SNMP is called Se*t*. It is actually a read-after-write operation, so it automatically returns a Get_Response. It is not called a Set_Response because it is exactly the same as performing a Get operation after the Set. It is assumed that you will only be writing (setting) limited amounts of information; thus, there is no Set_Next operation. After all, this was to be a simple network management protocol.

The final operation of SNMP is the trap function, which is an unsolicited event report from the device to the network manager. These traps are typically used to advise the network manager of an action that the device took without having been told to do so.

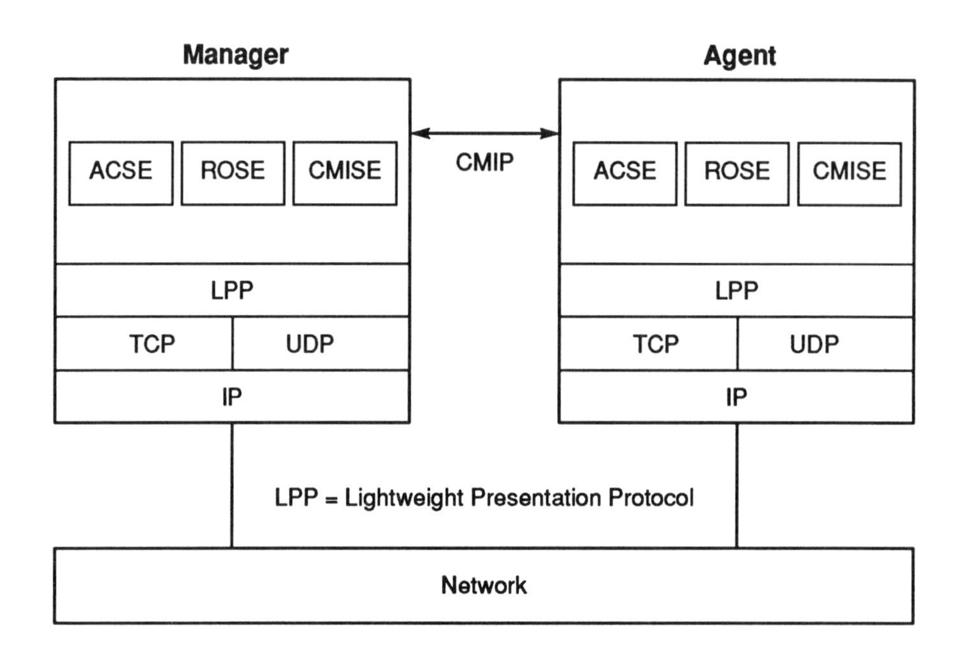


*Illustration courtesy of Learning Group International*

**FIGURE 8-6** CMOT provides OSI network management over TCP/IP networks.

SNMP has become the dominant network management approach in the TCP/IP community. It has been implemented by all major vendors of IP routers, multi-protocol routers, and many LAN bridges.

An alternative TCP/IP community network management approach that uses OSI network management protocols is CMIS Over TCP/IP (CMOT). In this approach, the CMIS/CMIP service/protocol operates over a minimal presentation layer and then over TCP/IP as shown in Figure 8-6. The intent again is to manage TCP/IP devices, usually meaning IP routers and LAN bridges. While CMOT is accepted equally as well as SNMP by the TCP/IP internet engineering board, CMOT has not found its way into actual products that need to be managed. So far, SNMP has been the approach of choice for vendor products.

CMOT may be an intermediate step between SNMP and OSI network management, but unless it provides some major advantage, it seems more likely that network users and developers will stick with SNMP until OSI is available.

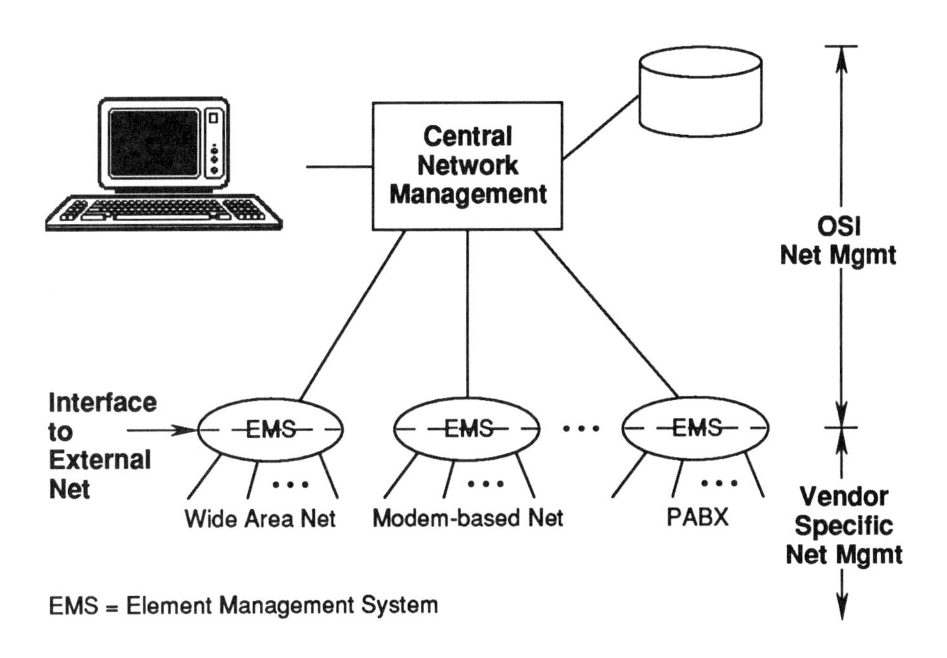


*Illustration courtesy of Learning Group International*

**FIGURE 8-7** The management of non-OSI networks can be integrated with OSI management.

A third approach that is being adopted by some vendors is to use the CMIS/CMIP OSI service/protocol between the network manager and an intermediate station called an element management system (EMS). The EMS converts between the OSI network management primitives and proprietary network management. This approach is shown in Figure 8-7.

# NETWORK MANAGEMENT SECURITY SERVICES

One rather isolated aspect of OSI network management is the security management capabilities that are to be provided. These capabilities can be expressed in terms of security services.

OSI security services are located in the security addendum to the OSI reference model and are called out in CCITT recommendation X.800, "OSI Security Architecture." These security services are particularly pervasive at the application layer. In fact, all five of the OSI security services (i.e., authentication, access control, data confidentiality, data integrity, and non-repudiation) are listed as services that could be provided by the application layer. These services are discussed later in this section. Only the network and transport layers also have a significant number of possible security services, and neither of them provides non-repudiation.

One of the principal reasons that the application layer receives such high marks as a location for security services is that it is in the best position to really know what needs to be protected and against what threats. At lower layers, this understanding is lost. Each of the five security services is discussed in the paragraphs that follow.

Authentication is provided for a number of network access needs, including that required for file transfer, virtual terminal access, and remote procedure calls. This is done at the initiation of an application layer connection. Authentication is based on something known (such as passwords), something possessed (such as a magnetic stripe badge), or something about the user (such as a fingerprint verification by a reader device). Passwords are by far the most common authentication approach, but they have historically been a weak form because of the way they have been selected and used. Allowing a user to select a password and to decide when to change it results in poor passwords (e.g., names, license plate numbers) and infrequent changes. Enforced, periodic changes, with computer-generated, eight-character, non-word passwords provide much better authentication and individual accountability. There also may be a need for ongoing authentication for some applications, such as is implicit in the ability to encrypt and decrypt messages.

Access control is required to ensure that only authorized users and applications gain access to sensitive data. Lower layers typically do not convey the user identification that is necessary to provide individual user access controls and accountability, but they can control access between end systems on a network. Access control can be based on mandatory checks (e.g., using security labels on objects and security clearances for users) and on discretionary checks (e.g., access control lists).

Data confidentiality is frequently provided at lower layers by encrypting the entire data field of packets and, in some cases, encrypting the headers as well. The application layer has the option of encrypting either the entire application data field or performing selective field encryption. The latter might significantly reduce the overhead because of the encryption/decryption operations, particularly when they are performed in software. However, the trust requirement is substantial in this case. The software must be trusted to always encrypt the selected fields and to perform the encryption correctly.

Software-based or controlled encryption is particularly important with electronic messaging systems such as X.400. These systems present an especially difficult problem for conventional cryptographic systems in which encrypt/decrypt keys are changed on a daily basis. If an electronic mail message is sent on Monday, when the day's key is Key(M), and if the message is not read until Friday, when the day's key is Key(F), how can users communicate? The typical answer to this dilemma in today's encryption technology is to get away from the use of simple one-day-at-a-time, symmetric keys and to go to a combination of asymmetric and symmetric keying. The body part of the message would be encrypted in a conventional symmetric key crypto system such as the Data Encryption Standard (DES). The key used for this encryption would be generated by a random number generator; it would be included with the body part of the message and encrypted in the public key of the recipient(s). Each possible recipient has a public key, which anyone can obtain, and a secret key that it alone knows. The DES key is encrypted in each recipient's public key and stored with the body part of the message. Each recipient can therefore decrypt the DES key and then can use it to decrypt the message.

The weak link in the scheme described is in the trustworthiness of the public keys. How do you know that you are not being given bogus public keys by some network source that wants to be able to read the messages? The solution here again is in the public key technology. A trusted source generates certificates that include the desired public key. These certificates are encrypted in the trusted site's private key. Any other site can decrypt the certificate, but only the trusted site could have encrypted it. This is a form of electronic signature.

Data integrity usually means that any attempt to modify the data in transit will be detected with a very high probability. This can be achieved at lower layers (such as the network or transport layers) by using a cryptographic error check. Because the lower layers do not know which fields of information are in need of protection, they must protect the integrity of every field. Here again, the application layer can reduce this overhead by applying integrity mechanisms only to those fields that need such protection.

The last security service, non-repudiation, has two forms. First, it can mean that the recipient who actually got the message cannot later successfully claim that the message was never received. Alternatively, non-repudiation may mean that the sender cannot later successfully claim not to have sent the message. Proof of receipt or transmittal is usually by means of an electronic signature using public key cryptography. Each user of the network has both a public key and a private key. Messages that are encrypted in the public key can only be decrypted by the owner of the private key. Messages that are encrypted in the private key can be read by anyone, but they could only be sent by the individual who possesses the private key. This provides the basis for the electronic signature. Several variations build on this basic concept.

## Summary and Conclusions

The application layer provides a wealth of opportunities for introducing security into the networks. The OSI recommendations for the placement of security services indicate that the application layer is a prime candidate for implementing security. In some cases, the network or transport layers are also considered possible locations for security services and mechanisms. However, implementer agreements and actual software products are not readily available yet. Much work remains to be done to ensure that differing implementations of security services and mechanisms do not create multi-vendor interoperability problems. That is what will happen if vendor X performs encryption as an option at the transport layer and vendor Y does it at the network layer, or if any of the other security services and mechanisms are implemented differently. There are many opportunities to destroy interoperability!

# 9

# EVOLVING OSI DEVELOPMENTS

Open Systems Interconnection (OSI) developments will continue for the foreseeable future. Capabilities that are already in some stage of standardization will be expanded. Other added capabilities will be entirely new developments. OSI standards development will change from the formalization of existing technological approaches such as reliable transmission protocols and consistent distributed data base updates to include new technological developments as part of the standardization process. This can be seen in other recent high technology standards developments such as Fiber Distributed Data Interface (FDDI) local area networks (LANs).

In the meantime, a number of extensions to the current evolving standards will be incorporated. Especially important examples of these developments are the expanded directory services and network management standards. These developments are in one stage or another of the formalization process. Extensions to file transfer, access, and management (FTAM) are also planned to allow simultaneous reads and writes to a file, file directory manipulation capability, and the ability to specify different levels of access control to portions of files.

A number of other areas are in much more formative stages of development. These include remote data base access, especially in mixed data base management environments, with remote data base management systems, replicated data, and various access methods. Office document architectures are also being developed for the exchange of documents in an OSI environment. Other developments include graphics with a variety of methods for representing graphics and images across diverse systems. These standards could certainly embody the current state of the art in representing information to users at high-performance workstations.

Additional standardization work will undoubtedly come about with regard to conformance testing of OSI protocols. However, the importance of conformance testing remains somewhat controversial. How important is it that an implementation of a protocol (or an entire protocol suite) successfully interoperate with a test protocol suite? It certainly does not guarantee interoperability with another protocol or protocol suite, even one that has passed the same conformance test. The closest analogies are Underwriter's Laboratories' Seal of Approval, which says that "we tested it, and it didn't short out or burn up" or the *Good Housekeeping* Seal of Approval, which says that you get your money back if the product was defective. What does one actually expect from conformance testing? Much remains to be done.

Developments in network security are just getting underway as cost justification and product availability are still being sorted out. The secure data network system (SDNS) incorporates OSI protocols and may address this need for both classified and unclassified-but-sensitive applications, especially in government and government-contract instances. It is hoped that the choices of layers for the differing security services and the approaches for each service will be limited to a manageable number as government and industry develop SDNS products.

Almost all the original OSI developments are connection-oriented protocols. Only the LAN data link and the internet protocol (IP) are exceptions. One can expect a number of additional connectionless OSI protocols to be developed, especially in areas such as shared file access across LANs. The commercial popularity of connectionless protocols such as the Sun Microsystem Network File System™, which is now an industry standard, will influence similar developments as an OSI standard. It may be that FTAM could serve this need, but the relative performance may well dictate the need for a better way. Additional connectionless support (such as for network management and directory services) may follow suit.

Application program interfaces for OSI applications are currently being developed in a few cases and can be expected in a large number of others in the future. This will promote the profitability of applications programs, as well as interoperability across vendor platforms. The combination of portability and interoperability provides greater freedom in multivendor networking, and additional options of vendor platforms.

There are also needs that will be filled by OSI standards for intercommunications between the different *islands* that OSI itself has created. These islands are particularly evident at the network and transport layers. The two layers tend to be closely coupled, with one camp preferring the Transport Protocol (TP) Class zero (0) or 2 over the X.25 approach, and the other preferring the TP Class 4/internet protocol approach. How can they intercommunicate? One *ad hoc* approach, which may become standardized, is the *transport bridge*. In this scheme end-to-end communications between a TP Class zero (0) or 2 over an X.25 system and a TP Class 4/IP system go through an intermediate system (bridge) that removes session layer packets from one form of encapsulation and places them in the other form of encapsulation. This is not a bridge in the sense of a media access control sublayer LAN bridge, but the general intent is the same. Unfortunately, the transport bridge is not transparent and suffers from a loss of end-to-end integrity mechanisms. It is also in direct violation of a prime directive of the OSI Reference Model that one should not have relay devices at the transport layer. Though one may expect another visit from the protocol police, one can at least plead insanity! Who would think that OSI would produce such divergent and incompatible approaches for something so fundamental as the network and transport layers? Your only concern will be whether to plead insanity for yourself or the OSI developers!

Another troublesome aspect of the OSI protocols has been the complexity added due to the committee aspect of doing business and to the desire for backward compatibility. This is especially evident at the session layer where the vast array of protocol data unit structures, rules for combining data units, and state machines lead to considerable confusion and complexity. Can this sort of problem escape the standards? There *are* precedents. The first versions of X.25 included an unworkable form of datagram support. It is history; forget it! It also included an awkward and potentially deadlock-prone data link protocol, the asynchronous response mode. It has been relegated to the *also ran* category. Maybe the same will apply to some of the excessively complex and awkward parts of current OSI protocols as time and experience allow a *survival-of-the-fittest* approach to the OSI evolution.

Another variation that is apt to occur concerns vendor enhancements. If all vendors provide OSI networking, why should one select vendor X's approach over vendor Y's approach? One reason might be performance, while another might be demonstrated robustness. But vendors are likely to make this comparison turn out in their own favor by providing proprietary enhancements beyond the OSI standards. This almost sounds like a contradiction. How can one have proprietary enhancements to a standard? There are many examples in everyday life in which this seems to be the case. One can purchase a telephone from any number of companies, plug it into the same jack, and still expect it to work. However, one might purchase a telephone with special features such as an intercom, which is beyond the standard. When one wishes to purchase additional telephones, has the situation changed? Can one still purchase any standard telephone and simply plug it in? Yes and no. If the added feature has become sufficiently important, one may once again be locked into a single-vendor solution.

As the development toward an OSI environment continues, environments such as DECnet, IBM's System Network Architecture (SNA), or Transmission Control Protocol/Internet Protocol (TCP/IP) are gradually being left behind. This always raises the matter of the transition. This is one of the expected future problems, and several solutions have been proposed. One of the most common is to operate with *dual stacks*, e.g., running either DECnet or TCP/IP in addition to the OSI stack for some period of time. Another proposal is to add the OSI session, presentation, and application protocols on top of TCP/IP and to run both TCP and OSI applications in this manner. Yet another approach is to develop gateways between two protocol stacks. This has been done for the TCP/IP and OSI electronic messaging and file transfer protocols. It is also mentioned in the IBM literature for interoperability between an SNA network and an OSI network. The SNA network becomes the end system in this case. That appears to be a perfectly legitimate interpretation of an end system.

Integrated Services Digital Network (ISDN) should also be mentioned, as well as its impact on OSI. Aside from reinterpreting a few of the lower-layer OSI approaches, ISDN is simply another way of delivering the bits. It can be used just as any other delivery mechanism without any significant difference or perturbation to OSI. Probably the biggest change to OSI was the need to extend the addressing capability of X.25 to include ISDN addresses. ISDN provides circuit switching instead of packet switching, but in today's world of *fast packet switching*, *frame relay*, and *cell relay*, it is difficult to tell the difference. It becomes a non-issue at the higher layers.

The development of network communications and applications standards continues with no end in sight. So far, the standards have been of general utility. Additional standards directed to the concerns of smaller segments of industry and government can be expected. Banking is one such example. There are undoubtedly many more. Special needs should make themselves known in the standards development committees. Standards come about when some company or agency wants them badly enough to chair the committees and make the development happen.

Standards are extremely beneficial. Generating more standards in more application areas can break proprietary locks on certain areas of industry. There will be reluctance on the part of those who currently benefit from these proprietary products. Such people will claim that the very nature of the standardization process, which typically takes at least five years to finalize, ensures that the end result will be near obsolescence. This claim is countered by examples in which the end result is state-of-the-art. Many good examples can be found in local area network technology. The 100 Mbps Fiber Distributed Data Interface was an advanced technology when it became standardized. Similarly, the metropolitan area network (MAN) is based on the leading edge of fast packet switching technology. Other impressive examples are those that apply to the upper-layer protocols, especially those that provide application services. For example, FTAM can be considered state-of-the-art. Few of today's operating systems and file systems can take advantage of all its features. This is probably also true of other application protocols.

FTAM is an ambitious protocol development. Attempting to develop one file-handling protocol to cover all applications borders on a research program as much as a protocol standardization topic. It certainly does not lock the world into the more limited predecessor approaches.

Virtual terminal service (VTS) has significant improvements beyond its predecessors, but probably not to the scale of FTAM. Because a basic problem addressed by VTS is handling terminal devices that are not state-of-the-art, little need exists to stretch technology too far. On the other hand, VTS also is to be used by workstations and other advanced devices that wish to perform remote logins to other network resources. VTS does more than merely support *dumb terminals*.

The transaction processing standard builds on IBM's LU 6.2 transaction protocol, but the standard extends it considerably. It uses state-of-the-art transaction integrity mechanisms. The same arguments can be made for essentially all evolving application protocols. The OSI standardization program should not result in inferior methods in the network applications.

How modern the standards are and will continue to be depends on how standards continue to evolve. Nothing is static in the world of network protocols. New standards will eventually replace the current ones. Keeping track of this dynamic situation can help one plan for the necessary transitions that will occur. Migration strategies will be required as an integral part of subsequent protocol developments. Users of these protocols should insist upon having such migration strategies provided, and they should be included in the user's long-term plans and budgets.

One thing seems certain. Networking has created enormous opportunities for those involved in its development and application.

# GLOSSARY & ACRONYMS

## A

AARE — A-Associate Response.

AARQ — A-Associate Request.

ABRT — A-Abort.

abstract syntax (AS) — A data structure, typically an application layer PDU.

abstract syntax notation.one (ASN.1) — An OSI notation for describing abstract syntax.

access control — Ensuring that user access to network resources is only as authorized.

ACID — atomicity, consistency, isolation, and durability.

acknowledgment (ACK) — An indication that a message was received.

activity — An identified operation at the session layer such as the transmission of an electronic message.

address — A network location, expressed as a number, or an internal service access point.

American National Standards Institute (ANSI) — A U.S. standards body; the U.S. representative to ISO.

AOW — Asia-Oceania Workshop.

AP — application program.

APDU — application protocol data unit.

API — application program interface.

application context — A collection of application service elements and the rules for their interactions making up an application entity.

application entity (AE) — The OSI application layer processes.

application service element (ASE) — A collection of related services that are grouped together in one standard.

ARPA — Advanced Research Projects Agency.

ASCII — Basic American Standard Code for Information Interchange.

association — Roughly, the equivalent of a connection at the application layer; more specifically, the use of a presentation layer connection by the application layer.

association control service element (ACSE) — A grouping of application services to establish and release associations.

asynchronous — Meaning *not synchronous*, i.e., not knowing when an event such as a packet arrival will occur.

atomic action — An operation that is either completed in its entirety or not at all.

attributes — Values associated with an object, e.g., the attributes of a file such as its name and owner.

AU — access unit.

authentication — Proving that a user is who he/she claims to be.

authority and format indicator (AFI) — The field of an NSAP that indicates how the address is formatted.

availability — The fraction of time that a network (or service) is capable of operating as expected.

AWG — American Wire Gauge.

## B

basic activity subset (BAS) — A combination of session layer functional units to support activities, e.g., the transfer of electronic messages.

basic combined subset (BCS) — A combination of session layer functional units for minimal support of connections and half- or full-duplex operation.

basic encoding rules (BER) — The rules associated with ASN.1 for determining the concrete transfer syntax.

basic synchronization subset (BSS) — A combination of session layer functional units to support major and/or minor synchronization.

blocking — Placing two or more NSAPs into one NPDU.

bridge — A LAN interconnection device that operates at the media access control (MAC) sublayer.

## C

C/R — command/response.

CASE — common application service element.

CATV — cable television.

CCA — conceptual communications area.

CCR — commitment, concurrency, and recovery.

CD — collision detection.

CDM — code division multiplexing.

CGM — Computer Graphics Metafile.

class — A term that indicates a grouping or an alternate form of service.

CLNP — connectionless network protocol.

CLTS — connectionless transport service.

CMOT — CMIS Over TCP/IP.

common management information protocol (CMIP) — A protocol utilized in OSI network management.

common management information service (CMIS) — The service utilized in OSI network management.

common management information service element (CMISE) — The application layer service utilized by network management.

concatenation — Placing two or more NPDUs into one (N-1)SDU.

concrete syntax — The actual representation of data sent across the network.

confirmed — An operation in OSI that has the full request-indication-response-confirmation handshake.

connection — A relationship between two entities that is established to provide an agreed upon service.

connection-oriented network service (CONS) — The service provided by a network connection, typically that of X.25.

connectionless — Communications without prior establishment of a connection.

constraint set — A limited form of file operation in file transfer, access, and management.

Consultative Committee for International Telephone and Telegraph (CCITT) — An International Standards-making group.

Corporation for Open Systems (COS) — An organization primarily concerned with OSI conformance testing.

CRC — cyclic redundancy check.

CSMA — carrier sense multiple access.

CTS — clear to send.

## D

DAP — directory access protocol.

DAS — dual attached station.

Data Encryption Standard (DES) — An algorithm for data encryption/decryption.

data circuit-termination equipment (DCE) — CCITT term for the endpoints of a communications circuit, including modems and X.25 packet switches.

data network identification code (DNIC) — The country code and network code fields of an X.121 address.

data terminal equipment (DTE) — The CCITT term for data processing equipment including terminals and computers.

DC1 — device control 1 (=XON).

DC3 — device control 3 (=XOFF).

defined context set (DCS) — A set of defined presentation layer contexts.

delay — Measure of the time required for a data unit to get across the network.

DIB — directory information base.

directory — A service that provides name-to-address mappings and related services.

distinguished name — The global name of an entity.

DIT — directory information tree.

DLE — data link escape.

document type — An FTAM categorization of information having the same constraint set, data type, and concrete transfer syntax.

domain-specific part (DSP) — The local option portion of an NSAP address.

Draft International Standard (DIS) — The stage of the ISO standardization process before a full International Standard (IS).

draft proposal (DP) — A stage of the ISO standardization process during which many changes can be expected; precedes the DIS.

DSA — directory system agent.

DSAP — destination service access point.

DSE — data switching equipment.

DTAM — document transfer, access, and management.

DUA — directory user agent.

## E

EBCDIC — Extended Binary Coded Decimal Interchange Code.

EDIFACT — EDI for Administration, Commerce, and Transportation.

EIA — Electronics Industries Association.

Electronic Data Interchange (EDI) — An emerging standard for the exchange of procurement documents.

EMA — DEC's Enterprise Management Architecture.

EMS — element management system.

encapsulation — Placing one PDU as the data in another PDU.

encryption — To protect information by making it meaningless unless one has the decrypt key.

end system (ES) — A system (typically but not limited to a single computer) that implements all seven layers of OSI.

end-to-end — Services between end systems, as opposed to services with an intermediate system.

EOT — end of TSDU.

EPA — Enhanced Performance Architecture.

ES–IS — end system–intermediate system.

European Computer Manufacturers Association (ECMA) — An influential group in OSI.

EWOS — European Workshop for Open Systems.

expedited data — Data that are to be sent and processed as quickly as possible without regard for flow control.

# F

facility — A grouping of services, sometimes for the purposes of negotiation.

fast select — The X.25 facility for transaction support.

FCS — frame check sequence.

FDDI — Fiber Distributed Data Interface.

FDM — frequency division multiplexing.

file access data unit (FADU) — A unit of information that can be manipulated independently.

file transfer, access, and management (FTAM) — The OSI file operation protocol.

FIPS — Federal Information Processing Standard.

flow control — The ability of a receiver to regulate the rate at which data are sent to it.

frame — The name often utilized at the data link layer for a PDU.

FSK — frequency shift keying.

FTP — file transfer protocol.

functional unit — A negotiable portion of the services of an upper layer protocol.

# G

gateway — A term that has many variations in its meanings; generally utilized to refer to a device that couples two kinds of networks together.

Government OSI Profile (GOSIP) — A Government directive on the procurement of OSI networking.

# H

HDLC — high-level data link control.

# I

ICD — international code designator.

initial domain identifier (IDI) — The portion of the initial domain part of an NSAP address that identifies the address domain and the address authority.

initial domain part (IDP) — The portion of an NSAP address containing the information about how to interpret domain-specific part.

Institute of Electrical and Electronics Engineers (IEEE) — An industry organization that develops LAN standards.

Integrated Services Digital Network (ISDN) — An evolving set of voice and data physical through network layer standards by CCITT.

integrity — A property of data that indicates that it has not been corrupted.

intermediate system (IS) — System operation that relays information on towards its ultimate destination.

International Alphabet 5 (IA5) — The international equivalent of ASCII but with some different symbols such as for currency.

International Standards Organization (ISO) — A voluntary, international group that initiated OSI.

internetworking — Connecting networks (subnets) together.

interpersonal message — The defined body parts of an electronic message.

interworking — The OSI term for internetworking.

IP — Internet Protocol.

IPDU — internet protocol data unit.

IS–IS — intermediate system–intermediate system.

ISP — international standardized profile.

# L

LAP — link access procedure.

LAPB — link access procedure balanced.

LAPD — link access procedure D channel.

layer — A modular and hierarchical component of the OSI approach to networking.

length indicator (LI) — A field in the protocol control information that indicates its length.

LLC — logical link control.

LPP — lightweight presentation protocol.

local area network (LAN) — Typically a small, high-speed, user-owned network.

LSAP — link service access point.

## M

major synchronization point — An OSI session layer service that stops the flow of data until the confirmation that previous data is safely stored.

MAN — metropolitan area network.

management information base (MIB) — A database of objects that can be managed by the network management protocols.

MAP — Manufacturing Automation Protocol.

MAU — medium attachment unit.

media access control (MAC) — A sublayer of LAN protocols.

message handling system (MHS) — A system for the generation, delivery, and retrieval of electronic messages.

message store (MS) — A part of X.400 that provides longer term storage of messages.

message transfer agent (MTA) — The delivery portion of X.400.

minor synchronization point — An OSI session layer service that does not require that the flow of data stop until confirmed.

MMS — Manufacturing Message Specification.

modem — A contraction of modulator/demodulator; used for data transmission over an analog telephone network.

MOTIS — Message-Oriented Text Interchange System.

## N

N-layer — A general reference to an arbitrary OSI layer.

National Institute of Standards and Technology (NIST) — A major U.S. standards organization involved in OSI.

network service access point (NSAP) — Sufficient addressing information to identify the user of a network service.

NFS — network file system.

NPDU — network protocol data unit.

NRZI — Non-Return to Zero Inverted.

## O

octet — An eight-bit data unit (byte).

ODA — Office Document Architecture.

ODIF — Office Document Interchange Format.

Open Systems Interconnection (OSI) — Developments of networking for multi-vendor interoperability.

options — May be optional portions of the implementation or optional portions of any given PDU.

## P

P/F — poll/final.

PABX — private automatic branch exchange.

packet — General term for a data unit sent across the network; in OSI, a PDU.

packet assembler/disassembler (PAD) — A network device that interfaces terminals to an X.25 network.

PCM — pulse code modulation.

PDU — protocol data unit.

peer — An entity at the same protocol layer (or sublayer).

permanent virtual circuit (PVC) — An X.25 connection that is always available for immediate usage.

PGI — parameter group identifier .

PI — parameter identifier .

PLP — packet layer protocol.

post, telephone, and telegraph (PTT) — A government monopoly organization.

PPDU — presentation protocol data unit.

presentation context — An abstract syntax and a selected transfer syntax.

presentation context identifier (PCI) — A number associated with a specific presentation context.

profile — A selected set of standards at each of the OSI layers.

protocol — A set of rules and conventions for communications.

protocol control information (PCI) — The control (header) portion of a PDU.

protocol data unit (PDU) — The control and data portion of a data unit; a packet.

protocol machine — The state machine that defines the protocol operation.

PSAP — presentation service access point.

PSDU — presentation service data unit.

PSK — phase shift keying.

public key — An asymmetric encryption approach in which one key is made public and the other is kept secret.

## Q

quality of service (QOS) — Expressing the desired communications characteristics such as allowable delay and required throughput.

## R

RDN — relative distinguished name.

recommendation — The term utilized by CCITT for its standards.

reference model — A high-level architectural description.

reject (Rej) — A response when something received was unexpected.

relay — To pass information on, as done by a router between two networks.

reliable transfer service element (RTSE) — An application layer service that provides checkpoint/recovery mechanisms.

remote operation (RO) — Invoking an operation on another computer.

remote operations service element (ROSE) — An application layer service that provides a transaction-like capability across the net.

remote procedure call (RPC) — Calling a program (procedure) from across the network.

reset — To reestablish a predefined state at both ends of a connection.

responder — The end of a connection that responds to a connection request.

RLRE — A-Release Response.

RLRQ — A-Release Request.

RNR — receiver not ready.

router — A relay device at the internet (SNICP) sublayer.

routing — Finding the best path across a network or internetwork.

RPC — remote procedure recall.

RR — receiver ready.

RS — recommended standard.

RTORQ — RTSE open request.

RTS — request to send.

## S

SABM — set asynchronous balanced mode.

SAS — single attached stations.

SDNS — secure data network system.

SE — service element.

segmentation — Cutting data into manageable size units for transmission.

sequence — A grouping in which order is important.

service access point (SAP) — An internal location (address) where the services of a layer are provided.

service data unit (SDU) — The unit of data that is passed to a service access point.

service primitive — One of a set of generic calls that the user of a layer makes to access the desired service.

set — A grouping, usually without regard to ordering.

SGML — Standardized General Mark-up Language.

SI — SPDU identifier.

SMAE — system management application entity.

SMASE — system management application service element.

SNMP — simple network management protocol.

SNPA — subnetwork point of attachment.

source routing — When the end system prescribes the set of intermediate systems along a path.

SPDU — session protocol data unit.

SPF — shortest path first.

SRej — selective reject.

SS — session service.

SSAP — session service access point.

ST — straight tip.

STE — signaling terminal equipment.

STDM — statistical time division multiplexing.

subnetwork — The OSI term to represent a single network.

subnetwork access protocol (SNAP) — A sublayer within the network layer to provide access (interface) to a network, e.g., X.25.

subnetwork dependent convergence protocol (SNDCP) — A sublayer within the network layer to augment the service of a network.

subnetwork independent convergence protocol (SNICP) — A sublayer within the network layer to provide communications across any networks.

switched virtual circuit (SVC) — The same as a virtual call in X.25.

synchronization — To provide consistent control information (such as sequence numbers) to both parties of a connection.

synchronous — Knowing when an event (such as receiving a packet in response to a poll) will occur.

syntax — The format and structure of data.

System Network Architecture (SNA) — IBM's proprietary networking approach.

# T

TCP — Transmission Control Protocol.

TDM — time division multiplexing.

TEPI — terminal endpoint identifier.

TFTP — trivial file transfer protocol.

throughput — The sustainable data rate at which information can be sent and received.

title — The permanent identifier of an entity.

token — An object, the ownership of which allows one to perform a given operation.

TOP — Technical and Office Protocol.

TP — transaction processing.

TP — transport protocol.

TPDU — transport protocol data unit.

transfer syntax (TS) — The representation of data as it is transferred across the network.

transparent — Not having to recognize or deal with a network mechanism, e.g., being able to send arbitrary data even though some bit patterns have special control significance.
TS — transport service.
TSAP — transport service access point.
TSDU — transport service data unit.
two-way alternate (TWA) — Half-duplex flow of information.
two-way simultaneous (TWS) — Full-duplex flow of information.
type (tag), length, value (TLV) — A form of self-representation of data.
typed data — Data that can be sent in a two-way alternate communications without having the token.

## U

user — A person or entity that utilizes the services of a layer.
user agent (UA) — The portion of X.400 that relates to the preparation of electronic messages.
user element (UE) — The overlap portion between a user's application program and the OSI application layer.
UTP — unshielded twisted pair (telephone) wiring .

## V

virtual — Giving the appearance of having characteristics beyond that of a physical device.
virtual call (VC) — An X.25 connection that is established as needed.
virtual circuit — A network connection with enhanced properties such as error recovery.
virtual filestore — A generalized representation of a file server.
virtual terminal service (VTS) — The OSI application service to support remote login from a wide variety of terminal types.

## W

WAN — wide area network.
window — A mechanism that allows one or more PDUs to be sent without having to wait for a response from the receiving side.

## X

XID — exchange identification.
XNS — Xerox Network System.
XPDU — X protocol data unit.

# APPENDIX: OSI STANDARDS

## THE OSI REFERENCE MODEL

Open Systems Interconnection (ISO) 7498
CCITT Recommendation X.200

| | |
|---|---|
| ISO 7498-1 | Basic Reference Model *[published 84-10-15]* |
| ISO 7498-2 | Security Architecture *[final text 88-07-19]* |
| ISO 7498-3 | Naming and Addressing *[published 89-03-1]* |
| ISO 7498-4 | Management Framework *[published 89-11-15]* |
| ISO 7498-1/Add. 1 | Addendum 1: Connectionless Data Transmission *[published 87-07-15]* |
| ISO 7498-1/PDAM2 | Addendum 2: Multipeer Data Transmission *[suspended]* |
| ISO 7498-1/Cor. 1 | Technical Corrigendum 1 *[published 88-12-15]* |

## LAYER INDEPENDENT STANDARDS

| | |
|---|---|
| ISO TR 8509<br>CCITT X.210 | OSI Service Conventions *[published 87-09-01]* |
| ISO PDTR 10730 | Tutorial on Naming and Addressing |
| ISO CD 10731 | Conventions for the Definition of OSI Services |

### Formal Description Techniques

| | |
|---|---|
| ISO 8807 | LOTOS — A Formal Description Technique Based on the Temporal Ordering of Observational Behaviour *[published 89-02-15]* |

Chapin, Lyman, "Status of Standards," *Computer Communication Review*, ACM Special Interest Group on Data Communication, January 1991. Reprinted by permission of the publisher.

| | |
|---|---|
| ISO 8807/PDAM1 | Amendment 1: Graphical Representation (G-LOTOS) |
| ISO 9074 | ESTELLE — A Formal Description Technique Based on an Extended State Transition Model *[published 89-07-15]* |
| ISO 9074/PDAM1 | Amendment 1: ESTELLE Tutorial |
| ISO 9496 | CCITT High-Level Language (CHILL) *[published 89-08-01]* |
| ISO DTR 10167 | Guidelines for the Application of Estelle, LOTOS, and SDL *[ballot closed 90-06-01]* |

## Conformance Testing

| | |
|---|---|
| ISO 9646-1 | OSI Conformance Testing Methodology and Framework, Part 1: General Concepts |
| ISO 9646-2 | Part 2: Abstract Test Suite Specification |
| ISO DIS 9646-3 | Part 3: Tree and Tabular Combined Notation *[ballot closed 90-07-01]* |
| ISO 9646-4 | Part 4: Test Realization |
| ISO 9646-5 | Part 5: Requirements on Test Laboratories and Their Clients for the Conformance Assessment Process |
| ISO DP 9646-6 | Part 6: Test Laboratory Operations *[working draft]* |

## Registration Authorities

| | |
|---|---|
| ISO DIS 9834-1 | Procedures for Specific OSI Registration Authorities, Part 1: General Procedures *[ballot closed 91-02-01]* |
| ISO DIS 9834-2 | Part 2: Registration Procedures for OSI Document Types *[ballot closed 91-02-01]* |
| ISO 9834-3 | Part 3: Procedures for the Assignment of Object Identifier Component Values for Joint ISO — CCITT Use *[published 90-09-27]* |
| ISO DIS 9834-4 | Part 4: Registration of VTE — Profiles *[second DIS ballot closed 91-02-01]* |
| ISO DIS 9834-5 | Part 5: Registration of VT Control Objects *[second DIS ballot closed 91-02-01]* |
| ISO DIS 9834-6 | Part 6: Registration of Application Process Titles and Application Entity Titles *[ballot closed 91-02-01]* |

## Abstract Syntax Notation

| | |
|---|---|
| ISO 8824<br>CCITT X.208 | Specification of Abstract Syntax Notation 1 (ASN.1) *[published 87-12-15]* |
| ISO 8824/Add. 1 | Addendum 1: ASN.1 Extensions |
| ISO 8825<br>CCITT X.209 | Specification of Basic Encoding Rules for Abstract Syntax Notation 1 (ASN.1) *[published 87-11-15]* |
| ISO 8825/Add. 1 | Addendum 1: ASN.1 Extensions |

## Security

| | |
|---|---|
| ISO CD 10181-1 | OSI Security Model, Part 1: Security Framework |
| ISO CD 10181-2 | OSI Security Model, Part 2: Authentication Framework |

# MULTI-LAYER STANDARDS (PROFILES)

| | |
|---|---|
| ISO TR 10000-1 | International Standardized Profiles, Part 1: Taxonomy Framework *[published 90-07-16]* |
| ISO TR 10000-2 | Part 2: Taxonomy of Profiles *[published 90-07-16]* |
| ISO DISP 10607-1 | International Standardized Profile AFT nn — File Transfer, Access, and Management, Part 1: Specification of ACSE, Presentation, and Session protocols for the use of FTAM *[ballot closed 90-07-26]* |
| ISO DISP 10607-2 | Part 2: Definition of document types, constraint sets, and syntaxes *[ballot closed 90-07-26]* |
| ISO DISP 10607-3 | Part 3: AFT11 — Simple file transfer service (unstructured) *[ballot closed 90-07-26]* |
| ISO PDISP 10608-1 | International Standardized Profile TA — Connection-mode Transport Service over Connectionless Network Service, Part 1: General Overview and Subnetwork-independent Requirements *[ballot closed 90-12-13]* |
| ISO PDISP 10608-2 | Part 2: TA51 Profile Including Subnetwork-dependent Requirements for CSMA/CD LANs *[ballot closed 90-12-13]* |
| ISO PDISP 10608-5 | Part 5: TA1111/TA1121 Profiles Including Subnetwork dependent Requirements for X.25 Packet Switched Data Networks Using Switched Virtual Circuits *[ballot closed 90-12-13]* |

| | |
|---|---|
| ISO DISP 10609-1 | International Standardized Profiles TB, TC, TD, and TE — Connection-mode Transport Service over Connection-mode Network Service, Part 1: Subnetwork-type Independent Requirements for Group TB *[ballot closed 90-12-13]* |
| ISO DISP 10609-2 | Part 2: Subnetwork-type Independent Requirements for Group TC *[ballot closed 90-12-13]* |
| ISO DISP 10609-3 | Part 3: Subnetwork-type Independent Requirements for Group-TD *[ballot closed 90-12-13]* |
| ISO DISP 10609-4 | Part 4: Subnetwork-type Independent Requirements for Group TE *[ballot closed 90-12-13]* |
| ISO DISP 10609-5 | Part 5: Definition of Profile TB 1111 /TB 1121 *[ballot closed 90-12-13]* |
| ISO DISP 10609-6 | Part 6: Definition of Profile TC 1111/TC 1121 *[ballot closed 90-12-13]* |
| ISO DISP 10609-7 | Part 7: Definition of Profile TD 1111/TD 1121 *[ballot closed 90-12-13]* |
| ISO DISP 10609-8 | Part 8: Definition of Profile TE 1111/TE 1121 *[ballot closed 90-12-13]* |
| ISO DISP 10609-9 | Part 9: Subnetwork-type Dependent Requirements for Network Layer, Data Link Layer, and Physical Layer Concerning Permanent Access to a Packet Switched Data Network Using Virtual Call *[ballot closed 90-12-13]* |

# APPLICATION LAYER STANDARDS

| | |
|---|---|
| ISO 9545<br>CCITT X.207 | Application Layer Structure *[published 89-12-15]* |
| ISO 9545/PDAM1 | Amendment 1: Connectionless Operation *[working draft]* |

## Association Control (ACSE)

| | |
|---|---|
| ISO 8649<br>CCITT X.217 | Service Definition for the Association Control Service Element *[published 88-12-15]* |
| ISO 8649/DAM1 | Amendment 1: Peer-entity Authentication during Association Establishment |
| ISO 8649/DAM2 | Amendment 2: Connectionless ACSE Service |

| | |
|---|---|
| ISO 8650<br>CCITT X.227 | Protocol Specification for the Association Control Service Element *[published 88-12-15]* |
| ISO 8650/DAM1 | Amendment 1: Peer-entity Authentication during Association Establishment |
| ISO 8650/PDAM2 | Amendment 2: PICS Proforma *[awaiting PDAM ballot]* |
| ISO 10035 | Connectionless ACSE Protocol Specification |
| ISO DIS 10169-1 | Conformance Test Suite for the ACSE Protocol, Part 1: Test Suite Structure and Test Purposes *[ballot closed 90-10-19]* |

## Commitment, Concurrency, and Recovery (CCR)

| | |
|---|---|
| ISO 9804<br>CCITT X.237 | Service Definition for the Commitment, Concurrency, and Recovery Service Element |
| ISO 9804/PDAM1 | Amendment 1: Service Enhancements |
| ISO 9804/PDAM2 | Amendment 2: Support for Session Mapping Changes |
| ISO 9805<br>CCITT X.247 | Protocol Specification for the Commitment, Concurrency, and Recovery Service Element |
| ISO 9805/PDAM1 | Amendment 1: Service Enhancements |
| ISO 9805/PDAM2 | Amendment 2: PICS Proforma |

## Reliable Transfer (RTS)

| | |
|---|---|
| ISO 9066-1<br>CCITT X.218 | Reliable Transfer, Part 1: Model and Service Definition *[published 89-11-15]* |
| ISO 9066-2<br>CCITT X.228 | Part 2: Protocol Specification *[published 89-11-15]* |

## Remote Operations (ROS)

| | |
|---|---|
| ISO 9072-1<br>CCITT X.219 | Remote Operations, Part 1: Model, Notation, and Service Definition *[published 89-11-15]* |
| ISO 9072-2<br>CCITT X.229 | Part 2: Protocol Specification *[published 89-11-15]* |

## Management

| | |
|---|---|
| ISO 9595<br>CCITT X.710 | Common Management Information Service (CMIS) Definition *[published 90-07-16]* |
| ISO 9595/DAM1 | Amendment 1: Cancel/Get |
| ISO 9595/DAM2 | Amendment 2: Add, Remove, and Set To Default |
| ISO 9595/PDAM3 | Amendment 3: Support for Allomorphism |
| ISO 9596<br>CCITT X.711 | Common Management Information Protocol (CMIP) Specification *[published 90-7-16]* |
| ISO 9596/DAM1 | Amendment 1: Cancel/Get |
| ISO 9596/DAM2 | Amendment 2: Add, Remove, and Set To Default |
| ISO 9596/PDAM3 | Amendment 3: Support for Allomorphism |
| ISO 9596/PDAM4 | Amendment 4: PICS Proforma |
| ISO DIS 10040<br>CCITT X.701 | Systems Management Overview |
| ISO DIS 10164-1<br>CCITT X.730 | Systems Management, Part 1: Object Management Function *[awaiting DIS ballot]* |
| ISO DIS 10164-2<br>CCITT X.731 | Part 2: State Management Function *[awaiting DIS ballot]* |
| ISO DIS 10164-3<br>CCITT X.732 | Part 3: Attributes for Representing Relationships *[awaiting DIS ballot]* |
| ISO DIS 10164-4<br>CCITT X.733 | Part 4: Alarm Reporting Function *[awaiting DIS ballot]* |
| ISO DIS 10164-5<br>CCITT X.734 | Part 5: Event Report Management Function *[awaiting DIS ballot]* |
| ISO DIS 10164-6<br>CCITT X.735 | Part 6: Log Control Function *[awaiting DIS ballot]* |
| ISO DIS 10164-7<br>CCITT X.736 | Part 7: Security Alarm Reporting Function *[awaiting DIS ballot]* |
| ISO CD 10164-8<br>CCITT X.740 | Part 8: Security Audit Trail Function |
| ISO CD 10164-9<br>CCITT X.741 | Part 9: Objects and Attributes for Access Control |
| ISO CD 10164-10<br>CCITT X.742 | Part 10: Accounting Meter Function |

| | |
|---|---|
| ISO CD 10164-11<br>CCITT X.739 | Part 11: Workload Monitoring Function |
| ISO CD 10164-*sm*<br>CCITT X.744 | Part *sm*: Software Management Function *[working draft]* |
| ISO CD 10164-*tc*<br>CCITT X.737 | Part *tc*: Confidence and Diagnostic Test Classes *[working draft]* |
| ISO CD 10164-*ms*<br>CCITT X.738 | Part *ms*: Measurement Summarization Function *[working draft]* |
| ISO CD 10164-*tm*<br>CCITT X.745 | Part *tm*: Test Management Function *[working draft]* |
| ISO CD 10164-*ti*<br>CCITT X.743 | Part *ti*: Time Management Function *[working draft]* |
| ISO DIS 10165-1<br>CCITT X.720 | Structure of Management Information, Part 1: Management Information Model *[awaiting DIS ballot]* |
| ISO DIS 10165-2<br>CCITT X.721 | Part 2: Definition of Management Information (replaces original parts 2 and 3) *[awaiting DIS ballot]* |
| ISO DIS 10165-4<br>CCITT X.722 | Part 4: Guidelines for the Definition of Managed Objects *[awaiting DIS ballot]* |

## File Transfer, Access, and Management (FTAM)

| | |
|---|---|
| ISO 8571-1 | File Transfer, Access, and Management (FTAM), Part 1: General Introduction *[published 88-10-01]* |
| ISO 8571-1/DAM1 | Amendment 1: Filestore Management *[ballot closed 91-03-01]* |
| ISO 8571-1/PDAM2 | Amendment 2: Overlapped Access |
| ISO 8571-2 | Part 2: The Virtual Filestore Definition *[published 88-10-01]* |
| ISO 8571-2/DAM1 | Amendment 1: Filestore Management *[ballot closed 91-03-01]* |
| ISO 8571-2/PDAM2 | Amendment 2: Overlapped Access |
| ISO 8571-3 | Part 3: The File Service Definition *[published 88-10-01]* |
| ISO 8571-3/DAM1 | Amendment 1: Filestore Management *[ballot closed 91-03-01]* |
| ISO 8571-3/PDAM2 | Amendment 2: Overlapped Access |

| | |
|---|---|
| ISO 8571-4 | Part 4: The File Protocol Specification *[published 88-10-01]* |
| ISO 8571-4/DAM1 | Amendment 1: Filestore Management *[ballot closed 91-03-01]* |
| ISO 8571-4/PDAM2 | Amendment 2: Overlapped Access |
| ISO 8571-5 | Part 5: PICS Proforma *[awaiting publication]* |
| ISO CD 10170-1 | Conformance Test Suite for the FTAM Protocol, Part 1: Test Suite Structure and Test Purposes *[second CD ballot closed 90-03-23]* |

## Virtual Terminal (VT)

| | |
|---|---|
| ISO 9040 | Virtual Terminal Service — Basic Class *[final text 88-08-23]* |
| ISO 9040/Add. 1 | Addendum 1: Extended Facility Set *[final text 88-09-21]* |
| ISO 9040/DAM2 | Amendment 2: Additional Functional Units *[ballot closed 91-03-01]* |
| ISO 9041 | Virtual Terminal Protocol — Basic Class *[final text distributed 89-03-01]* |
| ISO 9041/Add. 1 | Addendum 1: Extended Facility Set *[final text distributed 89-03-01]* |
| ISO 9041/DAM2 | Amendment 2: Additional Functional Units *[ballot closed 91-03-01]* |
| ISO 9041/PDAM3 | Amendment 3: PICS Proforma |

## Job Transfer and Manipulation (JTM)

| | |
|---|---|
| ISO 8831 | JTM Concepts and Services *[published 89-07-01]* |
| ISO 8832 | Specification of the Basic Class Protocol for JTM *[published 89-07-01]* |
| ISO 8832/DAM1 | Amendment 1: Full Class Protocol for Job Transfer and Manipulation *[ballot closed 91-03-01]* |

## The Directory

| | |
|---|---|
| ISO DIS 9594-1<br>CCITT X.500 | The Directory, Part 1: Overview of Concepts, Models, and Services *[final text 88-12-01]* |

| | |
|---|---|
| ISO 9594-1/PDAM1 | Amendment 1: Replication, Schema, and Access Control *[awaiting PDAM ballot]* |
| ISO DIS 9594-2<br>CCITT X.501 | Part 2: Information Framework *[final text 88-12-01]* |
| ISO 9594-2/PDAM1 | Amendment 1: Access Control *[awaiting second PDAM ballot]* |
| ISO 9594-2/PDAM2 | Amendment 2: Schema *[awaiting PDAM ballot]* |
| ISO 9594-2/PDAM3 | Amendment 3: Replication *[awaiting PDAM ballot]* |
| ISO DIS 9594-3<br>CCITT X.511 | Part 3: Access and System Services Definition *[final text 88-12-01]* |
| ISO 9594-3/PDAM1 | Amendment 1: Access Control *[awaiting second PDAM ballot]* |
| ISO 9594-3/PDAM2 | Amendment 2: Replication, Schema, and Enhan-ced Search *[awaiting PDAM ballot]* |
| ISO DIS 9594-4<br>CCITT X.518 | Part 4: Procedures for Distributed Operation *[final text 88-12-01]* |
| ISO 9594-4/PDAM1 | Amendment 1: Access Control *[awaiting second PDAM ballot]* |
| ISO 9594-4/PDAM2 | Amendment 2: Replication, Schema, and Enhan-ced Search *[awaiting PDAM ballot]* |
| ISO DIS 9594-5<br>CCITT X.519 | Part 5: Access and System Protocols Specification *[final text 88-12-01]* |
| ISO 9594-5/PDAM1 | Amendment 1: Replication *[awaiting PDAM ballot]* |
| ISO DIS 9594-6<br>CCITT X.520 | Part 6: Selected Attribute Types *[final text 88-12-01]* |
| ISO 9594-6/PDAM1 | Amendment 1: Schema *[awaiting PDAM ballot]* |
| ISO DIS 9594-7<br>CCITT X.521 | Part 7: Selected Object Classes *[final text 88-12-01]* |
| ISO 9594-7/PDAM1 | Amendment 1: Schema *[awaiting PDAM ballot]* |
| ISO DIS 9594-8<br>CCITT X.509 | Part 8: Authentication Framework *[final text 88-12-01]* |
| ISO 9594-8/PDAM1 | Amendment 1: Access Control *[awaiting PDAM ballot]* |
| ISO CD 9594-9 | Part 9: Replication and Knowledge Management *[awaiting CD ballot]* |

## Message Handling (MHS)

| | |
|---|---|
| ISO DIS 10021-1<br>CCITT X.400 | Message Oriented Text Interchange System (MOTIS) [Message Handling], Part 1: System and Service Overview *[was 8505-1; ballot closed 88-09-30]* |
| ISO DIS 10021-2<br>CCITT X.402 | Part 2: Overall Architecture *[was 8505-2; ballot closed 88-09-30]* |
| CCITT X.403 | Message Handling: Conformance Testing *[final tex in preparation]* |
| ISO DIS 10021-3<br>CCITT X.407 | Part 3: Abstract Service Definition Conventions *[was 8505-4; ballot closed 88-09-30]* |
| CCITT X.408 | Message Handling: Encoded Information Type Conversion Rules *[final text in preparation]* |
| ISO DIS 10021-4<br>CCITT X.411 | Part 4: Message Transfer System — Abstract Service Definition and Procedures *[was 8883-1; ballot closed 88-09-30]* |
| ISO DIS 10021-5<br>CCITT X.413 | Part 5: Message Store — Abstract Service Definition *[ballot closed 88-12-30]* |
| ISO DIS 10021-6<br>CCITT X.419 | Part 6: Protocol Specifications *[was 8883-2; ballot closed 88-09-30]* |
| ISO DIS 10021-7<br>CCITT X.420 | Part 7: Interpersonal Messaging System *[was 9065; ballot closed 88-09-30]* |

## Office Document Architecture (ODA)
## Office Document Interchange Format (ODIF)
## Document Transfer, Access, and Manipulation (DTAM)

| | |
|---|---|
| CCITT T.400 | Document Transfer, Access, and Manipulation (DTAM) — General Introduction |
| ISO 8613-1<br>CCITT T.411 | Text and Office Systems — Office Document Architecture and Interchange Format, Part 1: Introduction and General Principles *[published 89-09-01]* |
| ISO 8613-1/DAM1 | Amendment 1: Document Application Profile Proforma and Notation *[ballot closed 90-07-01]* |
| ISO 8613-1/DAM2 | Amendment 2: Conformance Testing Methodology |
| ISO 8613-2<br>CCITT T.412 | Part 2: Document Structures *[published 89-09-01]* |

| | |
|---|---|
| ISO 8613-4<br>CCITT T.414 | Part 4: Document Profile *[published 89-09-02]* |
| ISO 8613-4/PDAM1 | Amendment 1: Additive Extensions for Filing and Retrieval Attributes |
| ISO 8613-4/PDAM2 | Amendment 2: Document Application Profile Proforma and Notation *[ballot closed 89-09-15]* |
| ISO 8613-5<br>CCITT T.415 | Part 5: Document Interchange Format *[published 89-09-01]* |
| ISO 8613-6<br>CCITT T.416 | Part 6: Character Content Architectures *[published 89-09-01]* |
| ISO 8613-7<br>CCITT T.417 | Part 7: Raster Graphics Content Architectures *[published 89-09-01]* |
| ISO 8613-7/DAM1 | Amendment 1: Tiled Raster Graphics Content Architectures |
| ISO 8613-8<br>CCITT T.418 | Part 8: Geometric Graphics Content Architectures *[published 89-09-01]* |
| ISO CD 8613-9 | Part 9: Audio Content Architectures *[new work item]* |
| ISO CD 8613-10 | Part 10: Formal Specifications |
| ISO 8613-10/DAM1 | Amendment 1: Formal Specification of the Document Profile *[ballot closed 91-03-01]* |
| ISO 8613-10/DAM2 | Amendment 2: Formal Specification of the Raster Graphics Content Architectures *[ballot closed 91-03-01]* |
| ISO CD 10033 | Text and Office Systems — Office Document Interchange, Flexible Disks *[ballot closed 88-09-19]* |
| CCITT T.419 | Document Transfer, Access, and Manipulation (DTAM) — Composite Graphics Content Architectures |
| CCITT T.431 | Document Transfer, Access, and Manipulation (DTAM) — Introduction and General Principles |
| CCITT T.432 | Document Transfer, Access, and Manipulation (DTAM) — Service Definition |
| CCITT T.433 | Document Transfer, Access, and Manipulation (DTAM) — Protocol Specification |
| CCITT T.441 | Document Transfer, Access, and Manipulation (DTAM) — Operational Structure |

## Remote Database Access (RDA)

| | |
|---|---|
| ISO CD 9579-1 | Remote Database Access, Part 1: General Model, Services, and Protocol |
| ISO CD 9579-2 | Part 2: SQL Specialization |

## Transaction Processing (TP)

| | |
|---|---|
| ISO DIS 10026-1 | Distributed Transaction Processing, Part 1: Model |
| ISO DIS 10026-2 | Part 2: Service Definition |
| ISO DIS 10026-3 | Part 3: Transaction Processing Protocol Specification |
| ISO CD 10026-4 | Part 4: PICS Proforma |
| ISO CD 10026-5 | Part 5: Application Context Proforma |

## Computer Graphics Metafile (CGM)

| | |
|---|---|
| ISO 8632-1 | Metafile for the Storage and Transfer of Picture Description Information, Part 1: Functional Specification *[published 87-08-01]* |
| ISO 8632-1/DAM1 | Amendment 1: Audit Trail Metafile |
| ISO 8632-1/PDAM2 | Amendment 2: 3D Static Picture Capture Metafile |
| ISO 8632-2 | Part 2: Character Encoding *[published 87-08-01]* |
| ISO 8632-3 | Part 3: Binary Encoding *[published 87-08-01]* |
| ISO 8632-4 | Part 4: Clear Text Encoding *[published 87-08-01]* |

## Graphical Kernel System (GKS)

| | |
|---|---|
| ISO 7942 | Graphical Kernel System Functional Description *[published 1985]* |
| ISO 7942/DAM1 | Amendment 1: Audit Trail Metafile |
| ISO 8651-1 | GKS Language Bindings, Part 1: FORTRAN *[published 88-10-11]* |
| ISO 8651-2 | Part 2: Pascal *[published 88-10-11]* |
| ISO 8651-3 | Part 3: Ada *[published 88-10-11]* |

| | |
|---|---|
| ISO DIS 8651-4 | Part 4: C *[ballot closed 90-12-02]* |
| ISO 8805 | Graphical Kernel System for Three Dimensions (GKS-3D) Functional Description *[published 88-10-11]* |
| ISO DIS 8806 | Graphical Kernel System for Three Dimensions (GKS-3D) Language Bindings, Part 4: C *[ballot closed 90-12-02]* |
| ISO TR 9973 | Registration of Graphical Items *[published 88-10-11]* |

## Programmer's Hierarchical Interactive Graphics Interface (PHIGS)

| | |
|---|---|
| ISO 9592-1 | Programmer's Hierarchical Interactive Graphics Interface, Part 1: Functional Description *[published 89-05-21]* |
| ISO 9592-1/Am. 1 | Amendment 1: PHIGS Plus Support |
| ISO 9592-2 | Part 2: Archive File Format *[published 89-05-21]* |
| ISO 9592-2/Am. 1 | Amendment 1: PHIGS Plus Support |
| ISO 9592-3 | Part 3: Clear-text Encoding for Archive File *[published 89-05-21]* |
| ISO 9592-3/Am. 1 | Amendment 1: PHIGS Plus Support |
| ISO DIS 9592-4 | Part 4: PHIGS Plus *[ballot closed 90-09-01]* |
| ISO 9593-1 | PHIGS Language Bindings, Part 1: FORTRAN *[published 90-08-22]* |
| ISO DIS 9593-2 | Part 2: Pascal *[awaiting DIS ballot]* |
| ISO 9593-3 | Part 3: ADA *[published 90-07-16]* |
| ISO DIS 9593-4 | Part 4: C *[ballot closed 91-03-21]* |

## Graphical Device Interfaces

| | |
|---|---|
| ISO DIS 9636-1 | Interfacing Techniques for Dialogues with Graphical Devices — Functional Specification, Part 1: Overview, Profiles, and Conformance *[ballot closed 90-09-08]* |
| ISO DIS 9636-2 | Part 2: Control *[ballot closed 90-09-08]* |
| ISO DIS 9636-3 | Part 3: Output *[ballot closed 90-09-08]* |
| ISO DIS 9636-4 | Part 4: Segments *[ballot closed 90-09-08]* |

| | |
|---|---|
| ISO DIS 9636-5 | Part 5: Input and Echoing *[ballot closed 90-09-08]* |
| ISO DIS 9636-6 | Part 6: Raster *[ballot closed 90-09-08]* |

## Fonts, Text Composition, and Page Layout

| | |
|---|---|
| ISO 8879 | Standard Generalized Markup Language *[published 86-10-15]* |
| ISO 8879/Am. 1 | Amendment 1 *[published 88-07-01]* |
| ISO 9069 | SGML Document Interchange Format (SDIF) *[published 88-09-15]* |
| ISO 9070 | Registration Procedures for Public Text Owner Identifiers *[published 90-02-01]* |
| ISO DIS 9541-1 | Font and Character Information Interchange, Part 1: Architecture *[second DIS ballot closed 90-11-17]* |
| ISO DIS 9541-2 | Part 2: Interchange Format *[second DIS ballot closed 90-11-17]* |
| ISO CD 9541-3 | Part 3: Glyph Shape Representations *[working draft]* |
| ISO TR 9573 | Techniques for Using SGML *[published 88-12-01]* |
| ISO DIS 10036 | Procedure for Registration of Glyph and Glyph Collection Identifiers *[ballot closed 90-11-17]* |
| ISO TR 10037 | Guidelines for SGML Syntax-Directed Editing Systems *[awaiting publication]* |
| ISO CD 10179 | Document Style Semantics and Specification Language (DSSSL) *[awaiting CD ballot]* |
| ISO CD 10180 | Standard Page Description Language *[awaiting CD ballot]* |

## Manufacturing Message Service (MMS)

| | |
|---|---|
| ISO DIS 9506-1 | Industrial Automation Systems — Systems Integration and Communications — Manufacturing Message Specification, Part 1: Service Definition *[ballot closed 88-08-14]* |
| ISO DIS 9506-2 | Part 2: Protocol Specification *[ballot closed 88-08-14]* |

## Distributed Office Applications (DOA)

| | |
|---|---|
| ISO DIS 10031-1 | Distributed Office Applications, Part 1: General Model *[ballot closed 89-10-12]* |

| | |
|---|---|
| ISO DIS 10031-2 | Part 2: Referenced Data Transfer *[ballot closed 89-10-12]* |

## Electronic Data Interchange (EDI)

| | |
|---|---|
| ISO 9735 | EDIFACT Syntax Rules *[published 88-07-01]* |

## Banking Information Interchange

| | |
|---|---|
| ISO CD 9955 | Methodology and Guidelines for the Development of Application Protocols for Banking Information Interchange |

## Library Applications

| | |
|---|---|
| ISO CD 10160 | Documentation — Interlibrary Loan Service Definition *[ballot closed 88-11-07]* |
| ISO CD 10161 | Documentation — Interlibrary Loan Protocol Specification *[ballot closed 88-11-07]* |
| ISO CD 10162 | Documentation — Application Service for Information Systems — Bibliographic Search, Retrieval, and Update Service *[ballot closed 88-11-07]* |
| ISO CD 10163 | Documentation — Application Protocol for Information Systems — Bibliographic Search, Retrieval, and Update Protocol *[ballot closed 88-11-07]* |

## Document Filing and Retrieval

| | |
|---|---|
| ISO DIS 10166-1 | Document Filing and Retrieval, Part 1: Abstract Service Definition and Procedures *[ballot closed 90-05-26]* |
| ISO DIS 10166-2 | Part 2: Protocol Specification *[ballot closed 90-05-26]* |

# PRESENTATION LAYER STANDARDS

| | |
|---|---|
| ISO 8822<br>CCITT X.216 | Connection-Oriented Presentation Service Definition *[published 88-08-15]* |
| ISO 8822/DAM1 | Amendment 1: Connectionless-mode Presentation Service *[ballot closed 89-10-13]* |

| | |
|---|---|
| ISO 8822/PDAM2 | Amendment 2: Support of Session Symmetric Synchronization Service |
| ISO 8822/PDAM3 | Amendment 3: Unlimited User Data |
| ISO 8822/PDAM4 | Amendment 4: Procedures for Registration of Abstract Syntaxes |
| ISO 8823<br>CCITT X.226 | Connection-Oriented Presentation Protocol Specification *[published 88-08-15]* |
| ISO 8823/DAM1 | Amendment 1: Presentation PICS *[ballot closed 89-12-22]* |
| ISO 8823/PDAM2 | Amendment 2: Support of Session Symmetric Synchronization Service |
| ISO 8823/PDAM3 | Amendment 3: Unlimited User Data |
| ISO 8823/PDAM4 | Amendment 4: Procedures for Registration of Transfer Syntaxes |
| ISO 9576 | Connectionless Presentation Protocol Specification *[published 1990]* |

# SESSION LAYER STANDARDS

| | |
|---|---|
| ISO 8326<br>CCITT X.215 | Basic Connection-Oriented Session Service Definition *[published 87-08-15]* |
| ISO 8326/Add. 1 | Addendum 1: Session Symmetric Synchronization *[final text 88-12-01]* |
| ISO 8326/Add. 2 | Addendum 2: Incorporation of Unlimited User Data *[final text 88-06-27]* |
| ISO 8326/DAM3 | Amendment 3: Connectionless Session Service *[ballot closed 88-11-19]* |
| ISO 8326/Am. 1 | Amendment 1 |
| ISO 8327<br>CCITT X.225 | Basic Connection-Oriented Session Protocol Specification *[published 87-08-15]* |
| ISO 8327/Add. 1 | Addendum 1: Session Symmetric Synchronization *[final text 88-12-01]* |
| ISO 8327/Add. 2 | Addendum 2: Incorporation of Unlimited User Data *[final text 88-06-27]* |
| ISO 8327/DAM3 | Amendment 3: PICS Proforma |

| | |
|---|---|
| ISO 9548 | Connectionless Session Protocol *[published 1989]* |
| ISO TR 9571 | LOTOS Description of the Session Service *[published 89-11-01]* |
| ISO TR 9572 | LOTOS Description of the Session Protocol *[published 89-11-01]* |
| ISO DIS 10168-1 | Conformance Test Suite for the Session Protocol, Part 1: Test Suite Structure and Test Purposes *[ballot closed 90-10-19]* |
| ISO CD 10168-4 | Part 4: Test Management Protocol Specification |

# TRANSPORT LAYER STANDARDS

| | |
|---|---|
| ISO 8072<br>CCITT X.214 | Transport Service Definition *[published 86-06-15]* |
| ISO 8072/Add. 1 | Addendum 1: Connectionless-mode Transmission *[published 86-06-15]* |
| ISO 8073<br>CCITT X.224 | Connection-Oriented Transport Protocol Specification *[second edition published 88-12-15]* |
| ISO 8073/Add. 1 | Addendum 1: Network Connection Management Subprotocol (NCMS) *[published 88-12-01]* |
| ISO 8073/Add. 2 | Addendum 2: Class 4 Operation over Connectionless Network Service *[published 89-09-15]* |
| ISO 8073/DAM3 | Amendment 3: Protocol Implementation Conformance Statement Proforma *[ballot closed 91-04-11]* |
| ISO 8073/DAM4 | Amendment 4: Transport Protocol Enhancements *[awaiting DAM ballot]* |
| ISO 8073/Cor. 1 | Technical Corrigendum 1 *[published 90-01-15]* |
| ISO 8073/Cor. 2 | Technical Corrigendum 2 *[published 90-05-01]* |
| ISO 8073/Cor. 3 | Technical Corrigendum 3 *[published 90-06-01]* |
| ISO 8602 | Protocol for Providing the Connectionless-mode Transport Service *[published 87-12-15]* |
| ISO PDTR 10023 | LOTOS Description of ISO 8072 *[awaiting decision concerning further progression]* |
| ISO CD 10024 | LOTOS Description of ISO 8073 *[working draft]* |

### Conformance Testing

| | |
|---|---|
| ISO DIS 10025-1 | Transport Protocol Conformance Testing, Part 1: General Principles |
| ISO CD 10025-2 | Part 2: Test Suite Structure and Test Purposes |
| ISO CD xxxxx | Transport Test Management Protocol *[awaiting CD ballot]* |

### Management

| | |
|---|---|
| ISO CD 10736 | Specification of the Elements of Management Information Related to OSI Transport Layer Standards *[ballot closed 91-03-09]* |

### Security

| | |
|---|---|
| ISO CD yyyyy | Transport Layer Security Protocol *[awaiting CD ballot]* |

## NETWORK LAYER STANDARDS

| | |
|---|---|
| ISO 8348<br>CCITT X.213 | Network Service Definition *[published 87-04-15]* |
| ISO 8348/Add. 1 | Addendum 1: Connectionless-mode Transmission *[published 87-04-15]* |
| ISO 8348/Add. 2 | Addendum 2: Network Layer Addressing *[published 88-06-01]* |
| ISO 8348/Add. 3 | Addendum 3: Additional Features of the Network Service *[published 88-10-15]* |
| ISO 8348/PDAM4 | Amendment 4: Removal of the Preferred Decimal Encoding of the NSAP Address *[awaiting PDAM ballot]* |
| ISO 8648 | Internal Organization of the Network Layer *[published 88-02-15]* |
| ISO 8648/Cor. 1 | Technical Corrigendum 1 *[awaiting publication]* |
| ISO 8880-1 | Protocol Combinations to Provide and Support the OSI Network Service, Part 1: General Principles *[final text 88-10-21]* |

ISO 8880-2 | Part 2: Provision and Support of the Connection-mode Network Service *[final text 88-10-21]*

ISO 8880-2/DAM1 | Amendment 1: Addition of the ISDN Environment *[awaiting DAM ballot]*

ISO 8880-2/PDAM2 | Amendment 2: Addition of the PSTN and CSDN Environments *[awaiting PDAM ballot]*

ISO 8880-3 | Part 3: Provision and Support of the Connectionless Network Service *[final text 88-10-21]*

ISO TR 9577 | Protocol Identification in the Network Layer *[published 90-10-15]*

ISO TR 10172 | Network/Transport Protocol Interworking Specification *[published 90-10-15]*

## Internetwork Protocol

ISO 8473 | Protocol for Providing the Connectionless-mode Network Service (Internetwork Protocol) *[published 88-12-15]*

ISO 8473/Add. 3 | Addendum 3: Provision of the Underlying Service Assumed by ISO 8473 over Subnetworks that Provide the OSI Data Link Service *[published 89-09-01]*

ISO 8473/PDAMx | Amendment x: PICS Proforma *[new work item]*

ISO 8473/PDAMy | Amendment y: Provision of the Underlying Service Assumed by ISO 8473 over ISDN Circuit-switched B-channels *[new work item]*

ISO PDTR xxxx | ESTELLE Formal Description of ISO 8473 *[awaiting PDTR ballot]*

## X.25 Packet Level Protocol

ISO 8208 | X.25 Packet Layer Protocol for Data Terminal Equipment *[second edition published 90-03-15]*

ISO 8208/Am. 1 | Amendment 1: Alternative Logical Channel Identifier Assignment *[published 90-09-15]*

ISO 8208/Am. 3 | Amendment 3: Static Conformance Requirements *[published 90-10-12]*

| | |
|---|---|
| ISO 8878<br>CCITT X.223 | Use of X.25 to Provide the Connection-Oriented Network Service *[published 87-09-01]* |
| ISO 8878/Add. 1 | Addendum: Priority *[published 90-06-15]* |
| ISO 8878/Add. 2 | Addendum 2: Use of an X.25 PVC to Provide the OSI CONS *[published 90-06-15]* |
| ISO 8878/DAM3 | Amendment 3: Conformance *[ballot closed 90-11-03]* |
| ISO 8878/PDAM4 | Amendment 4: PICS Proforma *[awaiting second PDAM ballot]* |
| ISO 8878/Cor. 1 | Technical Corrigendum 1 *[published 90-03-01]* |
| ISO 8878/Cor. 2 | Technical Corrigendum 2 *[published 90-06-15]* |
| ISO 8878/Cor. 3 | Technical Corrigendum 3 *[awaiting publication]* |
| ISO 8881 | Use of the X.25 Packet Level Protocol in Local Area Networks *[published 89-12-01]* |
| ISO DIS 8882-1 | X.25 DTE Conformance Testing, Part 1: General Principles *[awaiting second DIS ballot]* |
| ISO 8882-3 | X.25 DTE Conformance Testing, Part 3: Packet Level Conformance Suite *[awaiting publication]* |
| ISO TR 10029 | Operation of an X.25 Interworking Unit *[published 89-03-15]* |
| ISO DIS 10177 | Intermediate System Support of the OSI CONS using ISO 8208 in Accordance with ISO 10028 *[ballot closed 91-02-23]* |
| ISO DIS 10588 | Use of X.25 PLP in Conjunction with X.21 /$X.21_{bis}$ to Provide the OSI CONS *[awaiting DIS ballot]* |
| ISO CD 10732 | Use of X.25 PLP to provide the OSI CONS over the telephone network *[ballot closed 91-02-20]* |

## Routing

| | |
|---|---|
| ISO 9542 | End System to Intermediate System Routing Information Exchange Protocol for Use in Conjunction with the Protocol for the Provision of the Connectionless-mode Network Service *[published 88-08-15]* |
| ISO 9542/Cor. 1 | Technical Corrigendum 1 *[awaiting publication]* |
| ISO 9542/PDAM1 | Amendment 1: Dynamic Discovery of OSI NSAP Addresses by End Systems *[new work item]* |

| | |
|---|---|
| ISO TR 9575 | OSI Routing Framework *[published 90-06-01]* |
| ISO DIS 10028-1 | Definition of the Relaying Functions of a Network Layer Intermediate System, Part 1: Connection-mode Network Service *[awaiting DIS ballot]* |
| ISO CD 10028-2 | Part 2: Connectionless Network Service *[awaiting CD ballot]* |
| ISO 10030 | End System to Intermediate System Routing Information Exchange Protocol for Use in Conjunction with ISO 8878 *[final text 90-10-22]* |
| ISO 10030/PDAM1 | Amendment 1: Dynamic Discovery of OSI NSAP Addresses by End Systems *[new work item]* |
| ISO 10030/PDAM3 | Amendment 3: Specification of IS-SNARE interactions *[ballot closed 91-02-08]* |
| ISO CD 10030-2 | End System to Intermediate System Routing Information Exchange Protocol for Use in Conjunction with ISO 8878, Part 2: PICS Proforma *[awaiting CD ballot]* |
| ISO DIS 10589 | Intermediate System to Intermediate System Routing Information Exchange Protocol for Use in Conjunction with ISO 8473 *[awaiting DIS ballot]* |

## Management

| | |
|---|---|
| ISO CD 10733 | Specification of the Elements of Management Information Related to OSI Network Layer Standards *[ballot closed 91-03-29]* |

## Security

| | |
|---|---|
| ISO CD yyyyy | Network Layer Security *[working draft]* |

## ISDN

| | |
|---|---|
| ISO 9574 | Provision of the OSI Connection-mode Network Service by Packet-mode Terminal Equipment Connected to an ISDN *[published 89-12-15]* |
| ISO 9574/DAM1 | Amendment 1: Provision of CONS over an ISDN Circuit-Switched Channel Connecting Directly to the Remote Terminal *[awaiting DAM ballot]* |

# DATA LINK LAYER STANDARDS

| | |
|---|---|
| ISO DIS 8886<br>CCITT X.212 | Data Link Service Definition *[third DIS ballot closed 88-09-16]* |
| ISO DIS 9234 | Industrial Asynchronous Data Link for Two-way Simultaneous or Two-way Alternate Mode |

## High-level Data Link Control (HDLC)

| | |
|---|---|
| ISO DIS 3309 | High-level Data Link Control (HDLC) — Frame Structure *[second DIS ballot closed 90-10-26]* |
| ISO 3309/Add. 1 | Addendum 1: Start/Stop Transmission *[final text 90-03-12]* |
| ISO 3309/DAM2 | Amendment 2: Extended Transparency Options for Start/Stop Transmission *[awaiting DAM ballot]* |
| ISO 3309/PDAM3 | Amendment 3: Seven-bit Transparency Option for Start/Stop Transmission *[ballot closed 91-03-10]* |
| ISO DIS 4335 | HDLC — Consolidation of Elements of Procedures *[second DIS ballot closed 90-10-26]* |
| ISO 4335/Add. 1 | Addendum 1 (no title; contains UI and SREJ extensions) *[published 87-08-01]* |
| ISO 4335/Add. 2 | Addendum 2: Enhancement of the XID Function Utility |
| ISO 4335/Add. 3 | Addendum 3: Start/Stop Transmission *[final text 90-03-12]* |
| ISO 4335/DAM4 | Amendment 4: Multi-Selective Reject Option *[ballot closed 90-11-24]* |
| ISO 7478 | Multi-link Procedures *[third edition published 84-07-01]* |
| ISO 7478/Cor. 1 | Technical Corrigendum 1 *[published 89-03-01]* |
| ISO 7776 | HDLC — Description of the X.25 LAPB-compatible DTE Data Link Procedures *[published 86-12-15]* |
| ISO 7776/Cor. 1 | Technical Corrigendum 1 *[published 89-4-1]* |
| ISO 7776/Cor. 2 | Technical Corrigendum 2 *[published 89-9-1]* |
| ISO 7776/DAM1 | Amendment 1: PICS Proforma *[awaiting DAM ballot]* |

| | |
|---|---|
| ISO DIS 7809 | HDLC — Consolidation of Classes of Procedures *[second DIS ballot closed 90-10-26]* |
| ISO 7809/Add. 1 | Addendum 1 (no title; contains UI extensions) *[published 87-06-15]* |
| ISO 7809/Add. 2 | Addendum 2: Description of Optional Functions *[published 87-06-15]* |
| ISO 7809/Add. 3 | Addendum 3: Start/Stop Transmission *[final text 90-03-12]* |
| ISO 7809/DAM5 | Amendment 5: Connectionless Class of Procedures *[awaiting DAM ballot]* |
| ISO 7809/DAM6 | Amendment 6: Extended Transparency Options for Start/Stop Transmission *[awaiting DAM ballot]* |
| ISO 7809/DAM7 | Amendment 7: Multi-Selective Reject Option *[ballot closed 90-11-24]* |
| ISO 7809/PDAM9 | Amendment 9: Seven-bit Transparency Option for Start/Stop Transmission *[ballot closed 91-03-10]* |
| ISO 8471 | HDLC Balanced Classes of Procedures-Data Link Layer Address Resolution/Negotiation in Switched Environments *[published 87-04-01]* |
| ISO 8885 | HDLC — General Purpose XID Frame Information Field Content and Format *[published 87-08-15]* |
| ISO 8885/Add. 1 | Addendum 1: Additional Operational Parameters for the Parameter Negotiation Data Link Layer Subfield and Definition of a Multilink Parameter Negotiation Data Link Layer Subfield *[published 89-10-01]* |
| ISO 8885/Add. 2 | Addendum 2: Start/Stop Transmission *[final text 90-03-12]* |
| ISO 8885/DAM3 | Amendment 3: Definition of a Private Parameter Negotiation Data Link Layer Subfield *[second DAM ballot closed 91-04-11]* |
| ISO 8885/DAM4 | Amendment 4: Extended Transparency Options for Start/Stop Transmission *[awaiting DAM ballot]* |
| ISO 8885/DAM5 | Amendment 5: Multi-Selective Reject Option *[ballot closed 90-11-17]* |
| ISO 8885/PDAM6 | Amendment 6: Seven-bit Transparency Option for Start/Stop Transmission *[ballot closed 91-03-10]* |

ISO 8885/PDAM7 — Amendment 7: Frame Check Sequence Negotiation Using the Parameter Negotiation Subfield *[ballot closed 90-08-21]*

ISO TR 10171 — List of Standard Data Link Layer Protocols that Utilize High-level Data Link Control (HDLC) Classes of Procedures *[awaiting publication]*

ISO 10171/PDAM1 — Amendment 1: Registration of XID Format Identifiers and Private Parameter Set Identifiers *[ballot closed 91-03-10]*

## Basic Mode

ISO 1155 — Use of Longitudinal Parity to Detect Errors in Information Messages *[second edition published 78-11-15]*

ISO 1177 — Character Structure for Start/Stop and Synchronous Character-Oriented Transmission *[second edition published 85-08-15]*

ISO 1745 — Basic Mode Control Procedures for Data Communication Systems *[published 75-02-01]*

ISO 2111 — Basic Mode Control Procedures — Code-Independent Information Transfer *[second edition published 85-02-01]*

ISO 2628 — Basic Mode Control Procedures — Complements *[published 73-06-01]*

ISO 2629 — Basic Mode Control Procedures-Conversational Information Message Transfer *[published 73-02-15]*

## Local Area Networks (LANs)

ISO 8802-1 — Local Area Networks, Part 1: Introduction

ISO DIS 8802-1E — Local Area Networks, Part 1: Introduction, Section E: System Load Protocol *[ballot closed 91-03-07]*

ISO 8802-2 — Part 2: Logical Link Control *[published 90-07-16]*

ISO 8802-2/DAM1 — Amendment 1: Flow Control Techniques for Bridged Local Area Networks *[ballot closed 88-11-19]*

ISO 8802-2/DAM2 — Amendment 2: Acknowledged connectionless-mode service, Type 3 operation *[ballot closed 90-05-02]*

| | |
|---|---|
| ISO 8802-2/PDAM3 | Amendment 3: PICS Proforma *[ballot closed 90-09-10]* |
| ISO 8802-2/DAM4 | Amendment 4: Editorial Changes and Technical Corrections *[ballot closed 90-11-24]* |
| ISO 8802-3 | Part 3: Carrier Sense Multiple Access with Collision Detection — Access Method and Physical Layer Specifications *[published 89-02-24]* |
| ISO 8802-3/DAM1 | Amendment 1: Medium Attachment Unit and Baseband Medium Specifications for Type 10BASE2 |
| ISO 8802-3/DAM2 | Amendment 2: Repeater Set and Repeater Unit Specification for use with 10BASE5 and 10BASE2 Networks |
| ISO 8802-3/DAM3 | Amendment 3: Broadband Medium Attachment Unit and Broadband Medium Specifications, Type 10BROAD36 *[ballot closed 90-10-28]* |
| ISO 8802-3/DAM4 | Amendment 4: Physical Medium, Medium Attachment, and Baseband Medium Specifications, Type 1BASE5 (StarLAN) *[ballot closed 91-01]* |
| ISO 8802-3/DAM5 | Amendment 5: Medium Attachment Unit and Baseband Medium Attachment Specification for a Vendor Independent Fiber Optic Inter-repeater Link |
| ISO 8802-3/DAM6 | Amendment 6: Summary of IEEE 802.3 First Maintenance Ballot *[awaiting DAM ballot]* |
| ISO 8802-3/PDAM7 | Amendment 7: LAN Layer Management *[awaiting PDAM ballot]* |
| ISO 8802-3/PDAM9 | Amendment 9: Physical Medium, Medium Attachment, and Baseband Medium Specifications, Type 10BaseT *[new work item]* |
| ISO 8802-4 | Part 4: Token-passing Bus Access Method and Physical Layer Specification |
| ISO DIS 8802-5 | Part 5: Token Ring Access Method and Physical Layer Specification *[second DIS ballot on consolidated document containing part 5 and its first three addenda closed 90-09-01]* |
| ISO 8802-5/PDAM1 | Amendment 1: 4 and 16 Mbit/s Specification *[ballot closed 89-01-13]* |

| | |
|---|---|
| ISO 8802-5/PDAM2 | Amendment 2: MAC Sublayer Enhancement *[ballot closed 89-11-10]* |
| ISO 8802-5/PDAM3 | Amendment 3: Management Entity Specification *[ballot closed 89-11-10]* |
| ISO 8802-5/DAM4 | Amendment 4: Source Routing MAC Bridge *[awaiting DAM ballot]* |
| ISO 8802-5/DAM5 | Amendment 5: PICS Proforma *[awaiting DAM ballot]* |
| ISO 8802-7 | Part 7: Slotted Ring Access Method and Physical Layer Specification *[final text distributed 89-07-13]* |
| ISO DIS 10038 | MAC Bridging *[awaiting DIS ballot]* |
| ISO 10038/PDAM1 | Amendment 1: Specification of Management Information for CMIP *[awaiting PDAM ballot]* |
| ISO 10038/PDAM2 | Amendment 2: Source Routing Supplement *[ballot closed 91-03-07]* |
| ISO 10039 | MAC Service Definition *[final text 90-10-26]* |
| ISO PDTR 10178 | The Structure and Coding of Link Service Access Point Addresses in Local Area Networks *[ballot closed 89-12-28]* |
| ISO PDTR 10734 | Guidelines for Bridged LAN Source Routing Operation by End Systems *[ballot closed 91-03-08]* |
| ISO PDTR 10735 | Standard Group MAC Addresses *[ballot closed 91-03-10]* |

## Fiber Distributed Data Interface (FDDI)

| | |
|---|---|
| ISO 9314-2 | Fiber Distributed Data Interface, Part 2: Medium Access Control *[published 89-05-01]* |
| ISO CD 9314-5 | Part 5: Hybrid Ring Control (FDDI-II) |

## Conformance Testing

| | |
|---|---|
| ISO DIS 8882-2 | X.25 DTE Conformance Testing, Part 2: Data Link Layer Test Suite *[awaiting DIS ballot]* |
| ISO DTR 10174 | Logical Link Control (Type 2 Operation) Test Purposes *[awaiting DTR ballot]* |

# PHYSICAL LAYER STANDARDS

| | |
|---|---|
| ISO 10022<br>CCITT X.211 | Physical Service Definition *[published 90-08-01]* |
| ISO TR 7477 | Arrangements for DTE to DTE Physical Connection Using V.24 and X.24 Interchange Circuits *[published 85-09-15]* |
| ISO DIS 7480 | Start-Stop Transmission Signal Quality at DTE-DCE Interfaces *[awaiting DIS ballot (second edition)]* |
| ISO 8480 | DTE-DCE Interface Backup Control Operation Using the 25 Pin Connector *[published 87-11-15]* |
| ISO 8481 | DTE to DTE Physical Connection Using X.24 Interchange Circuits with DTE-provided Timing *[published 86-09-15]* |
| ISO 8482 | Twisted Pair Multipoint Interconnections *[published 87-11-15]* |
| ISO 9067 | Automatic Fault Isolation Procedures Using Test Loops *[published 87-09-01]* |
| ISO 9543 | Synchronous Transmission Signal Quality at DTE-DCE Interfaces *[published 89-04-01]* |
| ISO 9549 | Galvanic Isolation of Balanced Interchange Circuits *[published 90-10-15]* |

## Fiber Distributed Data Interface (FDDI)

| | |
|---|---|
| ISO 9314-1 | Fiber Distributed Data Interface, Part 1: Physical Layer Protocol *[published 89-04-15]* |
| ISO 9314-3 | Part 3: Physical Layer Medium Dependent (PMD) *[published 90-08-01]* |
| ISO CD 9314-4 | Part 4: Single-Mode Fiber/Physical Layer Medium Dependent |

## Physical Connectors

| | |
|---|---|
| ISO 2110 | 25 Pole DTE-DCE Interface Connector and Contact Number Assignments *[third edition published 89-10-01]* |
| ISO 2110/DAM1 | Amendment 1: Interface Connector and Contact Number Assignments for a DTE/DCE Interface for Data Signalling Rates Above 20K Bits per Second *[ballot closed 90-12-28]* |

| | |
|---|---|
| ISO 2593 | 34 Pole DTE-DCE Interface Connector and Contact Number Assignments *[third edition awaiting publication]* |
| ISO 4902 | 37 Pole DTE-DCE Interface Connector and Contact Number Assignments *[second edition published 89-12-01]* |
| ISO 4903 | 15 Pole DTE-DCE Interface Connector and Contact Number Assignments *[second edition published 89-10-01]* |
| ISO 8877 | Interface Connector and Contact Assignments for ISDN Basic Access Interface at Reference Points S & T *[published 87-08-15]* |
| ISO 8877/DAM1 | Amendment 1: TE Connecting Cord *[awaiting second DAM ballot]* |
| ISO TR 9578 | Communication Interface Connectors Used in Local Area Networks *[final text 90-05-24]* |
| ISO DIS 10173 | ISDN Primary Access Connector at Reference Points S and T *[ballot closed 91-01-05]* |

# REFERENCES


Bebford, S., "Components of OSI: The OSI Directory Service," *ConneXions*, June 1989.

Berson, A., *APPC: Introduction to LU 6.2*, McGraw-Hill, 1990.

Black, U., *Physical Level Interfaces and Protocols*, IEEE Computer Society Press, 1988.

Black, U., "The X.25 Facilities," *Journal of Data & Computer Communications*, Fall 1989.

Black, U., *OSI: A Model for Computer Communications Standards*, Prentice-Hall, 1991.

Boland, T., *Government Open Systems Interconnection Profile Users' Guide*, National Institute of Standards and Technology, August 1989.

Cerf, V., "Prospects for Electronic Data Interchange," *Telecommunications*, January 1991.

Cerf, V. and K. Mills, "Explaining the Role of GOSIP," *RFC* 1169, Network Information Center, August 1990.

Chanson, S. and M. Goh, "Implementation of the ISO File Transfer, Access, and Management Protocol in the Unix Environment," *IEEE Computer Networking Symposium*, IEEE Computer Society Press, 1988.

Chappell, D., "Abstract Syntax Notation One (ASN.1)," *Journal of Data & Computer Communications*, Spring 1989.

Chappell, D., "Components of OSI: The Presentation Layer," *ConneXions: The Interoperability Report*, November 1989.

Chappell, D., "The OSI Virtual Terminal Protocol," *Communications Standards Management*, Auerbach Publishers, 1989.

Claiborne, J.D., *Mathematical Preliminaries for Computer Networking*, John Wiley & Sons, 1990.

Cole, G., *Computer Networking for Systems Programmers*, John Wiley & Sons, 1990.

Conard, J., "Bit-Oriented Data Link Protocols and Their Applications," *Journal of Data & Computer Communications,* Winter 1989.

Davidson, W., "Application Associations: The Key to Establishing OSI Conversations," *Communications Standards Management,* Auerbach Publishers, 1989.

Dixon, G., "Components of OSI: The Virtual Terminal ASE," *ConneXions,* February 1991.

Fisher, S., "The Latest GOSIP," *BYTE,* June 1990.

Fleischmann, E., "FTAM, FTP, and NFS Within an Enterprise Network," *ConnneXions,* November 1990.

Fong, K. and J. Reinstedler, "The Development of an OSI Application Layer Protocol Interface," *Computer Communications Review,* July 1989.

Galvin, J., "Components of OSI: Security Architecture," *ConnneXions,* August 1990.

Genilloud, G., "X.400 MHS: First Steps Towards an EDI Communication Standard," *Computer Communication Review,* April 1990.

Gregori, E., et al, "OSILAB: An OSI Prototyping Laboratory," *IEEE Computer Networking Symposium,* IEEE Computer Society Press, 1988.

Gross, P. and R. Nitzan, "Clarification of GOSIP," *ConneXions,* March 1990.

Halshall, J. and S. Shaw, *OSI Explained: End-to-End Computer Communications Standards*, John Wiley & Sons, 1988.

Heatley, S. and D. Stokesberry, "Measurement of a Transport Implementation Running Over an IEEE 802.3 Local Area Network," *IEEE Computer Networking Symposium,* IEEE Computer Society Press, 1988.

Huitema, C. and A. Doghri, "Defining Faster Transfer Syntaxes for the OSI Presentation Protocol," *Computer Communication Review,* October 1989.

Janas, J. and H. Wiehle, "On the State of Affairs in OSI Transaction Processing," *IEEE Computer Networking Symposium,* IEEE Computer Society Press, 1988.

Jones, V., *MAP/TOP Networking*, McGraw-Hill, 1988.

Knightson, K., T. Knowles, and J. Larmouth, *Standards for Open Systems Interconnection,* McGraw-Hill, 1988.

Madron, T., *LANs: Applications of IEEE/ANSI 802 Standards*, John Wiley & Sons, 1989.

Madron, T., *Local Area Networks: The Next Generation,* John Wiley & Sons, 1990.

Malamud, C., "X.400 and X.500 – International Communications Standards," *Network Computing,* January 1991.

Mantelman, L., "The Birth of OSI TP (Transaction Protocol)," *Data Communications Magazine,* November 1989.

Marks, L., "OSI Management: Interoperable Network Management Finally Arrives," *Open Systems Data Transfer,* December 1990.

Martin, J. and K. Chapman, *Local Area Networks, Architectures, and Implementations,* Prentice Hall, 1989.

Mazzaferro, J., "An Overview of FDDI," *Journal of Data & Computer Communications,* Summer 1990.

Miller, M., *LAN Protocol Handbook,* M&T Books, 1990.

Neufeld, G., "Descriptive Names in X.500," *Communications Architectures and Protocols,* ACM SIGCOM, September 1989.

Norris, R., "Electronic Data Interchange," *Communications Standards Management,* Auerbach Publishers, 1989.

Omnicom, "Progress on OSI Transaction Processing," *Open Systems Communication,* January 1991.

Omnicom, "Omnicom Special Report: The NIST OSI Implementors' Workshop (NIST-IW)," *Open Systems Applications,* March 1991.

Onions, J., "Components of OSI: The X.400 Message Handling System," *ConneXions,* May 1989.

Rose, M., "Components of OSI: The Application Layer Structure," *ConneXions: The Interoperability Report,* January 1990.

Rose, M., *The Simple Book: An Introduction to Management of TCP/IP–Based Internets,* Prentice Hall, 1991.

Rose, M., *The Open Book: A Practical Perspective on OSI,* Prentice Hall, 1990.

Scott, K., "X.400 Pushes the Envelope for Electronic Messaging," *Data Communications Magazine,* June 1990.

Soppe, M., "A Method for Testing Data Aspects of Protocol Implementations and Its Application to the OSI Session Layer," *IEEE Computer Networking Symposium,* IEEE Computer Society Press, 1988.

Spragins, J., J. Hammond, and K. Pawlikowski, *Telecommunications Protocols and Design,* Addison-Wesley, 1991.

Stallings, W., *Handbook of Computer Communications Standards, Volume 1: The Open Systems Interconnection (OSI) Model and OSI–Related Standards,* Macmillan Books, 1987.

Stallings, W., *Handbook of Computer Communications Standards, Volume 2: Local Area Networks,* Macmillan Books, 1987.

Tannenbaum, A., *Computer Networks,* Second Edition, Prentice Hall, 1988.

Tardo, J. "Communications Security Services and Protocols – Parts I and II," *Communications Standards Management,* Auerbach Publishers, 1989.

Truoel, K., "Components of OSI: File Transfer, Access, and Management (FTAM)," *ConneXions: The Interoperability Report,* April 1990.

Turner, S., "Public Key Encryption Using the RSA and SEEK Algorithms," *Journal of Data & Computer Communications,* Summer 1990.

Vair, D., "Components of OSI: X.25 – The Network, Data Link, and Physical Layers of the OSI Reference Model," *ConneXions,* December 1990.

Walter, M., "Progress Towards Interoperability," *Telecommunications,* January 1991.

Wilder, F., "Recommendation X.25: Changes for the 1988–1992 Cycle," *Data Communications Management,* Auerbach Publishers, Number 52-10-20, 1990.

# INDEX

## B



## C

## E



## F

## K



## L



## M

## N



## O



## P

## Q



## R

## T

## U



## V



## W



## X

## Y



## Z